Judy Gorman's

❖ BREADS OF NEW ENGLAND ❖

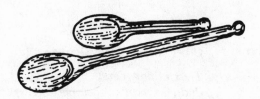

Other Books by Judy Gorman

The Culinary Craft
Judy Gorman's Vegetable Cookbook

Judy Gorman's

❖ BREADS OF NEW ENGLAND ❖

From biscuits to bagels, pizza to popovers — more than 500 easy-to-follow
recipes that capture the best of New England home baking.

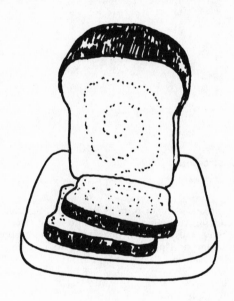

YANKEE® BOOKS
Camden, Maine

Cover design by Lurelle Cheverie
Front cover photograph by Ralph Copeland
Design and illustrations by Jill Shaffer
Food styling on cover by Kristie Scott
Printed and bound in the United States

Library of Congress Cataloging-in-Publication Data

Gorman, Judy.
    Judy Gorman's breads of New England.

    Includes index.
    1. Bread — New England. 2. Baking. I. Title.
II. Title: Breads of New England.
TX769-G59 1988   641.8'15'0974   88-36
ISBN 0-89909-348-5

10   9   8   7   6   5   4   3

❖ Contents ❖

❖ Introduction ❖

WHEN EDMUND and I were first married, I bought one of those old-fashioned, crank-type bread mixers that looks like a pail with a cover on top. My mother had always used one to mix yeast bread, and I considered it an essential piece of kitchen equipment.

That bread mixer was a simple yet ingenious contraption. To mix bread dough, you poured a quart or so of warm milk into the bottom of the pail. Some melted shortening and dissolved yeast were added, and in went the flour. Next you attached the dough hook and long-handled crank to the top of the pail by means of a brace. When the crank was turned, the ingredients joined together to form a smooth dough. But you didn't stop there. Slowly and continuously you turned the crank, which turned the dough hook,

which kneaded the bread. Finally, the cover of the pail was lowered over the crank and situated atop the brace, and the dough was set aside to rise.

The whole process was efficient and remarkably effortless. Dough for as many as eight loaves could be produced easily, without strenuous kneading. When the dough had risen, you simply turned the crank to deflate it and knead it briefly. All that was left to do was to turn the dough out and shape it into loaves.

As time went by, other bread-making equipment made its way into my kitchen: first a heavy-duty electric mixer with a dough hook attachment, then a food processor. But experiments with these tools left me unsatisfied. Somehow I always turned back to that hand-cranked mixer.

Home-baked bread was a staple in our household for many years. I always kept a generous supply of white, whole wheat, and oatmeal bread in the freezer at all times, so there was seldom any reason to purchase bread at the store. But times change. Our daughter reached the age of awareness, which is to say she found out that other kids ate sandwiches made from spongy, store-bought bread.

At first I stood my ground, reciting the nutritional merits of from-scratch bread and extolling the love that went into every loaf. Phooey. Who cares when you're the kid with the weird sandwich?

It was under that kind of pressure that I finally accepted store-bought bread as an inevitable part of life. At the same time I realized that making quantities of home-made loaves was no longer practical or necessary. So I retired my beloved mixer to the attic and set about experimenting with various ways to make one or two yeast loaves at a time.

The method that I found to be the most efficient and satisfying is the one I've suggested in this book. Basically, it involves beating the liquid ingredients with as much flour as you can stir in comfortably. When the dough becomes too stiff to manipulate with a wooden spoon, you turn it out onto a work surface and add the remaining flour by kneading it in. This technique gives you close control over the amount of flour incorporated, so the final loaves are less apt to be heavy and dense.

You will notice that three different types of flour are recommended throughout the recipes. "Bread flour" refers to high-gluten, multipurpose flour, such as King Arthur. This type of flour is recognized by its high protein content, which is listed in the nutritional information on the side of the package. "Bromated bread flour" is a high-gluten flour especially formulated for making yeast bread. It contains potassium bromate, a dough conditioner that strengthens gluten strands. This kind of flour is clearly labeled with the word "bromated," and it is an excellent choice for making free-standing loaves. "All-purpose" flour is generally lower in gluten-producing proteins than the other two types. Consequently, it is the best one to use for making biscuits and other breads with a tender crumb.

The recipes in this book call for dry, granular yeast, and the directions given are the traditional ones for dissolving the yeast in a small amount of warm water. Nevertheless, "rapid-rise" yeast, a relatively new item on the market, may be substituted by following the directions on the back of the yeast packet. If you do substitute, take special care to include the water designated for dissolving the traditional yeast in the total amount of liquid ingredients.

In addition to yeast breads, the New England culinary heritage is rich with breads of many other types. For that reason I have tried to present a broad spectrum of examples here. Recipes in this cookbook range from the jonnycakes and Boston brown bread of colonial times to more contemporary baked goods like bagels, pizza, and calzone. Also offered are such homespun favorites as muffins, biscuits, pancakes, and doughnuts.

Homemade breads have been an important element of Yankee cooking since the time of the earliest settlers. Traditionally they have been honest, wholesome breads and have included indigenous ingredients such as maple syrup, molasses, nuts, and dried fruits. Through the years, as the cuisine was shaped by different ethnic influences, the variety of components grew more diverse, and today's New England breads are just as apt to be made from up-to-the-minute ingredients such as yogurt and fresh gingerroot. What I hope to do with this book is to kindle an appreciation for these wonderful breads, which reflect the straightforward Yankee character so closely associated with the region.

❖ Yeast Breads ❖

OF ALL THE reasons people bake bread at home, necessity is surely the least compelling. Creative expression, emotional therapy, and physical exercise have all been put forth as motives, but I think the real reason is the pure sensual joy of working with yeast dough.

First, there is the pleasure of kneading. As you push the dough back and forth with rhythmic strokes, it comes alive under your hands. You can actually feel the limp, flaccid mass develop lively resiliency and a taut, satiny touch.

Then there is the aroma. When set aside to rise, yeast dough begins to ferment and give off alcohol. This produces the wonderful "yeasty" smell so closely associated with homemade bread. When the rising step is completed and the dough is put into a hot oven to bake, the fragrance becomes even more intense. Only a person of stone could ignore the appeal of that seductive scent.

Traditional advice cautions against slicing yeast bread that has just come out of the oven. And there is a degree of truth to the warning. Slicing a hot loaf does change the way the interior cools and slightly alters its consistency. But how can you resist? The damage is minimal, so go ahead. Cut off a nice thick slice of that piping hot loaf, slather it with butter, and enjoy!

Successful yeast bread is the result of favorable rising conditions, sufficient kneading, and the correct amount of flour. Due to the fact that atmospheric conditions change the extent to which flour absorbs liquid, the amounts of flour given in yeast bread recipes are necessarily vague. Usually the measurements suggested provide a leeway of ½ to ¾ cup. Always blend in the smaller amount first, kneading in the remainder only if necessary to prevent the dough from sticking. The best rule of thumb is to stop kneading in flour as soon as the dough is resilient enough to pull away from the work surface. Keep in mind that it is better to err on the side of too little flour than too much, because excessive flour creates a dense, leaden loaf.

Yeast breads store well, and it is therefore sensible to make three or four loaves at one time. When completely cool, transfer the loaves to plastic storage bags and secure with a wire twist. Use one loaf and freeze the rest. To defrost yeast bread, allow it to come to room temperature inside the plastic bag. If you wish to serve it warm, wrap the bread in aluminum foil and place it in a preheated 375°F. oven for 5 to 8 minutes. Warming a loaf of yeast bread in the microwave oven is not recommended.

Almond Orange Bread

MAKES ONE 9x5-INCH LOAF

A sunny, aromatic loaf moistened with orange-juice glaze.

½ cup milk
2 tablespoons honey
2 tablespoons butter or margarine
¾ teaspoon salt
½ cup freshly squeezed orange juice
1 tablespoon finely grated orange zest
½ teaspoon almond extract
1 package dry yeast, dissolved in ¼ cup warm
    water
1 large egg, beaten
3 to 3½ cups bread flour, scoop measured
½ cup toasted almonds, finely ground
3 tablespoons sugar

1. In a wide saucepan, combine the milk, honey, butter, and salt. Place over medium heat and stir until the butter is melted. Remove from the heat and stir in ¼ cup of the orange juice, the orange zest, and the almond extract. Transfer to a large mixing bowl.

2. When the mixture is barely warm to the touch, stir in the dissolved yeast and beaten egg. Add 1 cup of the flour and beat with a wooden spoon until smooth. Stir in the almonds. Gradually blend in additional flour until the dough becomes too difficult to stir. Turn out onto a floured surface and knead in as much of the remaining flour as necessary to form a cohesive dough. Continue kneading in flour until the dough is soft yet no longer sticks to the work surface. Transfer to a greased bowl and cover with a clean kitchen towel. Set aside to rise until double in bulk.

3. Generously grease a 9x5-inch loaf pan. Punch the dough down, then turn it out onto a floured surface. Shape it into a loaf and place it in the prepared pan. Cover and set aside to rise. When double in bulk, bake in a preheated 375°F. oven for 35 to 45 minutes, or until the crust is nicely browned. Combine the remaining ¼ cup orange juice and the sugar in a small saucepan. Bring to a gentle bubble and cook, uncovered, until slightly thickened. Brush over the surface of the warm loaf. Cool on a rack for 10 minutes, then turn out. ❖

Anadama Bread

MAKES 1 ROUND LOAF

A combination of cornmeal and molasses creates this New England classic. Serve warm in generously thick slices.

1½ cups cold water
⅓ cup molasses
2 tablespoons solid vegetable shortening
1 teaspoon salt
1 package dry yeast, dissolved in ¼ cup warm
    water

½ teaspoon baking soda
¾ cup yellow cornmeal
1½ cups whole wheat flour, scoop measured
3 to 3½ cups bread flour, preferably
  bromated, scoop measured

1. In a wide saucepan, combine the water, molasses, shortening, and salt. Place over medium heat and stir until the shortening is melted. Transfer to a large mixing bowl.

2. When the mixture is barely warm to the touch, stir in the dissolved yeast. Blend in the baking soda and cornmeal. Add the whole wheat flour and 1 cup of the bread flour and beat with a wooden spoon until smooth. Gradually blend in additional bread flour until the dough becomes too difficult to stir. Turn out onto a floured surface and knead in as much of the remaining bread flour as necessary to form a cohesive dough. Continue kneading in flour until the dough is soft yet no longer sticks to the work surface. Transfer to a greased bowl and cover with plastic wrap. Secure with an elastic band and set aside until double in bulk.

3. Generously grease a 9-inch round baking pan. Punch the dough down, then turn it out onto a floured surface. Shape it into a round loaf and place it in the pan. Cover loosely with plastic wrap and let rise. When double in bulk, bake in a preheated 375°F. oven for 35 to 40 minutes, or until the loaf sounds hollow when you tap the top. Cool on a rack for 5 minutes, then turn out.   ❖

Apple Wheat Bread

MAKES ONE 9x5-INCH LOAF

A hearty whole wheat loaf, enriched with bran and studded with fragrant chunks of fresh apple.

¾ cup warm water
2 tablespoons sugar
1 package dry yeast
1 cup 100% bran cereal (not flakes)
1 cup milk
2 tablespoons butter or margarine
¾ teaspoon salt

2 cups whole wheat flour, scoop measured
2 medium apples, peeled, cored, and coarsely
  chopped
½ cup raisins
1½ to 2 cups bread flour, scoop measured

1. In a large mixing bowl, combine the water, sugar, and yeast. Stir to dissolve the yeast, then add the bran. Blend well and set aside to soften.

2. In a wide saucepan, combine the milk, butter, and salt. Place over medium heat and stir until the butter is melted. Remove from the heat and allow to cool.

3. When the milk is barely warm to the touch, stir into the softened bran. Add the whole wheat flour, apples, and raisins. Stir to combine. Blend in enough of the bread flour to form a stiff dough. Turn out onto a floured surface and knead, working in as much of the remaining bread flour as necessary to form a cohesive dough. Continue kneading in bread flour until the dough is soft yet no longer sticks to the work surface. Transfer to a greased bowl and cover with plastic wrap. Secure with an elastic band and set aside to rise until double in bulk.

4. Generously grease a 9x5-inch loaf pan. Punch the dough down, then turn it out onto a floured surface. Shape it into a loaf and place it in the prepared pan. Cover loosely with plastic wrap and let rise. When double in bulk, bake in a preheated 375°F. oven for 35 to 45 minutes, or until the loaf sounds hollow when you tap the top. Cool on a rack for 5 minutes, then turn out.   ❖

Apricot Date Bread

MAKES TWO 9x5-INCH LOAVES

This is a wonderful breakfast bread. Cut into thick slices and toast lightly, then spread with unsalted butter.

2½ cups cold water
½ cup coarsely chopped dried apricots
½ cup coarsely chopped pitted dates
2 tablespoons butter or margarine
1 tablespoon sugar

1½ teaspoons salt

1 package dry yeast, dissolved in ¼ cup warm water

3 cups whole wheat flour, scoop measured

3 to 3½ cups bread flour, preferably bromated, scoop measured

1. In a wide saucepan, combine the water, apricots, and dates. Bring to a gentle bubble and cook, uncovered, until soft. Remove from the heat and add the butter, sugar, and salt. Stir to melt the butter. Transfer to a large mixing bowl.

2. When the mixture is barely warm to the touch, stir in the dissolved yeast. Add the whole wheat flour and beat with a wooden spoon. Stir in enough of the bread flour to form a stiff dough. Turn out onto a floured surface and knead, working in as much additional bread flour as necessary to form a cohesive dough. Continue kneading in bread flour until the dough is soft yet no longer sticks to the work surface. Transfer to a greased bowl and cover with plastic wrap. Secure with an elastic band and set aside to rise until double in bulk.

3. Generously grease two 9x5-inch loaf pans. Punch the dough down, then turn it out onto a floured surface. Shape it into 2 loaves and place them in the prepared pans. Cover loosely with plastic wrap and let rise. When double in bulk, bake in a preheated 350°F. oven for 50 minutes to 1 hour, or until the loaf sounds hollow when you tap the top. Cool on a rack for 5 minutes, then turn out.   ❖

Apricot Almond Swirl Loaf

MAKES ONE 9x5-INCH LOAF

Vibrant streaks of apricot filling turn this deceptively plain-looking loaf into an extraordinary bread. Offer warm slices with tea or coffee and plenty of softened butter.

1½ cups cold water

¼ cup sugar

1 pound dried apricots, coarsely chopped

1 teaspoon almond extract

½ cup coarsely chopped blanched almonds

1 cup milk

3 tablespoons honey

2 tablespoons butter or margarine

1 teaspoon salt

1 package dry yeast, dissolved in ¼ cup warm water

3 to 3½ cups bread flour, scoop measured

1. In a wide saucepan, combine the water, sugar, and apricots. Place over medium heat and bring to a gentle bubble. Cook, stirring, until the apricots are soft and the mixture takes on a thick, spreadable consistency. Remove from the heat and stir in the almond extract and almonds. Set aside to cool to room temperature.

2. In a separate saucepan, combine the milk, honey, butter, and salt. Place over medium heat and stir until the butter is melted. Transfer to a large mixing bowl.

3. When the milk mixture is barely warm to the touch, stir in the dissolved yeast. Add 1 cup of the flour and beat with a wooden spoon until smooth. Gradually blend in additional flour until the dough becomes too

---

To make an Apricot Almond Swirl Loaf, spread apricot filling to within 1 inch of the edges of the flattened dough. Starting at the short side, roll up into a loaf. After pinching to seal the seam, place in the prepared pan, seam side down.

difficult to stir. Turn out onto a floured surface and knead in as much of the remaining flour as necessary to form a cohesive dough. Continue kneading in flour until the dough is soft yet no longer sticks to the work surface. Transfer to a greased bowl and cover with a clean kitchen towel. Set aside to rise until double in bulk.

4. Generously grease a 9x5-inch loaf pan. Punch the dough down, then turn it out onto a floured surface. Roll into a 9x14-inch rectangle. Trim the edges to square off the rectangle. Lift the dough to loosen it from the work surface. Spread with the apricot filling to within 1 inch of the edges. Starting at the short side, roll up into a loaf. Pinch the long edges to seal the seam. Place in the prepared pan, seam side down. (See illustration on facing page.) Cover and set aside to rise. When double in bulk, bake in a preheated 375°F. oven for 35 to 45 minutes, or until the crust is nicely browned. Cool on a rack for 5 minutes, then turn out. ❖

Banana Bread

MAKES ONE 9x5-INCH LOAF

Mashed banana is an excellent source of dietary potassium and here contributes its comforting flavor to this tasty yeast loaf.

½ cup milk
¼ cup butter or margarine
2 tablespoons light brown sugar
¾ teaspoon salt
1 package dry yeast, dissolved in ¼ cup warm
    water
1 large egg, beaten
1 cup mashed banana
½ cup wheat germ
3 to 3½ cups bread flour, scoop measured

1. In a wide saucepan, combine the milk, butter, sugar, and salt. Place over medium heat and stir until the butter is melted. Transfer to a large mixing bowl.

2. When the mixture is barely warm to the touch, stir in the dissolved yeast and beaten egg. Blend in the banana and wheat germ. Add 1 cup of the flour and beat with a wooden spoon until smooth. Gradually blend in additional flour until the dough becomes too difficult to stir. Turn out onto a floured surface and knead in as much of the remaining flour as necessary to form a cohesive dough. Continue kneading in flour until the dough is soft yet no longer sticks to the work surface. Transfer to a greased bowl and cover with a clean kitchen towel. Set aside to rise until double in bulk.

3. Generously grease a 9x5-inch loaf pan. Punch the dough down, then turn it out onto a floured surface. Shape it into a loaf and place it in the prepared pan. Cover and set aside to rise. When double in bulk, bake in a preheated 375°F. oven for 35 to 45 minutes, or until the crust is nicely browned. Cool on a rack for 5 minutes, then turn out. ❖

Whole Kernel Barley Bread

MAKES ONE 9x5-INCH LOAF

Barley kernels, softened by simmering in water, contribute textural interest to this bread without the threat to your teeth often posed by hard kernels of grain.

1 cup cold water
⅓ cup quick-cooking barley
1 cup milk
¼ cup honey
2 tablespoons butter or margarine
1 teaspoon salt
1 package dry yeast, dissolved in ¼ cup warm
    water
1 large egg, beaten
2 cups whole wheat flour, scoop measured
1½ to 2 cups bread flour, scoop measured

1. Measure the water into a small saucepan and bring to a boil. Stir in the barley and return to the boil. Reduce the heat and simmer, uncovered, for 10 minutes, or until the kernels are tender but firm to the bite. Drain in a sieve and set aside.

2. In a wide saucepan, combine the milk, honey, butter, and salt. Place over medium heat and stir until the butter is melted. Transfer to a large mixing bowl.

3. When the mixture is barely warm to the touch, stir in the dissolved yeast and beaten egg. Add the whole wheat flour and beat with a wooden spoon until smooth. Stir in the barley. Stir in enough of the bread flour to form a stiff dough. Turn out onto a floured surface and knead, working in as much additional bread flour as necessary to form a cohesive dough. Continue kneading in bread flour until the dough is soft yet no longer sticks to the work surface. Transfer to a greased bowl and cover with plastic wrap. Secure with an elastic band and set aside to rise until double in bulk.

4. Generously grease a 9x5-inch loaf pan. Punch the dough down, then turn it out onto a floured surface. Shape it into a loaf and place it in the prepared pan. Cover loosely with plastic wrap and let rise. When double in bulk, bake in a preheated 350°F. oven for 50 minutes to 1 hour, or until the loaf sounds hollow when you tap the top. Cool on a rack for 5 minutes, then turn out.   ❖

Beer Cheese Bread

MAKES 1 ROUND LOAF

An earthy loaf to enjoy with soup or sandwiched with slices of warm baked ham slathered with grainy mustard.

2 cups beer, at room temperature
1 teaspoon sugar
1 teaspoon salt
1 tablespoon vegetable oil
1 package dry yeast, dissolved in ¼ cup warm water
4 to 4½ cups bread flour, preferably bromated, scoop measured
1 cup shredded sharp Cheddar cheese

1. In a large mixing bowl, combine the beer, sugar, salt, and vegetable oil. Stir to dissolve the sugar and salt. Blend in the dissolved yeast.

2. Add 2 cups of the flour and beat with a wooden spoon until smooth. Stir in the cheese and enough of the remaining flour to form a stiff dough. Turn out onto a floured surface and knead, working in as much additional flour as necessary to form a cohesive dough. Continue kneading in flour until the dough is soft yet no longer sticks to the work surface. Transfer to a greased bowl and cover with a clean kitchen towel. Set aside to rise until double in bulk.

3. Generously grease a baking sheet and sprinkle with cornmeal. Punch the dough down, then turn it out onto a floured surface. Shape it into a round loaf and place it on the prepared sheet. Cover and set aside to rise. When double in bulk, bake in a preheated 375°F. oven for 35 to 45 minutes, or until the crust is nicely browned. Transfer to a rack to cool.   ❖

Beer Rye Bread

MAKES 2 ROUND LOAVES

Molasses and beer join to create an outstanding dark rye bread.

2 cups beer
¼ cup solid vegetable shortening
½ cup dark molasses
1½ teaspoons salt
2 packages dry yeast, dissolved in ½ cup warm water
1 tablespoon caraway seeds
4 cups dark rye flour, scoop measured
2 to 2½ cups bread flour, preferably bromated, scoop measured

1. In a wide saucepan, combine the beer, shortening, molasses, and salt. Place over medium heat and stir until the shortening is melted. Transfer to a large mixing bowl.

2. When the mixture is barely warm to the touch, stir in the dissolved yeast. Add the caraway seeds and 2 cups of the rye flour and beat with a wooden spoon until smooth. Stir in the remaining 2 cups of the

rye flour and enough of the bread flour to form a stiff dough. Turn out onto a floured surface and knead, working in as much additional bread flour as necessary to form a cohesive dough. Continue kneading in bread flour until the dough is soft yet no longer sticks to the work surface. Transfer to a greased bowl and cover with plastic wrap. Secure with an elastic band and set aside to rise until double in bulk.

3. Generously grease a baking sheet and sprinkle with cornmeal. Punch the dough down, then turn it out onto a floured surface. Shape it into 2 round loaves and place them on the prepared sheet. Cover loosely with plastic wrap and let rise. When double in bulk, make 2 parallel slashes in the surface of each loaf. Bake in a preheated 375°F. oven for 35 to 45 minutes, or until the loaves sound hollow when you tap the tops. Transfer to a rack to cool.   ❖

Black Bread

MAKES 2 ROUND LOAVES

A dark, intensely flavored loaf based on a foundation of cooked cornmeal.

½ cup yellow cornmeal
¾ cup cold water
¾ cup boiling water
2 tablespoons butter or margarine
3 tablespoons dark brown sugar
1½ teaspoons salt
1 tablespoon caraway seeds
1 tablespoon unsweetened cocoa
1 tablespoon freeze-dried coffee
2 packages dry yeast, dissolved in ½ cup
    warm water
2 cups dark rye flour, scoop measured
1 cup whole wheat flour, scoop measured
2 to 2½ cups bread flour, preferably
    bromated, scoop measured
1 large egg white, beaten with 1 tablespoon
    cold water

1. In a large measuring cup, combine the cornmeal and cold water. Stir with a fork. To the water boiling in a saucepan, gradually add the cornmeal mixture. Stir the mixture

constantly over medium heat until thickened. Remove from the heat and blend in the butter, sugar, salt, caraway seeds, cocoa, and coffee. Transfer to a large mixing bowl.

2. When the mixture is barely warm to the touch, stir in the dissolved yeast. Add the rye flour and whole wheat flour and beat with a wooden spoon until smooth. Stir in enough of the bread flour to form a stiff dough. Turn out onto a floured surface and knead, working in as much additional bread flour as necessary to form a cohesive dough. Continue kneading in bread flour until the dough is soft yet no longer sticks to the work surface. Transfer to a greased bowl and cover with plastic wrap. Secure with an elastic band and set aside to rise until double in bulk.

3. Generously grease a baking sheet and sprinkle with cornmeal. Punch the dough down, then turn it out onto a floured surface. Shape it into 2 round loaves and place them on the prepared sheet. Cover loosely with plastic wrap and let rise. When double in bulk, brush on the beaten egg white and bake in a preheated 375°F. oven for 35 to 45 minutes, or until the loaves sound hollow when you tap the tops. Transfer to a rack to cool.   ❖

Bran Bread

MAKES ONE 9x5-INCH LOAF

A healthful, honey-scented bran loaf enriched with egg.

1 cup warm water
¼ cup sugar
1 package dry yeast
2 cups 100% bran cereal (not flakes)
½ cup milk
¼ cup honey
3 tablespoons butter or margarine
½ teaspoon salt
1 large egg, beaten
3 to 3½ cups bread flour, scoop measured

1. In a large mixing bowl, combine the water, sugar, and yeast. Stir to dissolve the

yeast, then add the bran. Blend well and set aside to soften.

2. In a wide saucepan, combine the milk, honey, butter, and salt. Place over medium heat and stir until the butter is melted. Remove from the heat and allow to cool.

3. When the milk mixture is barely warm to the touch, stir it into the softened bran. Blend in the beaten egg. Add 1 cup of the flour and beat with a wooden spoon until smooth. Gradually blend in additional flour until the dough becomes too difficult to stir. Turn out onto a floured surface and knead in as much of the remaining flour as necessary to form a cohesive dough. Continue kneading in flour until the dough is soft yet no longer sticks to the work surface. Transfer to a greased bowl and cover with plastic wrap. Secure with an elastic band and set aside to rise until double in bulk.

4. Generously grease a 9x5-inch loaf pan. Punch the dough down, then turn it out onto a floured surface. Shape it into a loaf and place it in the prepared pan. Cover loosely with plastic wrap and let rise. When double in bulk, bake in a preheated 375°F. oven for 35 to 45 minutes, or until the loaf sounds hollow when you tap the top. Cool on a rack for 5 minutes, then turn out.   ❖

Buckwheat Bread

MAKES TWO 9x5-INCH LOAVES

If you like buckwheat pancakes, you'll love this hearty, down-home bread. Try thick slices buttered lightly and toasted directly on a barbecue grill. Drizzle with maple syrup and serve with grilled pork sausage.

1 cup cold water
1 cup milk
2 tablespoons honey
2 tablespoons butter or margarine
1 teaspoon salt
1 package dry yeast, dissolved in ¼ cup warm water
1½ cups buckwheat flour, scoop measured

1½ cups whole wheat flour, scoop measured
3½ to 4 cups bread flour, preferably bromated, scoop measured

1. In a wide saucepan, combine the water, milk, honey, butter, and salt. Place over medium heat and stir until the butter is melted. Transfer to a large mixing bowl.

2. When the mixture is barely warm to the touch, stir in the dissolved yeast. Add the buckwheat flour and whole wheat flour and beat with a wooden spoon until smooth. Stir in enough of the bread flour to form a stiff dough. Turn out onto a floured surface and knead, working in as much additional bread flour as necessary to form a cohesive dough. Continue kneading in bread flour until the dough is soft yet no longer sticks to the work surface. Transfer to a greased bowl and cover with plastic wrap. Secure with an elastic band and set aside to rise until double in bulk.

3. Generously grease two 9x5-inch loaf pans. Punch the dough down, then turn it out onto a floured surface. Shape it into 2 loaves and place them in the prepared pans. Cover loosely with plastic wrap and let rise. When double in bulk, bake in a preheated 375°F. oven for 35 to 45 minutes, or until the loaves sound hollow when you tap the tops. Cool on a rack for 5 minutes, then turn out.   ❖

Buttermilk Bread

MAKES TWO 9x5-INCH LOAVES

Buttermilk is an old-time favorite ingredient in New England. Here it lends its pleasing character to white yeast bread.

1 cup cold water
¼ cup butter or margarine
1 tablespoon sugar
1½ teaspoons salt
1 cup buttermilk
1 package dry yeast, dissolved in ¼ cup warm water
6 to 6½ cups bread flour, scoop measured

1. In a wide saucepan, combine the water, butter, sugar, and salt. Place over medium heat and stir until the butter is melted. Transfer to a large mixing bowl and stir in the buttermilk.

2. When the mixture is barely warm to the touch, stir in the dissolved yeast. Add 2 cups of the flour and beat with a wooden spoon until smooth. Gradually blend in additional flour until the dough becomes too difficult to stir. Turn out onto a floured surface and knead in as much of the remaining flour as necessary to form a cohesive dough. Continue kneading in flour until the dough is soft yet no longer sticks to the work surface. Transfer to a greased bowl and cover with a clean kitchen towel. Set aside to rise until double in bulk.

3. Generously grease two 9x5-inch loaf pans. Punch the dough down, then turn it out onto a floured surface. Shape it into 2 loaves and place them in the prepared pans. Cover and set aside to rise. When double in bulk, bake in a preheated 375°F. oven for 35 to 45 minutes, or until the crust is nicely browned. Cool on a rack for 5 minutes, then turn out. ❖

Buttermilk Egg Braid

MAKES 2 BRAIDED LOAVES

This golden braided loaf is as beautiful as it is delicious. The high proportion of eggs creates a rich, seductive texture and taste.

1¾ cups buttermilk
¼ cup butter or margarine, melted
¼ cup sugar
1 teaspoon salt
1 package dry yeast, dissolved in ¼ cup warm water
3 large eggs, beaten
6 to 6½ cups bread flour, scoop measured
1 teaspoon cold water
2 tablespoons sesame seeds

1. In a large mixing bowl, combine the buttermilk, melted butter, sugar, and salt. Stir in the dissolved yeast. Transfer 2 tablespoons of the beaten egg to a measuring cup and add the remainder to the milk mixture. Blend well.

2. Add 2 cups of the flour and beat with a wooden spoon until smooth. Gradually blend in additional flour until the dough becomes too difficult to stir. Turn out onto a floured surface and knead in as much of the

To make a braided loaf, cut the dough into 6 portions. Dust with flour and roll each portion into a 14-inch rope. Take up 3 of the ropes and form into a braid. Pinch the ends together to seal. Transfer to the prepared baking sheet. Repeat with the other 3 ropes.

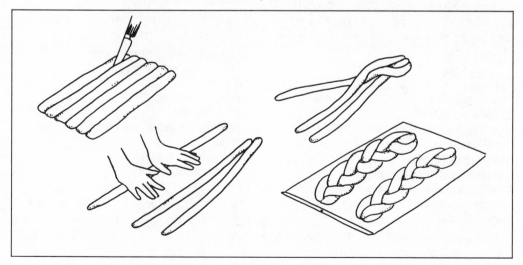

remaining flour as necessary to form a cohesive dough. Continue kneading in flour until the dough is soft yet no longer sticks to the work surface. Transfer to a greased bowl and cover with a clean kitchen towel. Allow the dough to rise until double in bulk.

3. Generously grease a baking sheet. Punch the dough down and press into a flat rectangle. Using a serrated knife, cut the dough lengthwise into 6 equal portions. Dust with flour and roll each portion with the palms of your hands into a 14-inch rope. Take up 3 of the ropes and form into a braid. Pinch the ends together to seal. Transfer to the prepared baking sheet. Repeat with the other 3 ropes. (See illustration on previous page.) Cover and set aside to rise. When double in bulk, mix the reserved beaten egg with the water and brush over the surface of the braids. Sprinkle on the sesame seeds and bake in a preheated 375°F. oven for 25 to 35 minutes, or until the crust is nicely browned. Transfer to a rack to cool.   ❖

Cardamom Fruit Bread

MAKES TWO 9x5-INCH LOAVES

Traditionally considered a holiday bread, this fruit-filled loaf is marvelous any time of year. Stock up on candied fruit at Christmastime and store in the freezer to use during the months when it is not readily available.

1⅓ cups milk
½ cup butter or margarine
½ cup sugar
1 teaspoon salt
2 packages dry yeast, dissolved in ½ cup warm water
3 large eggs, beaten
2 teaspoons ground cardamom
6 to 6½ cups bread flour, scoop measured
1 cup mixed candied fruit, finely chopped
½ cup raisins

1. In a wide saucepan, combine the milk, butter, sugar, and salt. Place over medium heat and stir until the butter is melted. Transfer to a large mixing bowl.

2. When the mixture is barely warm to the touch, stir in the dissolved yeast, beaten egg, and cardamom. Blend well. Add 2 cups of the flour and beat with a wooden spoon until smooth. Stir in the candied fruit and raisins. Gradually blend in additional flour until the dough becomes too difficult to stir. Turn out onto a floured surface and knead in as much of the remaining flour as necessary to form a cohesive dough. Continue kneading in flour until the dough is soft yet no longer sticks to the work surface. Transfer to a greased bowl and cover with a clean kitchen towel. Set aside to rise until double in bulk.

3. Generously grease two 9x5-inch loaf pans. Punch the dough down, then turn it out onto a floured surface. Shape it into 2 loaves and place them in the prepared pans. Cover and set aside to rise. When double in bulk, bake in a preheated 375°F. oven for 35 to 45 minutes, or until the crust is nicely browned. Cool on a rack for 5 minutes, then turn out.   ❖

Cheddar Onion Bread

MAKES 1 ROUND LOAF

Bits of tender onion spark this cheese-flavored loaf.

3 tablespoons butter or margarine
1 medium onion, finely chopped
1½ cups milk
1 tablespoon sugar
1 teaspoon salt
1 package dry yeast, dissolved in ½ cup warm water
4 to 4½ cups bread flour, preferably bromated, scoop measured
2 cups shredded Cheddar cheese

1. Melt the butter in a wide saucepan. Add the onion and cook, stirring, over medium heat until the onion is soft and translucent. Remove from the heat. Add the milk, sugar,

and salt, and stir to dissolve the sugar. Transfer to a large mixing bowl.

2. Stir in the dissolved yeast. Add 2 cups of the flour and beat with a wooden spoon until smooth. Stir in the shredded cheese. Gradually blend in additional flour until the dough becomes too difficult to stir. Turn out onto a floured surface and knead in as much of the remaining flour as necessary to form a cohesive dough. Continue kneading in flour until the dough is soft yet no longer sticks to the work surface. Transfer to a greased bowl and cover with plastic wrap. Secure with an elastic band and set aside to rise until double in bulk.

3. Generously grease a baking sheet and sprinkle with cornmeal. Punch the dough down, then turn it out onto a floured surface. Shape it into a round loaf and place it on the prepared sheet. Cover loosely with plastic wrap and let rise. When double in bulk, bake in a preheated 375°F. oven for 30 to 40 minutes, or until the crust is nicely browned. Transfer to a rack to cool.   ❖

Whole Wheat Cheese Bread

MAKES TWO 9x5-INCH LOAVES

Slices of this hearty, nutritious bread make a welcome after-school snack. Toast and spread with chunky peanut butter.

1 cup milk
2 tablespoons butter or margarine
3 tablespoons dark brown sugar
1½ teaspoons salt
2 packages dry yeast, dissolved in 1 cup warm water
1 large egg, beaten
3 cups whole wheat flour, scoop measured
1 cup wheat germ
1 cup shredded Cheddar cheese
2 to 2½ cups bread flour, preferably bromated, scoop measured

1. In a wide saucepan, combine the milk, butter, sugar, and salt. Place over medium heat and stir until the butter is melted. Transfer to a large mixing bowl.

2. When the mixture is barely warm to the touch, stir in the dissolved yeast and beaten egg. Add the whole wheat flour and beat with a wooden spoon until smooth. Stir in the wheat germ and shredded cheese and enough of the bread flour to form a stiff dough. Turn out onto a floured surface and knead, working in as much additional bread flour as necessary to form a cohesive dough. Continue kneading in bread flour until the dough is soft yet no longer sticks to the work surface. Transfer to a greased bowl and cover with plastic wrap. Secure with an elastic band and set aside to rise until double in bulk.

3. Generously grease two 9x5-inch loaf pans. Punch the dough down, then turn it out onto a floured surface. Shape it into 2 loaves and place them in the prepared pans. Cover loosely with plastic wrap and let rise. When double in bulk, bake in a preheated 375°F. oven for 35 to 45 minutes, or until the loaves sound hollow when you tap the tops. Cool on a rack for 5 minutes, then turn out.   ❖

Cinnamon Swirl Loaf

MAKES ONE 9x5-INCH LOAF

The unique swirl design in this loaf is created by rolling the dough up in two directions instead of just one. First the dough is rolled from the long side, then from the short side to produce a cinnamon-ripple effect.

1½ cups milk
½ cup honey
¼ cup butter or margarine
1½ teaspoons salt
½ cup quick-cooking rolled oats
1 package dry yeast, dissolved in ¼ cup warm water
¼ cup wheat bran
¼ cup wheat germ
3¾ to 4¼ cups bread flour, scoop measured
¼ cup granulated sugar
¼ cup light brown sugar
1 teaspoon cinnamon

1. In a wide saucepan, combine the milk, honey, butter, and salt. Place over medium heat and stir until the butter is melted. Remove from the heat and stir in the oats. Transfer to a large mixing bowl.

2. When the mixture is barely warm to the touch, stir in the dissolved yeast. Blend in the wheat bran and wheat germ. Add 1 cup of the flour and beat with a wooden spoon until smooth. Gradually blend in additional flour until the dough becomes too difficult to stir. Turn out onto a floured surface and knead in as much of the remaining flour as necessary to form a cohesive dough. Continue kneading in flour until the dough is soft yet no longer sticks to the work

To make a Cinnamon Swirl loaf, press the dough into a flat oval and sprinkle on half the sugar mixture. Starting from the long side, roll the dough into a cylinder. Pinch to seal the seam. Press the cylinder into a flat oval and sprinkle on the remaining sugar mixture. Then, starting from the point of the oval, roll up into a loaf and pinch to seal the seam. Transfer to the prepared pan, seam side down.

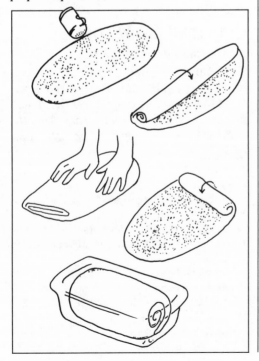

surface. Transfer to a greased bowl and cover with a clean kitchen towel. Set aside to rise until double in bulk.

3. Generously grease a 9x5-inch loaf pan. In a small bowl, combine the granulated sugar, brown sugar, and cinnamon, and stir with a fork to blend. Punch the dough down, then turn it out onto a floured surface. Press the dough into a flat oval. Sprinkle on half the sugar mixture. Starting from the long side, roll the dough into a cylinder. Pinch to seal the seam. Press the cylinder into a flat oval. Sprinkle on the remaining sugar mixture. Then, starting from the point of the oval, roll up into a loaf. Again, pinch to seal the seam. Transfer to the prepared pan, seam side down. (See illustration.) Cover and set aside to rise. When double in bulk, bake in a preheated 350°F. oven for 50 minutes to 1 hour, or until the crust is nicely browned. Cool on a rack for 5 minutes, then turn out.   ❖

Crusty Sourdough Bread

MAKES 2 LONG LOAVES

Aromatic and full-flavored, these loaves are excellent with fish chowder or chili.

1 cup warm water
1 package dry yeast
1 tablespoon sugar
1 teaspoon salt
2 cups water-based sourdough starter (p. 51), at room temperature
4½ to 5 cups bread flour, preferably bromated, scoop measured

1. Measure the warm water into a large mixing bowl. Sprinkle on the yeast and stir to dissolve. Blend in the sugar and salt. Add the sourdough starter and mix well.

2. Add 2 cups of the flour and beat with a wooden spoon until smooth. Gradually blend in additional flour until the dough becomes too difficult to stir. Turn out onto a floured surface and knead in as much of the remaining flour as necessary to form a co-

hesive dough. Continue kneading in flour until the dough is soft yet no longer sticks to the work surface. Transfer to a greased bowl and cover with plastic wrap. Secure with an elastic band and set aside to rise until double in bulk.

3. Punch down the dough and turn it out onto a floured surface. Knead vigorously until the dough is smooth and resilient. Return to the greased bowl. Cover and let rise until double in bulk.

4. Generously grease two 16-inch baguette pans and sprinkle them with cornmeal. Punch the dough down, then turn it out onto a floured surface. Shape it into two 16-inch loaves and place them in the prepared pans. Cover loosely with plastic wrap and let rise. When double in bulk, bake in a preheated 425°F. oven for 25 to 30 minutes, or until the the crust is nicely browned. Remove from the pans and transfer to a rack to cool. ❖

Coriander Bread

MAKES 1 ROUND LOAF

Because it is baked in a soufflé dish, this spicy loaf comes out exceptionally high. Cut in wedges to serve, or divide the loaf in half and then cut the halves into slices.

¾ cup milk
¼ cup honey
¼ cup butter or margarine
1 teaspoon salt
1 package dry yeast, dissolved in ¼ cup warm water
1 large egg, beaten
1 teaspoon finely grated orange zest
2 tablespoons ground coriander
¼ teaspoon cinnamon
⅛ teaspoon ground ginger
⅛ teaspoon ground cloves
3½ to 4 cups bread flour, scoop measured

1. In a wide saucepan, combine the milk, honey, butter, and salt. Place over medium heat and stir until the butter is melted. Transfer to a large mixing bowl.

2. When the mixture is barely warm to the touch, stir in the dissolved yeast and beaten egg. Blend in the orange zest, coriander, cinnamon, ginger, and cloves. Add 1 cup of the flour and beat with a wooden spoon until smooth. Gradually blend in additional flour until the dough becomes too difficult to stir. Turn out onto a floured surface and knead in as much of the remaining flour as necessary to form a cohesive dough. Continue kneading in flour until the dough is soft yet no longer sticks to the work surface. Transfer to a greased bowl and cover with plastic wrap. Secure with an elastic band and set aside to rise until double in bulk.

3. Generously grease an 8-cup soufflé dish. Punch the dough down. Shape into a round loaf and place in the prepared dish. Cover loosely with plastic wrap and let rise. When double in bulk, bake in a preheated 350°F. oven for 40 to 50 minutes, or until the crust is nicely browned. Brush the surface with a small amount of melted butter. Cool on a rack for 5 minutes, then turn out. ❖

Cornmeal Herb Bread

MAKES ONE 9x5-INCH LOAF

A dash of basil and oregano lends excitement to this whole wheat and cornmeal loaf.

1 cup milk
¼ cup honey
1 tablespoon solid vegetable shortening
1 teaspoon salt
1 package dry yeast, dissolved in ¼ cup warm water
1 teaspoon dried basil
1 teaspoon dried oregano
1 cup yellow cornmeal
1½ cups whole wheat flour, scoop measured
1½ to 2 cups bread flour, preferably bromated, scoop measured

1. In a wide saucepan, combine the milk, honey, shortening, and salt. Place over me-

dium heat and stir until the shortening is melted. Transfer to a large mixing bowl.

2. When the mixture is barely warm to the touch, stir in the dissolved yeast. Blend in the basil and oregano. Add the cornmeal and whole wheat flour and beat with a wooden spoon until smooth. Stir in enough of the bread flour to form a stiff dough. Turn out onto a floured surface and knead, working in as much additional bread flour as necessary to form a cohesive dough. Continue kneading in bread flour until the dough is soft yet no longer sticks to the work surface. Transfer to a greased bowl and cover with plastic wrap. Secure with an elastic band and set aside to rise until double in bulk.

3. Generously grease a 9x5-inch loaf pan. Punch the dough down, then turn it out onto a floured surface. Shape it into a loaf and place it in the prepared pan. Cover loosely with plastic wrap and let rise. When double in bulk, bake in a preheated 375°F. oven for 35 to 45 minutes, or until the loaf sounds hollow when you tap the top. Cool on a rack for 5 minutes, then turn out.   ❖

Sesame Cornmeal Bread

MAKES 1 ROUND LOAF

A high, round cornmeal loaf flecked with toasted sesame seeds.

½ cup water
2 tablespoons butter or margarine
2 tablespoons sugar
1 teaspoon salt
½ cup buttermilk
1 package dry yeast, dissolved in ¼ cup warm water
1 cup yellow cornmeal
5 tablespoons toasted sesame seeds
2½ to 3 cups bread flour, scoop measured
1 large egg white, beaten with 1 tablespoon cold water

1. In a wide saucepan, combine the water, butter, sugar, and salt. Place over medium heat and stir until the butter is melted. Re-

move from the heat and stir in the buttermilk. Transfer to a large mixing bowl.

2. When the mixture is barely warm to the touch, stir in the dissolved yeast. Blend in the cornmeal and 4 tablespoons of the sesame seeds. Add 1 cup of the flour and beat with a wooden spoon until smooth. Gradually blend in additional flour until the dough becomes too difficult to stir. Turn out onto a floured surface and knead in as much of the remaining flour as necessary to form a cohesive dough. Continue kneading in flour until the dough is soft yet no longer sticks to the work surface. Transfer to a greased bowl and cover with plastic wrap. Secure with an elastic band and set aside to rise until double in bulk.

3. Generously grease a 9-inch round baking pan. Punch the dough down, then turn it out onto a floured surface. Shape it into a round loaf and place it in the prepared pan. Cover loosely with plastic wrap and let rise. When double in bulk, brush with the beaten egg white and sprinkle the surface with the remaining tablespoon of sesame seeds. Bake in a preheated 350°F. oven for 50 minutes to 1 hour, or until the loaf sounds hollow when you tap the top. Cool on a rack for 5 minutes, then turn out. Complete cooling on the rack.   ❖

Raised Corn Bread

MAKES 1 ROUND LOAF

A sunny yellow round of yeast corn bread. For added flavor, stir in fennel or cumin seeds.

1 cup milk
¼ cup butter or margarine
¼ cup sugar
1 teaspoon salt
1 package dry yeast, dissolved in ½ cup warm water
1 large egg, beaten
1½ cups yellow cornmeal
1 tablespoon fennel or cumin seeds (optional)

2¾ to 3¼ cups bread flour, preferably bromated, scoop measured

1. In a wide saucepan, combine the milk, butter, sugar, and salt. Place over medium heat and stir until the butter is melted. Transfer to a large mixing bowl.

2. When the mixture is barely warm to the touch, stir in the dissolved yeast and beaten egg. Add the cornmeal and beat with a wooden spoon until smooth. Blend in the fennel or cumin seeds. Gradually blend in the bread flour until the dough becomes too difficult to stir. Turn out onto a floured surface and knead in as much of the remaining flour as necessary to form a cohesive dough. Continue kneading in flour until the dough is soft yet no longer sticks to the work surface. Transfer to a greased bowl and cover with plastic wrap. Secure with an elastic band and set aside to rise until double in bulk.

3. Punch the dough down and turn out onto a floured surface. Knead vigorously until the dough is smooth and resilient. Return to the greased bowl. Cover and let rise until double in bulk.

4. Generously grease a baking sheet and sprinkle with cornmeal. Punch the dough down, then turn it out onto a floured surface. Shape it into a round loaf and place it on the prepared sheet. Cover loosely with plastic wrap and let rise. When double in bulk, bake in a preheated 425°F. oven for 30 to 40 minutes, or until the crust is nicely browned. Brush the surface with solid vegetable shortening that has been melted. Remove from the sheet and transfer to a rack to cool. ❖

Cottage Cheese and Chive Bread

MAKES ONE 9x5-INCH LOAF

Cottage cheese is the surprise ingredient in this chive-lively loaf. This bread is a fine companion for fresh fruit salad.

1 large egg
1 cup small-curd cottage cheese
¼ cup butter or margarine, melted
1 teaspoon sugar
1 teaspoon salt
1 package dry yeast, dissolved in ½ cup warm water
¼ cup wheat germ
2 tablespoons chopped fresh chives
2½ to 3 cups bread flour, scoop measured

1. In a wide saucepan, beat the egg and cottage cheese until well blended. Stir in the melted butter, sugar, and salt. Blend in the dissolved yeast, wheat germ, and chives.

2. Add 1 cup of the flour and beat with a wooden spoon until smooth. Gradually blend in additional flour until the dough becomes too difficult to stir. Turn out onto a floured surface and knead in as much of the remaining flour as necessary to form a cohesive dough. Continue kneading in flour until the dough is soft yet no longer sticks to the work surface. Transfer to a greased bowl and cover with a clean kitchen towel. Set aside to rise until double in bulk.

3. Generously grease a 9x5-inch loaf pan. Punch the dough down, then turn it out onto a floured surface. Shape it into a loaf and place it in the prepared pan. Cover and set aside to rise. When double in bulk, bake in a preheated 375°F. oven for 35 to 45 minutes, or until the crust is nicely browned. Cool on a rack for 5 minutes, then turn out. Complete cooling on the rack. ❖

Cracked Wheat Molasses Bread

MAKES TWO 9x5-INCH LOAVES

Cracked wheat fermented with molasses overnight creates a robust flavor with sourdough overtones. This is not a bread for sissies.

2 cups warm water, plus ¼ cup
2 packages dry yeast
⅓ cup molasses
2 tablespoons light brown sugar

¾ cup coarse cracked wheat
5 to 5½ cups bread flour, preferably
　　bromated, scoop measured
1 teaspoon salt
1 tablespoon vegetable oil
1 cup quick-cooking rolled oats
⅓ cup wheat germ

1. In a large mixing bowl, combine 2 cups of the water and 1 package of the yeast. Stir to dissolve the yeast, then add the molasses, sugar, cracked wheat, and 1 cup of the flour. Cover with a clean kitchen towel and set in a warm, draft-free place overnight.

2. Dissolve the remaining package of yeast in the remaining ¼ cup warm water. Add to the cracked wheat mixture and stir to blend. Stir in the salt, oil, oats, and wheat germ. Stir in 1 more cup of the flour and beat with a wooden spoon until smooth. Gradually blend in additional flour until the dough becomes too difficult to stir. Turn out onto a floured surface and knead in as much of the remaining flour as necessary to form a cohesive dough. Continue kneading in flour until the dough is soft yet no longer sticks to the work surface. Transfer to a greased bowl and cover with plastic wrap. Secure with an elastic band and set aside to rise until double in bulk.

3. Generously grease two 9x5-inch loaf pans. Punch the dough down, then turn it out onto a floured surface. Shape it into 2 loaves and place them in the prepared pans. Cover loosely with plastic wrap and let rise. When double in bulk, bake in a preheated 375°F. oven for 35 to 45 minutes, or until the loaves sound hollow when you tap the tops. Cool on a rack for 5 minutes, then turn out. Complete cooling on the rack.　❖

Date Swirl Loaf

MAKES ONE 9x5-INCH LOAF

Layers of flavorful dates swirl through this light-textured whole wheat bread.

2¼ cups cold water
¼ cup sugar

1 pound dates, coarsely chopped
¾ cup milk
3 tablespoons honey
3 tablespoons butter or margarine
1 teaspoon salt
1 package dry yeast, dissolved in ¼ cup warm
　　water
2 cups whole wheat flour, scoop measured
2 to 2½ cups bread flour, preferably
　　bromated, scoop measured

1. In a wide saucepan, combine 1½ cups of the water with the sugar and dates. Place over medium heat and bring to a gentle bubble. Cook, stirring, until the dates are soft and the mixture takes on a thick, spreadable consistency. Remove from the heat and allow to cool to room temperature.

2. In a separate saucepan, combine the remaining ¾ cup water with the milk, honey, butter, and salt. Place over medium heat and stir until the butter is melted. Transfer to a large mixing bowl.

3. When the mixture is barely warm to the touch, stir in the dissolved yeast. Add the whole wheat flour and beat with a wooden spoon until smooth. Gradually blend in the bread flour until the dough becomes too difficult to stir. Turn out onto a floured surface and knead in as much of the remaining bread flour as necessary to form a cohesive dough. Continue kneading in bread flour until the dough is soft yet no longer sticks to the work surface. Transfer to a greased bowl and cover with a clean kitchen towel. Set aside to rise until double in bulk.

4. Generously grease a 9x5-inch loaf pan. Punch the dough down, then turn it out onto a floured surface. Roll into a 9x14-inch rectangle. Trim the edges to square off the rectangle. Lift the dough to loosen it from the work surface. Spread with the date filling to within 1 inch of the edges. Starting at the short side, roll up into a loaf. Pinch the long edges to seal the seam. Place the dough, seam side down, in the prepared pan. (See illustration on page 12.) Cover and set aside to rise. When double in bulk, bake in a preheated 375°F. oven for 35 to 45 min-

utes, or until the crust is nicely browned. Cool on a rack for 5 minutes, then turn out. ❖

Dill Seed Bread

MAKES ONE 9x5-INCH LOAF

Dill seeds impart a unique character to this cottage cheese loaf. Offer thin slices with shrimp or salmon salad.

½ cup cold water
2 tablespoons honey
1 tablespoon butter or margarine
1 teaspoon salt
1 package dry yeast, dissolved in ¼ cup warm water
1 large egg, beaten
1 cup small-curd cottage cheese
1 tablespoon dill seeds
3 to 3½ cups bread flour, scoop measured

1. In a wide saucepan, combine the water, honey, butter, and salt. Place over medium heat and stir until the butter is melted. Transfer to a large mixing bowl.

2. When the mixture is barely warm to the touch, stir in the dissolved yeast and beaten egg. Blend in the cottage cheese and dill seeds. Add 1 cup of the flour and beat with a wooden spoon until smooth. Gradually blend in additional flour until the dough becomes too difficult to stir. Turn out onto a floured surface and knead in as much of the remaining flour as necessary to form a cohesive dough. Continue kneading in flour until the dough is soft yet no longer sticks to the work surface. Transfer

to a greased bowl and cover with a clean kitchen towel. Set aside to rise until double in bulk.

3. Generously grease a 9x5-inch loaf pan. Punch the dough down, then turn it out onto a floured surface. Shape it into a loaf and place it in the prepared pan. Cover and set aside to rise. When double in bulk, bake in a preheated 375°F. oven for 35 to 45 minutes, or until the crust is nicely browned. Cool on a rack for 5 minutes, then turn out. Complete cooling on the rack. ❖

Granola Bread

MAKES ONE 9x5-INCH LOAF

This coarsely textured bread makes the most wonderful breakfast toast. Light eaters especially appreciate the fact that two thin slices give them a satisfying start to the day.

½ cup cold water
½ cup milk
2 tablespoons butter or margarine
¼ cup light brown sugar
¾ teaspoon salt
1 package dry yeast, dissolved in ¼ cup warm water
1½ cups granola cereal, crushed
1½ cups whole wheat flour, scoop measured
2 to 2½ cups bread flour, preferably bromated, scoop measured

1. In a wide saucepan, combine the water, milk, butter, sugar, and salt. Place over medium heat and stir until the butter is melted. Transfer to a large mixing bowl.

2. When the mixture is barely warm to the touch, stir in the dissolved yeast. Blend in the granola and whole wheat flour. Beat thoroughly. Gradually blend in the bread flour until the dough becomes too difficult to stir. Turn out onto a floured surface and knead in as much of the remaining bread flour as necessary to form a cohesive dough. Continue kneading in bread flour until the dough is soft yet no longer sticks to the work surface. Transfer to a greased

bowl and cover with plastic wrap. Secure with an elastic band and set aside to rise until double in bulk.

3. Generously grease a 9x5-inch loaf pan. Punch the dough down, then turn it out onto a floured surface. Shape it into a loaf and place it in the prepared pan. Cover loosely with plastic wrap and let rise. When double in bulk, bake in a preheated 375°F. oven for 35 to 45 minutes, or until the loaf sounds hollow when you tap the top. Cool on a rack for 5 minutes, then turn out. Complete cooling on the rack.   ❖

Honeyed French Bread

MAKES 2 LONG LOAVES

A small amount of honey lends flavor and moisture to this French-style loaf.

2 cups milk
2 tablespoons honey
2 tablespoons butter or margarine
1½ teaspoons salt
1 package dry yeast, dissolved in ¼ cup warm
   water
5 to 6 cups bread flour, preferably bromated,
   scoop measured
1 large egg, beaten with 1 tablespoon cream

1. In a wide saucepan, combine the milk, honey, butter, and salt. Place over medium heat and stir until the butter is melted. Transfer to a large mixing bowl.

2. When the mixture is barely warm to the touch, stir in the dissolved yeast. Add 2 cups of the flour and beat with a wooden spoon until smooth. Gradually blend in additional flour until the dough becomes too difficult to stir. Turn out onto a floured surface and knead in as much of the remaining flour as necessary to form a cohesive dough. Continue kneading in flour until the dough is soft yet no longer sticks to the work surface. Transfer to a greased bowl and cover with plastic wrap. Secure with an elastic band and set aside to rise until double in bulk.

3. Generously grease a baking sheet and sprinkle with cornmeal. Punch the dough down, then turn it out onto a floured surface. Shape it into 2 long, French-style loaves and place them on the prepared sheet. Cover loosely with plastic wrap and let rise. When the loaves have doubled in bulk, brush the surface with the beaten egg. Bake in a preheated 400°F. oven for 30 to 40 minutes, or until the crust is nicely browned. Remove from the sheet and transfer to a rack to cool.   ❖

Honey Walnut Swirl Loaf

MAKES ONE 9x5-INCH LOAF

Shaping this loaf by rolling up the dough from both sides to the center creates a pinwheel pattern when the bread is sliced.

1 cup milk
½ cup butter or margarine
¼ cup granulated sugar
1 teaspoon salt
1 package dry yeast, dissolved in ¼ cup warm
   water
2 large eggs, beaten
4 to 4½ cups bread flour, scoop measured
½ cup honey
½ cup light brown sugar
¾ cup coarsely chopped walnuts

1. In a wide saucepan, combine the milk, ¼ cup of the butter, the granulated sugar, and the salt. Place over medium heat and stir until the butter is melted. Transfer to a large mixing bowl.

2. When the mixture is barely warm to the touch, stir in the dissolved yeast and beaten egg. Add 2 cups of the flour and beat with a wooden spoon until smooth. Gradually blend in additional flour until the dough becomes too difficult to stir. Turn out onto a floured surface and knead in as much of the remaining flour as necessary to form a cohesive dough. Continue kneading in flour until the dough is soft yet no longer sticks to the work surface. Transfer to a greased bowl and cover with a clean kitchen towel. Set aside to rise until double in bulk.

3. Generously grease a 9x5-inch loaf pan. In a small saucepan, combine the remaining ¼ cup butter and the honey. Heat gently, just until the butter is melted. Set aside. Punch the dough down, then turn it out onto a floured surface. Roll into a 9x14-inch rectangle. Trim the edges to square off the rectangle. Lift the dough to loosen it from the work surface. Spread with the honey mixture to within 1 inch of the edges. Sprinkle on the brown sugar and walnuts. Starting at the short side, roll up the dough to the center. Repeat with the other side. Pinch the dough together to seal the seam and place in the prepared pan, seam side down. (See illustration.) Cover and set aside to rise. When double in bulk, bake in a preheated 375°F. oven for 35 to 45 minutes, or until the crust is nicely browned. Cool on a rack for 5 minutes, then turn out. Complete cooling on the rack.   ❖

To make a Honey Walnut Swirl Loaf, roll the dough into a 9x14-inch rectangle, spread with the honey mixture, and sprinkle on the brown sugar and walnuts. Starting at the short side, roll up the dough to the center. Repeat with the other side. Pinch the dough together to seal the seam and place in the prepared pan, seam side down.

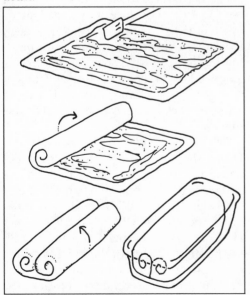

Honey Twist

MAKES 2 ROUND LOAVES

Luscious coils of honey-filled sweet bread make an attractive centerpiece for Sunday brunch.

1 cup milk
¾ cup butter or margarine
¼ cup sugar
1 teaspoon salt
1 package dry yeast, dissolved in ¼ cup warm water
2 large eggs, beaten
4 to 4½ cups bread flour, scoop measured
¼ cup honey
1 cup confectioners' sugar
1 large egg white

1. In a wide saucepan, combine the milk, ¼ cup of the butter, the sugar, and the salt. Place over medium heat and stir until the butter is melted. Transfer to a large mixing bowl.

2. When the mixture is barely warm to the touch, stir in the dissolved yeast and the beaten egg. Add 2 cups of the flour and beat with a wooden spoon until smooth. Gradually blend in additional flour until the dough becomes too difficult to stir. Turn out onto a floured surface and knead in as much of the remaining flour as necessary to form a cohesive dough. Continue kneading in flour until the dough is soft yet no longer sticks to the work surface. Transfer to a greased bowl and cover with a clean kitchen towel. Set aside to rise until double in bulk.

3. Generously grease two 9-inch pie pans. In a mixing bowl, beat the remaining ½ cup butter and the honey until fluffy. Gradually beat in the confectioners' sugar. Add the egg white and blend well. Set aside. Punch the dough down, then turn it out onto a floured surface. Roll the dough into a 12x18-inch rectangle. Trim the edges to square off the rectangle. Lift the dough to loosen it from the work surface. With a serrated knife, cut the dough in half lengthwise to form two 6x18-inch rectangles. Spread each rectan-

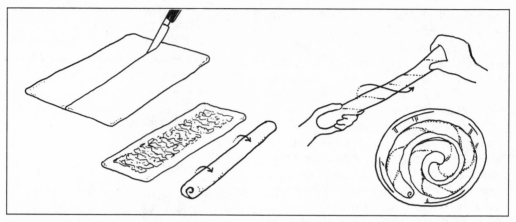

To make a Honey Twist, cut the rolled dough in half lengthwise. Spread each rectangle with ⅓ of the honey mixture. Roll up tightly to form 2 ropes. Take up 1 rope and twist, coiling the dough into the prepared pie pan. Leave generous spaces in the coil for the dough to expand.

gle with ⅓ of the honey mixture to within 1 inch of the edges. Roll up tightly to form 2 ropes. Take up 1 rope and twist, coiling the dough into the prepared pie pan. Repeat with the remaining rope. Leave generous spaces in the coil for the dough to expand. (See illustration.) Cover and set aside to rise. When double in bulk, bake in a preheated 375°F. oven for 25 to 30 minutes, or until golden brown. Remove from the oven and brush the surface with the remaining honey mixture. Cool on a rack for 5 minutes, then turn out. Complete cooling on the rack.   ❖

Herbed Ricotta Bread

MAKES ONE 9x5-INCH LOAF

Fresh herbs add immeasurable flavor to this savory loaf. An excellent choice for a spring picnic.

2 large eggs
1½ cups ricotta
¼ cup butter or margarine, melted
2 tablespoons sugar
1 teaspoon salt
1 package dry yeast, dissolved in ¼ cup warm water
1 tablespoon chopped fresh basil
1 tablespoon chopped fresh oregano
1 tablespoon chopped fresh rosemary

3½ to 4 cups bread flour, scoop measured
1 large egg yolk, beaten with 1 tablespoon cold water

1. Beat the eggs in a large mixing bowl. Add the ricotta, melted butter, sugar, and salt, and blend thoroughly. Stir in the dissolved yeast. Add the basil, oregano, and rosemary, and mix well.

2. Add 1 cup of the flour and beat with a wooden spoon until well incorporated. Gradually blend in additional flour until the dough becomes too difficult to stir. Turn out onto a floured surface and knead in as much of the remaining flour as necessary to form a cohesive dough. Continue kneading in flour until the dough is soft yet no longer sticks to the work surface. Transfer to a greased bowl and cover with a clean kitchen towel. Set aside to rise until double in bulk.

3. Generously grease a 9x5-inch loaf pan. Punch the dough down, then turn it out onto a floured surface. Shape it into a loaf and place it in the prepared pan. Cover and set aside to rise. When double in bulk, brush the surface with the beaten egg yolk and bake in a preheated 375°F. oven for 35 to 45 minutes, or until the crust is golden brown. Cool on a rack for 5 minutes, then turn out. Complete cooling on the rack.   ❖

Herbed Whole Wheat Bread

MAKES 1 ROUND LOAF

Perfumed with rosemary, this earthy loaf is a delicious partner for grilled chicken or lamb.

1 cup warm water
1 package dry yeast
1 tablespoon sugar
1 teaspoon salt
2 teaspoons dried rosemary, crushed with a mortar and pestle
2 cups whole wheat flour, scoop measured
1½ to 2 cups bread flour, preferably bromated, scoop measured

1. In a large mixing bowl, combine the water, yeast, and sugar. Stir to dissolve the yeast, then blend in the salt and rosemary.

2. Add the whole wheat flour and beat with a wooden spoon until smooth. Gradually blend in some of the bread flour until the dough becomes too difficult to stir. Turn out onto a floured surface and knead in as much of the remaining bread flour as necessary to form a cohesive dough. Continue kneading in bread flour until the dough is soft yet no longer sticks to the work surface. Transfer to a greased bowl and cover with plastic wrap. Secure with an elastic band and set aside to rise until double in bulk.

3. Generously grease a baking sheet. Punch the dough down, then turn it out onto a floured surface. Shape it into a round loaf and place it on the prepared sheet. Cover loosely with plastic wrap and let rise. When double in bulk, bake in a preheated 375°F. oven for 35 to 45 minutes, or until the loaf sounds hollow when you tap the top. Remove from the sheet and transfer to a rack to cool. ❖

Honey Wheat Bread

MAKES 1 ROUND LOAF

Baked in a buttered casserole, this whole wheat loaf makes a generous round.

1 cup milk
½ cup honey
⅓ cup solid vegetable shortening
1½ teaspoons salt
1 package dry yeast, dissolved in ½ cup warm water
2 large eggs, beaten
½ cup wheat bran
2 cups whole wheat flour, scoop measured
2½ to 3 cups bread flour, preferably bromated, scoop measured

1. In a wide saucepan, combine the milk, honey, shortening, and salt. Place over medium heat and stir until the shortening is melted. Transfer to a large mixing bowl.

2. When the mixture is barely warm to the touch, stir in the dissolved yeast and beaten egg. Add the wheat bran and whole wheat flour and beat with a wooden spoon until smooth. Gradually blend in the bread flour until the dough becomes too difficult to stir. Turn out onto a floured surface and knead in as much of the remaining bread flour as necessary to form a cohesive dough. Continue kneading in bread flour until the dough is soft yet no longer sticks to the work surface. Transfer to a greased bowl and cover with plastic wrap. Secure with an elastic band and set aside to rise until double in bulk.

3. Generously grease a bowl-shaped 3-quart casserole. Punch the dough down, then turn it out onto a floured surface. Shape it into a round loaf and place it in the prepared dish. Cover loosely with plastic wrap and let rise. When double in bulk, bake in a preheated 375°F. oven for 35 to 45 minutes, or until the loaf sounds hollow when you tap the top. Cool on a rack for 5 minutes, then turn out. Complete cooling on the rack. ❖

Kasha Bread

MAKES TWO 9x5-INCH LOAVES

Kasha is the toasted version of buckwheat groats. It is available in bulk at health-food stores or sold in 1-pound boxes in large supermarkets. It is fre-

quently found with items used in Jewish cuisine, such as jars of chave, rather than with other grains.

1 cup kasha
1 large egg, beaten
2 cups hot water
1½ cups milk
⅓ cup molasses
2 tablespoons vegetable oil
1 teaspoon salt
2 packages dry yeast, dissolved in ½ cup
  warm water
½ cup rye flour, scoop measured
3½ to 4 cups bread flour, preferably
  bromated, scoop measured

1. In a wide saucepan, combine the kasha and beaten egg. Stir over medium heat until the grains become separate. Add the hot water and bring to a boil. Simmer, uncovered, for 20 minutes, or until the kasha is tender. Remove from the heat and stir in the milk, molasses, oil, and salt. Transfer to a large mixing bowl to cool.

2. When the mixture is barely warm to the touch, stir in the dissolved yeast. Add the rye flour and 2 cups of the bread flour, and beat with a wooden spoon until smooth. Gradually blend in additional bread flour until the dough becomes too difficult to stir. Turn out onto a floured surface and knead in as much of the remaining bread flour as necessary to form a cohesive dough. Continue kneading in bread flour until the dough is soft yet no longer sticks to the work surface. Transfer to a greased bowl and cover with plastic wrap. Secure with an elastic band and set aside to rise until double in bulk.

3. Generously grease two 9x5-inch loaf pans. Punch the dough down, then turn it out onto a floured surface. Shape it into 2 loaves and place them in the prepared pans. Cover loosely with plastic wrap and let rise. When double in bulk, bake in a preheated 350°F. oven for 50 minutes to 1 hour, or until the loaves sound hollow when you tap the tops. Cool on a rack for 5 minutes, then turn out. Complete cooling on the rack.   ❖

Lemon Bread

MAKES ONE 9x5-INCH LOAF

Zingy lemon bread, replete with golden raisins, is the perfect loaf to serve for a summer luncheon.

⅔ cup freshly squeezed lemon juice
¼ cup butter or margarine, melted
3 tablespoons sugar
¾ teaspoon salt
1 package dry yeast, dissolved in ½ cup warm
  water
2 large eggs, beaten
1 tablespoon finely grated lemon zest
4 to 4½ cups bread flour, scoop measured
¾ cup golden raisins

1. In a large mixing bowl, combine the lemon juice, melted butter, sugar, and salt. Stir in the dissolved yeast and beaten egg. Blend in the lemon zest. Add 1 cup of the flour and beat with a wooden spoon until smooth. Stir in the raisins.

2. Gradually blend in additional flour until the dough becomes too difficult to stir. Turn out onto a floured surface and knead in as much of the remaining flour as necessary to form a cohesive dough. Continue kneading in flour until the dough is soft yet no longer sticks to the work surface. Transfer to a greased bowl and cover with a clean kitchen towel. Set aside to rise until double in bulk.

3. Generously grease a 9x5-inch loaf pan. Punch the dough down, then turn it out onto a floured surface. Shape it into a loaf and place it in the prepared pan. Cover and set aside to rise. When double in bulk, bake in a preheated 375°F. oven for 35 to 45 min-

utes, or until the crust is nicely browned. Cool on a rack for 5 minutes, then turn out. Complete cooling on the rack. ❖

Maple Oatmeal Bread

MAKES TWO 9x5-INCH LOAVES

Hot from the oven, this homey loaf con-jures up visions of a snug New England kitchen on a snowy morning.

1 cup quick-cooking rolled oats
1 cup pure maple syrup
4 tablespoons butter or margarine, cut into
  small pieces
¾ cup boiling water
1 cup strong coffee
½ cup sugar
1 teaspoon salt
1 package dry yeast, dissolved in ¼ cup warm
  water
2 large eggs, beaten
5½ to 6 cups bread flour, preferably
  bromated, scoop measured

1. In a large mixing bowl, combine the oats, maple syrup, and butter. Pour on the boiling water and stir to melt the butter. Blend in the coffee, sugar, and salt. Allow to cool.

2. When the mixture is barely warm to the touch, stir in the dissolved yeast and beaten egg. Add 2 cups of the flour and beat with a wooden spoon until smooth. Gradu-ally blend in additional flour until the dough becomes too difficult to stir. Turn out onto a floured surface and knead in as much of the remaining flour as necessary to form a cohesive dough. Continue knead-ing in flour until the dough is soft yet no longer sticks to the work surface. Transfer to a greased bowl and cover with plastic wrap. Secure with an elastic band and set aside to rise until double in bulk.

3. Generously grease two 9x5-inch loaf pans. Punch the dough down, then turn it out onto a floured surface. Shape it into 2 loaves and place them in the prepared pans. Cover loosely with plastic wrap and let rise.

When double in bulk, bake in a preheated 375°F. oven for 35 to 45 minutes, or until the loaves sound hollow when you tap the tops. Cool on a rack for 5 minutes, then turn out. Complete cooling on the rack. ❖

Maple Whole Wheat Bread

MAKES ONE 9x5-INCH LOAF

The enticing flavor of maple syrup comple-ments the robust character of whole wheat. A sturdy loaf for cold-weather feasting.

1½ cups cold water
¼ cup milk
¼ cup pure maple syrup
3 tablespoons butter or margarine
1 teaspoon salt
1 package dry yeast, dissolved in ¼ cup warm
  water
4 to 4½ cups whole wheat flour, scoop
  measured

1. In a wide saucepan, combine the water, milk, maple syrup, butter, and salt. Place over medium heat and stir until the butter is melted. Transfer to a large mixing bowl to cool.

2. When the mixture is barely warm to the touch, stir in the dissolved yeast. Add 2 cups of the flour and beat with a wooden spoon until smooth. Gradually blend in ad-ditional flour until the dough becomes too difficult to stir. Turn out onto a floured sur-face and knead in as much of the remaining flour as necessary to form a cohesive dough. Continue kneading in flour until the dough is soft yet no longer sticks to the work surface. Transfer to a greased bowl and cov-er with plastic wrap. Secure with an elastic band and set aside to rise until double in bulk.

3. Punch down the dough and turn out onto a floured surface. Knead vigorously until the dough is smooth and resilient. Re-turn to the greased bowl. Cover with plastic wrap and let rise until double in bulk.

4. Generously grease a 9x5-inch loaf pan. Punch the dough down, then turn it out onto a floured surface. Shape it into a loaf and place it in the prepared pan. Cover loosely with plastic wrap and let rise. When double in bulk, bake in a preheated 400°F. oven for 40 to 50 minutes, or until the loaf sounds hollow when you tap the top. Cool on a rack for 5 minutes, then turn out. Complete cooling on the rack.   ❖

Honey Millet Bread

MAKES TWO 9x5-INCH LOAVES

Look for ground millet in health-food stores. Also, you can grind whole millet in a blender to achieve the texture needed for this bread.

1 cup milk
⅓ cup honey
2 tablespoons butter or margarine
1½ teaspoons salt
2 packages dry yeast, dissolved in 1 cup warm water
1 cup ground millet
2 cups whole wheat flour, scoop measured
3½ to 4 cups bread flour, preferably bromated, scoop measured

1. In a wide saucepan, combine the milk, honey, butter, and salt. Place over medium heat and stir until the butter is melted. Transfer to a large mixing bowl.

2. When the mixture is barely warm to the touch, stir in the dissolved yeast. Add the millet and whole wheat flour and beat with a wooden spoon until smooth. Gradually blend in the bread flour until the dough becomes too difficult to stir. Turn out onto a floured surface and knead in as much of the remaining bread flour as necessary to form a cohesive dough. Continue kneading in bread flour until the dough is soft yet no longer sticks to the work surface. Transfer to a greased bowl and cover with plastic wrap. Secure with an elastic band and set aside to rise until double in bulk.

3. Generously grease two 9x5-inch loaf pans. Punch the dough down, then turn it out onto a floured surface. Shape it into 2 loaves and place them in the prepared pans. Cover loosely with plastic wrap and let rise. When double in bulk, bake in a preheated 375°F. oven for 35 to 45 minutes, or until the loaves sound hollow when you tap the tops. Cool on a rack for 5 minutes, then turn out. Complete cooling on the rack.   ❖

Molasses Multigrain Bread

MAKES TWO 9x5-INCH LOAVES

Substantial, satisfying loaves for hearty eaters and lovers of full-bodied bread.

1½ cups milk
½ cup molasses
¼ cup butter or margarine
¼ cup sugar
1½ teaspoons salt
2 packages dry yeast, dissolved in ½ cup warm water
2 large eggs, beaten
½ cup quick-cooking rolled oats
½ cup wheat germ
½ cup 100% bran cereal (not flakes)
2 cups whole wheat flour, scoop measured
3½ to 4 cups bread flour, preferably bromated, scoop measured

1. In a wide saucepan, combine the milk, molasses, butter, sugar, and salt. Place over medium heat and stir until the butter is melted. Transfer to a large mixing bowl.

2. When the mixture is barely warm to the touch, stir in the dissolved yeast and beaten egg. Add the oats, wheat germ, bran cereal, and whole wheat flour. Beat with a wooden spoon until smooth. Gradually blend in the bread flour until the dough becomes too difficult to stir. Turn out onto a floured surface and knead in as much of the remaining bread flour as necessary to form a cohesive dough. Continue kneading in bread flour until the dough is soft yet no longer sticks to the work surface. Transfer to a greased bowl and cover with plastic

wrap. Secure with an elastic band and set aside to rise until double in bulk.

3. Generously grease two 9x5-inch loaf pans. Punch the dough down, then turn it out onto a floured surface. Shape it into 2 loaves and place them in the prepared pans. Cover loosely with plastic wrap and let rise. When double in bulk, bake in a preheated 375°F. oven for 35 to 45 minutes, or until the loaves sound hollow when you tap the tops. Cool on a rack for 5 minutes, then turn out. Complete cooling on the rack. ❖

Molasses Wheat Bread

MAKES ONE 9x5-INCH LOAF

The down-home flavor of molasses infuses this loaf with earthy goodness.

1¼ cups milk
¼ cup molasses
2 tablespoons sugar
1 teaspoon salt
1 package dry yeast, dissolved in ¼ cup warm water
1 large egg, beaten
2 tablespoons vegetable oil
½ cup wheat germ
2 cups whole wheat flour, scoop measured
2 to 2½ cups bread flour, preferably bromated, scoop measured

1. In a wide saucepan, combine the milk, molasses, sugar, and salt. Place over medium heat and stir until the molasses liquefies. Transfer to a large mixing bowl to cool.

2. When the mixture is barely warm to the touch, stir in the dissolved yeast and beaten egg. Blend in the oil. Add the wheat germ and whole wheat flour, and beat with a wooden spoon until smooth. Gradually blend in the bread flour until the dough becomes too difficult to stir. Turn out onto a floured surface and knead in as much of the remaining bread flour as necessary to form a cohesive dough. Continue kneading in bread flour until the dough is soft yet no longer sticks to the work surface. Transfer to a greased bowl and cover with plastic

wrap. Secure with an elastic band and set aside to rise until double in bulk.

3. Generously grease a 9x5-inch loaf pan. Punch the dough down, then turn it out onto a floured surface. Shape it into a loaf and place it in the prepared pan. Cover loosely with plastic wrap and let rise. When double in bulk, bake in a preheated 375°F. oven for 35 to 45 minutes, or until the loaf sounds hollow when you tap the top. Cool on a rack for 5 minutes, then turn out. Complete cooling on the rack. ❖

Hearty Multigrain Bread

MAKES 2 ROUND LOAVES

Sunflower seeds contribute nutty flavor to this densely textured loaf.

2 cups milk
⅔ cup honey
2 tablespoons molasses
¼ cup butter or margarine
1½ teaspoons salt
2 packages dry yeast, dissolved in ½ cup warm water
½ cup rye flour, scoop measured
3 cups whole wheat flour, scoop measured
½ cup sunflower seeds
¼ cup wheat germ
¼ cup 100% bran cereal flakes
3½ to 4 cups bread flour, preferably bromated, scoop measured

1. In a wide saucepan, combine the milk, honey, molasses, butter, and salt. Place over medium heat and stir until the butter is melted. Transfer to a large mixing bowl to cool.

2. When the mixture is barely warm to the touch, stir in the dissolved yeast. Add the rye flour and whole wheat flour and beat with a wooden spoon until smooth. Stir in the sunflower seeds, wheat germ, and bran flakes. Gradually blend in the bread flour until the dough becomes too difficult to stir. Turn out onto a floured surface and knead in as much of the remaining bread flour as necessary to form a cohesive dough. Con-

tinue kneading in bread flour until the dough is soft yet no longer sticks to the work surface. Transfer to a greased bowl and cover with plastic wrap. Secure with an elastic band and set aside to rise until double in bulk.

3. Generously grease a baking sheet and sprinkle with cornmeal. Punch the dough down, then turn it out onto a floured surface. Shape it into 2 round loaves and place them on the prepared sheet. Cover loosely with plastic wrap and let rise. When double in bulk, bake in a preheated 375°F. oven for 35 to 45 minutes, or until the loaves sound hollow when you tap the tops. Remove from the sheet and transfer to a rack to cool. ❖

Oatmeal Molasses Bread

MAKES 2 ROUND LOAVES

Round loaves of molasses-scented oatmeal bread to serve with hearty winter casseroles.

1 cup warm water
2 packages dry yeast
1 cup milk
¼ cup molasses
1 cup quick-cooking rolled oats
¼ cup butter or margarine, melted
1½ teaspoons salt
2 large eggs, beaten
5½ to 6 cups bread flour, preferably
    bromated, scoop measured

1. Measure the water into a large mixing bowl. Sprinkle on the yeast and stir to dissolve. Blend in the milk and molasses. Add the oats, melted butter, salt, and beaten egg. Blend thoroughly.

2. Add 2 cups of the flour and beat with a wooden spoon until smooth. Gradually blend in additional flour until the dough becomes too difficult to stir. Turn out onto a floured surface and knead in as much of the remaining flour as necessary to form a cohesive dough. Continue kneading in flour until the dough is soft yet no longer sticks to the work surface. Transfer to a greased

bowl and cover with a clean kitchen towel. Allow the dough to rise until double in bulk.

3. Generously grease a baking sheet. Punch the dough down, then turn it out onto a floured surface. Shape it into 2 round loaves and place them on the prepared sheet. Cover and set aside to rise. When double in bulk, bake in a preheated 375°F. oven for 35 to 45 minutes, or until the loaves sound hollow when you tap the tops. Remove from the sheet and transfer to a rack to cool. ❖

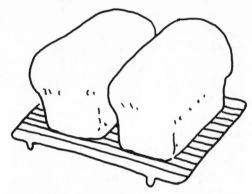

Oatmeal Bread

MAKES TWO 9x5-INCH LOAVES

Satisfy your longing for old-fashioned oatmeal bread with this honey-scented loaf.

1 cup cold water
1 cup milk
2 tablespoons honey
2 tablespoons butter or margarine
1½ teaspoons salt
1 package dry yeast, dissolved in ¼ cup warm
    water
2 cups whole wheat flour, scoop measured
1 cup quick-cooking rolled oats
3½ to 4 cups bread flour, scoop measured

1. In a wide saucepan, combine the water, milk, honey, butter, and salt. Place over medium heat and stir until the butter is melted. Transfer to a large mixing bowl to cool.

2. When the mixture is barely warm to the touch, stir in the dissolved yeast. Add the whole wheat flour and beat with a wooden spoon until smooth. Stir in the oats. Gradually blend in the bread flour until the

dough becomes too difficult to stir. Turn out onto a floured surface and knead in as much of the remaining bread flour as necessary to form a cohesive dough. Continue kneading in bread flour until the dough is soft yet no longer sticks to the work surface. Transfer to a greased bowl and cover with a clean kitchen towel. Allow the dough to rise until double in bulk.

3. Generously grease two 9x5-inch loaf pans. Punch the dough down, then turn it out onto a floured surface. Shape it into 2 loaves and place them in the prepared pans. Cover and set aside to rise. When double in bulk, bake in a preheated 375°F. oven for 35 to 45 minutes, or until the loaves sound hollow when you tap the tops. Cool on a rack for 5 minutes, then turn out. Complete cooling on the rack.   ❖

Peanut Butter Rye Bread

MAKES 2 OBLONG LOAVES

For cooks who grew up loving peanut butter spread on rye bread, this loaf offers the best of both worlds.

1½ cups water
½ cup smooth peanut butter
2 tablespoons molasses
2 tablespoons sugar
1½ teaspoons salt
2 packages dry yeast, dissolved in ½ cup warm water
3 cups rye flour, scoop measured
1 cup dry roasted, unsalted peanuts, coarsely chopped
3 to 3½ cups bread flour, preferably bromated, scoop measured

1. In a wide saucepan, combine the water, peanut butter, molasses, sugar, and salt. Place over medium heat and stir until the peanut butter is melted. Transfer to a large mixing bowl to cool.

2. When the mixture is barely warm to the touch, stir in the dissolved yeast. Add the rye flour and beat with a wooden spoon until smooth. Stir in the peanuts. Gradual-

ly blend in the bread flour until the dough becomes too difficult to stir. Turn out onto a floured surface and knead in as much of the remaining bread flour as necessary to form a cohesive dough. Continue kneading in bread flour until the dough is soft yet no longer sticks to the work surface. Transfer to a greased bowl and cover with plastic wrap. Secure with an elastic band and set aside to rise until double in bulk.

3. Generously grease a baking sheet. Punch the dough down, then turn it out onto a floured surface. Shape it into 2 oblong loaves and place them on the prepared sheet. Cover loosely with plastic wrap and let rise. When double in bulk, bake in a preheated 375°F. oven for 35 to 45 minutes, or until the loaves sound hollow when you tap the tops. Remove from the sheet and transfer to a rack to cool.   ❖

Peanut Whole Wheat Bread

MAKES ONE 9x5-INCH LOAF

A liberal sprinkling of coarsely chopped peanuts gives crunch to this enjoyable whole wheat bread.

1 cup milk
⅓ cup smooth peanut butter
2 tablespoons sugar
1 teaspoon salt
1 package dry yeast, dissolved in ¼ cup warm water
1 large egg, beaten
2 cups whole wheat flour, scoop measured
1 cup coarsely chopped unsalted roasted peanuts
1½ to 2 cups bread flour, scoop measured

1. In a wide saucepan, combine the milk, peanut butter, sugar, and salt. Place over medium heat and stir until the peanut butter is melted. Transfer to a large mixing bowl to cool.

2. When the mixture is barely warm to the touch, stir in the dissolved yeast and beaten egg. Add the whole wheat flour and beat with a wooden spoon until smooth. Stir in the peanuts. Gradually blend in the

bread flour until the dough becomes too difficult to stir. Turn out onto a floured surface and knead in as much of the remaining bread flour as necessary to form a cohesive dough. Continue kneading in bread flour until the dough is soft yet no longer sticks to the work surface. Transfer to a greased bowl and cover with plastic wrap. Secure with an elastic band and set aside to rise until double in bulk.

3. Generously grease a 9x5-inch loaf pan. Punch the dough down, then turn it out onto a floured surface. Shape it into a loaf and place it in the prepared pan. Cover loosely with plastic wrap and let rise. When double in bulk, bake in a preheated 375°F. oven for 35 to 45 minutes, or until the loaf sounds hollow when you tap the top. Cool on a rack for 5 minutes, then turn out. Complete cooling on the rack.   ❖

Poppy Seed Swirl Loaf

MAKES ONE 9x5-INCH LOAF

A filling of poppy seeds and honey, sparked with lemon, twines throughout this attractive loaf.

4 tablespoons poppy seeds
1 tablespoon honey
4 teaspoons sugar
1 teaspoon freshly squeezed lemon juice
1 large egg, separated
2 teaspoons cold water
1 cup milk
2 tablespoons butter or margarine
1 teaspoon salt
1 package dry yeast, dissolved in ¼ cup warm
    water
3 to 3½ cups bread flour, scoop measured

1. In a small saucepan, combine 3 tablespoons of the poppy seeds, the honey, 1 teaspoon of the sugar, and the lemon juice. Place over medium heat and stir until the honey liquefies. Remove from the heat. Whisk the egg yolk in a small bowl with 1 teaspoon of the cold water. Gradually whisk in the hot poppy seed mixture. Return the

mixture to the saucepan and place over low heat. Cook, stirring, until thickened. Set aside to cool to room temperature.

2. In a wide saucepan, combine the milk, butter, remaining 3 teaspoons sugar, and salt. Place over medium heat and stir until the butter is melted. Transfer to a large mixing bowl to cool.

3. When the mixture is barely warm to the touch, stir in the dissolved yeast. Add 1 cup of the flour and beat with a wooden spoon until smooth. Gradually blend in additional flour until the dough becomes too difficult to stir. Turn out onto a floured surface and knead in as much of the remaining flour as necessary to form a cohesive dough. Continue kneading in flour until the dough is soft yet no longer sticks to the work surface. Transfer to a greased bowl and cover with a clean kitchen towel. Set aside to rise until double in bulk.

4. Generously grease a 9x5-inch loaf pan. Punch the dough down, then turn it out onto a floured surface. Roll it into a 9x14-inch rectangle. Trim the edges to square off the rectangle. Lift the dough to loosen it from the work surface. Spread with the poppy seed mixture to within 1 inch of the edges. Starting with the short side, roll up the dough and pinch the long edge to seal the seam. Place, seam side down, in the prepared pan. (See illustration on page 12.) Cover and set aside to rise. When double in bulk, whisk the egg white with the remaining teaspoon cold water and brush over the surface. Sprinkle on the remaining tablespoon poppy seeds. Bake in a preheated 375°F. oven for 35 to 45 minutes, or until the crust is nicely browned. Cool on a rack for 5 minutes, then turn out. Complete cooling on the rack.   ❖

Portuguese Sweet Bread

MAKES 2 ROUND LOAVES

Richly glazed rounds of egg-enriched bread. Serve warm for brunch or spread thin slices with herbed butter to accompany a luncheon salad.

1 cup milk
½ cup butter or margarine
1 cup sugar
1 teaspoon salt
1 package dry yeast, dissolved in ¼ cup warm
  water
3 large eggs, beaten
5 to 6 cups bread flour, scoop measured
1 teaspoon cold water

1. In a wide saucepan, combine the milk, butter, sugar, and salt. Place over medium heat and stir until the butter is melted. Transfer to a large mixing bowl to cool.

2. When the mixture is barely warm to the touch, stir in the dissolved yeast. Measure out 2 tablespoons of the beaten egg and set aside. Blend the remainder into the milk mixture. Add 2 cups of the flour and beat with a wooden spoon until smooth. Gradually blend in additional flour until the dough becomes too difficult to stir. Turn out onto a floured surface and knead in as much of the remaining flour as necessary to form a cohesive dough. Continue kneading in flour until the dough is soft yet no longer sticks to the work surface. Transfer to a greased bowl and cover with a clean kitchen towel. Set aside to rise until double in bulk.

3. Generously grease two 9-inch round baking pans. Punch the dough down, then turn it out onto a floured surface. Shape it into 2 round, flat loaves. Place in the prepared pans and pat the dough so that it

touches the sides of the pans. Cover and set aside to rise. When double in bulk, whisk the reserved egg with the cold water and brush over the surface. Bake in a preheated 350°F. oven for 30 to 40 minutes, or until the crust is golden brown. Cool on a rack for 5 minutes, then turn out. Complete cooling on the rack. ❖

Pumpernickel Bread

MAKES 2 ROUND LOAVES

These relatively light-textured, molasses-scented loaves are flecked with caraway seeds and make good sandwiches.

1 cup cold water
½ cup molasses
2 tablespoons solid vegetable shortening
1½ teaspoons salt
2 packages dry yeast, dissolved in ½ cup
  warm water
2 tablespoons caraway seeds
2¾ cups rye flour, scoop measured
3 to 3½ cups bread flour, preferably
  bromated, scoop measured

1. In a wide saucepan, combine the water, molasses, shortening, and salt. Place over medium heat and stir until the shortening is melted. Transfer to a large mixing bowl to cool.

2. When the mixture is barely warm to the touch, stir in the dissolved yeast. Blend in the caraway seeds. Add the rye flour and beat with a wooden spoon until smooth. Gradually blend in the bread flour until the dough becomes too difficult to stir. Turn out onto a floured surface and knead in as much of the remaining bread flour as necessary to form a cohesive dough. Continue kneading in bread flour until the dough is soft yet no longer sticks to the work surface. Transfer to a greased bowl and cover with plastic wrap. Secure with an elastic band and set aside to rise until double in bulk.

3. Generously grease a baking sheet and sprinkle with cornmeal. Punch the dough down, then turn it out onto a floured sur-

face. Shape it into 2 round loaves and place them on the prepared sheet. Cover loosely with plastic wrap and let rise. When double in bulk, bake in a preheated 375°F. oven for 35 to 45 minutes, or until the loaves sound hollow when you tap the tops. Remove from the sheet and transfer to a rack to cool. ❖

Raisin Pumpernickel Bread

MAKES 2 OBLONG LOAVES

In this recipe, pumpernickel dough rises twice to give it added flavor with a hint of sour tang.

1 cup milk
½ cup molasses
2 tablespoons butter or margarine
1½ teaspoons salt
2 packages dry yeast, dissolved in ½ cup
    warm water
2½ cups dark rye flour, scoop measured
¾ cup raisins
2 tablespoons finely grated orange zest
3½ to 4 cups bread flour, preferably
    bromated, scoop measured

1. In a wide saucepan, combine the milk, molasses, butter, and salt. Place over medium heat and stir until the butter is melted. Transfer to a large mixing bowl to cool.

2. When the mixture is barely warm to the touch, stir in the dissolved yeast. Add the rye flour and beat with a wooden spoon until smooth. Stir in the raisins and orange zest. Gradually blend in the bread flour until the dough becomes too difficult to stir. Turn out onto a floured surface and knead in as much of the remaining bread flour as necessary to form a cohesive dough. Continue kneading in bread flour until the dough is soft yet no longer sticks to the work surface. Transfer to a greased bowl and cover with plastic wrap. Secure with an elastic band and set aside to rise until double in bulk.

3. Punch down the dough and turn it out onto a floured surface. Knead vigorously until the dough is smooth and resilient. Re-turn to the greased bowl. Cover and let rise until double in bulk.

4. Generously grease a baking sheet and sprinkle with cornmeal. Punch the dough down, then turn it out onto a floured surface. Shape it into 2 oblong loaves and place them on the prepared sheet. Cover loosely with plastic wrap and let rise. When double in bulk, bake in a preheated 375°F. oven for 35 to 45 minutes, or until the loaves sound hollow when you tap the tops. Remove from the sheet and transfer to a rack to cool. ❖

Spiced Raisin Pumpernickel

MAKES 1 ROUND LOAF

A dense, chewy loaf bursting with spicy flavor and aroma.

½ cup warm water
1 package dry yeast
¼ cup molasses
1 cup unflavored yogurt
3½ cups dark rye flour, scoop measured
1 cup cold water
3 tablespoons butter or margarine
1 teaspoon salt
1 ounce unsweetened chocolate
1 teaspoon cinnamon
½ teaspoon allspice
½ teaspoon ground ginger
¾ cup raisins
2½ to 3 cups bread flour, preferably
    bromated, scoop measured

1. In a large mixing bowl, combine the warm water and yeast and stir to dissolve. Blend in the molasses, then stir in the yogurt. Add 1½ cups of the rye flour and stir until smooth. Cover the bowl with plastic wrap and secure with an elastic band. Set aside for 1½ hours, or until the bubbling action slows and the mixture begins to collapse on itself.

2. In a wide saucepan, combine the cold water, butter, salt, and chocolate. Place over medium heat and stir until the butter and chocolate are melted. Stir into the yeast mixture. Stir in the cinnamon, allspice,

and ginger. Add the remaining 2 cups rye flour and beat with a wooden spoon until smooth. Stir in the raisins. Gradually blend in the bread flour until the dough becomes too difficult to stir. Turn out onto a floured surface and knead in as much of the remaining bread flour as necessary to form a cohesive dough. Continue kneading in bread flour until the dough is soft yet no longer sticks to the work surface. Transfer to a greased bowl and cover with plastic wrap. Secure with an elastic band and set aside to rise until double in bulk.

3. Generously grease an 8-inch springform pan. Punch the dough down, then turn it out onto a floured surface. Shape it into a round loaf and place it in the prepared pan. Cover loosely with plastic wrap and let rise. When double in bulk, bake in a preheated 375°F. oven for 35 to 45 minutes, or until the loaf sounds hollow when you tap the top. Cool on a rack for 5 minutes, then release the sides of the pan. Turn the loaf out and transfer to a rack to complete cooling. ❖

Raisin Braid

MAKES 2 BRAIDED LOAVES

These beautiful loaves are rich with eggs and butter and studded with raisins.

1 cup milk
6 tablespoons butter or margarine
½ cup sugar
1½ teaspoons salt
1 package dry yeast, dissolved in ¼ cup warm
  water
3 large eggs, beaten
6 to 6½ cups bread flour, scoop measured
¾ cup raisins
1 teaspoon cold water

1. In a wide saucepan, combine the milk, butter, sugar, and salt. Place over medium heat and stir until the butter is melted. Transfer to a large mixing bowl to cool.

2. When the mixture is barely warm to the touch, stir in the dissolved yeast. Measure out 2 tablespoons of the beaten egg

and set aside in a glass measuring cup. Stir the remainder into the yeast mixture. Add 2 cups of the flour and beat with a wooden spoon until smooth. Stir in the raisins. Gradually blend in additional flour until the dough becomes too difficult to stir. Turn out onto a floured surface and knead in as much of the remaining flour as necessary to form a cohesive dough. Continue kneading in flour until the dough is soft yet no longer sticks to the work surface. Transfer to a greased bowl and cover with a clean kitchen towel. Set aside to rise until double in bulk.

3. Generously grease a baking sheet. Punch the dough down and press into a flat rectangle. Using a serrated knife, cut the dough lengthwise into 6 equal portions. Dust with flour and roll each portion with the palms of your hands into a 10-inch rope. Take up 3 of the ropes and form into a braid. Pinch the ends together to seal. Transfer to the prepared sheet. (See illustration on page 17.) Repeat with the other 3 ropes. Cover and set aside to rise. When double in bulk, mix the reserved beaten egg with the cold water and brush over the surface. Bake in a preheated 375°F. oven for 25 to 30 minutes, or until the crust is nicely browned. Remove from the sheet and transfer to a rack to cool. ❖

Caraway Rye Bread

MAKES 2 OBLONG LOAVES

This is the familiar caraway loaf that is so popular as a foundation for ham and pastrami sandwiches.

2 cups milk
⅓ cup molasses
2 tablespoons butter or margarine
2 teaspoons salt
1 package dry yeast, dissolved in ¼ cup warm
  water
1 tablespoon caraway seeds
3 cups rye flour, scoop measured
3 to 3½ cups bread flour, preferably
  bromated, scoop measured

1. In a wide saucepan, combine the milk, molasses, butter, and salt. Place over medium heat and stir until the butter is melted. Transfer to a large mixing bowl to cool.

2. When the mixture is barely warm to the touch, stir in the dissolved yeast. Blend in the caraway seeds. Add the rye flour and beat with a wooden spoon until smooth. Gradually blend in the bread flour until the dough becomes too difficult to stir. Turn out onto a floured surface and knead in as much of the remaining bread flour as necessary to form a cohesive dough. Continue kneading in bread flour until the dough is soft yet no longer sticks to the work surface. Transfer to a greased bowl and cover with plastic wrap. Secure with an elastic band and set aside to rise until double in bulk.

3. Generously grease a baking sheet and sprinkle with cornmeal. Punch the dough down, then turn it out onto a floured surface. Shape it into 2 oblong loaves and place them on the prepared sheet. Cover loosely with plastic wrap and let rise. When double in bulk, bake in a preheated 375°F. oven for 35 to 45 minutes, or until the loaves sound hollow when you tap the tops. Remove from the sheet and transfer to a rack to cool. ❖

Deli Rye Bread

MAKES 1 OBLONG LOAF

Sourdough starter gives this rye bread a deep, sour flavor and tantalizing aroma.

1½ cups warm water
2 tablespoons molasses
1 cup water-based sourdough starter (p. 51), not necessarily at room temperature
½ cup yellow cornmeal
1½ cups rye flour, scoop measured
1 package dry yeast, dissolved in ¼ cup warm water
2 tablespoons solid vegetable shortening, melted
1 teaspoon salt
3½ to 4 cups bread flour, preferably bromated, scoop measured

1. In a large mixing bowl, combine the water and molasses, and stir to blend. Add the sourdough starter, cornmeal, and rye flour, and beat with a wooden spoon until smooth. Cover the bowl with plastic wrap and secure with an elastic band. Allow to stand at room temperature for 24 hours.

2. Stir in the dissolved yeast, melted shortening, salt, and 1 cup of the bread flour. Gradually blend in additional bread flour until the dough becomes too difficult to stir. Turn out onto a floured surface and knead in as much of the remaining bread flour as necessary to form a cohesive dough. Continue kneading in bread flour until the dough is soft yet no longer sticks to the work surface. Transfer to a greased bowl and cover with plastic wrap. Secure with an elastic band and set aside to rise until double in bulk.

3. Generously grease a baking sheet and sprinkle with cornmeal. Punch the dough down, then turn it out onto a floured surface. Shape it into an oblong loaf and place it on the prepared sheet. Cover loosely with plastic wrap and let rise. When double in bulk, bake in a preheated 375°F. oven for 35 to 45 minutes, or until the loaf sounds hollow when you tap the top. Remove from the sheet and transfer to a rack to cool. ❖

Fennel Rye Bread

MAKES 1 OBLONG LOAF

Fennel seeds add remarkable flavor to this rye bread. I've suggested a conservative amount — feel free to add more if you like.

½ cup cold water
½ cup milk
2 tablespoons molasses
2 tablespoons light brown sugar
1 teaspoon salt
1 package dry yeast, dissolved in ¼ cup warm water
1½ teaspoons fennel seeds
⅓ cup yellow cornmeal

2 cups rye flour, scoop measured

1½ cups to 2 cups bread flour, preferably bromated, scoop measured

1. In a wide saucepan, combine the water, milk, molasses, sugar, and salt. Place over medium heat and stir until the molasses liquefies. Transfer to a large mixing bowl to cool.

2. When the mixture is barely warm to the touch, stir in the dissolved yeast. Blend in the fennel seeds. Add the cornmeal and rye flour and beat with a wooden spoon until smooth. Gradually blend in the bread flour until the dough becomes too difficult to stir. Turn out onto a floured surface and knead in as much of the remaining bread flour as necessary to form a cohesive dough. Continue kneading in bread flour until the dough is soft yet no longer sticks to the work surface. Transfer to a greased bowl and cover with plastic wrap. Secure with an elastic band and set aside to rise until double in bulk.

3. Generously grease a baking sheet and sprinkle with cornmeal. Punch the dough down, then turn it out onto a floured surface. Shape it into an oblong loaf and place it on the prepared sheet. Cover loosely with plastic wrap and let rise. When double in bulk, bake in a preheated 375°F. oven for 35 to 45 minutes, or until the loaf sounds hollow when you tap the top. Remove from the sheet and transfer to a rack to cool. ❖

Candied Orange Rye

MAKES TWO 9x5-INCH LOAVES

The flavor of candied orange peel is a unique addition to this full-bodied dark rye bread.

1 cup milk
½ cup water
⅓ cup molasses
⅓ cup dark brown sugar
¼ cup butter or margarine
1½ teaspoons salt

2 packages dry yeast, dissolved in ½ cup warm water

1 teaspoon anise seeds

3 cups dark rye flour, scoop measured

½ cup candied orange peel, very finely chopped

3 to 3½ cups bread flour, preferably bromated, scoop measured

1. In a wide saucepan, combine the milk, water, molasses, sugar, butter, and salt. Place over medium heat and stir until the butter is melted. Transfer to a large mixing bowl to cool.

2. When the mixture is barely warm to the touch, stir in the dissolved yeast. Blend in the anise seeds. Add 2 cups of the rye flour and beat with a wooden spoon until smooth. Stir in the candied orange peel and the remaining cup of rye flour. Gradually blend in the bread flour until the dough becomes too difficult to stir. Turn out onto a floured surface and knead in as much of the remaining bread flour as necessary to form a cohesive dough. Continue kneading in bread flour until the dough is soft yet no longer sticks to the work surface. Transfer to a greased bowl and cover with plastic wrap. Secure with an elastic band and set aside to rise until double in bulk.

3. Generously grease two 9x5-inch loaf pans. Punch the dough down, then turn it out onto a floured surface. Shape it into 2 loaves and place them in the prepared pans. Cover loosely with plastic wrap and let rise. When double in bulk, bake in a preheated 375°F. oven for 35 to 45 minutes, or until the loaves sound hollow when you tap the tops. Cool on a rack for 5 minutes, then turn out. Complete cooling on the rack. ❖

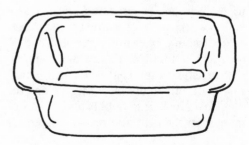

Peasant Rye Bread

MAKES 2 OBLONG LOAVES

The exceptional crackly crust on this loaf is created with a cornstarch glaze.

3 cups warm water
2 packages dry yeast
¼ cup molasses
2 tablespoons cider vinegar
1½ teaspoons salt
4 cups dark rye flour, scoop measured
2 tablespoons caraway seeds
3 cups whole wheat flour, scoop measured
1 to 1½ cups bread flour, preferably
   bromated, scoop measured
½ teaspoon cornstarch
½ cup cold water

1. Measure the warm water into a large mixing bowl. Sprinkle on the yeast and stir to dissolve. Add the molasses, vinegar, and salt. Stir to blend.

2. Add 2 cups of the rye flour and beat with a wooden spoon until smooth. Blend in the caraway seeds. Stir in the remaining 2 cups rye flour and the whole wheat flour. Gradually blend in the bread flour until the dough becomes too difficult to stir. Turn out onto a floured surface and knead in as much of the remaining bread flour as necessary to form a cohesive dough. Continue kneading in bread flour until the dough is soft yet no longer sticks to the work surface. Transfer to a greased bowl and cover with plastic wrap. Secure with an elastic band and set aside to rise until double in bulk.

3. Generously grease a baking sheet and sprinkle with cornmeal. Punch the dough down, then turn it out onto a floured surface. Shape it into two oblong loaves and place them on the prepared sheet. Cover loosely with plastic wrap and let rise. When double in bulk, bake in a preheated 375°F. oven for 30 minutes. Meanwhile, combine the cornstarch and cold water in a small saucepan. Stir to dissolve, then place over high heat. Cook until bubbly and clear. Remove from the heat and brush, while still hot, over the surface of the loaves. (If the cornstarch mixture cools and thickens, simply reheat until it liquefies.) Continue baking the loaves for 10 to 15 minutes, or until they sound hollow when you tap the tops. Remove from the sheet and transfer to a rack to cool.   ❖

Refrigerator Rye

MAKES 1 ROUND LOAF

In this recipe, the dough is partially mixed and then allowed to sit overnight in the refrigerator, giving the finished bread a slightly sour character.

1 cup milk
2 tablespoons solid vegetable shortening
¼ cup dark brown sugar
1 teaspoon salt
2 packages dry yeast, dissolved in 1 cup warm
   water
2 cups rye flour, scoop measured
1 tablespoon caraway seeds
2 cups whole wheat flour, scoop measured
¾ to 1¼ cups bread flour, preferably
   bromated, scoop measured

1. In a wide saucepan, combine the milk, shortening, sugar, and salt. Place over medium heat and stir until the shortening is melted. Transfer to a large mixing bowl to cool.

2. When the mixture is barely warm to the touch, stir in the dissolved yeast. Add the rye flour and beat with a wooden spoon until smooth. Blend in the caraway seeds. Stir in the whole wheat flour. Cover the bowl with plastic wrap and secure with an elastic band. Place the bowl in the refrigerator and let stand overnight.

3. Turn the dough out onto a floured surface and knead in as much of the bread flour as necessary to form a cohesive dough. Continue kneading in bread flour until the dough is soft yet no longer sticks to the work surface. Transfer to a greased bowl and cover with plastic wrap. Secure

with an elastic band and set aside to rise until double in bulk.

4. Generously grease a baking sheet and sprinkle with cornmeal. Punch the dough down, then turn it out onto a floured surface. Shape it into a round loaf and place it on the prepared sheet. Cover loosely with plastic wrap and let rise. When double in bulk, bake in a preheated 375°F. oven for 35 to 45 minutes, or until the loaf sounds hollow when you tap the top. Remove from the sheet and transfer to a rack to cool. ❖

Sweet Potato Rye Bread

MAKES 1 ROUND LOAF

Mashed sweet potato combines with the assertive flavor of reduced beer to produce a deliciously different loaf of rye bread.

Two 12-ounce bottles beer
2 tablespoons molasses
2 tablespoons honey
2 tablespoons sugar
1½ teaspoons salt
1 package dry yeast, dissolved in ¼ cup warm water
1 cup mashed, baked sweet potato
3 cups rye flour, scoop measured
1 tablespoon caraway seeds
3 to 3½ cups bread flour, preferably bromated, scoop measured

1. In a wide saucepan, boil the beer gently until it is reduced to 2 cups. Add the molasses, honey, sugar, and salt, and stir over medium heat until the molasses and honey are liquefied. Transfer to a large mixing bowl to cool.

2. When the mixture is barely warm to the touch, stir in the dissolved yeast. Blend in the sweet potato. Add the rye flour and beat with a wooden spoon until smooth. Blend in the caraway seeds. Gradually blend in the bread flour until the dough becomes too difficult to stir. Turn out onto a floured surface and knead in as much of the remaining bread flour as necessary to form

a cohesive dough. Continue kneading in bread flour until the dough is soft yet no longer sticks to the work surface. Transfer to a greased bowl and cover with plastic wrap. Secure with an elastic band and set aside to rise until double in bulk.

3. Generously grease a baking sheet and sprinkle with cornmeal. Punch the dough down, then turn it out onto a floured surface. Shape it into a round loaf and place it on the prepared sheet. Cover loosely with plastic wrap and let rise. When double in bulk, slash a cross design in the surface with a razor blade. Bake in a preheated 375°F. oven for 35 to 45 minutes, or until the loaf sounds hollow when you tap the top. Remove from the sheet and transfer to a rack to cool. ❖

Sausage Bread

MAKES 2 LONG LOAVES

Hot Italian sausage is crumbled and sautéed, then incorporated into a hearty yeast loaf.

1 pound hot Italian sausage, casings removed
1 cup milk
¼ cup butter or margarine
2 tablespoons sugar
1 teaspoon salt
1 package dry yeast, dissolved in ¼ cup warm water
2 large eggs, beaten
4 to 4½ cups bread flour, preferably bromated, scoop measured

1. Crumble the sausage and place it in a small skillet with a nonstick surface. Stir over medium-high heat until no longer pink. Using a slotted spoon, transfer the sausage to a bowl. Cover and refrigerate.

2. In a wide saucepan, combine the milk, butter, sugar, and salt. Place over medium heat and stir until the butter is melted. Transfer to a large mixing bowl to cool.

3. When the mixture is barely warm to the touch, stir in the dissolved yeast and beaten egg. Add 2 cups of the flour and beat

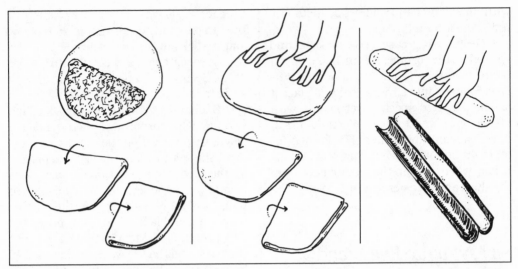

To make Sausage Bread, roll the dough into a 14-inch circle. Sprinkle the cooked sausage over half the dough. Bring up the other half of the dough to cover the sausage. Fold in half again to form a quarter circle. Press down on the dough to flatten and create a rough circle. Dust with flour to prevent sticking, and repeat by folding the circle in half and then into quarters again. Cut the dough in half and shape into two 18-inch loaves.

with a wooden spoon until smooth. Gradually blend in additional flour until the dough becomes too difficult to stir. Turn out onto a floured surface and knead in as much of the remaining flour as necessary to form a cohesive dough. Continue kneading in flour until the dough is soft yet no longer sticks to the work surface. Transfer to a greased bowl and cover with a clean kitchen towel. Set aside to rise until double in bulk.

4. Generously grease two 18-inch baguette pans. Punch the dough down, then turn it out onto a floured surface. Roll the dough into a 14-inch circle. Sprinkle the cooked sausage over half the dough. Bring up the other half of the dough to cover the sausage. Fold in half again to form a quarter circle. Press down on the dough to flatten and create a rough circle. Dust with flour to prevent sticking, and repeat by folding the circle in half and then into quarters again. Divide the dough in half and shape into two 18-inch loaves. Place in the prepared pans and cover with a clean kitchen towel. (See illustration above.) Set aside to rise. When double in bulk, bake in a preheated 400°F. oven for 30 to 40 minutes, or until the loaves are nicely browned. Remove from the pans and transfer to a rack to cool. ❖

Italian Sausage and Cheese Loaf

MAKES 1 LOAF

Filled with hot sausage and provolone cheese, and shaped like a jelly roll, this wonderful loaf is a picnic lunch of its own. Slice and offer with chilled, sliced tomatoes and olive salad.

2 cups warm water
2 packages dry yeast
1 teaspoon sugar
1 teaspoon salt
4½ to 5 cups bread flour, preferably bromated, scoop measured
1½ pounds hot Italian sausage, casings removed
¼ cup freshly grated Romano cheese
2 teaspoons dried oregano

½ pound provolone cheese, thinly sliced
1 large egg, beaten with 1 tablespoon cold
  water

1. Measure the warm water into a large mixing bowl. Sprinkle on the yeast and stir to dissolve. Blend in the sugar and salt. Add 2 cups of the flour and stir with a wooden spoon until smooth. Gradually blend in additional flour until the dough becomes too difficult to stir. Turn out onto a floured surface and knead in as much of the remaining flour as necessary to form a cohesive dough. Continue kneading in flour until the dough is soft yet no longer sticks to the work surface. Transfer to a greased bowl and cover with plastic wrap. Secure with an elastic band and set aside to rise until double in bulk.

2. Crumble the sausage and place it in a small skillet with a nonstick surface. Stir over medium-high heat until no longer

To make an Italian Sausage and Cheese Loaf, sprinkle the dough with Romano cheese, sausage, and oregano. Arrange the provolone cheese slices over the sausage, allowing them to overlap. Starting with the long side, roll the dough up tightly. Pinch the long edge to seal the seam. Pinch the ends and tuck under.

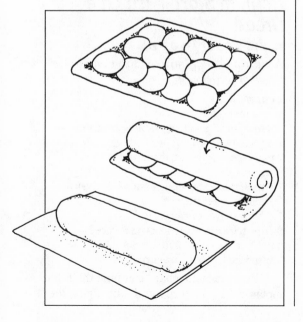

pink. Using a slotted spoon, transfer the sausage to a bowl and set aside.

3. Generously grease a baking sheet and sprinkle with cornmeal. Punch the dough down, then turn it out onto a floured surface. Roll the dough out into a 12x18-inch rectangle. Trim the edges to square off the rectangle. Lift the dough to loosen it from the work surface. Sprinkle the dough with the Romano cheese. Scatter the sausage over the dough to within 1 inch of the edges. Sprinkle on the oregano. Arrange the provolone cheese slices over the sausage, allowing them to overlap. Starting with the long side, roll the dough up tightly. Pinch the long edge to seal the seam. Pinch the ends and tuck under. (See illustration on this page.) Cover loosely with plastic wrap and let rise. When double in bulk, brush the surface with the beaten egg and bake in a preheated 450°F. oven for 20 to 30 minutes, or until the crust is nicely browned. Remove from the sheet and transfer to a rack to cool. ❖

Multiseed Loaf

MAKES ONE 9x5-INCH LOAF

A quartet of seeds lends crunchy texture to this whole wheat loaf.

1¼ cups milk
¼ cup molasses
3 tablespoons butter or margarine
1 teaspoon salt
2 packages dry yeast, dissolved in ½ cup
  warm water
4 to 4½ cups whole wheat flour, scoop
  measured
½ cup sunflower seeds
⅓ cup millet
¼ cup sesame seeds
2 tablespoons poppy seeds

1. In a wide saucepan, combine the milk, molasses, butter, and salt. Place over medium heat and stir until the butter is melted. Transfer to a large mixing bowl to cool.

2. When the mixture is barely warm to the touch, stir in the dissolved yeast. Add 2

cups of the flour and beat with a wooden spoon until smooth. Stir in the sunflower seeds, millet, sesame seeds, and poppy seeds. Gradually blend in additional flour until the dough becomes too difficult to stir. Turn out onto a floured surface and knead in as much of the remaining flour as necessary to form a cohesive dough. Continue kneading in flour until the dough is soft yet no longer sticks to the work surface. Transfer to a greased bowl and cover with plastic wrap. Secure with an elastic band and set aside to rise until double in bulk.

3. Generously grease a 9x5-inch loaf pan. Punch the dough down, then turn it out onto a floured surface. Shape it into a loaf and place it in the prepared pan. Cover loosely with plastic wrap and let rise. When double in bulk, bake in a preheated 375°F. oven for 35 to 45 minutes, or until the loaf sounds hollow when you tap the top. Cool on a rack for 5 minutes, then turn out. Complete cooling on the rack.   ❖

Triticale Honey Raisin Bread

MAKES TWO 9x5-INCH LOAVES

Triticale is a newly developed hybrid grain that is a cross between wheat and rye. It produces a dense, flavorful loaf and is most commonly found in health-food stores.

1 cup cold water
1 cup milk
⅓ cup honey
1½ teaspoons salt
2 packages dry yeast, dissolved in ½ cup warm water
¼ cup vegetable oil
3 cups triticale flour, scoop measured
1 cup raisins
3½ to 4 cups bread flour, preferably bromated, scoop measured

1. In a wide saucepan, combine the water, milk, honey, and salt. Place over medium heat and stir until the honey liquefies. Transfer to a large mixing bowl to cool.

2. When the mixture is barely warm to the touch, stir in the dissolved yeast. Blend in the oil. Add 2 cups of the triticale flour and beat with a wooden spoon until smooth. Stir in the raisins and the remaining cup of triticale flour. Gradually blend in the bread flour until the dough becomes too difficult to stir. Turn out onto a floured surface and knead in as much of the remaining bread flour as necessary to form a cohesive dough. Continue kneading in bread flour until the dough is soft yet no longer sticks to the work surface. Transfer to a greased bowl and cover with plastic wrap. Secure with an elastic band and set aside to rise until double in bulk.

3. Generously grease two 9x5-inch loaf pans. Punch the dough down, then turn it out onto a floured surface. Shape it into 2 loaves and place them in the prepared pans. Cover loosely with plastic wrap and let rise. When double in bulk, bake in a preheated 375°F. oven for 35 to 45 minutes, or until the loaves sound hollow when you tap the tops. Cool on a rack for 5 minutes, then turn out. Complete cooling on the rack.   ❖

Herman Starter Triticale Bread

MAKES 2 OBLONG LOAVES

A sturdy, satisfying loaf with lusty undertones of sourdough.

1 cup milk
½ cup molasses
2 tablespoons solid vegetable shortening
1½ teaspoons salt
2 packages dry yeast, dissolved in ½ cup warm water
1 cup Herman sourdough starter (p. 49), at room temperature
1 tablespoon caraway seeds
3 cups triticale flour, scoop measured
3 to 3½ cups bread flour, preferably bromated, scoop measured

1. In a wide saucepan, combine the milk, molasses, shortening, and salt. Place over

medium heat and stir until the shortening is melted. Transfer to a large mixing bowl to cool.

2. When the mixture is barely warm to the touch, stir in the dissolved yeast. Blend in the sourdough starter and the caraway seeds. Add 2 cups of the triticale flour and beat with a wooden spoon until smooth. Stir in the remaining cup of triticale flour. Gradually blend in the bread flour until the dough becomes too difficult to stir. Turn out onto a floured surface and knead in as much of the remaining bread flour as necessary to form a cohesive dough. Continue kneading in bread flour until the dough is soft yet no longer sticks to the work surface. Transfer to a greased bowl and cover with plastic wrap. Secure with an elastic band and set aside to rise until double in bulk.

3. Generously grease a baking sheet and sprinkle with cornmeal. Punch the dough down, then turn it out onto a floured surface. Shape it into 2 oblong loaves and place them on the prepared sheet. Cover loosely with plastic wrap and let rise. When double in bulk, make 3 parallel slashes on the diagonal across the surface of each loaf with a razor blade. Bake in a preheated 375°F. oven for 35 to 45 minutes, or until the loaves sound hollow when you tap the tops. Remove from the sheet and transfer to a rack to cool.   ❖

Turkey Stuffing Bread

MAKES ONE 9x5-INCH LOAF

A great way to create a unique and delicious stuffing for your next holiday bird.

½ cup water
½ cup milk
2 tablespoons solid vegetable shortening
2 teaspoons sugar
1 teaspoon salt

1 package dry yeast, dissolved in ¼ cup warm water
½ cup yellow cornmeal
2 tablespoons dehydrated onion flakes
2 tablespoons dried parsley
1 teaspoon dried sage
½ teaspoon dried thyme
½ teaspoon dried rosemary
3 to 3½ cups bread flour, scoop measured

1. In a wide saucepan, combine the water, milk, shortening, sugar, and salt. Place over medium heat and stir until the shortening is melted. Transfer to a large mixing bowl to cool.

2. When the mixture is barely warm to the touch, stir in the dissolved yeast. Blend in the cornmeal, onion flakes, parsley, sage, thyme, and rosemary. Add 2 cups of the flour and beat with a wooden spoon until smooth. Gradually blend in additional flour until the dough becomes too difficult to stir. Turn out onto a floured surface and knead in as much of the remaining flour as necessary to form a cohesive dough. Continue kneading in flour until the dough is soft yet no longer sticks to the work surface. Transfer to a greased bowl and cover with a clean kitchen towel. Set aside to rise until double in bulk.

3. Generously grease a 9x5-inch loaf pan. Punch the dough down, then turn it out onto a floured surface. Shape it into a loaf and place it in the prepared pan. Cover and set aside to rise. When double in bulk, bake in a preheated 375°F. oven for 35 to 45 minutes, or until the crust is nicely browned. Cool on a rack for 5 minutes, then turn out. Complete cooling on the rack.

4. To make stuffing, cut the bread into thin slices and then into cubes. Scatter the bread cubes over the bottom of a jelly-roll pan and place in a 250°F. oven for 30 minutes, or until dry and crisp. Allow to cool. You will have 8 cups of bread cubes, or enough to make stuffing for a 16- to 18-pound turkey. Combine with your favorite stuffing ingredients.   ❖

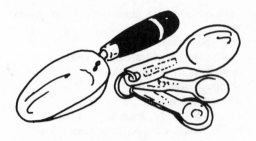

Wheat Germ Bread

MAKES 2 ROUND LOAVES

Wheat germ contributes its nutritious benefits and nubbly texture to these plump round loaves.

½ cup water
1 cup milk
⅓ cup honey
1½ teaspoons salt
2 packages dry yeast, dissolved in ½ cup
   warm water
2 tablespoons vegetable oil
1 cup wheat germ
5½ to 6 cups bread flour, preferably
   bromated, scoop measured

1. In a wide saucepan, combine the water, milk, honey, and salt. Place over medium heat and stir until the honey liquefies. Transfer to a large mixing bowl to cool.

2. When the mixture is barely warm to the touch, stir in the dissolved yeast. Blend in the oil. Add the wheat germ and 1 cup of the flour. Beat with a wooden spoon until smooth. Gradually blend in additional flour until the dough becomes too difficult to stir. Turn out onto a floured surface and knead in as much of the remaining flour as necessary to form a cohesive dough. Continue kneading in flour until the dough is soft yet no longer sticks to the work surface. Transfer to a greased bowl and cover with a clean kitchen towel. Allow the dough to rise until double in bulk.

3. Generously grease a baking sheet and sprinkle with cornmeal. Punch the dough down, then turn it out onto a floured surface. Shape it into 2 round loaves and place them on the prepared sheet. Cover and set aside to rise. When double in bulk, bake in a preheated 375°F. oven for 35 to 45 minutes, or until the crust is nicely browned. Remove from the sheet and transfer to a rack to cool.   ❖

White Bread

MAKES TWO 9x5-INCH LOAVES

This recipe has been passed down through our family for generations. Its special flavor is the result of using lard, but solid vegetable shortening may be substituted if you wish.

1 cup cold water
1 cup milk
2 tablespoons lard
2 tablespoons sugar
1½ teaspoons salt
1 package dry yeast, dissolved in ¼ cup warm
   water
6 to 6½ cups bread flour, scoop measured

1. In a wide saucepan, combine the water, milk, lard, sugar, and salt. Place over medium heat and stir until the lard is melted. Transfer to a large mixing bowl.

2. When the mixture is barely warm to the touch, stir in the dissolved yeast. Add 2 cups of the flour and beat with a wooden spoon until smooth. Gradually blend in additional flour until the dough becomes too difficult to stir. Turn out onto a floured surface and knead in as much of the remaining flour as necessary to form a cohesive dough. Continue kneading in flour until the dough is soft yet no longer sticks to the work surface. Transfer to a greased bowl and cover with a clean kitchen towel. Set aside to rise until double in bulk.

3. Generously grease two 9x5-inch loaf pans. Punch the dough down, then turn it out onto a floured surface. Shape it into 2 loaves and place them in the prepared pans. Cover and set aside to rise. When double in bulk, bake in a preheated 400°F. oven for 15 minutes. Reduce the heat and bake at 350°F. for 45 minutes, or until the crust is

nicely browned. Cool on a rack for 5 minutes, then turn out. Complete cooling on the rack. ❖

Herman Sourdough Starter

This milk-based sourdough starter has become extremely popular with New England cooks. Endlessly versatile, it can be incorporated into yeast breads, quick breads, muffins, pancakes, bagels, and other recipes.

2 cups milk
2 cups all-purpose flour, scoop measured
1 cup sugar
1 package dry yeast, dissolved in ¼ cup warm water

1. In a large glass or ceramic bowl, combine 1 cup of the milk, 1 cup of the flour, the sugar, and the dissolved yeast. Using a nonmetal spoon, beat until smooth and creamy. Stir in the remaining 1 cup milk and 1 cup flour. Cover with a clean kitchen towel and set in a moderately warm spot (about 70°F.). Let stand for 24 hours, at which point the batter should smell pleasantly sour.

2. Transfer to a tightly covered glass or plastic container and place in the refrigerator. Stir with a nonmetal spoon once a day for 5 days.

3. To use the starter, measure out what you need and let it come to room temperature. Replenish it with equal parts of flour and milk, plus half a part of sugar. (For example, if you remove 1 cup of starter, stir in ½ cup flour, ½ cup milk, and ¼ cup sugar.) The starter may be stored in the refrigerator indefinitely, but flavor develops best when the batter is used and replenished often. ❖

Herman Starter White Bread

MAKES TWO 9x5-INCH LOAVES

White bread with complex flavor and full-bodied texture. Try it sliced thick and grilled over an open fire to serve with steak.

1½ cups milk
2 tablespoons solid vegetable shortening
2 tablespoons sugar
1½ teaspoons salt
1 package dry yeast, dissolved in ¼ cup warm water
1 cup Herman sourdough starter (see recipe above), at room temperature
5½ to 6 cups bread flour, scoop measured

1. In a wide saucepan, combine the milk, shortening, sugar, and salt. Place over medium heat and stir until the shortening is melted. Transfer to a large mixing bowl to cool.

2. When the mixture is barely warm to the touch, stir in the dissolved yeast. Blend in the sourdough starter. Add 2 cups of the flour and beat with a wooden spoon until smooth. Gradually blend in additional flour until the dough becomes too difficult to stir. Turn out onto a floured surface and knead in as much of the remaining flour as necessary to form a cohesive dough. Continue kneading in flour until the dough is soft yet no longer sticks to the work surface. Transfer to a greased bowl and cover with a clean kitchen towel. Set aside to rise until double in bulk.

3. Generously grease two 9x5-inch loaf pans. Punch the dough down, then turn it out onto a floured surface. Shape it into 2 loaves and place them in the prepared pans. Cover and set aside to rise. When double in bulk, bake in a preheated 375°F. oven for 35 to 45 minutes, or until the crust is nicely browned. Cool on a rack for 5 minutes, then turn out. Complete cooling on the rack. ❖

Whole Wheat Cottage Cheese Bread

MAKES TWO 9x5-INCH LOAVES

Cottage cheese creates a whole wheat loaf that is moist yet lightly textured.

1½ cups milk
2 tablespoons butter or margarine
2 tablespoons sugar
1½ teaspoons salt
2 packages dry yeast, dissolved in ½ cup
   warm water
1 cup small-curd cottage cheese
3 cups whole wheat flour, scoop measured
3 to 3½ cups bread flour, preferably
   bromated, scoop measured

1. In a wide saucepan, combine the milk, butter, sugar, and salt. Place over medium heat and stir until the butter is melted. Transfer to a large mixing bowl to cool.

2. When the mixture is barely warm to the touch, stir in the dissolved yeast. Blend in the cottage cheese. Add 2 cups of the whole wheat flour and beat with a wooden spoon until smooth. Stir in the remaining cup of whole wheat flour. Gradually blend in the bread flour until the dough becomes too difficult to stir. Turn out onto a floured surface and knead in as much of the remaining bread flour as necessary to form a cohesive dough. Continue kneading in bread flour until the dough is soft yet no longer sticks to the work surface. Transfer to a greased bowl and cover with plastic wrap. Secure with an elastic band and set aside to rise until double in bulk.

3. Generously grease two 9x5-inch loaf pans. Punch the dough down, then turn it out onto a floured surface. Shape it into 2 loaves and place them in the prepared pans. Cover loosely with plastic wrap and let rise. When double in bulk, bake in a preheated 375°F. oven for 35 to 45 minutes, or until the loaves sound hollow when you tap the tops. Cool on a rack for 5 minutes, then turn out. Complete cooling on the rack. ❖

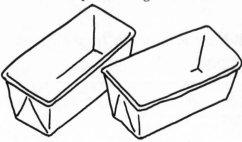

Whole Wheat Fennel Bread

MAKES 1 OBLONG LOAF

Whole wheat and fennel make a terrific flavor combination. This bread is particularly good sliced thin and toasted. Allow to cool and serve unbuttered as an accompaniment to chilled chicken salad.

1 cup cold water
½ cup milk
3 tablespoons molasses
2 tablespoons butter or margarine
1 teaspoon salt
1 package dry yeast, dissolved in ¼ cup warm
   water
1½ teaspoons fennel seeds
3 cups whole wheat flour, scoop measured
1 to 1½ cups bread flour, preferably
   bromated, scoop measured

1. In a wide saucepan, combine the water, milk, molasses, butter, and salt. Place over medium heat and stir until the butter is melted. Transfer to a large mixing bowl to cool.

2. When the mixture is barely warm to the touch, stir in the dissolved yeast. Blend in the fennel seeds. Add 2 cups of the whole wheat flour and beat with a wooden spoon until smooth. Stir in the remaining cup of whole wheat flour. Gradually blend in the bread flour until the dough becomes too difficult to stir. Turn out onto a floured surface and knead in as much of the remaining bread flour as necessary to form a cohesive dough. Continue kneading in bread flour until the dough is soft yet no longer sticks to the work surface. Transfer to a greased bowl and cover with plastic wrap. Secure with an elastic band and set aside to rise until double in bulk.

3. Generously grease a baking sheet and sprinkle with cornmeal. Punch the dough down, then turn it out onto a floured surface. Shape it into an oblong loaf and place it on the prepared sheet. Cover loosely with plastic wrap and let rise. When double in bulk, bake in a preheated 375°F. oven for

35 to 45 minutes, or until the loaf sounds hollow when you tap the top. Remove from the sheet and transfer to a rack to cool. ❖

Shredded Wheat Molasses Bread

MAKES TWO 9x5-INCH LOAVES

Shredded wheat bread is a perennial New England favorite. You'll love its natural, nutty, wholesome taste.

3 shredded wheat biscuits
1¾ cups boiling water
⅓ cup molasses
3 tablespoons solid vegetable shortening
1 tablespoon sugar
1½ teaspoons salt
½ cup milk
1 package dry yeast, dissolved in ¼ cup warm water
5½ to 6 cups bread flour, scoop measured

1. Place the shredded wheat biscuits in a large mixing bowl. Pour on the boiling water. Add the molasses, shortening, sugar, and salt. Stir to liquefy the molasses. Blend in the milk and let stand.

2. When the mixture is barely warm to the touch, stir in the dissolved yeast. Add 2 cups of the flour and beat with a wooden spoon until smooth. Gradually blend in additional flour until the dough becomes too difficult to stir. Turn out onto a floured surface and knead in as much of the remaining flour as necessary to form a cohesive dough. Continue kneading in flour until the dough is soft yet no longer sticks to the work surface. Transfer to a greased bowl and cover with a clean kitchen towel. Set aside to rise until double in bulk.

3. Generously grease two 9x5-inch loaf pans. Punch the dough down, then turn it out onto a floured surface. Shape it into 2 loaves and place them in the prepared pans. Cover and set aside to rise. When double in bulk, bake in a preheated 375°F. oven for 35 to 45 minutes, or until the crust is nicely browned. Brush the loaves with solid vegetable shortening that has been melted. Cool on a rack for 5 minutes, then turn out. Complete cooling on the rack. ❖

Water-Based Sourdough Starter

Water, enriched with potatoes, forms the basis for this sourdough starter. It may be used to make crusty breads, soft loaves, biscuits, and pancakes.

2 large baking potatoes, peeled and cut in half
2 tablespoons sugar
1 package dry yeast, dissolved in ¼ cup warm water
3 cups all-purpose flour, scoop measured
1 cup warm water

1. Place the potatoes in a large saucepan with enough water to cover. Boil gently until the potatoes fall apart. Do not drain. Force through a sieve, liquid and all, and allow to cool to room temperature.

2. Add water to the potatoes if necessary to make 2 cups. Pour into a large glass or ceramic bowl. Using a nonmetal spoon, stir in the sugar, dissolved yeast, and 2 cups of the flour. Beat until smooth and creamy. Cover with a clean kitchen towel and set in a moderately warm spot (about 70°F.). Let stand for 24 hours, at which point the batter should smell pleasantly sour. Stir in the remaining cup of flour and the warm water. Cover with the towel and let stand at room temperature for 2 to 3 days. The longer it stands, the more assertive the flavor. Transfer the starter to a tightly covered glass or plastic container and store in the refrigerator.

3. To use the starter, measure out what you need and allow it to come to room temperature. Replenish with equal parts of flour and water. (For example, if you remove 1 cup of starter, stir in ½ cup flour and ½ cup water.) The starter may be stored in the refrigerator indefinitely, but flavor develops best when the batter is used and replenished often. ❖

❖ Rolls, Buns, and Bagels ❖

SOONER OR later it must occur to all of us that, beyond being something good to eat, food is an amazingly strong link to the past and to people we have loved. I think I first realized this in connection with my grandmother's rolls.

Every Thanksgiving, for as far back as I can remember, my grandmother made her special rolls for the family feast. At first I loved them because they were so delicious. But as time passed those rolls took on a greater significance. My cousins and I were taught how to bake them, and they became an invisible thread from one generation to another. Today, although she has been dead for many years and the family group has splintered, the smell of those rolls coming out of the oven never fails to bring back vivid memories of my grandmother.

The practice of making homemade rolls always existed in New England to a limited degree, but it gained rapid acceptance during the mid-nineteenth century, when a chef at the famous Parker House hotel in Boston introduced pocketbook rolls. These rounds of dough folded over into a purselike configuration became an overnight sensation. Housewives all over the region tried to duplicate the Parker House recipe, and homemade yeast rolls became a fashionable part of "company dinner."

Buns, which were traditionally a sweet roll served at breakfast, attracted similar attention from Yankee cooks. The increased availability of reliable packaged yeast and the development of refined flour contributed to an interest in making homemade buns. Bagels are a relative newcomer to New England, yet they are nonetheless quite popular. Bagels are eaten with cream cheese or split and toasted to be served with butter and jam. Bagels are usually eaten for breakfast or as a snack.

Rolls are customarily made from a rich dough containing milk, eggs, and butter. They may be formed into attractive shapes, or the dough may simply be rolled into small balls and baked in muffin tins. Buns are usually luxurious spheres of dough stuffed with sweet delicacies, although they may also be large, straightforward rolls that serve as the foundation for an excellent sandwich.

Bagels are butter-rich, ring-shaped breads prepared in a unique way. Before they are baked, slightly risen bagels are submerged in simmering water and poached gently for two minutes. This brief encounter with hot water moistens the outer dough and prevents the crust from turning crisp during baking. The result is a soft, chewy outer surface and a dense inner crumb.

Rolls, buns, and bagels all store quite well, although they are at their best when eaten freshly made. They also freeze successfully. In fact, every Thanksgiving I prepare a double batch of rolls ahead of time and store them in the freezer to cut down on last-minute fuss (something my grandmother never considered). Rolls, buns, and bagels should be frozen in airtight plastic bags secured with a wire twist. Defrost them at room temperature, inside the sealed bag. If you wish to warm them, wrap tightly in aluminum foil and place in a preheated 375°F. oven for 5 to 8 minutes, or until piping hot. Rolls, buns, and bagels may also be warmed in a microwave oven. Wrap them in absorbent paper and heat gently on medium power for 30 seconds to 2 minutes, depending on the quantity. Do not heat on high power because that toughens their consistency.

Buckwheat Rolls

MAKES 12

Buckwheat flour contributes its appealing wholesomeness to these easy-to-prepare rolls.

1½ cups warm water
1 package dry yeast
¼ cup light brown sugar
½ teaspoon salt
2 tablespoons vegetable oil
1 cup buckwheat flour, scoop measured
1 cup whole wheat flour, scoop measured
¾ cup all-purpose flour, scoop measured

1. Measure the warm water into a large mixing bowl. Sprinkle in the yeast and stir to dissolve. Blend in the sugar and salt. Stir in the vegetable oil. Add the buckwheat flour and whole wheat flour and beat with a wooden spoon until smooth. Stir in the all-purpose flour. Cover the bowl with plastic wrap and secure with an elastic band. Set aside to rise until double in bulk.

2. Generously grease 12 muffin cups. Stir the dough down and spoon into the prepared cups, filling them two-thirds full. Cover loosely with plastic wrap and let rise. When double in bulk, bake in a preheated 375°F. oven for 20 to 25 minutes, or until crusted and lightly browned. Cool on a rack for 5 minutes, then turn out. Serve immediately or complete cooling on the rack.   ❖

Buttermilk Pocket Rolls

MAKES 32

These are Sunday-dinner rolls. Serve for family feasts with roast turkey or fried chicken.

1 cup buttermilk
½ cup butter or margarine, melted
3 tablespoons sugar

¾ teaspoon salt
½ teaspoon baking soda
1 package dry yeast, dissolved in ¼ cup warm
  water
3 to 3½ cups all-purpose flour, scoop
  measured

1. In a large mixing bowl, combine the buttermilk, 2 tablespoons of the melted butter, the sugar, the salt, and the baking soda. Stir in the dissolved yeast. Add 1 cup of the flour and beat with a wooden spoon until smooth. Gradually blend in additional flour until the dough becomes too difficult to stir. Turn out onto a floured surface and knead in as much of the remaining flour as necessary to form a cohesive dough. Continue kneading in flour until the dough is soft yet no longer sticks to the work surface. Transfer to a greased bowl and cover with a clean kitchen towel. Let the dough rise until double in bulk.

2. Pour 2 tablespoons of the remaining butter into a 9x13-inch baking dish. Tilt the dish to coat the bottom. Punch the dough down, then turn it out onto a floured surface. Roll to a ⅜-inch thickness. Cut out rounds with a 2¼-inch biscuit cutter. Brush the rounds with the remaining 4 tablespoons butter. Fold the rounds in half to form semicircles and place in the prepared baking dish. Cover and set aside to rise. When double in bulk, bake in a preheated 375°F. oven for 20 to 25 minutes, or until nicely browned. Cool on a rack for 5 minutes, then turn out. Serve immediately or complete cooling on the rack.   ❖

Quick Buttermilk Rolls

MAKES 12

The flavor combination of buttermilk and lard is particularly reminiscent of old New England. You may, however, substitute butter for the lard.

3 to 3½ cups all-purpose flour, scoop
  measured

3 tablespoons sugar
¾ teaspoon salt
¾ teaspoon baking powder
¼ teaspoon baking soda
¼ cup lard
1 cup buttermilk
1 package dry yeast, dissolved in ¼ cup warm
  water

1. In a large mixing bowl, combine 3 cups of the flour with the sugar, salt, baking powder, and baking soda. Whisk to blend thoroughly. Add the lard and cut in with a knife until the mixture is crumbly. Pour in the buttermilk and the dissolved yeast. Stir to blend into a soft dough. Turn out onto a floured surface and knead in as much of the remaining flour as necessary to form a cohesive dough. Cover and let rest for 10 minutes.

2. Generously grease 12 muffin cups. Using the palms of your hands, roll the dough into an 18-inch rope. Cut the rope into twelve 1½-inch pieces. Shape each piece into a ball by rolling between the palms of your hands. Place in the prepared muffin cups. Cover with a clean kitchen towel and set aside to rise. When double in bulk, bake in a preheated 400°F. oven for 18 to 20 minutes, or until nicely browned. Cool on a rack for 5 minutes, then turn out. Serve immediately or complete cooling on the rack.   ❖

Buttery Pull-Apart Rolls

MAKES 20

Also called Fan Tans, these beautiful rolls are created by stacking thin strips of buttered dough in muffin cups.

1½ cups buttermilk
½ cup butter or margarine, melted
⅓ cup sugar
1 teaspoon salt
½ teaspoon baking soda
1 package dry yeast, dissolved in ¼ cup warm
  water
4 to 4½ cups all-purpose flour, scoop
  measured

1. In a large mixing bowl, combine the buttermilk, ¼ cup of the melted butter, the sugar, the salt, and the baking soda. Stir in the dissolved yeast. Add 2 cups of the flour and beat with a wooden spoon until smooth. Gradually blend in additional flour until the dough becomes too difficult to stir. Turn out onto a floured surface and knead in as much of the remaining flour as necessary to form a cohesive dough. Continue kneading in flour until the dough is soft yet no longer sticks to the work surface. Transfer to a greased bowl and cover with a clean kitchen towel. Set aside to rise until double in bulk.

2. Generously grease 20 muffin cups. Punch the dough down, then roll it into a 15-inch square. Trim the edges to square off the dough. Lift the dough to loosen it from the work surface. Brush the surface with

To make Buttery Pull-Apart Rolls, use a pastry wheel to cut the dough into 10 strips, 1½ inches wide. Stack 5 strips on top of one another and cut into 1½-inch pieces. Place, cut side down, in the prepared muffin cups.

the remaining ¼ cup butter. Using a pastry wheel, cut the dough into 10 strips, 1½ inches wide. Stack 5 strips on top of one another and cut into 1½-inch pieces. Place, cut side down, in the prepared muffin cups. (See illustration.) Cover and set aside to rise. When double in bulk, bake in a preheated 400°F. oven for 20 to 25 minutes, or until nicely browned. Cool on a rack for 5 minutes, then turn out. Serve immediately or complete cooling on the rack. ❖

Cheddar Cornmeal Rolls

MAKES 24

The dough for these Cheddar-flavored rolls is simply spooned into muffin cups. No kneading, no shaping — they're supergood and superquick.

1¾ cups milk
2 tablespoons butter or margarine, cut into small pieces
¼ cup sugar
1 teaspoon salt
1 package dry yeast, dissolved in ¼ cup warm water
1 large egg, beaten
1 cup shredded Cheddar cheese
½ cup yellow cornmeal
4 cups all-purpose flour, scoop measured

1. In a wide saucepan, combine the milk, butter, sugar, and salt. Place over medium heat and stir until the butter is melted. Transfer to a large mixing bowl to cool.

2. When the mixture is barely warm to the touch, stir in the dissolved yeast and beaten egg. Blend in the cheese and cornmeal. Add 2 cups of the flour and beat with a wooden spoon until smooth. Stir in the remaining 2 cups flour. Cover the bowl with plastic wrap and secure with an elastic band. Set aside to rise until double in bulk.

3. Generously grease 24 muffin cups. Stir the dough down and spoon into the prepared cups, filling them two-thirds full. Cover loosely with plastic wrap and let rise. When double in bulk, bake in a preheated

375°F. oven for 20 to 25 minutes, or until nicely browned. Cool on a rack for 5 minutes, then turn out. Serve immediately or complete cooling on the rack. ❖

Caramel Pecan Rolls

MAKES 15

Nothing could be more reassuring on a cold, rainy morning than these sticky buns warm from the oven.

¾ cup milk
½ cup butter or margarine
¼ cup granulated sugar
¾ teaspoon salt
1 package dry yeast, dissolved in ¼ cup warm water
2 large eggs, beaten
3 cups all-purpose flour, scoop measured
1 teaspoon cinnamon
½ cup light brown sugar
2 tablespoons dark corn syrup
1 tablespoon water
½ cup coarsely chopped pecans

1. In a wide saucepan, combine the milk, ¼ cup of the butter, the granulated sugar, and the salt. Place over medium heat and stir until the butter is melted. Transfer to a large mixing bowl to cool.

2. When the mixture is barely warm to the touch, stir in the dissolved yeast and beaten egg. Add 1 cup of the flour and the cinnamon, and beat with a wooden spoon until smooth. Stir in the remaining 2 cups flour. (The dough will be moist and sticky.) Cover the bowl with plastic wrap and secure with an elastic band. Set aside to rise until double in bulk.

3. In a small saucepan, combine the remaining ¼ cup butter with the brown sugar, corn syrup, and water. Stir over medium heat until the butter melts and the sugar dissolves. Generously grease a 9x13-inch baking dish. Pour in the sugar syrup and tilt the dish to coat the bottom. Sprinkle on the pecans. Stir the dough down and drop by generous spoonfuls into the prepared baking dish, placing 3 dollops across and 5

dollops down. Cover with plastic wrap and let rise. When double in bulk, bake in a preheated 375°F. oven for 20 to 25 minutes, or until nicely browned. Cool on a rack for 10 minutes, then invert and turn out. Serve immediately or complete cooling on the rack. ❖

Herman Starter Cinnamon Rolls

MAKES 18

The fragrance of these cinnamon-filled rolls will take you back to your childhood. Cinnamon toast was wonderful, but it was never like this.

2 cups Herman sourdough starter (p. 49), at room temperature
½ cup butter or margarine, melted
½ cup granulated sugar
1 teaspoon salt
½ teaspoon baking soda
1 package dry yeast, dissolved in ¼ cup warm water
2 to 2½ cups all-purpose flour, scoop measured
1 teaspoon cinnamon
1 cup light brown sugar
½ cup coarsely chopped walnuts

1. In a large mixing bowl, combine the sourdough starter, ¼ cup of the melted butter, ¼ cup of the granulated sugar, the salt, and the baking soda. Stir to blend.

2. Add the dissolved yeast and 1 cup of the flour, and beat with a wooden spoon until smooth. Gradually blend in additional flour until the dough becomes too difficult to stir. Turn out onto a floured surface and knead in as much of the remaining flour as necessary to form a cohesive dough. Continue kneading in flour until the dough is soft yet no longer sticks to the work surface. Transfer to a greased bowl and cover with a clean kitchen towel. Set aside to rise until double in bulk.

3. In a small bowl, whisk together the remaining ¼ cup granulated sugar and the cinnamon. Set aside. Pour 2 tablespoons of

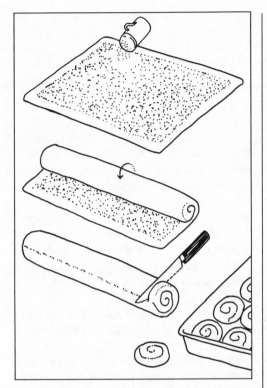

To make Herman Starter Cinnamon Rolls and similar filled rolls or buns, roll the dough into a rectangle. Distribute the filling over the dough to within 1 inch of the edges. Starting at the long side, roll the dough up. Pinch the long edges to seal the seam. Cut the roll with a serrated knife and place, cut side down, in the prepared pan or muffin tin.

the remaining butter into a 9x13-inch baking dish. Tilt to coat the bottom of the dish. Sprinkle the brown sugar over the butter, then scatter on the walnuts. Punch the dough down, then turn it out onto a floured surface. Roll into a 12x15-inch rectangle. Trim the edges to square off the rectangle. Lift the dough to loosen it from the work surface. Brush the surface lightly with the remaining 2 tablespoons butter. Distribute the cinnamon-sugar over the butter to within 1 inch of the edges. Starting at the long side, roll the dough up. Pinch the long edges to seal the seam. Using a serrated knife, cut the roll into 18 pieces, each about

1¼ inches thick. Place, cut side down, in the prepared pan. (See illustration.) Cover with a towel and set aside to rise. When double in bulk, bake in a preheated 350°F. oven and bake for 30 to 35 minutes, or until nicely browned. Place on a rack to cool for 10 minutes, then invert and turn out. Serve immediately or complete cooling on the rack.   ❖

Easy Crescent Rolls

MAKES 24

These yummy dinner rolls resemble croissants in shape, but they have a softer texture and are not such a chore to make.

1¼ cups milk
¼ cup solid vegetable shortening
¼ cup sugar
1 teaspoon salt
1 package dry yeast, dissolved in ¼ cup warm
   water
1 large egg, beaten
4 to 4½ cups all-purpose flour, scoop
   measured
¼ cup butter or margarine, softened

1. In a wide saucepan, combine the milk, shortening, sugar, and salt. Place over medium heat and stir until the shortening is melted. Transfer to a large mixing bowl to cool.

2. When the mixture is barely warm to the touch, stir in the dissolved yeast and beaten egg. Add 2 cups of the flour and beat with a wooden spoon until smooth. Gradually blend in additional flour until the dough becomes too difficult to stir. Turn out onto a floured surface and knead in as much of the remaining flour as necessary to form a cohesive dough. Continue kneading in flour until the dough is soft yet no longer sticks to the work surface. Transfer to a greased bowl and cover with a clean kitchen towel. Set aside to rise until double in bulk.

3. Generously grease 2 baking sheets. Punch the dough down, then turn it out onto a floured surface. Divide into 2 equal

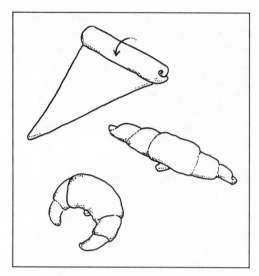

To make crescent rolls or twists, cut each circle of dough into 12 triangles. Starting at the wide end, roll each triangle toward the point. Bend slightly to form a crescent shape. Place, point down, on the prepared baking sheets.

portions. Pat each portion into a flat round, then roll into a 14-inch circle. Spread each circle generously with the softened butter. Cut each circle into 12 triangles. Starting at the wide end, roll each triangle toward the point. Bend slightly to form a crescent shape and place, point down, on the prepared baking sheets. (See illustration.) Cover and set aside to rise. When double in bulk, bake in a preheated 375°F. oven for 20 to 25 minutes, or until nicely browned. Remove from the sheets and serve immediately, or cool on a rack.   ❖

Quick Dinner Rolls

MAKES 12

These easy-to-prepare rolls rise only once, so they can be made in half the usual time.

½ cup milk
2 tablespoons butter or margarine
2 tablespoons sugar
½ teaspoon salt

1 package dry yeast, dissolved in ½ cup warm water
1 large egg, beaten
3 to 3½ cups all-purpose flour, scoop measured
1 large egg white, beaten with 2 teaspoons cold water
Poppy seeds

1. In a wide saucepan, combine the milk, butter, sugar, and salt. Place over medium heat and stir until the butter is melted. Transfer to a large mixing bowl to cool.

2. When the mixture is barely warm, stir in the dissolved yeast and beaten egg. Add 3 cups of the flour and stir to form a soft dough. Turn out onto a floured surface and knead in as much of the remaining flour as necessary to form a cohesive dough. Cover and let rest 10 minutes.

3. Generously grease 12 muffin cups. Using the palms of your hands, roll the dough into an 18-inch rope. Cut the rope into twelve 1½-inch pieces. Shape each piece into a ball by rolling between the palms of your hands. Place in the prepared muffin cups. Cover with a clean kitchen towel and set aside to rise. When double in bulk, brush the surface with the egg white and sprinkle on the poppy seeds. Place in a preheated 400°F. oven and bake for 18 to 20 minutes, or until nicely browned. Cool on a rack for 5 minutes, then turn out. Serve immediately or complete cooling on the rack.   ❖

Herman Sourdough Dinner Rolls

MAKES 32

An irresistible aroma rises from these rolls, and they disappear in minutes.

¾ cup cold water
¼ cup butter or margarine
¼ cup sugar
1 teaspoon salt
1 package dry yeast, dissolved in ¼ cup warm water

2 large eggs, beaten
1 cup Herman sourdough starter (p. 49), at
  room temperature
3½ to 4 cups all-purpose flour, scoop
  measured

1. In a wide saucepan, combine the water, butter, sugar, and salt. Place over medium heat and stir until the butter is melted. Transfer to a large mixing bowl to cool.

2. When the mixture is barely warm to the touch, stir in the dissolved yeast and beaten egg. Blend in the sourdough starter. Add 1 cup of the flour and beat with a wooden spoon until smooth. Gradually blend in additional flour until the dough becomes too difficult to stir. Turn out onto a floured surface and knead in as much of the remaining flour as necessary to form a cohesive dough. Continue kneading in flour until the dough is soft yet no longer sticks to the work surface. Transfer to a greased bowl and cover with plastic wrap. Secure with an elastic band and set aside to rise until double in bulk.

3. Generously grease two 9-inch round baking pans. Punch the dough down, then turn it out onto a floured surface. Divide in half. Roll each half into a 16-inch rope with the palms of your hands. Cut each rope into sixteen 1-inch pieces. Shape each piece into a ball by rolling between the palms of your hands. Place in the prepared pans. Cover loosely with plastic wrap and let rise. When double in bulk, place in a preheated 375°F. oven and bake for 20 to 25 minutes, or until nicely browned. Cool on a rack for 5 minutes, then turn out. Serve immediately or complete cooling on the rack.   ❖

Herb Cheese Twists

MAKES 24

Savory rolls with the enticing aroma of freshly snipped chives.

1¼ cups milk
6 tablespoons butter or margarine

2 tablespoons sugar
1 teaspoon salt
1 package dry yeast, dissolved in ¼ cup warm
  water
1 large egg, beaten
4 to 4½ cups all-purpose flour, scoop
  measured
¼ cup freshly grated Parmesan cheese
2 tablespoons chopped fresh parsley
2 tablespoons chopped fresh chives

1. In a wide saucepan, combine the milk, 4 tablespoons of the butter, the sugar, and the salt. Place over medium heat and stir until the butter is melted. Transfer to a large mixing bowl to cool.

2. When the mixture is barely warm to the touch, stir in the dissolved yeast and beaten egg. Add 2 cups of the flour and beat with a wooden spoon until smooth. Gradually blend in additional flour until the dough becomes too difficult to stir. Turn out onto a floured surface and knead in as much of the remaining flour as necessary to form a cohesive dough. Continue kneading in flour until the dough is soft yet no longer sticks to the work surface. Transfer to a greased bowl and cover with a clean kitchen towel. Set aside to rise until double in bulk.

3. Generously grease 2 baking sheets. Melt the remaining 2 tablespoons butter and set aside. Punch the dough down, then turn it out onto a floured surface. Divide into 2 equal portions. Pat each portion into a flat round, then roll into a 14-inch circle. Brush each circle lightly with the melted butter. Sprinkle on the cheese, then distribute the parsley and chives evenly over the surface. Cut each circle into 12 triangles. Starting at the wide end, roll each triangle toward the point. Place, point down, on the prepared baking sheets. (See illustration on page 58.) Cover and set aside to rise. When double in bulk, bake in a preheated 375°F. oven for 20 to 25 minutes, or until nicely browned. Remove from the sheet and serve immediately, or cool on a rack.   ❖

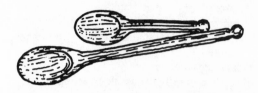

Honey-Glazed Pan Rolls

MAKES 15

Moist with melted butter and honey, these easy-to-make rolls are wonderful for breakfast or snacks.

1 cup milk
3 tablespoons honey
6 tablespoons butter or margarine
1 teaspoon salt
1 package dry yeast, dissolved in ¼ cup warm
　　water
2 large eggs
3½ cups all-purpose flour, scoop measured
⅓ cup confectioners' sugar

1. In a wide saucepan, combine the milk, 2 tablespoons of the honey, 4 tablespoons of the butter, and the salt. Place over medium heat and stir until the butter is melted. Transfer to a large mixing bowl to cool.

2. When the mixture is barely warm to the touch, stir in the dissolved yeast. Separate one egg, reserving the white. Beat the yolk and the remaining egg, and blend into the yeast mixture. Add 1 cup of the flour and beat with a wooden spoon until smooth. Stir in the remaining 2½ cups flour. The dough will be moist and sticky. Cover the bowl with plastic wrap and secure with an elastic band. Set aside and let rise until double in bulk.

3. Melt the remaining 2 tablespoons of butter and place in a small bowl. Add the remaining tablespoon of honey and the confectioners' sugar. Whisk to blend. Add the reserved egg white and beat until well mixed. Set aside.

4. Generously grease a 9x13-inch baking dish. Stir the dough down and drop by generous spoonfuls into the prepared baking dish, placing 3 dollops across and 5 dollops

down. Drizzle half the honey mixture over the surface. Cover with plastic wrap and let rise. When double in bulk, drizzle on the remaining honey mixture and bake in a preheated 350°F. oven for 25 to 30 minutes, or until nicely browned. Cool on a rack for 10 minutes. Serve immediately or complete cooling in the pan.　　　　　❖

Jam Roll-ups

MAKES 24

Layered with jam and walnuts, these delicate rolls are a special treat fresh from the oven for breakfast.

½ cup warm water
1 package dry yeast
½ cup evaporated milk
¼ cup butter or margarine, melted
¼ cup sugar
1 teaspoon salt
2 large eggs, beaten
4 to 4½ cups all-purpose flour, scoop
　　measured
¼ cup apricot or peach jam
½ cup finely chopped walnuts
2 teaspoons cold water

1. Measure the warm water into a large mixing bowl. Sprinkle on the yeast and stir to dissolve. Blend in the milk, melted butter, sugar, and salt. Measure out 2 tablespoons of the beaten egg and place in a glass measuring cup. Set aside. Blend the remaining egg into the yeast mixture.

2. Add 2 cups of the flour and beat with a wooden spoon until smooth. Gradually blend in additional flour until the dough becomes too difficult to stir. Turn out onto a floured surface and knead in as much of the remaining flour as necessary to form a cohesive dough. Continue kneading in flour until the dough is soft yet no longer sticks to the work surface. Transfer to a greased bowl and cover with a clean kitchen towel. Set aside to rise until double in bulk.

3. Generously grease 2 baking sheets. Punch the dough down, then turn it out

onto a floured surface. Divide into 2 equal portions. Pat each portion into a flat round, then roll into a 14-inch circle. Spread each circle with 2 tablespoons of jam, then scatter the walnuts over the surface. Cut each circle into 12 triangles. Starting at the wide end, roll each triangle toward the point. Place, point down, on the prepared baking sheets. (See illustration on page 58.) Cover and set aside to rise. When double in bulk, whisk the reserved egg with the cold water and brush over the surface. Bake in a preheated 375°F. oven for 20 to 25 minutes, or until nicely browned. Remove from the sheet and serve immediately, or cool on a rack. ❖

Lemony Pan Rolls

MAKES 15

Lively with fresh lemon juice, these soft dinner rolls pair admirably with tarragon-scented roast chicken.

¾ cup milk
6 tablespoons butter or margarine
¼ cup sugar
¾ teaspoon salt
1 package dry yeast, dissolved in ¼ cup warm water
2 large eggs, beaten
¼ cup freshly squeezed lemon juice
1 tablespoon finely grated lemon zest
3 cups all-purpose flour, scoop measured

1. In a wide saucepan, combine the milk, 4 tablespoons of the butter, the sugar, and the salt. Place over medium heat and stir until the butter is melted. Transfer to a large mixing bowl to cool.

2. When the mixture is barely warm to the touch, stir in the dissolved yeast and beaten egg. Blend in the lemon juice and lemon zest. Add 1 cup of the flour and beat with a wooden spoon until smooth. Stir in the remaining 2 cups flour. The dough will be moist and sticky. Cover the bowl with plastic wrap and secure with an elastic band. Set aside to rise until double in bulk.

3. Melt the remaining 2 tablespoons butter and pour into a 9x13-inch baking dish. Tilt to coat the bottom of the dish. Stir the dough down and drop by generous spoonfuls into the prepared baking dish, placing 3 dollops across and 5 dollops down. Cover with plastic wrap and let rise. When double in bulk, bake in a preheated 375°F. oven for 20 to 25 minutes, or until nicely browned. Cool on a rack for 5 minutes, then turn out. Serve immediately or complete cooling on the rack. ❖

Oatmeal Rolls

MAKES 18

These marvelous slice-and-bake rolls are shaped quickly by dividing the dough into two lengths and then cutting each length into thick rounds.

1 cup milk
4 tablespoons butter or margarine
1 tablespoon sugar
1 teaspoon salt
1 package dry yeast, dissolved in ¼ cup warm water
2 large eggs, beaten
1 cup quick-cooking rolled oats
1 cup whole wheat flour, scoop measured
2 to 2½ cups bread flour, scoop measured

1. In a wide saucepan, combine the milk, 2 tablespoons of the butter, the sugar, and the salt. Place over medium heat and stir until the butter is melted. Transfer to a large mixing bowl to cool.

2. When the mixture is barely warm to the touch, stir in the dissolved yeast and beaten egg. Add the oats and whole wheat flour, and beat with a wooden spoon until smooth. Gradually blend in the bread flour until the dough becomes too difficult to stir. Turn out onto a floured surface and knead in as much of the remaining bread flour as necessary to form a cohesive dough. Continue kneading in bread flour until the

dough is soft yet no longer sticks to the work surface. Transfer to a greased bowl and cover with plastic wrap. Secure with an elastic band and set aside to rise until double in bulk.

3. Generously grease a baking sheet. Melt the remaining 2 tablespoons butter and set aside. Punch the dough down, then turn it out onto a floured surface. Divide in half. Roll each half into a 12-inch rope. Cut each rope into 9 rounds, each about 1¼ inches thick. Place the rounds, cut side down, on the prepared baking sheet. Brush the surface with the melted butter. Lightly scatter rolled oats over the surface. Bake in a preheated 375°F. oven for 20 to 25 minutes, or until nicely browned. Remove from the sheet and cool on a rack.   ❖

Potato Rolls

MAKES 32

Meltingly tender, these delightful dinner rolls are a welcome part of any holiday feast.

3 medium baking potatoes, peeled and
  quartered
½ cup honey
¼ cup butter or margarine
1 tablespoon sugar
1 teaspoon salt
1 package dry yeast, dissolved in ¼ cup warm
  water
2 large eggs, beaten
4 to 4½ cups bread flour, scoop measured

1. Place the potatoes in a large saucepan and add enough cold water to cover. Bring to a boil and cook gently until tender. Drain the potatoes, reserving 1 cup of the cooking water. Return the reserved water to the saucepan. Mash the potatoes and set aside.

2. Add the honey, butter, sugar, and salt to the water in the saucepan. Place over medium heat and stir until the butter is melted. Transfer to a large mixing bowl to cool.

3. When the mixture is barely warm to the touch, stir in the dissolved yeast and

beaten egg. Blend in the mashed potato. Add 2 cups of the flour and beat with a wooden spoon until smooth. Gradually blend in additional flour until the dough becomes too difficult to stir. Turn out onto a floured surface and knead in as much of the remaining flour as necessary to form a cohesive dough. Continue kneading in flour until the dough is soft yet no longer sticks to the work surface. Transfer to a greased bowl and cover with a clean kitchen towel. Set aside to rise until double in bulk.

4. Generously grease two 9-inch round baking pans. Punch the dough down, then turn it out onto a floured surface. Divide in half. Roll each half into a 16-inch rope with the palms of your hands. Cut each rope into sixteen 1-inch pieces. Shape each piece into a ball by rolling between the palms of your hands. Place in the prepared pans. Cover and set aside to rise. When double in bulk, bake in a preheated 400°F. oven for 20 to 25 minutes, or until nicely browned. Cool on a rack for 5 minutes, then turn out. Serve immediately or complete cooling on the rack.   ❖

Herman Sourdough Rye Rolls

MAKES 32

Soft rye rolls, tangy with sourdough flavor, to go with a dinner of ham or corned beef.

1 cup cold water
2 tablespoons molasses
¼ cup solid vegetable shortening
1 tablespoon sugar
1 teaspoon salt
1 package dry yeast, dissolved in ¼ cup warm
  water
1 cup Herman sourdough starter (p. 49), at
  room temperature
1 tablespoon caraway seeds
2 cups dark rye flour, scoop measured
2 to 2½ cups bread flour, preferably
  bromated, scoop measured

1. In a wide saucepan, combine the water, molasses, shortening, sugar, and salt. Place over medium heat and stir until the shortening is melted. Transfer to a large mixing bowl to cool.

2. When the mixture is barely warm to the touch, stir in the dissolved yeast. Blend in the sourdough starter. Stir in the caraway seeds. Add the rye flour and beat with a wooden spoon until smooth. Gradually blend in the bread flour until the dough becomes too difficult to stir. Turn out onto a floured surface and knead in as much of the remaining bread flour as necessary to form a cohesive dough. Continue kneading in bread flour until the dough is soft yet no longer sticks to the work surface. Transfer to a greased bowl and cover with plastic wrap. Secure with an elastic band and set aside to rise until double in bulk.

3. Generously grease two 9-inch round baking pans. Punch the dough down, then turn it out onto a floured surface. Divide in half. Roll each half into a 16-inch rope with the palms of your hands. Cut each rope into sixteen 1-inch pieces. Shape each piece into a ball by rolling between the palms of your hands. Place in the prepared pans. Cover loosely with plastic wrap and let rise. When double in bulk, bake in a preheated 375°F. oven for 20 to 25 minutes, or until crusted and lightly browned. Remove from the oven and brush the surface with a small amount of melted butter. Cool on a rack for 5 minutes, then turn out. Serve immediately or complete cooling on the rack.   ❖

Sourdough Pan Rolls

MAKES 15

Dropped by spoonfuls into a buttered baking dish, these rolls are simple to prepare, but taste like they took you all day.

½ cup milk
6 tablespoons butter or margarine
¼ cup sugar

1 teaspoon salt
1 package dry yeast, dissolved in ½ cup warm water
1 large egg, beaten
1 cup water-based sourdough starter (p. 51), at room temperature
3½ cups all-purpose flour, scoop measured

1. In a wide saucepan, combine the milk, 4 tablespoons of the butter, the sugar, and the salt. Place over medium heat and stir until the butter is melted. Transfer to a large mixing bowl to cool.

2. When the mixture is barely warm to the touch, stir in the dissolved yeast and beaten egg. Blend in the sourdough starter. Add 2 cups of the flour and beat with a wooden spoon until smooth. Stir in the remaining 1½ cups flour. Cover the bowl with plastic wrap and secure with an elastic band. Set aside and let rise until double in bulk.

3. Melt the remaining 2 tablespoons butter and pour into a 9x13-inch baking dish. Tilt to coat the bottom of the dish. Stir the dough down and drop by generous spoonfuls into the prepared baking dish, placing 3 dollops across and 5 dollops down. Cover with plastic wrap and let rise. When double in bulk, bake in a preheated 375°F. oven for 20 to 25 minutes, or until nicely browned. Cool on a rack for 5 minutes, then turn out. Serve immediately or complete cooling on the rack.   ❖

Sweet Potato Whole Wheat Rolls

MAKES 24

Mashed, baked sweet potato contributes considerable vitamin A to these nutritious rolls.

1 cup milk
¼ cup honey
¼ cup butter or margarine
1 teaspoon salt
1 package dry yeast, dissolved in ¼ cup warm water

1 large egg, beaten
1 cup mashed, baked sweet potato
3 cups whole wheat flour, scoop measured
1 to 1½ cups bread flour, preferably
   bromated, scoop measured

1. In a wide saucepan, combine the milk, honey, butter, and salt. Place over medium heat and stir until the butter is melted. Transfer to a large mixing bowl to cool.

2. When the mixture is barely warm to the touch, stir in the dissolved yeast and beaten egg. Blend in the mashed sweet potato. Add 2 cups of the whole wheat flour and beat with a wooden spoon until smooth. Stir in the remaining cup of whole wheat flour. Gradually blend in the bread flour until the dough becomes too difficult to stir. Turn out onto a floured surface and knead in as much of the remaining bread flour as necessary to form a cohesive dough. Continue kneading in bread flour until the dough is soft yet no longer sticks to the work surface. Transfer to a greased bowl and cover with plastic wrap. Secure with an elastic band and set aside to rise until double in bulk.

3. Generously grease a 9x13-inch baking dish. Punch the dough down, then turn it out onto a floured surface. Divide in half. Roll each half into a 12-inch rope with the palms of your hands. Cut each rope into twelve 1-inch pieces. Shape each piece into a ball by rolling between the palms of your hands. Place in the prepared dish. Cover

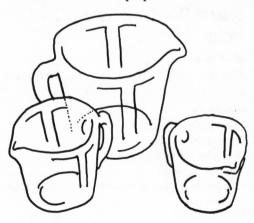

with plastic wrap and let rise. When double in bulk, bake in a preheated 375°F. oven for 25 to 30 minutes, or until lightly browned. Remove from the oven and brush the surface with a small amount of melted butter. Cool on a rack for 5 minutes, then turn out. Serve immediately or complete cooling on the rack.   ❖

Crusty Water Rolls

MAKES 12

These large rolls are a New England favorite for sandwiches or for breakfast with butter and jam.

1½ cups warm water
1 package dry yeast
1½ teaspoons salt
3½ to 4 cups bread flour, preferably
   bromated, scoop measured
1 large egg white, beaten with 1 tablespoon
   cold water
Poppy seeds

1. Measure the warm water into a large mixing bowl. Sprinkle on the yeast and stir to dissolve. Blend in the salt. Add 2 cups of the flour and beat with a wooden spoon until smooth. Gradually blend in additional flour until the dough becomes too difficult to stir. Turn out onto a floured surface and knead in as much of the remaining flour as necessary to form a cohesive dough. Continue kneading in flour until the dough is soft yet no longer sticks to the work surface. Transfer to a greased bowl and cover with plastic wrap. Secure with an elastic band and set aside to rise until double in bulk.

2. Generously grease a baking sheet and sprinkle with cornmeal. Punch the dough down, then turn it out onto a floured surface. Divide into 12 equal portions. Shape each portion into a ball and place on the prepared sheet. Flatten each ball slightly with floured fingertips. Cover loosely with plastic wrap and let rise. When double in bulk, brush the surface with the beaten egg

white and sprinkle on the poppy seeds. Bake in a preheated 450°F. oven for 15 to 20 minutes, or until nicely browned. Remove from the sheet and cool on a rack. ❖

Wheat Germ Sandwich Rolls

MAKES 12

For a sandwich that's a handful, start with these easy, quick rolls.

1¾ cups milk
¼ cup butter or margarine
2 tablespoons light brown sugar
1 teaspoon salt
1 package dry yeast, dissolved in ¼ cup warm
   water
2 large eggs, beaten
1 cup wheat germ
4½ to 5 cups bread flour, preferably
   bromated, scoop measured
1 tablespoon cold water

1. In a wide saucepan, combine the milk, butter, sugar, and salt. Place over medium heat and stir until the butter is melted. Transfer to a large mixing bowl to cool.

2. When the mixture is barely warm to the touch, stir in the dissolved yeast. Measure out 2 tablespoons of the beaten egg. Transfer to a glass measuring cup and set aside. Blend the remaining egg into the yeast mixture. Stir in the wheat germ. Add 2 cups of the flour and beat with a wooden spoon until smooth. Gradually blend in additional flour until the dough becomes too difficult to stir. Turn out onto a floured surface and knead in as much of the remaining flour as necessary to form a cohesive dough. Continue kneading in flour until the dough is soft yet no longer sticks to the work surface. Cover and let rest for 10 minutes.

3. Generously grease a baking sheet and sprinkle with cornmeal. Divide the dough into 12 equal portions and then shape each portion into a ball. Flatten each ball slightly with floured fingertips. Place 3 inches apart on the prepared sheet. Cover loosely

with plastic wrap and set aside to rise until double in bulk. Whisk the reserved egg with the cold water and brush over the surface. Sprinkle with additional wheat germ if you wish. Bake in a preheated 375°F. oven for 20 to 25 minutes, or until nicely browned. Remove from the pan and transfer to a rack to cool. ❖

Whole Wheat Ricotta Rolls

MAKES 12

Soft, tender dinner rolls to serve piping hot with hearty soup.

1 large egg
½ cup ricotta cheese
2 tablespoons butter or margarine, melted
2 tablespoons sugar
1 teaspoon salt
1 package dry yeast, dissolved in ½ cup warm
   water
1 tablespoon sesame seeds
2 to 2½ cups whole wheat flour, scoop
   measured

1. Beat the egg in a large mixing bowl. Add the ricotta, melted butter, sugar, and salt. Blend thoroughly. Stir in the dissolved yeast and sesame seeds.

2. Add 1 cup of the flour and beat with a wooden spoon until smooth. Gradually blend in the remaining flour until the dough becomes too difficult to stir. Turn out onto a floured surface and knead in as much of the remaining flour as necessary to form a cohesive dough. Continue kneading in flour until the dough is soft yet no longer sticks to the work surface. Transfer to a greased bowl and cover with plastic wrap. Secure with an elastic band and set aside to rise until double in bulk.

3. Generously grease 12 muffin cups. Punch the dough down, then turn it out onto a floured surface. Using the palms of your hands, roll the dough into an 18-inch rope. Cut the rope into twelve 1½-inch pieces. Shape each piece into a ball by roll-

ing between the palms of your hands. Place in the prepared muffin cups. Cover loosely with plastic wrap and let rise. When double in bulk, bake in a preheated 375°F. oven for 20 to 25 minutes, or until lightly browned. Cool on a rack for 5 minutes, then turn out. Serve immediately or complete cooling on the rack.   ❖

Anise Buns

MAKES 24

Tender sweet rolls redolent of anise seeds. Serve at breakfast or for tea.

¾ cup milk
3 tablespoons butter or margarine
⅓ cup sugar
¾ teaspoon salt
1 package dry yeast, dissolved in ¼ cup warm
   water
2 large eggs, beaten
1 tablespoon anise seeds
3½ to 4 cups all-purpose flour, scoop
   measured
2 teaspoons cold water

1. In a wide saucepan, combine the milk, butter, sugar, and salt. Place over medium heat and stir until the butter is melted. Transfer to a large mixing bowl to cool.

2. When the mixture is barely warm to the touch, stir in the dissolved yeast. Measure out 2 tablespoons of the beaten egg and transfer to a glass measuring cup. Blend the remaining egg into the yeast mixture. Stir in the anise seeds. Add 2 cups of the flour and beat with a wooden spoon until smooth. Gradually blend in additional flour until the dough becomes too difficult to stir. Turn out onto a floured surface and knead in as much of the remaining flour as necessary to form a cohesive dough. Continue kneading in flour until the dough is soft yet no longer sticks to the work surface. Transfer to a greased bowl and cover with a clean kitchen towel. Set aside to rise until double in bulk.

3. Generously grease a 9x13-inch baking dish. Punch the dough down, then turn it out onto a floured surface. Divide in half. Roll each half into a 12-inch rope with the palms of your hands. Cut each rope into twelve 1-inch pieces. Shape each piece into a ball by rolling between the palms of your hands. Place in the prepared baking dish. Cover and let rise. When double in bulk, whisk the reserved egg with the cold water and brush over the surface. Sprinkle on additional anise seeds if you wish. Bake in a preheated 375°F. oven for 20 to 25 minutes, or until nicely browned. Cool on a rack for 5 minutes, then turn out. Serve immediately or complete cooling on the rack.   ❖

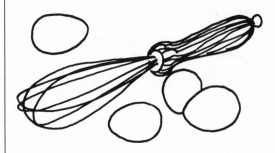

Bath Buns

MAKES 16

These gorgeous sugar-crusted buns are said to have originated at the famous spa in Bath, England. Sweet, rich, and densely textured, they are packed with currants and bits of candied orange peel.

1½ cups buttermilk
½ cup butter or margarine, melted
¼ cup granulated sugar, plus 2 tablespoons
1 teaspoon salt
1 package dry yeast, dissolved in ¼ cup warm
   water
2 large eggs, beaten
4 to 4½ cups bread flour, scoop measured
¾ cup dried currants
¼ cup finely chopped candied orange peel
¼ cup medium or whipping cream
2 tablespoons coarse sugar (or crushed sugar
   cubes)

1. In a large mixing bowl, combine the buttermilk, the melted butter, ¼ cup of the granulated sugar, and the salt. Stir in the dissolved yeast and beaten egg. Add 2 cups of the flour and beat with a wooden spoon until smooth. Stir in the currants and orange peel. Gradually blend in additional flour until the dough becomes too difficult to stir. Turn out onto a floured surface and knead in as much of the remaining flour as necessary to form a cohesive dough. Continue kneading in flour until the dough is soft yet no longer sticks to the work surface. Transfer to a greased bowl and cover with plastic wrap. Secure with an elastic band and set aside to rise until double in bulk.

2. Generously grease 2 baking sheets. Punch the dough down, then turn it out onto a floured surface. Divide into 16 equal portions. Shape each portion into a ball and place on the prepared sheets. Flatten each ball slightly with floured fingertips. Cover loosely with plastic wrap and let rise. When double in bulk, combine the cream and the remaining 2 tablespoons granulated sugar in a small saucepan. Heat gently until the sugar dissolves, but do not boil. Brush over the surface of the dough, then sprinkle on the coarse sugar. Bake in a preheated 375°F. oven for 20 to 25 minutes, or until nicely browned. Remove from the sheets and serve immediately, or cool on a rack.   ❖

Cinnamon Raisin Buns

MAKES 18

Raisin-filled buns, scented with cinnamon and brushed with a confectioners' sugar glaze.

1 cup milk
½ cup butter or margarine
½ cup granulated sugar
1 teaspoon salt
1 package dry yeast, dissolved in ¼ cup warm water

1 large egg, beaten
4 to 4½ cups bread flour, scoop measured
½ cup light brown sugar
1½ teaspoons cinnamon
¾ cup raisins
1 cup confectioners' sugar
4 teaspoons cold milk

1. In a wide saucepan, combine the 1 cup of milk, ¼ cup of the butter, the sugar, and the salt. Place over medium heat and stir until the butter is melted. Transfer to a large mixing bowl to cool.

2. When the mixture is barely warm to the touch, stir in the dissolved yeast and beaten egg. Add 2 cups of the flour and beat with a wooden spoon until smooth. Gradually blend in additional flour until the dough becomes too difficult to stir. Turn out onto a floured surface and knead in as much of the remaining flour as necessary to form a cohesive dough. Continue kneading in flour until the dough is soft yet no longer sticks to the work surface. Transfer to a greased bowl and cover with a clean kitchen towel. Set aside to rise until double in bulk.

3. In a small bowl, whisk together the brown sugar and cinnamon. Melt the remaining ¼ cup butter and set aside. Generously grease a 9x13-inch baking dish. Punch the dough down, then turn it out onto a floured surface. Roll into a 12x18-inch rectangle. Trim the edges to square off the rectangle. Lift the dough to loosen it from the work surface. Brush the melted butter over the surface of the dough. Sprinkle on the brown sugar and cinnamon. Scatter the raisins over the sugar. Starting at the long side, roll the dough up. Pinch the edges to seal the seam. Using a serrated knife, cut the roll into eighteen 1-inch pieces. Place, cut side down, in the prepared baking dish. (See illustration on page 57.) Cover and set aside to rise. When double in bulk, bake in a preheated 375°F. oven for 20 to 25 minutes, or until nicely browned. Place on a rack to cool for 20 min-

utes. Combine the confectioners' sugar and cold milk in a small bowl and blend until smooth. Brush over the surface of the warm rolls with a pastry brush.   ❖

Hot Cross Buns

MAKES 24

Puffy spheres, studded with candied fruit and fragrant with classic spices. Hot Cross Buns are traditionally served at Easter, and the confectioners' sugar glaze is applied in the shape of a cross.

1 cup milk, plus 1 tablespoon
¼ cup butter or margarine
¼ cup sugar
1 teaspoon salt
1 package dry yeast, dissolved in ¼ cup warm water
2 large eggs, beaten
1 teaspoon cinnamon
½ teaspoon nutmeg
¼ teaspoon ground cloves
4 to 4½ cups bread flour, scoop measured
½ cup raisins
½ cup finely chopped mixed candied fruit
2 teaspoons cold water
1 cup confectioners' sugar
¼ teaspoon vanilla extract

1. In a wide saucepan, combine 1 cup of the milk with the butter, sugar, and salt. Place over medium heat and stir until the butter is melted. Transfer to a large mixing bowl to cool.

2. When the mixture is barely warm to the touch, stir in the dissolved yeast. Measure out 2 tablespoons of the beaten egg and transfer to a glass measuring cup. Set aside. Blend the remaining egg into the yeast mixture. Stir in the cinnamon, nutmeg, and cloves. Add 2 cups of the flour and beat with a wooden spoon until smooth. Stir in the raisins and candied fruit. Gradually blend in additional flour until the dough becomes too difficult to stir. Turn out onto a floured surface and knead in as much of the remaining flour as necessary to form a cohesive dough. Continue kneading in flour until the dough is soft yet no longer sticks to the work surface. Transfer to a greased bowl and cover with a clean kitchen towel. Set aside to rise until double in bulk.

3. Generously grease two 9-inch square baking pans. Punch the dough down, then turn it out onto a floured surface. Divide in half. Roll each half into a 12-inch rope with the palms of your hands. Cut each rope into twelve 1-inch pieces. Shape each piece into a ball by rolling between the palms of your hands. Place in the prepared pans. Cover and set aside to rise. When double in bulk, whisk the reserved egg with the cold water and brush over the surface. Bake in a preheated 375°F. oven for 20 to 25 minutes, or until nicely browned. Cool on a rack for 30 minutes. In a small bowl, combine the confectioners' sugar, the remaining 1 tablespoon milk, and the vanilla. Take up with a spoon and drizzle over the buns in the design of a cross. Allow the buns to cool in the pan.   ❖

Maple Walnut Sticky Buns

MAKES 12

Everyone enjoys sticky buns, and these are exceptionally delicious. Maple syrup, sparked with rum, creates the memorable filling.

1 cup milk
1 cup butter or margarine
¼ cup granulated sugar, plus 2 tablespoons
1 teaspoon salt
1 package dry yeast, dissolved in ¼ cup warm water
2 large eggs, beaten
4 to 4½ cups bread flour, scoop measured
½ cup pure maple syrup
¼ cup dark rum
½ cup light brown sugar
2 tablespoons dark corn syrup
1 tablespoon cold water
¾ cup coarsely chopped walnuts

1. In a wide saucepan, combine the milk, ¼ cup of the butter, ¼ cup of the granulated sugar, and the salt. Place over medium heat and stir until the butter is melted. Transfer to a large mixing bowl to cool.

2. When the mixture is barely warm to the touch, stir in the dissolved yeast and beaten egg. Add 2 cups of the flour and beat with a wooden spoon until smooth. Gradually blend in additional flour until the dough becomes too difficult to stir. Turn out onto a floured surface and knead in as much of the remaining flour as necessary to form a cohesive dough. Continue kneading in flour until the dough is soft yet no longer sticks to the work surface. Transfer to a greased bowl and cover with a clean kitchen towel. Set aside to rise until double in bulk.

3. Meanwhile, combine the maple syrup and rum in a small saucepan. Add ½ cup of the remaining butter and the remaining 2 tablespoons granulated sugar. Place over medium heat and stir until the butter melts. Boil gently for 1 minute. Set aside to cool slightly.

4. Generously grease a 9x13-inch baking dish. In a small saucepan, combine the remaining ¼ cup butter with the brown sugar, corn syrup, and cold water. Place over medium heat and stir until the butter melts and the sugar dissolves. Pour into the prepared baking pan and tilt the pan to coat the bottom.

5. Punch the dough down, then turn it out onto a floured surface. Roll into a 10x18-inch rectangle. Trim the edges to square off the rectangle. Lift the dough to loosen it from the work surface. Using the back of a spoon, spread the maple filling over the dough to within 1 inch of the edges. Sprinkle on the walnuts. Starting at the long side, roll the dough up. Pinch the edges to seal the seam. Using a serrated knife, cut the roll into twelve 1½-inch pieces. Place, cut side down, in the prepared baking dish. (See illustration on page 57.) Cover and set aside to rise. When double in bulk, bake in a preheated 375°F. oven for 20 to 25 minutes, or until nicely browned. Cool on a rack for 10 minutes, then invert and turn out. Serve at once or complete cooling on the rack. ❖

Orange-Filled Breakfast Buns

MAKES 12

Fresh orange juice forms the basis for the filling of these glorious buns. Serve with whipped unsalted butter.

1 cup milk
¾ cup butter or margarine
1¼ cups sugar
1 teaspoon salt
1 package dry yeast, dissolved in ¼ cup warm water
2 large eggs, beaten
4 to 4½ cups bread flour, scoop measured
½ cup freshly squeezed orange juice
2 tablespoons finely grated orange zest
¾ cup coarsely chopped pecans

1. In a wide saucepan, combine the milk, ¼ cup of the butter, ¼ cup of the sugar, and the salt. Place over medium heat and stir until the butter is melted. Transfer to a large mixing bowl to cool.

2. When the mixture is barely warm to the touch, stir in the dissolved yeast and beaten egg. Add 2 cups of the flour and beat with a wooden spoon until smooth. Gradually blend in additional flour until the dough becomes too difficult to stir. Turn out onto a floured surface and knead in as much of the remaining flour as necessary to form a cohesive dough. Continue kneading in flour until the dough is soft yet no longer sticks to the work surface. Transfer to a greased bowl and cover with a clean kitchen towel. Set aside to rise until double in bulk.

3. Meanwhile, combine the orange juice and orange zest in a small saucepan. Add the remaining cup of sugar and ½ cup but-

ter. Bring to a boil and cook, uncovered and without stirring, until the mixture reaches 238°F. on a candy thermometer (the soft-ball stage). Set aside to cool slightly.

4. Generously grease 12 muffin cups. Punch the dough down, then turn it out onto a floured surface. Roll into a 10x18-inch rectangle. Trim the edges to square off the rectangle. Lift the dough to loosen it from the work surface. Using the back of a spoon, spread the orange filling over the dough to within 1 inch of the edges. Sprinkle on the pecans. Starting at the long side, roll the dough up. Pinch the edges to seal the seam. Using a serrated knife, cut the roll into twelve 1½-inch pieces. Place, cut side down, in the prepared muffin cups. (See illustration on page 57.) Cover and set aside to rise. When double in bulk, bake in a preheated 375°F. oven for 20 to 25 minutes, or until nicely browned. Cool on a rack for 10 minutes, then invert and turn out. Serve at once or complete cooling on the rack. ❖

Rum Buns

MAKES 18

The enchanting flavor of dark rum infuses these coiled buns. Serve warm with mugs of cappuccino.

1 cup milk
½ cup butter or margarine
¼ cup granulated sugar
½ cup light brown sugar
1 teaspoon salt
1 package dry yeast, dissolved in ¼ cup warm
    water
1 large egg, beaten
5 tablespoons dark rum
4 to 4½ cups bread flour, scoop measured
½ teaspoon freshly grated nutmeg
1 cup confectioners' sugar
1 teaspoon cold milk

1. In a wide saucepan, combine the 1 cup of milk, ¼ cup of the butter, the granulated

sugar, ¼ cup of the brown sugar, and the salt. Place over medium heat and stir until the butter is melted. Transfer to a large mixing bowl to cool.

2. When the mixture is barely warm to the touch, stir in the dissolved yeast and beaten egg. Blend in 2 tablespoons of the rum. Add 2 cups of the flour and beat with a wooden spoon until smooth. Gradually blend in additional flour until the dough becomes too difficult to stir. Turn out onto a floured surface and knead in as much of the remaining flour as necessary to form a cohesive dough. Continue kneading in flour until the dough is soft yet no longer sticks to the work surface. Transfer to a greased bowl and cover with a clean kitchen towel. Set aside to rise until double in bulk.

3. Melt the remaining ¼ cup of butter in a small saucepan. Stir in the remaining ¼ cup brown sugar, 2 tablespoons of the remaining rum, and the nutmeg. Heat until the sugar dissolves. Bring to a gentle boil and cook for 1 minute. Set aside to cool slightly. Generously grease a 9x13-inch baking dish. Punch the dough down, then turn it out onto a floured surface. Roll into a 12x18-inch rectangle. Trim the edges to square off the rectangle. Lift the dough to loosen it from the work surface. Using the back of a spoon, spread the rum mixture over the dough to within 1 inch of the edges. Starting at the long side, roll the dough up. Pinch the edges to seal the seam. Cut with a

serrated knife into eighteen 1-inch pieces. Place, cut side down, in the prepared baking dish. (See illustration on page 57.) Cover and set aside to rise. When double in bulk, bake in a preheated 375°F. oven for 20 to 25 minutes, or until the tops are nicely browned. Cool on a rack for 30 minutes. Combine the confectioners' sugar, cold milk, and the remaining tablespoon of rum in a small bowl and blend until smooth. Drizzle over the tops of the cooled buns. ❖

Streusel Buns

MAKES 16

Plump sweet rolls filled with crumbly cinnamon streusel and topped with lemon-flavored glaze.

1 cup milk
6 tablespoons butter or margarine
2 tablespoons granulated sugar, plus ½ cup
1 teaspoon salt
1 package dry yeast, dissolved in ¼ cup warm water
3 to 3½ cups bread flour, scoop measured
½ cup light brown sugar
1 teaspoon cinnamon
½ cup finely chopped pecans
1½ cups confectioners' sugar
1 tablespoon freshly squeezed lemon juice
1 tablespoon finely grated lemon zest

1. In a wide saucepan, combine the milk, 3 tablespoons of the butter, 2 tablespoons of the granulated sugar, and the salt. Place over medium heat and stir until the butter is melted. Transfer to a large mixing bowl to cool.

2. When the mixture is barely warm to the touch, stir in the dissolved yeast. Add 1 cup of the flour and beat with a wooden spoon until smooth. Gradually blend in additional flour until the dough becomes too difficult to stir. Turn out onto a floured surface and knead in as much of the remaining flour as necessary to form a cohesive dough. Continue kneading in flour until the dough is soft yet no longer sticks to the work surface. Transfer to a greased bowl and cover with a clean kitchen towel. Set aside to rise until double in bulk.

3. In a small mixing bowl, combine the remaining ½ cup granulated sugar, the brown sugar, and the cinnamon. Whisk to blend thoroughly. Add the remaining 3 tablespoons butter and cut in with a knife until crumbly. Stir in the pecans and set aside.

4. Line 2 baking sheets with parchment paper. Punch the dough down, then turn it out onto a floured surface. Roll into a 12x16-inch rectangle. Trim the edges to square off the rectangle. Lift the dough to loosen it from the work surface. Scatter the streusel mixture over the dough to within 1 inch of the edges. Starting at the long side, roll the dough up. Pinch the edges to seal the seam. Using a serrated knife, cut the roll into sixteen 1-inch pieces. Place, cut side down and well apart, on the parchment-lined sheets. (See illustration on page 57.) Cover and set aside to rise. When double in bulk, bake in a preheated 425°F. oven for 15 to 20 minutes, or until nicely browned. Remove from the pan and cool on a rack.

5. In a small bowl, combine the confectioners' sugar, lemon juice, and lemon zest. Blend until smooth, then drizzle over the buns while still warm. ❖

Walnut Honey Buns

MAKES 12

When you turn these buns out of the pan, they are crowned with a golden honey syrup.

1 cup milk
¾ cup butter or margarine
¼ cup sugar
1 teaspoon salt
1 package dry yeast, dissolved in ¼ cup warm water

2 large eggs, beaten
4 to 4½ cups bread flour, scoop measured
½ cup honey
¾ cup coarsely chopped walnuts

1. In a wide saucepan, combine the milk, ¼ cup of the butter, the sugar, and the salt. Place over medium heat and stir until the butter is melted. Transfer to a large mixing bowl to cool.

2. When the mixture is barely warm to the touch, stir in the dissolved yeast and beaten egg. Add 2 cups of the flour and beat with a wooden spoon until smooth. Gradually blend in additional flour until the dough becomes too difficult to stir. Turn out onto a floured surface and knead in as much of the remaining flour as necessary to form a cohesive dough. Continue kneading in flour until the dough is soft yet no longer sticks to the work surface. Transfer to a greased bowl and cover with a clean kitchen towel. Set aside to rise until double in bulk.

3. Meanwhile, combine ¼ cup of the honey with ¼ cup of the remaining butter in a small saucepan. Heat until the butter melts and the honey liquefies. Generously grease a 9x13-inch baking dish. Pour in the warm honey mixture and tilt to coat the bottom. Sprinkle on the walnuts.

4. In the same pan, heat the remaining ¼ cup honey with the remaining ¼ cup butter. Set aside to cool slightly.

5. Punch the dough down, then turn it out onto a floured surface. Roll into a 10x18-inch rectangle. Trim the edges to square off the rectangle. Lift the dough to loosen it from the work surface. Using the back of a spoon, spread the honey butter over the dough to within 1 inch of the edges. Starting at the long side, roll the dough up. Pinch the edges to seal the seam. Using a serrated knife, cut the roll into twelve 1½-inch pieces. Place, cut side down, in the prepared baking dish. Cover and set aside to rise. (See illustration on page 57.) When double in bulk, bake in a preheated 375°F.

oven for 20 to 25 minutes, or until nicely browned. Cool on a rack for 10 minutes, then invert and turn out. Serve immediately or complete cooling on the rack.   ❖

Whole Wheat Sandwich Buns

MAKES 12

Whole wheat rolls make a nutritious base for sandwiches. Try these filled with watercress and grilled chicken breasts that have been chilled and thinly sliced, then tossed with lemon vinaigrette.

1½ cups warm water
1 package dry yeast
1½ teaspoons salt
2 cups whole wheat flour, scoop measured
1½ to 2 cups bread flour, preferably
**   bromated, scoop measured**

1. Measure the warm water into a large mixing bowl. Sprinkle on the yeast and stir to dissolve. Blend in the salt. Add the whole wheat flour and beat with a wooden spoon until smooth. Gradually blend in the bread flour until the dough becomes too difficult to stir. Turn out onto a floured surface and knead in as much of the remaining bread flour as necessary to form a cohesive dough. Continue kneading in bread flour until the dough is soft yet no longer sticks to the work surface. Transfer to a greased bowl and cover with plastic wrap. Secure with an elastic band and set aside to rise until double in bulk.

2. Generously grease a baking sheet and sprinkle with cornmeal. Punch the dough down, then turn it out onto a floured surface. Divide into 12 equal portions. Shape each portion into a ball and place on the prepared sheet. Flatten each ball slightly with floured fingertips. Cover loosely with plastic wrap and let rise. When double in bulk, bake in a preheated 375°F. oven for 20 to 25 minutes, or until lightly browned. Remove from the pan and cool on a rack. ❖

Beer Onion Bagels

MAKES 12

Bits of caramelized onion top these beer-flavored bagels. They are a great partner for chili or beef stew.

9 tablespoons butter or margarine
1 medium onion, finely chopped
1 teaspoon sugar, plus 3 tablespoons
1 cup beer
1 teaspoon salt
1 package dry yeast, dissolved in ¼ cup warm water
¼ cup freshly grated Parmesan cheese
4 to 4½ cups bread flour, preferably bromated, scoop measured

1. Melt 3 tablespoons of the butter in a small skillet. Add the onion and cook over low heat until limp. Sprinkle with 1 teaspoon of the sugar and continue cooking until the onion turns golden brown. Transfer to a small bowl and set aside to cool.

2. In a wide saucepan, combine the beer, the remaining 6 tablespoons butter, 2 tablespoons of the sugar, and the salt. Place over medium heat and stir until the butter is melted. Transfer to a large mixing bowl to cool.

3. When the mixture is barely warm to the touch, stir in the dissolved yeast. Blend in the cheese. Add 2 cups of the flour and beat with a wooden spoon until smooth. Gradually blend in additional flour until the dough becomes too difficult to stir. Turn out onto a floured surface and knead in as much of the remaining flour as necessary to form a cohesive dough. Dust with flour to prevent sticking and continue kneading vigorously until the dough is smooth and resilient. Transfer to a greased bowl and cover with plastic wrap. Secure with an elastic band and set aside to rise.

4. When the dough is light (do not wait for it to double), turn it out onto a floured surface. Using the palms of your hands, roll the dough into a 12-inch rope. Cut the dough into twelve 1-inch pieces. Shape each piece into a ball by rolling between the palms of your hands. Flatten the balls slightly with floured fingertips. Poke your index finger through the center of each ball and twirl the dough around your finger in such a way as to enlarge the hole. Transfer to a floured board. Cover loosely with plastic wrap and let rise for 30 minutes, or until puffed but not double in bulk.

5. Pour tap water into a 12-inch skillet to the depth of 2 inches. Add the remaining tablespoon of sugar and bring to a gentle bubble. Stir to dissolve the sugar. Using a slotted metal spatula, lower 3 bagels into the water and cook exactly 1 minute. Turn and cook 1 minute on the other side. Transfer to absorbent paper to drain. Repeat with the remaining bagels.

6. Preheat the oven to 400°F. Generously grease a baking sheet. Brush the surface of the bagels with the caramelized onion and place on the prepared sheet. Bake for 20 to 25 minutes, or until nicely browned. Remove from the sheet and cool on a rack. ❖

Bran Bagels

MAKES 12

Hearty, satisfying bagels to split and toast for a chilly morning's breakfast.

1 cup cold water, plus 1 teaspoon
¼ cup butter or margarine
3 tablespoons sugar
1 teaspoon salt
1 package dry yeast, dissolved in ¼ cup warm water
1 large egg, separated
2½ cups 100% bran cereal flakes
2½ to 3 cups bread flour, preferably bromated, scoop measured

1. In a wide saucepan, combine 1 cup of the water, the butter, 2 tablespoons of the sugar, and the salt. Place over medium heat and stir until the butter is melted. Transfer to a large mixing bowl to cool.

2. When the mixture is barely warm to the touch, stir in the dissolved yeast. Whisk

the egg white until foamy and set the yolk aside in a glass measuring cup. Blend the egg white into the yeast mixture. Stir in the bran flakes. Add 1 cup of the flour and beat with a wooden spoon until smooth. Gradually blend in additional flour until the dough becomes too difficult to stir. Turn out onto a floured surface and knead in as much of the remaining flour as necessary to form a cohesive dough. Dust with flour to prevent sticking and continue kneading vigorously until the dough is smooth and resilient. Transfer to a greased bowl and cover with plastic wrap. Secure with an elastic band and set aside to rise.

3. When the dough is light (do not wait for it to double), turn it out onto a floured surface. Using the palms of your hands, roll the dough into a 12-inch rope. Cut the dough into twelve 1-inch pieces. Shape each piece into a ball by rolling between the palms of your hands. Flatten the balls slightly with floured fingertips. Poke your index finger through the center of each ball and twirl the dough around your finger in such a way as to enlarge the hole. Transfer to a floured board. Cover loosely with plastic wrap and let rise for 30 minutes, or until puffed but not double in bulk.

4. Pour tap water into a 12-inch skillet to the depth of 2 inches. Add the remaining tablespoon of sugar and bring to a gentle bubble. Stir to dissolve the sugar. Using a slotted metal spatula, lower 3 bagels into the water and cook exactly 1 minute. Turn and cook 1 minute on the other side. Transfer to absorbent paper to drain. Repeat with the remaining bagels.

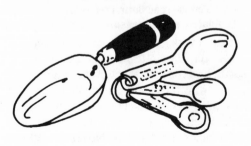

5. Preheat the oven to 400°F. Generously grease a baking sheet. Whisk the reserved egg yolk with the remaining teaspoon of cold water and brush over the surface of the bagels. Place on the prepared sheet. Bake for 20 to 25 minutes, or until nicely browned. Remove from the sheet and cool on a rack.   ❖

Egg Bagels

MAKES 12

Rich and inviting, these bagels are best when split and toasted. Serve with butter and jam.

1 cup cold water, plus 1 tablespoon
¼ cup butter or margarine
3 tablespoons sugar
1 teaspoon salt
1 package dry yeast, dissolved in ¼ cup warm water
3 large eggs, beaten
4 to 4½ cups bread flour, preferably bromated, scoop measured

1. In a wide saucepan, combine 1 cup of the water, the butter, 2 tablespoons of the sugar, and the salt. Place over medium heat and stir until the butter is melted. Transfer to a large mixing bowl to cool.

2. When the mixture is barely warm to the touch, stir in the dissolved yeast. Measure out 3 tablespoons of the beaten egg and set aside in a glass measuring cup. Blend the remaining egg into the yeast mixture. Add 2 cups of the flour and beat with a wooden spoon until smooth. Gradually blend in additional flour until the dough becomes too difficult to stir. Turn out onto a floured surface and knead in as much of the remaining flour as necessary to form a cohesive dough. Dust with flour to prevent sticking and continue kneading vigorously until the dough is smooth and resilient. Transfer to a greased bowl and cover with plastic wrap. Secure with an elastic band and set aside to rise.

3. When the dough is light (do not wait for it to double), turn it out onto a floured surface. Using the palms of your hands, roll the dough into a 12-inch rope. Cut the dough into twelve 1-inch pieces. Shape each piece into a ball by rolling between the palms of your hands. Flatten the balls slightly with floured fingertips. Poke your index finger through the center of each ball and twirl the dough around your finger in such a way as to enlarge the hole. Transfer to a floured board. Cover loosely with plastic wrap and let rise for 30 minutes, or until puffed but not double in bulk.

4. Pour tap water into a 12-inch skillet to the depth of 2 inches. Add the remaining tablespoon of sugar and bring to a gentle bubble. Stir to dissolve the sugar. Using a slotted metal spatula, lower 3 bagels into the water and cook exactly 1 minute. Turn and cook 1 minute on the other side. Transfer to absorbent paper to drain. Repeat with the remaining bagels.

5. Preheat the oven to 400°F. Generously grease a baking sheet. Whisk the reserved egg with the remaining tablespoon of cold water and brush over the surface of the bagels. Place on the prepared sheet. Bake for 20 to 25 minutes, or until nicely browned. Remove from the sheet and transfer to a rack to cool.   ❖

Honey Whole Wheat Bagels

MAKES 12

Honey and whole wheat make a favorite upcountry combination because of their wholesome goodness and comforting taste.

¾ cup cold water, plus 1 teaspoon
¼ cup honey
¼ cup butter or margarine
1 teaspoon salt
1 package dry yeast, dissolved in ¼ cup warm water
1 large egg, separated
2 cups whole wheat flour, scoop measured

2 to 2½ cups bread flour, preferably bromated, scoop measured
1 tablespoon sugar

1. In a wide saucepan, combine ¾ cup of the water with the honey, butter, and salt. Place over medium heat and stir until the butter is melted. Transfer to a large mixing bowl to cool.

2. When the mixture is barely warm to the touch, stir in the dissolved yeast. Whisk the egg white until foamy and set the yolk aside in a glass measuring cup. Blend the egg white into the yeast mixture. Add the whole wheat flour and beat with a wooden spoon until smooth. Gradually blend in the bread flour until the dough becomes too difficult to stir. Turn out onto a floured surface and knead in as much of the remaining bread flour as necessary to form a cohesive dough. Dust with bread flour to prevent sticking and continue kneading vigorously until the dough is smooth and resilient. Transfer to a greased bowl and cover with plastic wrap. Secure with an elastic band and set aside to rise.

3. When the dough is light (do not wait for it to double), turn it out onto a floured surface. Using the palms of your hands, roll the dough into a 12-inch rope. Cut the dough into twelve 1-inch pieces. Shape each piece into a ball by rolling between the palms of your hands. Flatten the balls slightly with floured fingertips. Poke your index finger through the center of each ball and twirl the dough around your finger in such a way as to enlarge the hole. Transfer to a floured board. Cover loosely with plastic wrap and let rise for 30 minutes, or until puffed but not double in bulk.

4. Pour tap water into a 12-inch skillet to the depth of 2 inches. Add the sugar and bring to a gentle bubble. Stir to dissolve the sugar. Using a slotted metal spatula, lower 3 bagels into the water and cook exactly 1 minute. Turn and cook 1 minute on the other side. Transfer to absorbent paper to drain. Repeat with the remaining bagels.

5. Preheat the oven to 375°F. Generously grease a baking sheet. Whisk the reserved egg yolk with the remaining teaspoon of cold water and brush over the surface of the bagels. Place on the prepared sheet. Bake for 20 to 25 minutes, or until nicely browned. Remove from the sheet and cool on a rack.   ❖

Herbed Bagels

MAKES 12

These are delicious for a picnic. Serve with cold fried chicken or a butterflied leg of lamb that has been grilled, refrigerated, and thinly sliced.

1 cup cold water
6 tablespoons butter or margarine
3 tablespoons sugar
1 teaspoon salt
1 package dry yeast, dissolved in ¼ cup warm
   water
1 tablespoon freeze-dried chives
1 teaspoon dried thyme
1 teaspoon dried chervil
4 to 4½ cups bread flour, preferably
   bromated, scoop measured
1 large egg, beaten with 1 teaspoon cold water

1. In a wide saucepan, combine the water, butter, 2 tablespoons of the sugar, and the salt. Place over medium heat and stir until the butter is melted. Transfer to a large mixing bowl to cool.

2. When the mixture is barely warm to the touch, stir in the dissolved yeast. Blend in the chives, thyme, and chervil. Add 2 cups of the flour and beat with a wooden spoon until smooth. Gradually blend in additional flour until the dough becomes too difficult to stir. Turn out onto a floured surface and knead in as much of the remaining flour as necessary to form a cohesive dough. Dust with flour to prevent sticking and continue kneading vigorously until the dough is smooth and resilient. Transfer to a greased bowl and cover with plastic wrap.

Secure with an elastic band and set aside to rise.

3. When the dough is light (do not wait for it to double), turn it out onto a floured surface. Using the palms of your hands, roll the dough into a 12-inch rope. Cut the dough into twelve 1-inch pieces. Shape each piece into a ball by rolling between the palms of your hands. Flatten the balls slightly with floured fingertips. Poke your index finger through the center of each ball and twirl the dough around your finger in such a way as to enlarge the hole. Transfer to a floured board. Cover loosely with plastic wrap and let rise for 30 minutes, or until puffed but not double in bulk.

4. Pour tap water into a 12-inch skillet to the depth of 2 inches. Add the remaining tablespoon of sugar and bring to a gentle bubble. Stir to dissolve the sugar. Using a slotted metal spatula, lower 3 bagels into the water and cook exactly 1 minute. Turn and cook 1 minute on the other side. Transfer to absorbent paper to drain. Repeat with the remaining bagels.

5. Preheat the oven to 400°F. Generously grease a baking sheet. Brush the surface of the bagels with the beaten egg and place on the prepared sheet. Bake for 20 to 25 minutes, or until nicely browned. Remove from the sheet and cool on a rack.   ❖

Milk Bagels

MAKES 12

These bagels have a soft, dense crumb with a beautiful brown crust.

1 cup milk
¼ cup butter or margarine
3 tablespoons sugar
1 teaspoon salt
1 package dry yeast, dissolved in ¼ cup warm
   water
1 large egg, separated
4 to 4½ cups bread flour, preferably
   bromated, scoop measured
1 teaspoon cold water

1. In a wide saucepan, combine the milk, butter, 2 tablespoons of the sugar, and the salt. Place over medium heat and stir until the butter is melted. Transfer to a large mixing bowl to cool.

2. When the mixture is barely warm to the touch, stir in the dissolved yeast. Whisk the egg white until foamy and set the yolk aside in a glass measuring cup. Blend the egg white into the yeast mixture. Add 2 cups of the flour and beat with a wooden spoon until smooth. Gradually blend in additional flour until the dough becomes too difficult to stir. Turn out onto a floured surface and knead in as much of the remaining flour as necessary to form a cohesive dough. Dust with flour to prevent sticking and continue kneading vigorously until the dough is smooth and resilient. Transfer to a greased bowl and cover with plastic wrap. Secure with an elastic band and set aside to rise.

3. When the dough is light (do not wait for it to double), turn it out onto a floured surface. Using the palms of your hands, roll the dough into a 12-inch rope. Cut the dough into twelve 1-inch pieces. Shape each piece into a ball by rolling between the palms of your hands. Flatten the balls slightly with floured fingertips. Poke your index finger through the center of each ball and twirl the dough around your finger in such a way as to enlarge the hole. Transfer to a floured board. Cover loosely with plastic wrap and let rise for 30 minutes, or until puffed but not double in bulk.

4. Pour tap water into a 12-inch skillet to the depth of 2 inches. Add the remaining tablespoon of sugar and bring to a gentle bubble. Stir to dissolve the sugar. Using a slotted metal spatula, lower 3 bagels into the water and cook exactly 1 minute. Turn and cook 1 minute on the other side. Transfer to absorbent paper to drain. Repeat with the remaining bagels.

5. Preheat the oven to 400°F. Generously grease a baking sheet. Whisk the reserved egg yolk with the cold water and brush over the surface of the bagels. Place on the prepared sheet. Bake for 20 to 25 minutes, or until nicely browned. Remove from the sheet and cool on a rack.   ❖

Raisin Bagels

MAKES 12

Kids love these raisin bagels for an after-school treat. Split and toast, then spread with chunky peanut butter.

1 cup cold water, plus 1 tablespoon
¼ cup butter or margarine
3 tablespoons sugar
1 teaspoon salt
1 package dry yeast, dissolved in ¼ cup warm water
3 large eggs, beaten
1 teaspoon cinnamon
½ teaspoon nutmeg
4 to 4½ cups bread flour, preferably bromated, scoop measured
½ cup raisins

1. In a wide saucepan, combine 1 cup of the water, the butter, 2 tablespoons of the sugar, and the salt. Place over medium heat and stir until the butter is melted. Transfer to a large mixing bowl to cool.

2. When the mixture is barely warm to the touch, stir in the dissolved yeast. Measure out 3 tablespoons of the beaten egg and set aside in a glass measuring cup. Blend the remaining egg into the yeast mixture. Stir in the cinnamon and nutmeg. Add 2 cups of the flour and beat with a wooden spoon until smooth. Stir in the raisins. Gradually blend in additional flour until the dough becomes too difficult to stir. Turn out onto a floured surface and knead in as much of the remaining flour as necessary to form a cohesive dough. Dust with flour to prevent sticking and continue kneading vigorously until the dough is smooth and resilient. Transfer to a greased bowl and cover with plastic wrap. Secure with an elastic band and set aside to rise.

3. When the dough is light (do not wait for it to double), turn it out onto a floured surface. Using the palms of your hands, roll the dough into a 12-inch rope. Cut the dough into twelve 1-inch pieces. Shape each piece into a ball by rolling between the palms of your hands. Flatten the balls slightly with floured fingertips. Poke your index finger through the center of each ball and twirl the dough around your finger in such a way as to enlarge the hole. Transfer to a floured board. Cover loosely with plastic wrap and let rise for 30 minutes, or until puffed but not double in bulk.

4. Pour tap water into a 12-inch skillet to the depth of 2 inches. Add the remaining tablespoon of sugar and bring to a gentle bubble. Stir to dissolve the sugar. Using a slotted metal spatula, lower 3 bagels into the water and cook exactly 1 minute. Turn and cook 1 minute on the other side. Transfer to absorbent paper to drain. Repeat with the remaining bagels.

5. Preheat the oven to 400°F. Generously grease a baking sheet. Whisk the reserved egg with the remaining tablespoon of cold water and brush over the surface of the bagels. Place on the prepared sheet. Bake for 20 to 25 minutes, or until nicely browned. Remove from the sheet and transfer to a rack to cool.   ❖

Rye Bagels

MAKES 12

Relish these rye bagels split, toasted, and sandwiched with warm baked ham.

1 cup cold water
6 tablespoons butter or margarine
3 tablespoons sugar
1 teaspoon salt
1 package dry yeast, dissolved in ¼ cup warm water
2 cups rye flour, scoop measured
2 tablespoons caraway seeds

2 to 2½ cups bread flour, preferably bromated, scoop measured
1 large egg white, beaten with 2 teaspoons cold water

1. In a wide saucepan, combine the water, butter, 2 tablespoons of the sugar, and the salt. Place over medium heat and stir until the butter is melted. Transfer to a large mixing bowl to cool.

2. When the mixture is barely warm to the touch, stir in the dissolved yeast. Add the rye flour and 1 tablespoon of the caraway seeds. Beat with a wooden spoon until smooth. Gradually blend in the bread flour until the dough becomes too difficult to stir. Turn out onto a floured surface and knead in as much of the remaining bread flour as necessary to form a cohesive dough. Dust with bread flour to prevent sticking and continue kneading vigorously until the dough is smooth and resilient. Transfer to a greased bowl and cover with plastic wrap. Secure with an elastic band and set aside to rise.

3. When the dough is light (do not wait for it to double), turn it out onto a floured surface. Using the palms of your hands, roll the dough into a 12-inch rope. Cut the dough into twelve 1-inch pieces. Shape each piece into a ball by rolling between the palms of your hands. Flatten the balls slightly with floured fingertips. Poke your index finger through the center of each ball and twirl the dough around your finger in such a way as to enlarge the hole. Transfer to a floured board. Cover loosely with plastic wrap and let rise for 30 minutes, or until puffed but not double in bulk.

4. Pour tap water into a 12-inch skillet to the depth of 2 inches. Add the remaining tablespoon of sugar and bring to a gentle bubble. Stir to dissolve the sugar. Using a slotted metal spatula, lower 3 bagels into the water and cook exactly 1 minute. Turn and cook 1 minute on the other side. Transfer to absorbent paper to drain. Repeat with the remaining bagels.

5. Preheat the oven to 400°F. Generously grease a baking sheet. Brush the surface of the bagels with the egg white and sprinkle on the remaining tablespoon of caraway seeds. Place on the prepared sheet. Bake for 20 to 25 minutes, or until nicely browned. Remove from the sheet and transfer to a rack to cool.   ❖

Water Bagels

MAKES 12

Water bagels have a lighter, chewier consistency than bagels made with milk or eggs.

1 cup cold water
6 tablespoons butter or margarine
3 tablespoons sugar
1 teaspoon salt
1 package dry yeast, dissolved in ¼ cup warm
   water
4 to 4½ cups bread flour, preferably
   bromated, scoop measured
1 large egg, beaten with 1 teaspoon cold water
Poppy seeds

1. In a wide saucepan, combine the water, butter, 2 tablespoons of the sugar, and the salt. Place over medium heat and stir until the butter is melted. Transfer to a large mixing bowl to cool.

2. When the mixture is barely warm to the touch, stir in the dissolved yeast. Add 2 cups of flour and beat with a wooden spoon until smooth. Gradually blend in additional flour until the dough becomes too difficult to stir. Turn out onto a floured surface and knead in as much of the remaining flour as necessary to form a cohesive dough. Dust with flour to prevent sticking and continue kneading vigorously until the dough is smooth and resilient. Transfer to a greased bowl and cover with plastic wrap. Secure with an elastic band and set aside to rise.

3. When the dough is light (do not wait for it to double), turn it out onto a floured surface. Using the palms of your hands, roll the dough into a 12-inch rope. Cut the dough into twelve 1-inch pieces. Shape each piece into a ball by rolling between the palms of your hands. Flatten the balls slightly with floured fingertips. Poke your index finger through the center of each ball and twirl the dough around your finger in such a way as to enlarge the hole. Transfer to a floured board. Cover loosely with plastic wrap and let rise for 30 minutes, or until puffed but not double in bulk.

4. Pour tap water into a 12-inch skillet to the depth of 2 inches. Add the remaining tablespoon of sugar and bring to a gentle bubble. Stir to dissolve the sugar. Using a slotted metal spatula, lower 3 bagels into the water and cook exactly 1 minute. Turn and cook 1 minute on the other side. Transfer to absorbent paper to drain. Repeat with the remaining bagels.

5. Preheat the oven to 400°F. Generously grease a baking sheet. Brush the surface of the bagels with the egg and sprinkle on the poppy seeds. Place on the prepared sheet. Bake for 20 to 25 minutes, or until nicely browned. Remove from the sheet and cool on a rack.   ❖

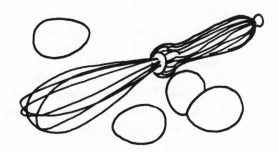

❖ Muffins and Popovers ❖

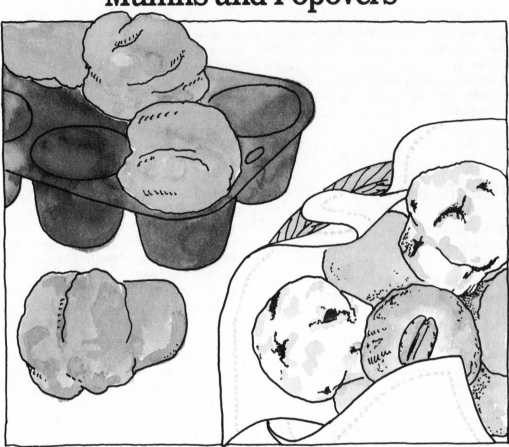

TO MY MIND, muffins are the quintessential New England bread. Honest and straightforward, muffins never pretend to be something they aren't.

The proper muffin is modestly sized with a gently rounded top. Its texture is light and crumbly, its taste faintly sweet. A judicious sprinkling of berries, nuts, or bits of fruit may be added, but always with a restrained hand. Overstuffed, oversweetened muffins belie the true nature of these simple breads.

The best way to prepare muffins is by the two-bowl method. That is to say, you combine the dry ingredients in a large bowl and the liquid ingredients in another bowl. Then you gently mix the two together, stirring only until the batter is moistened. A moderate amount of stirring ensures a tender con-sistency, so the batter should be blended by hand using a wooden spoon. Allow any lumps that occur to remain; they will dissipate during baking.

Whether or not to use muffin papers is a matter of personal taste and aesthetics. Some people like them because they eliminate the need for greasing the baking tins. I have never found the act of peeling the paper from a muffin particularly appealing, however, so I don't use them. Also, I prefer the slight crustiness that forms on the sides when muffins are baked directly in the pan.

Popovers are almost the direct opposite of muffins — flimsy shells puffed with hot air. But that doesn't mean they aren't delightful. Crisp, steaming popovers are a captivating delicacy.

The important point in preparing popovers is to avoid opening the oven door during baking. Popovers are leavened by steam. As the liquid in the batter heats, it turns to steam and creates the weblike interior characteristic of popovers. If you open the oven door, the cold air that enters the oven will convert the steam inside the popovers to water, causing them to collapse or become soggy. It is always a good idea to bake popovers at least 30 minutes before opening the oven door to check on them.

Popovers are best when eaten soon after baking. They don't store well, and I don't recommend freezing them. Muffins, however, freeze successfully and are the perfect bread for small families or a person living alone. After baking, allow the muffins to cool completely, then transfer them to a plastic freezer bag and secure it with a wire twist. Defrost in any number you choose. One or two muffins may be removed from the freezer the night before and then warmed to provide fresh-tasting treats for breakfast.

To heat muffins so that they retain their moisture, wrap them tightly in aluminum foil and place in a preheated 400°F. oven for approximately 5 minutes. Muffins may also be warmed in a microwave oven. Wrap each one individually in a paper towel and place in the microwave. Heat on high power. A single muffin will warm in 30 seconds, and two muffins take about 45 seconds. Do not double the time for each additional muffin because that would cause them to overheat and become tough. Instead, increase the amount of time by about half. Check for warmth, then microwave longer if needed.

Muffins make a warm, comforting gift for someone away from home. They pack easily and mail without breaking apart. If you have loved ones away at school, at camp, or serving in the armed forces, consider sending them a box of your very best homemade muffins.

Apple Cider Muffins

MAKES 12

One whiff of these muffins as they emerge from the oven calls up memories of autumn in New England.

1¼ cups whole wheat flour, scoop measured
¾ cup all-purpose flour, scoop measured
½ cup light brown sugar
1½ teaspoons baking powder
½ teaspoon baking soda
¾ teaspoon salt
½ teaspoon cinnamon
1 cup apple cider
1 large egg
¼ cup vegetable oil
½ cup coarsely chopped walnuts

1. Preheat the oven to 400°F. Generously grease 12 muffin cups or line with papers. Into a large mixing bowl, sift the whole wheat flour, all-purpose flour, brown sugar, baking powder, baking soda, salt, and cinnamon. Whisk to blend thoroughly.

2. In a separate bowl, whisk together the cider, egg, and vegetable oil. Make a well in the dry ingredients and pour in the egg mixture. Blend with a wooden spoon until a moist, lumpy batter is formed. Stir in the walnuts. Spoon into the prepared muffin cups and bake for 20 to 25 minutes, or until a wooden pick inserted in the center comes out clean. Cool on a rack for 5 minutes, then tilt the muffins on their sides or transfer them to the rack to complete cooling. ❖

Cinnamon Apple Muffins

MAKES 12

Chop the apples for these muffins, about the size of small blueberries. This will produce muffins with chunks of tender-crisp apple.

2 small tart green apples, peeled, cored, and coarsely chopped
Juice of half a lemon
2 cups all-purpose flour, scoop measured
½ cup sugar

1½ teaspoons baking powder
½ teaspoon baking soda
½ teaspoon salt
1 teaspoon cinnamon
¾ cup milk
1 large egg
¼ cup butter or margarine, melted
½ cup coarsely chopped walnuts

1. In a small bowl, toss the apples with the lemon juice and set aside. Preheat the oven to 400°F. Generously grease 12 muffin cups or line with papers. Combine the flour, sugar, baking powder, baking soda, salt, and cinnamon in a large mixing bowl. Whisk to blend thoroughly.

2. In a separate bowl, whisk together the milk, egg, and melted butter. Add the chopped apples and mix well. Make a well in the dry ingredients and pour in the egg mixture. Blend with a wooden spoon until a moist, lumpy batter is formed. Stir in the walnuts. Spoon into the prepared muffin cups and bake for 20 to 25 minutes, or until a wooden pick inserted in the center comes out clean. Cool on a rack for 5 minutes, then tilt the muffins on their sides or transfer them to the rack to complete cooling. ❖

Apple Streusel Muffins

MAKES 12

Apples and streusel have long been boon companions. Here they appear together in hearty, aromatic muffins.

2 tablespoons all-purpose flour, plus 2 cups, scoop measured
1 tablespoon light brown sugar, plus ¼ cup
¾ teaspoon cinnamon
1 tablespoon butter or margarine, cut into small pieces
¼ cup granulated sugar
2 teaspoons baking powder
½ teaspoon baking soda
½ teaspoon salt
1 cup buttermilk
1 large egg
¾ teaspoon vanilla extract

¼ cup vegetable oil
1 large apple, peeled, cored, and coarsely chopped

1. Into a small bowl, sift together 2 tablespoons of the flour, 1 tablespoon of the brown sugar, and ¼ teaspoon of the cinnamon. Whisk to blend and add the butter. Cut in with a knife until crumbly and set aside.

2. Preheat the oven to 400°F. Generously grease 12 muffin cups or line with papers. Into a large mixing bowl, sift the remaining 2 cups flour, ¼ cup brown sugar, and ½ teaspoon cinnamon, along with the granulated sugar, baking powder, baking soda, and salt. Whisk to blend thoroughly.

3. In a separate bowl, whisk together the buttermilk, egg, vanilla extract, and vegetable oil. Make a well in the dry ingredients and pour in the egg mixture. Blend with a wooden spoon until a moist, lumpy batter is formed. Stir in the chopped apple. Spoon into the prepared muffin cups and sprinkle on the reserved streusel. Bake for 20 to 25 minutes, or until a wooden pick inserted in the center comes out clean. Cool on a rack for 5 minutes, then tilt the muffins on their sides or transfer them to the rack to complete cooling. ❖

Apricot Rice Muffins

MAKES 12

These nutritious muffins are an excellent way to use up leftover brown rice.

1¼ cups whole wheat flour, scoop measured
⅓ cup light brown sugar
3 teaspoons baking powder
½ teaspoon salt
⅔ cup milk
2 large eggs
¼ cup vegetable oil
½ teaspoon almond extract
1 cup cooked brown rice
½ cup coarsely chopped dried apricots

1. Preheat the oven to 400°F. Generously grease 12 muffin cups or line with papers.

Sift the flour, sugar, baking powder, and salt into a large mixing bowl. Whisk to blend thoroughly.

2. In a separate bowl, whisk together the milk, eggs, vegetable oil, and almond extract. Make a well in the dry ingredients and pour in the egg mixture. Blend with a wooden spoon until a moist, lumpy batter is formed. Stir in the rice and apricots. Spoon into the prepared muffin cups and bake for 20 to 25 minutes, or until a wooden pick inserted in the center comes out clean. Cool on a rack for 5 minutes, then tilt the muffins on their sides or transfer them to the rack to complete cooling. ❖

Cinnamon Banana Muffins

MAKES 12

These muffins freeze exceptionally well. When they have cooled to room temperature, place the muffins in a plastic bag and secure with a wire twist. Defrost in the same bag or transfer to aluminum foil and wrap tightly. Place in a 350°F. oven and heat until soft and warm.

1 tablespoon sugar, plus ⅓ cup
1¼ teaspoons cinnamon
2 cups all-purpose flour, scoop measured
3 teaspoons baking powder
½ teaspoon salt
¾ cup milk
1 large egg
¼ cup vegetable oil
1 cup mashed banana (very ripe)

1. Preheat the oven to 400°F. Generously grease 12 muffin cups or line with papers. Combine 1 tablespoon of the sugar and ¼ teaspoon of the cinnamon. Mix well and set aside.

2. In a large mixing bowl, combine the flour with the remaining ⅓ cup sugar and 1 teaspoon cinnamon, along with the baking powder and salt. Whisk to blend thoroughly.

3. In a separate bowl, whisk together the milk, egg, and vegetable oil. Stir in the mashed banana. Make a well in the dry in-

gredients and pour in the egg mixture. Blend with a wooden spoon until a moist, lumpy batter is formed. Spoon into the prepared muffin cups and sprinkle on the cinnamon sugar. Bake for 20 to 25 minutes, or until a wooden pick inserted in the center comes out clean. Cool on a rack for 5 minutes, then tilt the muffins on their sides or transfer them to the rack to complete cooling. ❖

Banana Walnut Muffins

MAKES 12

These muffins are delicious served warm and spread with whipped cream cheese.

2 cups all-purpose flour, scoop measured
½ cup sugar
2 teaspoons baking powder
½ teaspoon baking soda
½ teaspoon salt
½ cup buttermilk
1 large egg
¼ cup vegetable oil
1 cup mashed banana (very ripe)
½ cup coarsely chopped walnuts

1. Preheat the oven to 400°F. Generously grease 12 muffin cups or line with papers. Combine the flour, sugar, baking powder, baking soda, and salt in a large mixing bowl. Whisk to blend thoroughly.

2. In a separate bowl, whisk together the buttermilk, egg, and vegetable oil. Stir in the mashed banana. Make a well in the dry ingredients and pour in the egg mixture. Blend with a wooden spoon until a moist, lumpy batter is formed. Stir in the walnuts. Spoon into the prepared muffin cups and bake for 20 to 25 minutes, or until a wooden pick inserted in the center comes out clean. Cool on a rack for 5 minutes, then tilt the muffins on their sides or transfer them to the rack to complete cooling. ❖

Blackberry Muffins

MAKES 12

To avoid gluey berry pockets, make sure the blackberries are dry before adding them to the batter. Rinse them under cold tap water, then scatter them on a double thickness of paper towels to drain. Pat gently to dry.

2 cups all-purpose flour, scoop measured
½ cup sugar, plus 2 tablespoons
3 teaspoons baking powder
¾ teaspoon salt
1 cup milk
1 large egg
¼ cup butter or margarine, melted
1 cup fresh blackberries, rinsed and gently
   patted dry

1. Preheat the oven to 400°F. Generously grease 12 muffin cups or line with papers. Combine the flour, ½ cup of the sugar, the baking powder, and the salt in a large mixing bowl. Whisk to blend thoroughly.

2. In a separate bowl, whisk together the milk, egg, and melted butter. Make a well in the dry ingredients and pour in the egg mixture. Blend with a wooden spoon until a moist, lumpy batter is formed. Gently stir in the blackberries. Spoon into the prepared muffin cups and sprinkle on the remaining 2 tablespoons sugar. Bake for 20 to 25 minutes, or until a wooden pick inserted in the center comes out clean. Cool on a rack for 5 minutes, then tilt the muffins on their sides or transfer them to the rack to complete cooling.   ❖

Blueberry Corn Muffins

MAKES 12

Crunchy corn muffins studded with juicy blueberries — a delightful surprise to the palate.

1½ cups all-purpose flour, scoop measured
¾ cup yellow cornmeal
½ cup sugar
3 teaspoons baking powder

½ teaspoon salt
⅔ cup milk
2 large eggs
¼ cup butter or margarine, melted
1 cup fresh blueberries, rinsed and gently
   patted dry

1. Preheat the oven to 425°F. Generously grease 12 muffin cups or line with papers. Combine the flour, cornmeal, sugar, baking powder, and salt in a large mixing bowl. Whisk to blend thoroughly.

2. In a separate bowl, whisk together the milk, eggs, and melted butter. Make a well in the dry ingredients and pour in the egg mixture. Blend with a wooden spoon until a moist, lumpy batter is formed. Stir in the blueberries. Spoon into the prepared muffin cups and bake for 20 to 25 minutes, or until a wooden pick inserted in the center comes out clean. Cool on a rack for 5 minutes, then tilt the muffins on their sides or transfer them to the rack to complete cooling.   ❖

Old-Fashioned Blueberry Muffins

MAKES 12

This recipe produces rough-textured muffins with nicely rounded tops that turn golden brown.

2 cups all-purpose flour, scoop measured
½ cup sugar
3 teaspoons baking powder
¾ teaspoon salt
¾ cup milk
1 large egg
¼ cup butter or margarine, melted
1 cup fresh blueberries, rinsed and gently
   patted dry

1. Preheat the oven to 425°F. Generously grease 12 muffin cups or line with papers. Combine the flour, sugar, baking powder, and salt in a large mixing bowl. Whisk to blend thoroughly.

2. In a separate bowl, whisk together the milk, egg, and melted butter. Make a well in

the dry ingredients and pour in the egg mixture. Blend with a wooden spoon until a moist, lumpy batter is formed. Stir in the blueberries. Spoon into the prepared muffin cups and bake for 20 to 25 minutes, or until a wooden pick inserted in the center comes out clean. Cool on a rack for 5 minutes, then tilt the muffins on their sides or transfer them to the rack to complete cooling. ❖

Blueberry Sour Cream Muffins

MAKES 12

When making these muffins, purchase the smallest blueberries you can find. They are most apt to have that tart aftertaste so reminiscent of berries picked in the wild.

2 cups all-purpose flour, scoop measured
¼ cup light brown sugar
2 teaspoons baking powder
½ teaspoon baking soda
½ teaspoon salt
½ teaspoon cinnamon
1 cup sour cream
2 tablespoons cold water
2 large eggs
1 cup fresh blueberries, rinsed and gently patted dry

1. Preheat the oven to 400°F. Generously grease 12 muffin cups or line with papers. Sift the flour, sugar, baking powder, baking soda, salt, and cinnamon into a large mixing bowl. Whisk to blend thoroughly.

2. In a separate bowl, whisk together the sour cream, cold water, and eggs. Make a well in the dry ingredients and pour in the egg mixture. Blend with a wooden spoon until a moist, lumpy batter is formed. Stir in the blueberries. Spoon into the prepared muffin cups and bake for 20 to 25 minutes, or until a wooden pick inserted in the center comes out clean. Cool on a rack for 5 minutes, then tilt the muffins on their sides or transfer them to the rack to complete cooling. ❖

Applesauce Bran Muffins

MAKES 12

Applesauce makes these bran muffins moist and delicious.

1¼ cups 100% bran cereal (not flakes)
⅔ cup milk
1 large egg
¼ cup butter or margarine, melted
⅔ cup prepared applesauce
¼ cup sugar
3 teaspoons baking powder
¾ teaspoon salt
1 cup all-purpose flour, scoop measured

1. Preheat the oven to 400°F. Generously grease 12 muffin cups or line with papers. Measure the bran into a large mixing bowl and pour on the milk. Set aside for 10 minutes to soften the bran. In a separate bowl, whisk together the egg and melted butter. Set aside.

2. Add the applesauce, sugar, baking powder, and salt to the softened bran. Stir to blend. Pour in the egg mixture and mix well. Sprinkle on the flour and blend with a wooden spoon until a moist, lumpy batter is formed. Spoon into the prepared muffin cups and bake for 20 to 30 minutes, or until a wooden pick inserted in the center comes out clean. Cool on a rack for 5 minutes, then tilt the muffins on their sides or transfer them to the rack to complete cooling. ❖

Old-Fashioned Bran Muffins

MAKES 12

A rough, crusty exterior gives these muffins a down-home look.

1⅓ cups 100% bran cereal (not flakes)
1 cup milk
½ cup light brown sugar
½ teaspoon salt
1 large egg
¼ cup vegetable oil
2 teaspoons baking powder
½ teaspoon baking soda
1⅓ cups all-purpose flour, scoop measured

1. Preheat the oven to 400°F. Generously grease 12 muffin cups or line with papers. Measure the bran into a large mixing bowl and pour on the milk. Add the sugar and salt, and stir to partially dissolve the sugar. Set aside for 10 minutes to soften the bran. In a separate bowl, whisk together the egg and vegetable oil. Set aside.

2. Add the baking powder and baking soda to the softened bran. Stir to mix well. Pour in the egg mixture and blend. Sprinkle on the flour and stir with a wooden spoon until a moist, lumpy batter is formed. Spoon into the prepared muffin cups and bake for 20 to 30 minutes, or until a wooden pick inserted in the center comes out clean. Cool on a rack for 5 minutes, then tilt the muffins on their sides or transfer them to the rack to complete cooling. ❖

Orange Bran Muffins

MAKES 12

Bran muffins moist with buttermilk and orange juice are a welcome addition to a country breakfast.

1 cup 100% bran cereal (not flakes)
½ cup freshly squeezed orange juice
½ cup light brown sugar
½ teaspoon salt
½ cup raisins
½ cup sour cream
1 large egg
¼ cup vegetable oil
1 tablespoon finely grated orange zest
2 teaspoons baking powder
½ teaspoon baking soda
1 cup all-purpose flour, scoop measured

1. Preheat the oven to 400°F. Generously grease 12 muffin cups or line with papers. Measure the bran into a large mixing bowl and pour on the orange juice. Add the sugar, salt, and raisins, and stir to partially dissolve the sugar. Set aside for 10 minutes to soften the bran. In a separate bowl, whisk together the sour cream, egg, and vegetable oil. Stir in the orange zest. Set aside.

2. Add the baking powder and baking soda to the softened bran. Stir to mix well. Pour in the egg mixture and blend. Sprinkle on the flour and stir with a wooden spoon until a moist, lumpy batter is formed. Spoon into the prepared muffin cups and bake for 20 to 25 minutes, or until a wooden pick inserted in the center comes out clean. Cool on a rack for 5 minutes, then tilt the muffins on their sides or transfer them to the rack to complete cooling. ❖

Peanut Butter Bran Muffins

MAKES 12

If you like peanut butter, you'll love these nutritious muffins. Have some on hand for healthful snacking.

1 cup 100% bran cereal (not flakes)
1 cup milk
⅓ cup chunky peanut butter
¼ cup light brown sugar
½ teaspoon salt
1 large egg
3 tablespoons vegetable oil
2 teaspoons baking powder
½ teaspoon baking soda
1 cup all-purpose flour, scoop measured

1. Preheat the oven to 400°F. Generously grease 12 muffin cups or line with papers.

Measure the bran into a large mixing bowl. Heat the milk and peanut butter in a small saucepan until the peanut butter softens and melts. Pour over the bran and stir. Add the sugar and salt, and blend to partially dissolve the sugar. Set aside for 10 minutes to soften the bran.

2. In a small bowl, whisk together the egg and vegetable oil. Add the baking powder and baking soda to the softened bran and stir to mix well. Pour in the egg mixture and blend. Sprinkle on the flour and stir with a wooden spoon until a moist, lumpy batter is formed. Spoon into the prepared muffin cups and bake for 20 to 25 minutes, or until a wooden pick inserted in the center comes out clean. Cool on a rack for 5 minutes, then tilt the muffins on their sides or transfer them to the rack to complete cooling. ❖

Carrot Nut Muffins

MAKES 12

These muffins are particularly good split lengthwise and toasted, then spread with softened cream cheese.

1 cup quick-cooking rolled oats
½ cup whole wheat flour, scoop measured
½ cup all-purpose flour, scoop measured
¼ cup light brown sugar
3 teaspoons baking powder
½ teaspoon salt
½ teaspoon cinnamon
⅔ cup milk
2 large eggs
¼ cup vegetable oil
1 cup shredded carrots
½ cup chopped walnuts

1. Preheat the oven to 400°F. Generously grease 12 muffin cups or line with papers. Measure the oats into a large mixing bowl. Sift in the whole wheat flour, all-purpose flour, sugar, baking powder, salt, and cinnamon. Whisk to blend thoroughly.

2. In a separate bowl, whisk together the milk, eggs, and vegetable oil. Make a well in the dry ingredients and pour in the egg mixture. Blend with a wooden spoon until a moist, lumpy batter is formed. Stir in the carrots and walnuts. Spoon into the prepared muffin cups and bake for 20 to 25 minutes, or until a wooden pick inserted in the center comes out clean. Cool on a rack for 5 minutes, then tilt the muffins on their sides or transfer them to the rack to complete cooling. ❖

Cream Cheese Muffins

MAKES 12

Serve these delicate, date-studded muffins with fruit salad for lunch.

2 cups all-purpose flour, scoop measured
½ cup sugar
3 teaspoons baking powder
½ teaspoon salt
6 ounces cream cheese, softened
2 large eggs
¼ cup butter or margarine, melted
⅔ cup milk
1 teaspoon vanilla extract
½ cup coarsely chopped pitted dates

1. Preheat the oven to 425°F. Generously grease 12 muffin cups or line with papers. Combine the flour, sugar, baking powder, and salt in a large mixing bowl. Whisk to blend thoroughly.

2. In a separate bowl, beat the cream cheese and eggs. Gradually beat in the melted butter and milk until smooth. Stir in the vanilla extract. Make a well in the dry ingredients and pour in the cream cheese mixture. Blend with a wooden spoon until a moist, lumpy batter is formed. Stir in the chopped dates. Spoon into the prepared muffin cups and bake for 20 to 25 minutes, or until a wooden pick inserted in the center comes out clean. Cool on a rack for 5 minutes, then tilt the muffins on their sides or transfer them to the rack to complete cooling. ❖

Caraway Cheddar Muffins

MAKES 12

These lusty cheese muffins are the perfect partner for bowls of steaming soup.

2 cups all-purpose flour, scoop measured
2 teaspoons sugar
3 teaspoons baking powder
¾ teaspoon salt
¼ teaspoon dry mustard
1 tablespoon caraway seeds
1 cup milk
1 large egg
¼ cup butter or margarine, melted
1 cup shredded sharp Cheddar cheese

1. Preheat the oven to 400°F. Generously grease 12 muffin cups or line with papers. Combine the flour, sugar, baking powder, salt, and dry mustard in a large mixing bowl. Whisk to blend thoroughly. Stir in the caraway seeds.

2. In a separate bowl, whisk together the milk, egg, and melted butter. Make a well in the dry ingredients and pour in the egg mixture. Blend with a wooden spoon until a moist, lumpy batter is formed. Stir in the Cheddar cheese. Spoon into the prepared muffin cups and bake for 20 to 25 minutes, or until a wooden pick inserted in the center comes out clean. Cool on a rack for 5 minutes, then tilt the muffins on their sides or transfer them to the rack to complete cooling.   ❖

Cherry Nut Muffins

MAKES 12

When tart red cherries are in season, be sure to try these delightful muffins. The perfect topping for them is whipped unsalted butter.

2 cups all-purpose flour, scoop measured
½ cup sugar
3 teaspoons baking powder
½ teaspoon salt
¾ cup milk
2 large eggs

¼ cup butter or margarine, melted
½ teaspoon vanilla extract
2 cups tart red cherries, pitted and coarsely chopped
½ cup chopped walnuts

1. Preheat the oven to 425°F. Generously grease 12 muffin cups or line with papers. Combine the flour, sugar, baking powder, and salt in a large mixing bowl. Whisk to blend thoroughly.

2. In a separate bowl, whisk together the milk, eggs, melted butter, and vanilla extract. Make a well in the dry ingredients and pour in the egg mixture. Blend with a wooden spoon until a moist, lumpy batter is formed. Stir in the cherries and walnuts. Spoon into the prepared muffin cups and bake for 20 to 25 minutes, or until a wooden pick inserted in the center comes out clean. Cool on a rack for 5 minutes, then tilt the muffins on their sides or transfer them to the rack to complete cooling.   ❖

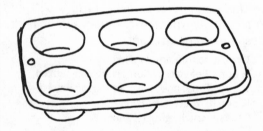

Basil Corn Muffins

MAKES 12

These are summer muffins. Chock-full of fresh corn kernels and enlivened with chopped fresh basil, they are delicious with fried chicken.

1¼ cups all-purpose flour, scoop measured
¾ cup yellow cornmeal
2 tablespoons sugar
3 teaspoons baking powder
¾ teaspoon salt
1 cup milk
1 large egg

¼ cup butter or margarine, melted
1 cup uncooked fresh corn kernels (about 2 large ears)
1 tablespoon chopped fresh basil

1. Preheat the oven to 400°F. Generously grease 12 muffin cups or line with papers. Combine the flour, cornmeal, sugar, baking powder, and salt in a large mixing bowl. Whisk to blend thoroughly.

2. In a separate bowl, whisk together the milk, egg, and melted butter. Make a well in the dry ingredients and pour in the egg mixture. Blend with a wooden spoon until a moist, lumpy batter is formed. Stir in the corn and basil. Spoon into the prepared muffin cups and bake for 20 to 25 minutes, or until a wooden pick inserted in the center comes out clean. Cool on a rack for 5 minutes, then tilt the muffins on their sides or transfer them to the rack to complete cooling.   ❖

Buttermilk Corn Muffins

MAKES 12

Buttermilk lends a country-kitchen air to these corn muffins.

1 cup yellow cornmeal
1 cup all-purpose flour, scoop measured
3 tablespoons sugar
2 teaspoons baking powder
½ teaspoon baking soda
½ teaspoon salt
1 cup buttermilk
1 large egg
¼ cup butter or margarine, melted

1. Preheat the oven to 400°F. Generously grease 12 muffin cups or line with papers. Combine the cornmeal, flour, sugar, baking powder, baking soda, and salt in a large mixing bowl. Whisk to blend thoroughly.

2. In a separate bowl, whisk together the buttermilk, egg, and melted butter. Make a well in the dry ingredients and pour in the egg mixture. Blend with a wooden spoon until a moist, lumpy batter is formed.

Spoon into the prepared muffin cups and bake for 20 to 25 minutes, or until a wooden pick inserted in the center comes out clean. Cool on a rack for 5 minutes, then tilt the muffins on their sides or transfer them to the rack to complete cooling.   ❖

Cranberry Corn Muffins

MAKES 12

Tangy flecks of bright red cranberries accent these corn muffins. Fresh cranberries are difficult to chop with a knife because they skitter all over the place. It's easier to use a food processor or a wooden bowl and a curved, two-handled knife called a mezzaluna.

¾ cup milk
¼ cup honey
¼ cup butter or margarine
1⅓ cups all-purpose flour, scoop measured
1 cup yellow cornmeal
2 tablespoons sugar
3 teaspoons baking powder
¾ teaspoon salt
1 large egg, beaten
1 cup fresh cranberries, finely chopped

1. Preheat the oven to 400°F. Generously grease 12 muffin cups or line with papers. Combine the milk, honey, and butter in a small saucepan and heat until the butter is melted. Set aside to cool.

2. In a large mixing bowl, combine the flour, cornmeal, sugar, baking powder, and salt. Whisk to blend thoroughly. Add the beaten egg to the cooled milk and stir.

3. Make a well in the dry ingredients and pour in the egg mixture. Blend with a wooden spoon until a moist, lumpy batter is formed. Stir in the chopped cranberries. Spoon into the prepared muffin cups and bake for 20 to 25 minutes, or until a wooden pick inserted in the center comes out clean. Cool on a rack for 5 minutes, then tilt the muffins on their sides or transfer them to the rack to complete cooling.   ❖

Crunchy Corn Muffins

MAKES 12

On May 27, 1986, the corn muffin became the official state muffin of Massachusetts. This recipe contains coarse cornmeal, often called polenta, so the final texture is exceptionally crunchy. Polenta is sold in Italian grocery stores and specialty food shops.

1¼ cups coarse cornmeal (polenta)
1¼ cups all-purpose flour, scoop measured
¼ cup sugar
3 teaspoons baking powder
¾ teaspoon salt
1 cup milk
2 large eggs
¼ cup butter or margarine, melted

1. Preheat the oven to 400°F. Generously grease 12 muffin cups or line with papers. Combine the cornmeal, flour, sugar, baking powder, and salt in a large mixing bowl. Whisk to blend thoroughly.

2. In a separate bowl, whisk together the milk, eggs, and melted butter. Make a well in the dry ingredients and pour in the egg mixture. Blend with a wooden spoon until a moist, lumpy batter is formed. Spoon into the prepared muffin cups and bake for 20 to 25 minutes, or until a wooden pick inserted in the center comes out clean. Cool on a rack for 5 minutes, then tilt the muffins on their sides or transfer them to the rack to complete cooling.   ❖

Sausage Corn Muffins

MAKES 12

Hearty breakfast muffins packed with chunks of pork sausage and accented with Parmesan cheese.

6 small breakfast sausages
3 tablespoons water
1 cup yellow cornmeal
1 cup all-purpose flour, scoop measured
¼ cup sugar
3 teaspoons baking powder

½ teaspoon salt
1 cup milk
2 large eggs
3 tablespoons vegetable oil
¼ cup freshly grated Parmesan cheese

1. In a small, uncovered skillet, cook the sausages in the water over medium-high heat until the water evaporates and the sausages are nicely browned. Remove from the heat and transfer the sausages to absorbent paper to drain. When the sausages are cool enough to handle, chop them coarsely.

2. Preheat the oven to 425°F. Generously grease 12 muffin cups or line with papers. Combine the cornmeal, flour, sugar, baking powder, and salt in a large mixing bowl. Whisk to blend thoroughly.

3. In a separate bowl, whisk together the milk, eggs, and vegetable oil. Make a well in the dry ingredients and pour in the egg mixture. Blend with a wooden spoon until a moist, lumpy batter is formed. Stir in the Parmesan cheese and chopped sausage. Spoon into the prepared muffin cups and bake for 20 to 25 minutes, or until a wooden pick inserted in the center comes out clean. Cool on a rack for 5 minutes, then tilt the muffins on their sides or transfer them to the rack to complete cooling.   ❖

Cranberry Almond Muffins

MAKES 12

Canned cranberry sauce may be successfully frozen. If you have any whole berry sauce left over from a holiday meal, freeze it to use in these muffins.

2 cups all-purpose flour, scoop measured
½ cup sugar
1 teaspoon baking powder
1 teaspoon baking soda
½ teaspoon salt
1 cup sour cream
1 large egg
¼ cup butter or margarine, melted

2 tablespoons milk
1 teaspoon almond extract
1 cup whole berry cranberry sauce

1. Preheat the oven to 400°F. Generously grease 12 muffin cups or line with papers. Combine the flour, sugar, baking powder, baking soda, and salt in a large mixing bowl. Whisk to blend thoroughly.

2. In a separate bowl, whisk together the sour cream, egg, melted butter, milk, and almond extract. Measure the cranberry sauce into a small bowl and stir with a fork to smooth it out.

3. Make a well in the dry ingredients and pour in the egg mixture. Blend with a wooden spoon until a moist, lumpy batter is formed. Stir in the cranberry sauce. Spoon into the prepared muffin cups and bake for 20 to 25 minutes, or until a wooden pick inserted in the center comes out clean. Cool on a rack for 5 minutes, then tilt the muffins on their sides or transfer them to the rack to complete cooling. ❖

Cranberry Orange Muffins

MAKES 12

The flavor combination of cranberry and orange has been a New England favorite for generations. Here the two join to create beautiful, aromatic muffins.

2 cups all-purpose flour, scoop measured
½ cup sugar
1½ teaspoons baking powder
½ teaspoon baking soda
½ teaspoon salt
¾ cup freshly squeezed orange juice
1 large egg
3 tablespoons butter or margarine, melted
1 tablespoon finely grated orange zest
1 cup fresh cranberries, coarsely chopped

1. Preheat the oven to 425°F. Generously grease 12 muffin cups or line with papers. Combine the flour, sugar, baking powder, baking soda, and salt in a large mixing bowl. Whisk to blend thoroughly.

2. In a separate bowl, whisk together the orange juice, egg, and melted butter. Stir in the orange zest. Make a well in the dry ingredients and pour in the egg mixture. Blend with a wooden spoon until a moist, lumpy batter is formed. Stir in the cranberries. Spoon into the prepared muffin cups and bake for 20 to 25 minutes, or until a wooden pick inserted in the center comes out clean. Cool on a rack for 5 minutes, then tilt the muffins on their sides or transfer them to the rack to complete cooling. ❖

Cranberry Upside-Down Muffins

MAKES 12

A syrupy glaze of fresh cranberries crowns these delicious muffins when you turn them out of the pan.

1½ cups fresh cranberries, coarsely chopped
1 cup sugar
2 cups all-purpose flour, scoop measured
3 teaspoons baking powder
½ teaspoon salt
½ teaspoon freshly grated nutmeg
1 cup milk
1 large egg
¼ cup butter or margarine, melted

1. In a small saucepan, combine the cranberries and ½ cup of the sugar. Toss to coat. Cover the pan and set it over low heat. Cook for 5 minutes, or until a bubbly syrup forms. Increase the heat and stir continuously until the mixture thickens. Remove from the heat and set aside.

2. Preheat the oven to 400°F. Generously butter 12 muffin cups. Spoon in enough of the cranberry mixture to cover the bottom of each cup. Combine the flour, the remaining ½ cup sugar, the baking powder, and the salt in a large mixing bowl. Add the nutmeg and whisk to blend thoroughly.

3. In a separate bowl, whisk together the milk, egg, and melted butter. Make a well in the dry ingredients and pour in the egg

mixture. Blend with a wooden spoon until a moist, lumpy batter is formed. Spoon into the prepared muffin cups and bake for 20 to 25 minutes, or until a wooden pick inserted in the center comes out clean. Cool on a rack for 5 minutes, then invert the muffin tin and transfer the muffins, glaze side up, to the rack to complete cooling.   ❖

Cranberry Whole Wheat Muffins

MAKES 12

Plump whole wheat muffins nubbly with chopped fresh cranberries.

1 cup fresh cranberries, coarsely chopped
6 tablespoons sugar
1¼ cups whole wheat flour, scoop measured
¾ cup all-purpose flour, scoop measured
½ cup yellow cornmeal
3 teaspoons baking powder
¾ teaspoon salt
1 cup milk
2 large eggs
¼ cup vegetable oil

1. In a small bowl, combine the chopped cranberries and 2 tablespoons of the sugar. Toss to coat and set aside.

2. Preheat the oven to 400°F. Generously grease 12 muffin cups or line with papers. Combine the whole wheat flour, all-purpose flour, cornmeal, and remaining 4 tablespoons sugar in a large mixing bowl. Add the baking powder and salt, and whisk to blend thoroughly.

3. In a separate bowl, whisk together the milk, eggs, and vegetable oil. Make a well in the dry ingredients and pour in the egg mixture. Blend with a wooden spoon until a moist, lumpy batter is formed. Stir in the chopped cranberries. Spoon into the prepared muffin cups and bake for 20 to 25 minutes, or until a wooden pick inserted in the center comes out clean. Cool on a rack for 5 minutes, then tilt the muffins on their sides or transfer them to the rack to complete cooling.   ❖

Red Currant Muffins

MAKES 12

The season for fresh red currants is very short, so don't hesitate. When you see them, buy them. Then enjoy their tart, zingy character in these tasty muffins.

2 cups all-purpose flour, scoop measured
⅔ cup sugar
3 teaspoons baking powder
½ teaspoon salt
¾ cup milk
2 large eggs
¼ cup butter or margarine, melted
1 cup fresh red currants, stemmed, rinsed, and gently patted dry

1. Preheat the oven to 425°F. Generously grease 12 muffin cups or line with papers. Combine the flour, sugar, baking powder, and salt in a large mixing bowl. Whisk to blend thoroughly.

2. In a separate bowl, whisk together the milk, eggs, and melted butter. Make a well in the dry ingredients and pour in the egg mixture. Blend with a wooden spoon until a moist, lumpy batter is formed. Stir in the currants. Spoon into the prepared muffin cups and bake for 20 to 25 minutes, or until a wooden pick inserted in the center comes out clean. Cool on a rack for 5 minutes, then tilt the muffins on their sides or transfer them to the rack to complete cooling.   ❖

Dill Cheese Muffins

MAKES 12

Dill-spiked muffins are wonderful with cold salmon or shrimp salad.

2 cups all-purpose flour, scoop measured
3 teaspoons baking powder
½ teaspoon salt
1 cup freshly grated Parmesan cheese
1 cup milk
1 large egg
¼ cup butter or margarine, melted
1 tablespoon chopped fresh dill leaves

1. Preheat the oven to 425°F. Generously grease 12 muffin cups or line with papers. Combine the flour, baking powder, and salt in a large mixing bowl. Whisk to blend thoroughly. Stir in the Parmesan cheese.

2. In a separate bowl, whisk together the milk, egg, and melted butter. Make a well in the dry ingredients and pour in the egg mixture. Blend with a wooden spoon until a moist, lumpy batter is formed. Stir in the dill. Spoon into the prepared muffin cups and bake for 20 to 25 minutes, or until a wooden pick inserted in the center comes out clean. Cool on a rack for 5 minutes, then tilt the muffins on their sides or transfer them to the rack to complete cooling. ❖

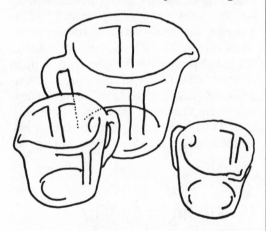

Whole Wheat Dill Muffins

MAKES 12

For a change of pace, offer dill-scented muffins with hot clam chowder.

1 cup whole wheat flour, scoop measured
1 cup all-purpose flour, scoop measured
3 teaspoons baking powder
¾ teaspoon salt
⅔ cup milk
½ cup small-curd cottage cheese
1 large egg
3 tablespoons butter or margarine, melted
1 tablespoon chopped fresh dill leaves

1. Preheat the oven to 400°F. Generously grease 12 muffin cups or line with papers. Combine the whole wheat flour, all-purpose flour, baking powder, and salt in a large mixing bowl. Whisk to blend thoroughly.

2. In a separate bowl, whisk together the milk, cottage cheese, egg, and melted butter. Make a well in the dry ingredients and pour in the cottage cheese mixture. Blend with a wooden spoon until a moist, lumpy batter is formed. Stir in the dill. Spoon into the prepared muffin cups and bake for 20 to 25 minutes, or until a wooden pick inserted in the center comes out clean. Cool on a rack for 5 minutes, then tilt the muffins on their sides or transfer them to the rack to complete cooling.   ❖

Fig Pecan Muffins

MAKES 12

Offer these muffins with lemon honey butter, made by beating together ½ cup softened butter, 1 tablespoon honey, and 1 tablespoon finely grated lemon zest.

2 cups all-purpose flour, scoop measured
⅓ cup sugar
2 teaspoons baking powder
½ teaspoon baking soda
½ teaspoon salt
1 cup buttermilk
1 large egg
¼ cup butter or margarine, melted
½ cup coarsely chopped dried figs
½ cup coarsely chopped pecans

1. Preheat the oven to 425°F. Generously grease 12 muffin cups or line with papers. Combine the flour, sugar, baking powder, baking soda, and salt in a large mixing bowl. Whisk to blend thoroughly.

2. In a separate bowl, whisk together the buttermilk, egg, and melted butter. Make a well in the dry ingredients and pour in the egg mixture. Blend with a wooden spoon until a moist, lumpy batter is formed. Stir in the figs and pecans. Spoon into the prepared muffin cups and bake for 20 to 25 minutes, or until a wooden pick inserted in the center comes out clean. Cool on a rack

for 5 minutes, then tilt the muffins on their sides or transfer them to the rack to complete cooling. ❖

Gingerbread Muffins

MAKES 12

What could be more inviting on a cold winter afternoon than spicy muffins, fragrant with ground ginger and molasses?

2 cups all-purpose flour, scoop measured
¼ cup light brown sugar
1½ teaspoons baking powder
½ teaspoon baking soda
½ teaspoon salt
1 teaspoon ground ginger
¾ cup buttermilk
1 large egg
¼ cup butter or margarine, melted
¼ cup molasses

1. Preheat the oven to 400°F. Generously grease 12 muffin cups or line with papers. Sift the flour, sugar, baking powder, baking soda, salt, and ginger into a large mixing bowl. Whisk to blend thoroughly.

2. In a separate bowl, whisk together the buttermilk, egg, melted butter, and molasses. Make a well in the dry ingredients and pour in the egg mixture. Blend with a wooden spoon until a moist, lumpy batter is formed. Spoon into the prepared muffin cups and bake for 20 to 25 minutes, or until a wooden pick inserted in the center comes out clean. Cool on a rack for 5 minutes, then tilt the muffins on their sides or transfer them to the rack to complete cooling. ❖

Graham Cracker Muffins

MAKES 12

Use packaged graham cracker crumbs if you're in a hurry, or crush your own. Plan on 9 graham crackers to make 1 cup of crumbs.

1½ cups all-purpose flour, scoop measured
⅓ cup light brown sugar
3 teaspoons baking powder
½ teaspoon salt
1 cup graham cracker crumbs
⅔ cup milk
1 large egg
¼ cup butter or margarine, melted
½ cup raisins

1. Preheat the oven to 400°F. Generously grease 12 muffin cups or line with papers. Sift the flour, sugar, baking powder, and salt into a large mixing bowl. Whisk to blend thoroughly. Stir in the graham cracker crumbs.

2. In a separate bowl, whisk together the milk, egg, and melted butter. Make a well in the dry ingredients and pour in the egg mixture. Blend with a wooden spoon until a moist, lumpy batter is formed. Stir in the raisins. Spoon into the prepared muffin cups and bake for 20 to 25 minutes, or until a wooden pick inserted in the center comes out clean. Cool on a rack for 5 minutes, then tilt the muffins on their sides or transfer them to the rack to complete cooling. ❖

Honey Ginger Muffins

MAKES 12

Bright bits of candied ginger add interest to these honey-flavored muffins.

⅓ cup honey
3 tablespoons butter or margarine
1¼ cups whole wheat flour, scoop measured
1 cup all-purpose flour, scoop measured
3 teaspoons baking powder
½ teaspoon salt
1 cup milk
1 large egg
½ cup coarsely chopped candied ginger

1. Preheat the oven to 400°F. Generously grease 12 muffin cups or line with papers. In a small saucepan, heat the honey and butter over medium heat until the butter is melted. Set aside.

2. Combine the whole wheat flour, all-purpose flour, baking powder, and salt in a large mixing bowl. Whisk to blend thoroughly. In a separate bowl whisk together the milk and egg. Stir in the cooled honey and butter.

3. Make a well in the dry ingredients and pour in the egg mixture. Blend with a wooden spoon until a moist, lumpy batter is formed. Stir in the candied ginger. Spoon into the prepared muffin cups and bake for 20 to 25 minutes, or until a wooden pick inserted in the center comes out clean. Cool on a rack for 5 minutes, then tilt the muffins on their sides or transfer them to the rack to complete cooling.   ❖

Honey-Glazed Muffins

MAKES 12

When you turn these muffins out of the pan, they glimmer with a beautiful honey glaze. Allow them to cool slightly and then serve upside-down on a decorative plate.

½ cup honey
5 tablespoons butter or margarine
2 cups all-purpose flour, scoop measured
⅓ cup light brown sugar
3 teaspoons baking powder
½ teaspoon salt
½ teaspoon cinnamon
1 cup milk
1 large egg
½ cup coarsely chopped pecans

1. Preheat the oven to 400°F. Generously butter 12 muffin cups. In a small saucepan, heat the honey and 1 tablespoon of the butter until the butter is melted. Divide the mixture among the 12 muffin cups, then tilt the pan so that the honey coats the bottom of each cup.

2. Sift the flour, sugar, baking powder, salt, and cinnamon into a large mixing bowl. Whisk to blend thoroughly. Melt the remaining 4 tablespoons butter and set aside.

3. In a separate bowl, whisk together the milk, egg, and melted butter. Make a well in the dry ingredients and pour in the egg mixture. Blend with a wooden spoon until a moist, lumpy batter is formed. Stir in the pecans. Spoon into the prepared muffin cups and bake for 20 to 25 minutes, or until a wooden pick inserted in the center comes out clean. Cool on a rack for 5 minutes, then invert the pan and turn out the muffins onto the rack to complete cooling.   ❖

Lemon Ginger Muffins

MAKES 12

The spicy flavor of grated gingerroot beautifully complements the tang of lemon juice. Offer these muffins with a seafood and pasta salad.

2 cups all-purpose flour, scoop measured
½ cup sugar
1½ teaspoons baking powder
½ teaspoon baking soda
½ teaspoon salt
½ cup freshly squeezed lemon juice
¼ cup cold water
1 large egg
¼ cup butter or margarine, melted
1 tablespoon finely grated lemon zest
1 tablespoon freshly grated gingerroot

1. Preheat the oven to 425°F. Generously grease 12 muffin cups or line with papers. Combine the flour, sugar, baking powder, baking soda, and salt in a large mixing bowl. Whisk to blend thoroughly.

2. In a separate bowl, whisk together the lemon juice, water, egg, and melted butter. Stir in the lemon zest and gingerroot. Make a well in the dry ingredients and pour in the egg mixture. Blend with a wooden spoon until a moist, lumpy batter is formed. Spoon into the prepared muffin cups and bake for 20 to 25 minutes, or until a wooden pick inserted in the center comes out clean. Cool on a rack for 5 minutes, then tilt the muffins on their sides or transfer them to the rack to complete cooling.   ❖

Maple Streusel Muffins

MAKES 12

Cinnamon streusel tops these maple syrup muffins.

2¼ cups all-purpose flour, scoop measured
6 tablespoons sugar
½ teaspoon cinnamon
2 tablespoons butter or margarine, cut into small pieces, plus ¼ cup
3 teaspoons baking powder
¾ teaspoon salt
⅔ cup milk
1 large egg
⅓ cup pure maple syrup
½ cup coarsely chopped walnuts

1. In a small bowl, combine ¼ cup of the flour, 2 tablespoons of the sugar, the cinnamon, and 2 tablespoons of the butter. Cut in the butter until the mixture is crumbly. Set aside. Melt the remaining ¼ cup butter and set aside.

2. Preheat the oven to 400°F. Generously grease 12 muffin cups or line with papers. In a large mixing bowl, combine the remaining 2 cups flour and 4 tablespoons sugar, along with the baking powder and salt. Whisk to blend thoroughly.

3. In a separate bowl, whisk together the milk, egg, melted butter, and maple syrup. Make a well in the dry ingredients and pour in the egg mixture. Blend with a wooden spoon until a moist, lumpy batter is formed. Stir in the walnuts. Spoon into the prepared muffin cups. Sprinkle on the streusel mixture. Bake for 20 to 25 minutes, or until a wooden pick inserted in the center comes out clean. Cool on a rack for 5 minutes, then tilt the muffins on their sides or transfer them to the rack to complete cooling. ❖

Mincemeat Muffins

MAKES 12

Mincemeat adds unexpected flavor to these savory muffins. Serve with roast pork or turkey.

2 cups all-purpose flour, scoop measured
½ cup light brown sugar
3 teaspoons baking powder
¾ teaspoon salt
¾ cup milk
1 large egg
¼ cup butter or margarine, melted
¾ cup prepared mincemeat
½ cup chopped walnuts

1. Preheat the oven to 400°F. Generously grease 12 muffin cups or line with papers. Sift the flour, sugar, baking powder, and salt into a large mixing bowl. Whisk to blend thoroughly.

2. In a separate bowl, whisk together the milk, egg, and melted butter. Stir in the mincemeat. Make a well in the dry ingredients and pour in the egg mixture. Blend with a wooden spoon until a moist, lumpy batter is formed. Stir in the walnuts. Spoon into the prepared muffin cups and bake for 20 to 25 minutes, or until a wooden pick inserted in the center comes out clean. Cool on a rack for 5 minutes, then tilt the muffins on their sides or transfer them to the rack to complete cooling. ❖

Oat Bran and Apple Muffins

MAKES 12

Oat bran has recently been hailed as one of the healthiest grains available. Here it is incorporated into cinnamon-flavored muffins bursting with chunks of apple.

1 cup all-purpose flour, scoop measured
½ cup light brown sugar
2 teaspoons baking powder
½ teaspoon baking soda
½ teaspoon salt
1 teaspoon cinnamon
1¼ cups oat bran
1 cup sour cream
2 tablespoons milk
1 large egg
¼ cup vegetable oil
1 cup peeled, cored, and coarsely chopped apple (about 2 small apples)

1. Preheat the oven to 400°F. Generously grease 12 muffin cups or line with papers. Sift the flour, sugar, baking powder, baking soda, salt, and cinnamon into a large bowl. Whisk to blend thoroughly. Stir in the oat bran.

2. In a separate bowl, whisk together the sour cream, milk, egg, and vegetable oil. Make a well in the dry ingredients and pour in the egg mixture. Blend with a wooden spoon until a moist, lumpy batter is formed. Stir in the apple. Spoon into the prepared muffin cups and bake for 20 to 25 minutes, or until a wooden pick inserted in the center comes out clean. Cool on a rack for 5 minutes, then tilt the muffins on their sides or transfer them to the rack to complete cooling.   ❖

Toasted Oat Muffins

MAKES 12

Toasting rolled oats accentuates their flavor and creates hearty muffins just right for winter fare.

1½ cups quick-cooking rolled oats
1 cup all-purpose flour, scoop measured
½ cup light brown sugar
3 teaspoons baking powder
¾ teaspoon salt
½ teaspoon cinnamon
¾ cup milk
1 large egg
¼ cup vegetable oil
¼ cup pure maple syrup

1. Preheat the oven to 350°F. Spread the rolled oats on the bottom of a jelly-roll pan. Place in the oven and bake for 10 to 15 minutes, or until lightly toasted. Remove and set aside.

2. Increase the oven temperature to 400°F. Generously grease 12 muffin cups or line with papers. Sift the flour, sugar, baking powder, salt, and cinnamon into a large bowl. Whisk to blend thoroughly. Stir in the toasted oats.

3. In a separate bowl, whisk together the milk, egg, vegetable oil, and maple syrup. Make a well in the dry ingredients and pour in the egg mixture. Blend with a wooden spoon until a moist, lumpy batter is formed. Spoon into the prepared muffin cups and bake for 20 to 25 minutes, or until a wooden pick inserted in the center comes out clean. Cool on a rack for 5 minutes, then tilt the muffins on their sides or transfer them to the rack to complete cooling.   ❖

Orange Date Muffins

MAKES 12

The flesh of a whole orange is used in these full-bodied, date-studded muffins.

1 large orange
½ cup freshly squeezed orange juice
½ cup sugar
1 large egg
¼ cup vegetable oil
2 cups all-purpose flour, scoop measured
2 teaspoons baking powder
½ teaspoon baking soda
½ teaspoon salt
½ cup coarsely chopped pitted dates

1. Preheat the oven to 425°F. Generously grease 12 muffin cups or line with papers. Remove the zest from the orange with a swivel-blade peeler. Place the zest in the container of a blender or processor. Remove the white pith from the orange and discard. Separate the flesh into segments and remove any seeds. Add the segments to the blender or processor. Add the orange juice

and sugar. Process briefly, until the zest is finely chopped. Add the egg and vegetable oil and process only until blended.

2. In a large mixing bowl, combine the flour, baking powder, baking soda, and salt. Whisk to blend thoroughly. Make a well in the dry ingredients and pour in the orange mixture. Blend with a wooden spoon until a moist, lumpy batter is formed. Stir in the dates. Spoon into the prepared muffin cups and bake for 20 to 25 minutes, or until a wooden pick inserted in the center comes out clean. Cool on a rack for 5 minutes, then tilt the muffins on their sides or transfer them to the rack to complete cooling. ❖

Orange Graham Muffins

MAKES 12

The comforting flavor of graham crackers makes these muffins irresistible.

1 cup all-purpose flour, scoop measured
¼ cup sugar
1½ teaspoons baking powder
½ teaspoon baking soda
½ teaspoon salt
1⅓ cups graham cracker crumbs
½ cup freshly squeezed orange juice
½ cup milk
1 large egg
¼ cup vegetable oil
1 tablespoon finely grated orange zest

1. Preheat the oven to 400°F. Generously grease 12 muffin cups or line with papers. Combine the flour, sugar, baking powder, baking soda, and salt in a large mixing bowl. Whisk to blend thoroughly. Stir in the graham cracker crumbs.

2. In a separate bowl, whisk together the orange juice, milk, egg, and vegetable oil. Stir in the orange zest. Make a well in the dry ingredients and pour in the egg mixture. Blend with a wooden spoon until a moist, lumpy batter is formed. Spoon into the prepared muffin cups and bake for 20 to 25 minutes, or until a wooden pick inserted

in the center comes out clean. Cool on a rack for 5 minutes, then tilt the muffins on their sides or transfer them to the rack to complete cooling. ❖

Orange Streusel Muffins

MAKES 12

What a way to start the day! Muffins made with freshly squeezed orange juice are topped with brown sugar streusel.

¼ cup all-purpose flour, plus 2 cups, scoop measured
2 tablespoons light brown sugar
½ teaspoon cinnamon
2 tablespoons butter or margarine, cut into small pieces, plus ¼ cup
½ cup granulated sugar
1 teaspoon baking powder
1 teaspoon baking soda
½ teaspoon salt
1 cup freshly squeezed orange juice
1 large egg
1 tablespoon finely grated orange zest
½ cup coarsely chopped walnuts

1. In a small bowl, combine the ¼ cup flour with the brown sugar, cinnamon, and the 2 tablespoons butter. Cut in the butter until the mixture is crumbly. Set aside. Melt the remaining ¼ cup butter.

2. Preheat the oven to 400°F. Generously grease 12 muffin cups or line with papers. In a large mixing bowl, combine the remaining 2 cups flour with the granulated sugar, baking powder, baking soda, and salt. Whisk to blend thoroughly.

3. In a separate bowl, whisk together the orange juice, egg, and melted butter. Stir in the orange zest. Make a well in the dry ingredients and pour in the egg mixture. Blend with a wooden spoon until a moist, lumpy batter is formed. Stir in the walnuts. Spoon into the prepared muffin cups. Sprinkle on the streusel mixture. Bake for 20 to 25 minutes, or until a wooden pick inserted in the center comes out clean. Cool

on a rack for 5 minutes, then tilt the muffins on their sides or transfer them to the rack to complete cooling. ❖

Cinnamon Peach Muffins

MAKES 12

Fresh peaches are peeled, halved, and cut into chunks for these unique muffins. Plan on two medium-size peaches to obtain one cup of small chunks.

2 cups all-purpose flour, scoop measured
¼ cup light brown sugar
¼ cup granulated sugar
3 teaspoons baking powder
½ teaspoon salt
1 teaspoon cinnamon
1 cup milk
1 large egg
¼ cup butter or margarine, melted
½ teaspoon almond extract
1 cup peeled, pitted, and coarsely chopped peaches

1. Preheat the oven to 400°F. Generously grease 12 muffin cups or line with papers. Sift the flour, brown sugar, granulated sugar, baking powder, salt, and cinnamon into a large mixing bowl. Whisk to blend the dry ingredients thoroughly.

2. In a separate bowl, whisk together the milk, egg, melted butter, and almond extract. Make a well in the dry ingredients and pour in the egg mixture. Blend with a wooden spoon until a moist, lumpy batter is formed. Stir in the peaches. Spoon into the prepared muffin cups and bake for 20 to 25 minutes, or until a wooden pick inserted in the center comes out clean. Cool on a rack for 5 minutes, then tilt the muffins on their sides or transfer them to the rack to complete cooling. ❖

Pear and Cornmeal Muffins

MAKES 12

Apples first come to mind when you think of fall fruits, but New England orchards are plentiful with pears at harvest time, too. Here they add flavor to cornmeal muffins made with unflavored yogurt.

1 cup all-purpose flour, scoop measured
1 cup yellow cornmeal
¼ cup sugar
2 teaspoons baking powder
½ teaspoon baking soda
½ teaspoon salt
1 cup unflavored yogurt
2 large eggs
¼ cup butter or margarine, melted
2 medium pears, peeled, cored, and coarsely chopped

1. Preheat the oven to 400°F. Generously grease 12 muffin cups or line with papers. Combine the flour, cornmeal, sugar, baking powder, baking soda, and salt in a large mixing bowl. Whisk to blend thoroughly.

2. In a separate bowl, whisk together the yogurt, eggs, and melted butter. Make a well in the dry ingredients and pour in the egg mixture. Blend with a wooden spoon until a moist, lumpy batter is formed. Stir in the pears. Spoon into the prepared muffin cups and bake for 20 to 25 minutes, or until a wooden pick inserted in the center comes out clean. Cool on a rack for 5 minutes, then tilt the muffins on their sides or transfer them to the rack to complete cooling. ❖

Fresh Pineapple Muffins

MAKES 12

Fresh pineapple isn't usually thought of in association with New England cookery, but early ship captains, plying the spice routes of the Caribbean, brought back pineapples as a special treat for their families. Here, chunks of fresh pineapple enliven delicate muffins.

2 cups all-purpose flour, scoop measured
½ cup sugar
2 teaspoons baking powder
½ teaspoon baking soda
½ teaspoon salt

½ teaspoon cinnamon
1 cup milk
1 large egg
¼ cup butter or margarine, melted
1 teaspoon vanilla extract
1 cup finely chopped fresh pineapple, drained
   in a sieve

1. Preheat the oven to 400°F. Generously grease 12 muffin cups or line with papers. Combine the flour, sugar, baking powder, baking soda, salt, and cinnamon in a large mixing bowl. Whisk to blend thoroughly.

2. In a separate bowl, whisk together the milk, egg, and melted butter. Stir in the vanilla. Make a well in the dry ingredients and pour in the egg mixture. Blend with a wooden spoon until a moist, lumpy batter is formed. Stir in the pineapple. Spoon into the prepared muffin cups and bake for 20 to 25 minutes, or until a wooden pick inserted in the center comes out clean. Cool on a rack for 5 minutes, then tilt the muffins on their sides or transfer them to the rack to complete cooling.   ❖

Pineapple Almond Muffins

MAKES 12

You needn't restrict these muffins to the breakfast table. They are healthful, yet sweet enough to pass for dessert, so wrap them up for your children's lunch.

2 cups all-purpose flour, scoop measured
½ cup light brown sugar
1 teaspoon baking powder
1 teaspoon baking soda
½ teaspoon salt
¾ cup canned crushed pineapple, well drained

Juice from the drained pineapple
Milk
1 large egg
¼ cup butter or margarine, melted
½ cup slivered almonds, chopped

1. Preheat the oven to 400°F. Generously grease 12 muffin cups or line with papers. Sift the flour, sugar, baking powder, baking soda, and salt into a large mixing bowl. Whisk to blend thoroughly.

2. Measure the reserved pineapple juice into a glass measuring cup and add enough milk to make ¾ cup. Whisk the egg and butter together in a small bowl. Stir in the pineapple juice. Make a well in the dry ingredients and pour in the egg mixture. Blend with a wooden spoon until a moist, lumpy batter is formed. Stir in the pineapple and almonds. Spoon into the prepared muffin cups and bake for 20 to 25 minutes, or until a wooden pick inserted in the center comes out clean. Cool on a rack for 5 minutes, then tilt the muffins on their sides or transfer them to the rack to complete cooling.   ❖

Plum Muffins

MAKES 12

If possible, use Laroda plums. They are wonderfully sweet, and it is not necessary to peel them.

2¼ cups all-purpose flour, scoop measured
½ cup sugar
3 teaspoons baking powder
¾ teaspoon salt
1 cup milk
1 large egg
¼ cup butter or margarine, melted
½ teaspoon almond extract
1 cup coarsely chopped fresh red plums
   (about ½ pound)

1. Preheat the oven to 425°F. Generously grease 12 muffin cups or line with papers. Combine the flour, sugar, baking powder, and salt in a large mixing bowl. Whisk to blend thoroughly.

2. In a separate bowl, whisk together the milk, egg, melted butter, and almond extract. Make a well in the dry ingredients and pour in the egg mixture. Blend with a wooden spoon until a moist, lumpy batter is formed. Stir in the plums. Spoon into the prepared muffin cups and bake for 20 to 25 minutes, or until a wooden pick inserted in the center comes out clean. Cool on a rack for 5 minutes, then tilt the muffins on their sides or transfer them to the rack to complete cooling. ❖

Pumpkin Walnut Muffins

MAKES 12

Spicy pumpkin muffins are a welcome addition to the Thanksgiving bread basket.

1¾ cups all-purpose flour, scoop measured
½ cup sugar
3 teaspoons baking powder
½ teaspoon salt
½ teaspoon cinnamon
½ teaspoon nutmeg
¼ teaspoon ground cloves
¾ cup milk
1 large egg
¼ cup butter or margarine, melted
¾ cup pumpkin purée
½ cup coarsely chopped walnuts

1. Preheat the oven to 400°F. Generously grease 12 muffin cups or line with papers. Combine the flour, sugar, baking powder, salt, cinnamon, nutmeg, and cloves in a large mixing bowl. Whisk to blend thoroughly.

2. In a separate bowl, whisk together the milk, egg, and melted butter. Stir in the pumpkin purée. Make a well in the dry ingredients and pour in the egg mixture. Blend with a wooden spoon until a moist, lumpy batter is formed. Stir in the walnuts. Spoon into the prepared muffin cups and bake for 20 to 25 minutes, or until a wooden pick inserted in the center comes out clean. Cool on a rack for 5 minutes, then tilt the muffins on their sides or transfer them to the rack to complete cooling. ❖

Raisin Spice Muffins

MAKES 12

As they bake, these muffins fill the house with the fragrance of traditional spices.

2 cups all-purpose flour, scoop measured
⅓ cup light brown sugar
3 teaspoons baking powder
½ teaspoon salt
1 teaspoon cinnamon
½ teaspoon nutmeg
½ teaspoon ground cloves
¾ cup milk
1 large egg
¼ cup vegetable oil
½ cup raisins

1. Preheat the oven to 400°F. Generously grease 12 muffin cups or line with papers. Sift the flour, sugar, baking powder, salt, cinnamon, nutmeg, and cloves into a large mixing bowl. Whisk to blend thoroughly.

2. In a separate bowl, whisk together the milk, egg, and vegetable oil. Make a well in the dry ingredients and pour in the egg mixture. Blend with a wooden spoon until a moist, lumpy batter is formed. Stir in the raisins. Spoon into the prepared muffin cups and bake for 20 to 25 minutes, or until a wooden pick inserted in the center comes out clean. Cool on a rack for 5 minutes, then tilt the muffins on their sides or transfer them to the rack to complete cooling. ❖

Butternut Squash Muffins

MAKES 12

Serve these muffins warm for breakfast with sausage and scrambled eggs.

1¾ cups all-purpose flour, scoop measured
¼ cup light brown sugar
2 tablespoons granulated sugar
3 teaspoons baking powder
¾ teaspoon salt
½ teaspoon mace
¾ cup milk
1 large egg

¼ cup butter or margarine, melted
¾ cup puréed butternut squash

1. Preheat the oven to 400°F. Generously grease 12 muffin cups or line with papers. Sift the flour, brown sugar, granulated sugar, baking powder, salt, and mace into a large mixing bowl. Whisk to blend the dry ingredients thoroughly.

2. In a separate bowl, whisk together the milk, egg, and melted butter. Stir in the butternut squash. Make a well in the dry ingredients and pour in the egg mixture. Blend with a wooden spoon until a moist, lumpy batter is formed. Spoon into the prepared muffin cups and bake for 20 to 25 minutes, or until a wooden pick inserted in the center comes out clean. Cool on a rack for 5 minutes, then tilt the muffins on their sides or transfer them to the rack to complete cooling.   ❖

Strawberry Muffins

MAKES 12

For best results, use strawberries that are firm and not quite at the peak of ripeness. Berries that are too ripe tend to be excessively juicy, and will cause the muffins to come out soggy.

2 cups whole strawberries
2 cups all-purpose flour, scoop measured
½ cup sugar
1½ teaspoons baking powder
½ teaspoon baking soda
½ teaspoon salt
¼ teaspoon freshly grated nutmeg
⅔ cup milk
2 large eggs
¼ cup butter or margarine, melted

1. Rinse, hull, and pat the strawberries dry. Quarter the berries, then cut them into small chunks. Scatter the chunks over absorbent paper and pat gently. Set aside.

2. Preheat the oven to 425°F. Generously grease 12 muffin cups or line with papers. Combine the flour, sugar, baking powder,

baking soda, salt, and nutmeg in a large mixing bowl. Whisk to blend thoroughly.

3. In a separate bowl, whisk together the milk, eggs, and melted butter. Make a well in the dry ingredients and pour in the egg mixture. Blend with a wooden spoon until a moist, lumpy batter is formed. Stir in the strawberries. Spoon into the prepared muffin cups and bake for 20 to 25 minutes, or until a wooden pick inserted in the center comes out clean. Cool on a rack for 5 minutes, then tilt the muffins on their sides or transfer them to the rack to complete cooling.   ❖

Sweet Potato Pecan Muffins

MAKES 12

Moist and cakelike in texture, these golden muffins make a nutritious after-school treat.

1¾ cups all-purpose flour, scoop measured
¼ cup light brown sugar
¼ cup granulated sugar
3 teaspoons baking powder
½ teaspoon salt
¾ cup milk
1 large egg
¼ cup butter or margarine, melted
¾ cup sweet potato purée (requires 1 large sweet potato)
½ cup coarsely chopped pecans

1. Preheat the oven to 400°F. Generously grease 12 muffin cups or line with papers. Sift the flour, brown sugar, granulated sugar, baking powder, and salt into a large mixing bowl. Whisk to blend thoroughly.

2. In a separate bowl, whisk together the milk, egg, and melted butter. Stir in the sweet potato purée. Make a well in the dry ingredients and pour in the egg mixture. Blend with a wooden spoon until a moist, lumpy batter is formed. Stir in the pecans. Spoon into the prepared muffin cups and bake for 20 to 25 minutes, or until a wooden pick inserted in the center comes out clean.

Cool on a rack for 5 minutes, then tilt the muffins on their sides or transfer them to the rack to complete cooling.   ❖

Shredded Wheat Muffins

MAKES 12

An old New England favorite. Offer these warm from the oven drizzled with pure maple syrup.

1 cup all-purpose flour, scoop measured
⅓ cup sugar
3 teaspoons baking powder
½ teaspoon salt
2 cups coarsely crumbled shredded wheat
¾ cup milk
1 large egg
¼ cup butter or margarine, melted

1. Preheat the oven to 425°F. Generously grease 12 muffin cups or line with papers. Combine the flour, sugar, baking powder, and salt in a large mixing bowl. Whisk to blend thoroughly. Stir in the shredded wheat.

2. In a separate bowl, whisk together the milk, egg, and melted butter. Make a well in the dry ingredients and pour in the egg mixture. Blend with a wooden spoon until a moist, lumpy batter is formed. Spoon into the prepared muffin cups and bake for 20 to 25 minutes, or until a wooden pick inserted in the center comes out clean. Cool on a rack for 5 minutes, then tilt the muffins on their sides or transfer them to the rack to complete cooling.   ❖

Whole Wheat Raisin Muffins

MAKES 12

Golden raisins have an exceptionally mild, sweet flavor because they are made from a delicate variety of grape called "Thompson seedless." They are the perfect foil for the earthy taste of whole wheat.

2 cups whole wheat flour, scoop measured
⅓ cup light brown sugar
3 teaspoons baking powder
½ teaspoon baking soda
½ teaspoon salt
½ teaspoon cinnamon
½ teaspoon nutmeg
1 cup buttermilk
1 large egg
¼ cup butter or margarine, melted
¾ cup golden raisins

1. Preheat the oven to 400°F. Generously grease 12 muffin cups or line with papers. Measure the whole wheat flour into a large mixing bowl. Sift in the sugar, baking powder, baking soda, and salt. Add the cinnamon and nutmeg, and whisk to blend the dry ingredients thoroughly.

2. In a separate bowl, whisk together the buttermilk, egg, and melted butter. Make a well in the dry ingredients and pour in the egg mixture. Blend with a wooden spoon until a moist, lumpy batter is formed. Stir in the raisins. Spoon into the prepared muffin cups and bake for 20 to 25 minutes, or until a wooden pick inserted in the center comes out clean. Cool on a rack for 5 minutes, then tilt the muffins on their sides or transfer them to the rack to complete cooling.   ❖

Yogurt Walnut Muffins

MAKES 12

A high proportion of wheat germ creates a densely textured effect. These muffins are delicious with cold raw carrot sticks and cottage cheese.

1 cup whole wheat flour, scoop measured
¼ cup light brown sugar
2 teaspoons baking powder
½ teaspoon baking soda
½ teaspoon salt
1 cup wheat germ
1 cup unflavored yogurt
1 large egg
3 tablespoons butter or margarine, melted
½ cup coarsely chopped walnuts

1. Preheat the oven to 400°F. Generously grease 12 muffin cups or line with papers. Measure the flour into a large mixing bowl. Sift in the sugar, baking powder, baking soda, and salt. Whisk to blend thoroughly. Stir in the wheat germ.

2. In a separate bowl, whisk together the yogurt, egg, and melted butter. Make a well in the dry ingredients and pour in the egg mixture. Blend with a wooden spoon until a moist, lumpy batter is formed. Stir in the walnuts. Spoon into the prepared muffin cups and bake for 20 to 25 minutes, or until a wooden pick inserted in the center comes out clean. Cool on a rack for 5 minutes, then tilt the muffins on their sides or transfer them to the rack to complete cooling. ❖

Zucchini Nut Muffins

MAKES 12

Shredded zucchini and crushed granola team up to create these satisfying summery muffins.

1 cup all-purpose flour, scoop measured
¼ cup light brown sugar
1½ teaspoons baking powder
½ teaspoon baking soda
¾ teaspoon salt
½ teaspoon cinnamon
½ teaspoon nutmeg
1 cup crushed granola cereal
⅔ cup milk
2 large eggs
¼ cup vegetable oil
¼ cup honey
1 cup shredded zucchini (about 1 small squash)
½ cup coarsely chopped walnuts

1. Preheat the oven to 400°F. Generously grease 12 muffin cups or line with papers. Sift the flour, sugar, baking powder, baking soda, salt, cinnamon, and nutmeg into a large mixing bowl. Whisk to blend thoroughly. Stir in the granola.

2. In a separate bowl, whisk together the milk, eggs, vegetable oil, and honey. Make a

well in the dry ingredients and pour in the egg mixture. Blend with a wooden spoon until a moist, lumpy batter is formed. Stir in the zucchini and walnuts. Spoon into the prepared muffin cups and bake for 20 to 25 minutes, or until a wooden pick inserted in the center comes out clean. Cool on a rack for 5 minutes, then tilt the muffins on their sides or transfer them to the rack to complete cooling. ❖

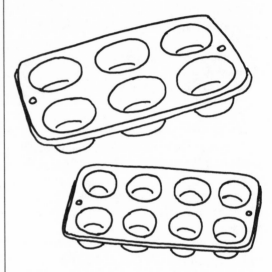

Bacon and Cheese Popovers

MAKES 12

Greasing the popover cups with bacon fat gives these cheesy popovers a hint of smoky bacon flavor.

3 tablespoons bacon fat
1 cup all-purpose flour, scoop measured
½ teaspoon salt
1 cup milk
2 large eggs
1 tablespoon butter or margarine, melted
½ cup finely grated Gruyère cheese

1. Preheat the oven to 425°F. Melt the bacon fat in a small saucepan. Generously grease 12 muffin or popover cups with the melted fat. Combine the flour and salt in a large mixing bowl. Whisk to blend the dry ingredients thoroughly.

2. In a separate bowl, whisk together the milk, eggs, and melted butter. Make a well in the dry ingredients and pour in the egg mixture. Beat with an electric hand mixer set on medium speed for exactly 2 minutes. Do not overbeat. The batter should be smooth and have the consistency of heavy cream. Stir in the cheese.

3. Pour into the prepared muffin or popover cups and immediately place in the hot oven. Reduce the temperature to 375°F. and bake for 35 to 45 minutes, or until puffed and browned. Loosen the popovers and tilt them in their cups. Pierce the side of each popover in several places with a wooden pick to allow steam to escape. Place in the turned-off oven for 5 minutes, leaving the door ajar. Serve immediately.   ❖

Country Popovers

MAKES 12

Brown and crispy outside, these popovers break open to reveal a moist, golden interior. Serve piping hot for breakfast, with honey or jam to spoon inside the airy nooks and crannies.

1 cup all-purpose flour, scoop measured
1 teaspoon sugar
¼ teaspoon salt
1 cup milk
2 large eggs
1 tablespoon butter or margarine, melted

1. Preheat the oven to 425°F. Generously grease 12 muffin or popover cups. Combine the flour, sugar, and salt in a large mixing bowl. Whisk to blend thoroughly.

2. In a separate bowl, whisk together the milk, eggs, and melted butter. Make a well in the dry ingredients and pour in the egg mixture. Beat with an electric hand mixer set on medium speed for exactly 2 minutes. Do not overbeat. The batter should be smooth and have the consistency of heavy cream.

3. Pour into the prepared muffin or popover cups and immediately place in the hot oven. Reduce the temperature to 375°F. and bake for 35 to 45 minutes, or until puffed and browned. Loosen the popovers and tilt them in their cups. Pierce the side of each popover in several places with a wooden pick to allow steam to escape. Place in the turned-off oven for 5 minutes, leaving the door ajar. Serve immediately.   ❖

Fresh Corn Popovers

MAKES 12

Kernels of fresh corn ground fine in a food processor give these popovers a delightful summery taste.

1 cup all-purpose flour, scoop measured
1 teaspoon sugar
½ teaspoon salt
½ cup fresh corn kernels (about 1 medium-size ear)
⅓ cup water
Milk
2 large eggs
1 tablespoon butter or margarine, melted

1. Preheat the oven to 425°F. Generously grease 12 muffin or popover cups. Combine the flour, sugar, and salt in a large mixing bowl. Whisk to blend thoroughly.

2. Place the corn in the bowl of a food processor. Add the water and whirl until the corn is finely chopped. Transfer to a sieve and drain, reserving the liquid. Set the corn aside. Measure the liquid and add enough milk to make 1 cup. Pour into the processor bowl. Add the eggs and melted butter, and whirl until blended.

3. Make a well in the dry ingredients and pour in the egg mixture. Beat with an electric hand mixer set on medium speed for exactly 2 minutes. Do not overbeat. The batter should be smooth and have the consistency of heavy cream. Stir in the ground corn.

4. Pour into the prepared muffin or popover cups and immediately place in the hot

oven. Reduce the temperature to 375°F. and bake for 35 to 45 minutes, or until puffed and browned. Loosen the popovers and tilt them in their cups. Pierce the side of each popover in several places with a wooden pick to allow steam to escape. Place in the turned-off oven for 5 minutes, leaving the door ajar. Serve immediately.   ❖

Garlic Basil Popovers

MAKES 12

Offer these garlic-flavored popovers for lunch with sliced fresh tomato and chilled tuna salad.

1 cup all-purpose flour, scoop measured
½ teaspoon salt
1 cup milk
2 large eggs
1 tablespoon butter or margarine, melted
1 clove garlic, pressed
2 teaspoons chopped fresh basil

1. Preheat the oven to 425°F. Generously grease 12 muffin or popover cups. Combine the flour and salt in a large mixing bowl. Whisk to blend thoroughly.

2. In a separate bowl, whisk together the milk, eggs, and melted butter. Stir in the garlic and basil. Make a well in the dry ingredients and pour in the egg mixture. Beat with an electric hand mixer set on medium speed for exactly 2 minutes. Do not overbeat. The batter should be smooth and have the consistency of heavy cream.

3. Pour into the prepared muffin or popover cups and immediately place in the hot oven. Reduce the temperature to 375°F. and bake for 35 to 45 minutes, or until puffed and browned. Loosen the popovers and tilt them in their cups. Pierce the side of each popover in several places with a wooden pick to allow steam to escape. Place in the turned-off oven for 5 minutes, leaving the door ajar. Serve immediately.   ❖

Herbed Popovers

MAKES 12

Serve these savory popovers with roast lamb or grilled chicken.

1 cup all-purpose flour, scoop measured
½ teaspoon salt
1 cup milk
2 large eggs
1 tablespoon butter or margarine, melted
2 teaspoons fresh thyme leaves

1. Preheat the oven to 425°F. Generously grease 12 muffin or popover cups. Combine the flour and salt in a large mixing bowl. Whisk to blend thoroughly.

2. In a separate bowl, whisk together the milk, eggs, and melted butter. Stir in the thyme. Make a well in the dry ingredients and pour in the egg mixture. Beat with an electric hand mixer set on medium speed for exactly 2 minutes. Do not overbeat. The batter should be smooth and have the consistency of heavy cream.

3. Pour into the prepared muffin or popover cups and immediately place in the hot oven. Reduce the temperature to 375°F. and bake for 35 to 45 minutes, or until puffed and browned. Loosen the popovers and tilt them in their cups. Pierce the side of each popover in several places with a wooden pick to allow steam to escape. Place in the turned-off oven for 5 minutes, leaving the door ajar. Serve immediately.   ❖

Lemon Walnut Popovers

MAKES 12

To crush the walnuts, place ¼ cup of walnut pieces in a blender. Whirl briefly, using the on-off switch. This should produce 2 tablespoons of very finely ground nuts.

1 cup all-purpose flour, scoop measured
1 teaspoon sugar
¼ teaspoon salt
1 cup milk
2 large eggs
1 tablespoon butter or margarine, melted

1 tablespoon finely grated lemon zest
2 tablespoons crushed walnuts

1. Preheat the oven to 425°F. Generously grease 12 muffin or popover cups. Combine the flour, sugar, and salt in a large mixing bowl. Whisk to blend thoroughly.

2. In a separate bowl, whisk together the milk, eggs, and melted butter. Stir in the lemon zest. Make a well in the dry ingredients and pour in the egg mixture. Beat with an electric hand mixer set on medium speed for exactly 2 minutes. Do not overbeat. The batter should be smooth and have the consistency of heavy cream. Stir in the crushed walnuts.

3. Pour into the prepared muffin or popover cups and immediately place in the hot oven. Reduce the temperature to 375°F. and bake for 35 to 45 minutes, or until puffed and browned. Loosen the popovers and tilt them in their cups. Pierce the side of each popover in several places with a wooden pick to allow steam to escape. Place in the turned-off oven for 5 minutes, leaving the door ajar. Serve immediately. ❖

Caraway Mustard Popovers

MAKES 12

These distinctive popovers are delicious served with slices of hot baked ham.

1 cup all-purpose flour, scoop measured
½ teaspoon salt
1 cup milk
2 large eggs
1 tablespoon butter or margarine, melted
2 teaspoons Dijon mustard
1½ teaspoons caraway seeds

1. Preheat the oven to 425°F. Generously grease 12 muffin or popover cups. Combine the flour and salt in a large mixing bowl. Whisk to blend thoroughly.

2. In a separate bowl, whisk together the milk, eggs, melted butter, and mustard. Make a well in the dry ingredients and pour in the egg mixture. Beat with an electric hand mixer set on medium speed for exactly 2 minutes. Do not overbeat. The batter should be smooth and have the consistency of heavy cream. Stir in the caraway seeds.

3. Pour into the prepared muffin or popover cups and immediately place in the hot oven. Reduce the temperature to 375°F. and bake for 35 to 45 minutes, or until puffed and browned. Loosen the popovers and tilt them in their cups. Pierce the side of each popover in several places with a wooden pick to allow steam to escape. Place in the turned-off oven for 5 minutes, leaving the door ajar. Serve immediately. ❖

Onion Popovers

MAKES 12

Hearty popovers to serve with soup. These are so good you can eat them plain, without butter.

3 tablespoons butter or margarine
1 small onion, very finely chopped
1 teaspoon sugar
¼ teaspoon paprika
1 cup all-purpose flour, scoop measured
½ teaspoon salt
1 cup milk
2 large eggs

1. Melt the butter in a small saucepan. Add the onion and sugar, and stir to coat. Cook over low heat until the onion is tender and beginning to turn golden brown. Remove from the heat and stir in the paprika. Set aside to cool.

2. Preheat the oven to 425°F. Generously grease 12 muffin or popover cups. Combine the flour and salt in a large mixing bowl. Whisk to blend thoroughly.

3. In a separate bowl, whisk together the milk and eggs. Stir in the onion. Make a well in the dry ingredients and pour in the egg mixture. Beat with an electric hand mixer set on medium speed for exactly 2 minutes. Do not overbeat. The batter should have the consistency of heavy cream.

4. Pour into the prepared muffin or popover cups and immediately place in the hot oven. Reduce the temperature to 375°F. and bake for 35 to 45 minutes, or until puffed and browned. Loosen the popovers and tilt them in their cups. Pierce the side of each popover in several places with a wooden pick to allow steam to escape. Place in the turned-off oven for 5 minutes, leaving the door ajar. Serve immediately.   ❖

Orange Spice Popovers

MAKES 12

Concentrated orange juice gives these spicy popovers an assertive orange flavor.

1 cup all-purpose flour, scoop measured
1 teaspoon sugar
¼ teaspoon salt
½ teaspoon cinnamon
¼ teaspoon nutmeg
1 cup milk
2 large eggs
1 tablespoon butter or margarine, melted
1 tablespoon frozen orange juice concentrate, thawed

1. Preheat the oven to 425°F. Generously grease 12 muffin or popover cups. Combine the flour, sugar, salt, cinnamon, and nutmeg in a large mixing bowl. Whisk to blend thoroughly.

2. In a separate bowl, whisk together the milk, eggs, melted butter, and orange juice concentrate. Make a well in the dry ingredients and pour in the egg mixture. Beat with an electric hand mixer set on medium speed for exactly 2 minutes. Do not overbeat. The batter should be smooth and have the consistency of heavy cream.

3. Pour into the prepared muffin or popover cups and immediately place in the hot oven. Reduce the temperature to 375°F. and bake for 35 to 45 minutes, or until puffed and browned. Loosen the popovers and tilt them in their cups. Pierce the side of each popover in several places with a wooden

pick to allow steam to escape. Place in the turned-off oven for 5 minutes, leaving the door ajar. Serve immediately.   ❖

Parmesan Popovers

MAKES 12

Snipped fresh chives add zest to these cheese-flavored popovers.

1 cup all-purpose flour, scoop measured
½ teaspoon salt
1 cup milk
2 large eggs
1 tablespoon butter or margarine, melted
1 tablespoon chopped fresh chives
½ cup freshly grated Parmesan cheese

1. Preheat the oven to 425°F. Generously grease 12 muffin or popover cups. Combine the flour and salt in a large mixing bowl. Whisk to blend thoroughly.

2. In a separate bowl, whisk together the milk, eggs, and melted butter. Make a well in the dry ingredients and pour in the egg mixture. Beat with an electric hand mixer set on medium speed for exactly 2 minutes. Do not overbeat. The batter should be smooth and have the consistency of heavy cream. Stir in the chives and cheese.

3. Pour into the prepared muffin or popover cups and immediately place in the hot oven. Reduce the temperature to 375°F. and bake for 35 to 45 minutes, or until puffed and browned. Loosen the popovers and tilt them in their cups. Pierce the side of each popover in several places with a wooden pick to allow steam to escape. Place in the turned-off oven for 5 minutes, leaving the door ajar. Serve immediately.   ❖

Whole Wheat Sage Popovers

MAKES 12

Whole wheat flour produces more densely textured popovers. Serve in place of rolls as an accompaniment to roast chicken or turkey.

⅔ cup whole wheat flour, scoop measured
⅓ cup all-purpose flour, scoop measured
½ teaspoon salt
1 cup milk
2 large eggs
1 tablespoon butter or margarine, melted
1½ teaspoons chopped fresh sage

1. Preheat the oven to 425°F. Generously grease 12 muffin or popover cups. Combine the whole wheat flour, all-purpose flour, and salt in a large mixing bowl. Whisk to blend thoroughly.

2. In a separate bowl, whisk together the milk, eggs, and melted butter. Stir in the sage. Make a well in the dry ingredients and pour in the egg mixture. Beat with an electric hand mixer set on medium speed for exactly 2 minutes. Do not overbeat. The batter should be smooth and have the consistency of heavy cream.

3. Pour into the prepared muffin or popover cups and immediately place in the hot oven. Reduce the temperature to 375°F. and bake for 35 to 45 minutes, or until puffed and browned. Loosen the popovers and tilt them in their cups. Pierce the side of each popover in several places with a wooden pick to allow steam to escape. Place in the turned-off oven for 5 minutes, leaving the door ajar. Serve immediately. ❖

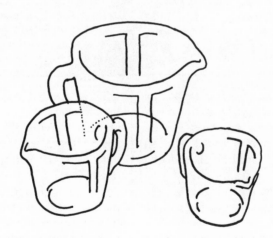

❖ Quick Breads ❖

LOOK OVER the bake-sale table at any New England country fair, and you will see row upon row of quick breads. There's zucchini bread, pumpkin bread, squash bread, banana bread, cranberry bread, and applesauce bread, to name only a few. Clearly, these soda-leavened loaves are the region's most popular type of homemade bread.

Just as the name implies, quick breads are easy to put together. But more than that, they serve a most important Yankee purpose — they are an excellent way for cooks to "use it up." Be it refrigerator leftovers or the remnants of a neighbor's harvest, any number of fruits and vegetables can be admirably incorporated into quick breads.

There are two basic methods for preparing these loaves. One is to cream butter or shortening with sugar, then gradually add the dry ingredients, alternating with a liquid. The other technique is similar to that used when making muffins: simply mix the dry and liquid ingredients together. Unlike muffin batter, which is best blended by hand, a quick bread may be prepared by using an electric mixer set at low speed.

Successful quick breads bake up moist and tender with a compact consistency. They are usually about 2 to 2½ inches high and have a soft crust with an attractive split running down the center of the loaf. For the best results, use a serrated knife for slicing, and be sure that the bread is thoroughly cooled before you begin. In fact, a loaf that has been cooled and then wrapped in aluminum foil for 24 hours can be cut into very thin slices without crumbling.

Quick breads are customarily served with butter or cream cheese, although I often eat them plain. Thin slices are delicious with hot tea, and thicker slices may be toasted to enjoy with coffee. Quick breads make a delightful addition to a holiday bread tray (cranberry and pumpkin bread being outstanding examples), and slices cut into narrow strips are a lovely side note to fruit or seafood salads.

Quick breads store remarkably well. A loaf that is tightly wrapped and kept at a cool room temperature will retain its freshness and flavor for as long as seven days. Quick breads freeze well, too. And since the recipes can be easily doubled, it is possible to make several loaves to freeze and have on hand at all times.

To freeze a quick bread, cool the loaf completely on a wire rack. Then, without wrapping it, put the loaf in a plastic freezer bag. Secure with a wire twist and place in the freezer. Defrost at room temperature inside the sealed bag. If you wish to serve quick bread warm, cut several slices and wrap them tightly in aluminum foil. Place the packet in a preheated 375°F. oven for 5 to 10 minutes.

Cheddar Cheese and Apple Bread

MAKES ONE 9x5-INCH LOAF

October brings crisp, tart apples to New England fruit stands. Try Rhode Island Greenings in this cheese-flavored loaf.

2¼ cups all-purpose flour, scoop measured
2 teaspoons baking powder
½ teaspoon baking soda
¾ teaspoon salt
½ cup butter or margarine, softened
⅔ cup sugar
2 large eggs

¼ cup milk
½ cup shredded Cheddar cheese
1 cup peeled, cored, and coarsely chopped tart apple

1. Preheat the oven to 350°F. Generously grease a 9x5-inch loaf pan. In a large mixing bowl, combine the flour, baking powder, baking soda, and salt. Whisk to blend the dry ingredients thoroughly.

2. In the bowl of an electric mixer, combine the butter and sugar. Beat at high speed until light and fluffy. Beat in the eggs, one at a time. With the mixer on low speed, sprinkle in the dry ingredients, alternating with the milk. Beat until well moistened. Stir in the cheese and apple.

3. Pour into the prepared pan and bake for 50 minutes to 1 hour, covering the loaf with aluminum foil during the last 10 minutes if necessary to prevent overbrowning. When a wooden pick inserted into the center comes out clean, transfer the bread to a cooling rack. Let stand for 10 minutes, then turn out. Cool completely before slicing. ❖

Lemon Apple Bread

MAKES ONE 9x5-INCH LOAF

A dash of fresh lemon enhances the apple flavor of this intriguing loaf. This is a wonderful bread to take to a bake sale.

2 cups all-purpose flour, scoop measured
1 teaspoon baking powder
1 teaspoon baking soda
¾ teaspoon salt
½ teaspoon cinnamon
½ teaspoon nutmeg
½ cup butter or margarine, softened
½ cup sour cream
1 cup sugar
2 large eggs
1 tablespoon freshly squeezed lemon juice
1 teaspoon vanilla extract
1 tablespoon finely grated lemon zest
1 cup peeled, cored, and coarsely chopped tart apple
½ cup raisins

1. Preheat the oven to 350°F. Generously grease a 9x5-inch loaf pan. In a large mixing bowl, combine the flour, baking powder, baking soda, salt, cinnamon, and nutmeg. Whisk to blend thoroughly.

2. In the bowl of an electric mixer, combine the butter and sour cream. Beat at high speed until light and fluffy. Gradually beat in the sugar. Add the eggs, beating them in one at a time. Blend in the lemon juice, vanilla, and lemon zest. With the mixer on low speed, sprinkle in the dry ingredients. Beat until well moistened. Stir in the apple and raisins.

3. Pour into the prepared pan and bake for 50 minutes to 1 hour, covering the loaf with aluminum foil during the last 10 minutes if necessary to prevent overbrowning. When a wooden pick inserted into the center comes out clean, transfer the bread to a cooling rack. Let stand for 10 minutes, then turn out. Cool completely before slicing. ❖

Spiced Apple Loaf

MAKES ONE 9x5-INCH LOAF

Cinnamon and nutmeg infuse this down-home loaf with traditional spicy flavor. Serve generous slices with ham and scrambled eggs.

2 cups all-purpose flour, scoop measured
1 teaspoon baking powder
1 teaspoon baking soda
¾ teaspoon salt
½ teaspoon cinnamon
½ teaspoon nutmeg
½ cup solid vegetable shortening
⅔ cup sugar
1 large egg
1 teaspoon vanilla extract
¾ cup buttermilk
2 cups peeled, cored, and coarsely chopped tart apple

1. Preheat the oven to 350°F. Generously grease a 9x5-inch loaf pan. In a large mixing bowl, combine the flour, baking powder,

baking soda, salt, cinnamon, and nutmeg. Whisk to blend thoroughly.

2. In the bowl of an electric mixer, combine the shortening and sugar. Beat at high speed until light and fluffy. Beat in the egg. Blend in the vanilla. With the mixer on low speed, sprinkle in the dry ingredients, alternating with the buttermilk. Beat until well moistened. Stir in the apple.

3. Pour into the prepared pan and bake for 50 minutes to 1 hour, covering the loaf with aluminum foil during the last 10 minutes if necessary to prevent overbrowning. When a wooden pick inserted into the center comes out clean, transfer the bread to a cooling rack. Let stand for 10 minutes, then turn out. Cool completely before slicing. ❖

Applesauce Raisin Bread

MAKES ONE 9x5-INCH LOAF

Moist with tart applesauce and studded with raisins, this hearty loaf evokes autumn memories of cider mills and baskets of apples lined up for sale by the side of the road.

2 cups all-purpose flour, scoop measured
2 teaspoons baking powder
½ teaspoon baking soda
½ teaspoon salt
1 teaspoon cinnamon
½ teaspoon nutmeg
½ cup solid vegetable shortening
1 cup sugar
2 large eggs
1 teaspoon vanilla extract
1 cup unsweetened applesauce
1 cup raisins
½ cup coarsely chopped walnuts

1. Preheat the oven to 350°F. Generously grease a 9x5-inch loaf pan. In a large bowl combine the flour, sugars, baking powder, baking soda, salt, cinnamon, and nutmeg. Whisk to blend thoroughly.

2. In the bowl of an electric mixer, combine the shortening and sugar. Beat at high speed until light and fluffy. Beat in the eggs,

one at a time. Blend in the vanilla. With the mixer on low speed, sprinkle in the dry ingredients, alternating with the applesauce. Beat until well moistened. Stir in the raisins and walnuts.

3. Pour into the prepared pan and bake for 50 minutes to 1 hour, covering the loaf with aluminum foil during the last 10 minutes if necessary to prevent overbrowning. When a wooden pick inserted into the center comes out clean, transfer the bread to a cooling rack. Let stand for 10 minutes, then turn out. Cool completely before slicing. ❖

Applesauce Nut Bread

MAKES ONE 9x5-INCH LOAF

A quick, nutritious loaf to offer as an after-school snack. Dust the top with confectioners' sugar if you like, and the kids will eat it instead of cake.

2 cups all-purpose flour, scoop measured
¾ cup sugar
2 teaspoons baking powder
½ teaspoon baking soda
½ teaspoon salt
½ teaspoon cinnamon
½ cup milk
1 large egg
¼ cup butter or margarine, melted
1 cup unsweetened applesauce
¾ cup coarsely chopped walnuts

1. Preheat the oven to 350°F. Generously grease a 9x5-inch loaf pan. In the bowl of an electric mixer, combine the flour, sugar, baking powder, baking soda, salt, and cinnamon. Run the mixer briefly on low speed to blend the dry ingredients.

2. In a separate bowl, whisk together the milk, egg, and melted butter. Stir in the applesauce. With the mixer set on low speed, gradually pour the egg mixture into the dry ingredients. Beat until well moistened. Stir in the walnuts.

3. Pour into the prepared pan and bake for 50 minutes to 1 hour, covering the loaf with aluminum foil during the last 10 min-

utes if necessary to prevent overbrowning. When a wooden pick inserted into the center comes out clean, transfer the bread to a cooling rack. Let stand for 10 minutes, then turn out. Cool completely before slicing. ❖

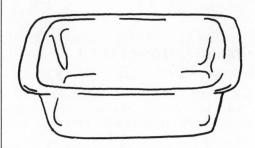

Apricot Date Bread

MAKES ONE 9x5-INCH LOAF

Succulent bits of apricots and dates accent this lovely loaf. Cut with a serrated knife for neat, attractive slices.

2 cups all-purpose flour, scoop measured
3 tablespoons granulated sugar
3 tablespoons light brown sugar
2 teaspoons baking powder
½ teaspoon baking soda
¾ teaspoon salt
1 large egg
¼ cup vegetable oil
1 cup boiling water
1 cup coarsely chopped dried apricots
½ cup coarsely chopped dates

1. Preheat the oven to 350°F. Generously grease a 9x5-inch loaf pan. In the bowl of an electric mixer, combine the flour, granulated sugar, brown sugar, baking powder, baking soda, and salt. Run the mixer briefly on low speed to blend the dry ingredients.

2. In a separate bowl, whisk together the egg and oil. Whisk in the water. With the mixer set on low speed, gradually pour the egg mixture into the dry ingredients. Beat until well moistened. Stir in the apricots and dates.

3. Pour into the prepared pan and bake for 50 minutes to 1 hour, covering the loaf

with aluminum foil during the last 10 minutes if necessary to prevent overbrowning. When a wooden pick inserted into the center comes out clean, transfer the bread to a cooling rack. Let stand for 10 minutes, then turn out. Cool completely before slicing. ❖

Apricot Orange Bread

MAKES ONE 9x5-INCH LOAF

The flavor combination of orange and apricot is especially pleasing. Offer slices of this loaf with softened cream cheese whipped with a small amount of finely grated orange zest.

2 cups all-purpose flour, scoop measured
1 cup sugar
2 teaspoons baking powder
½ teaspoon baking soda
½ teaspoon salt
½ cup freshly squeezed orange juice
⅓ cup cold water
2 large eggs
3 tablespoons butter or margarine, melted
½ cup coarsely chopped dried apricots
½ cup coarsely chopped walnuts

1. Preheat the oven to 350°F. Generously grease a 9x5-inch loaf pan. In the bowl of an electric mixer, combine the flour, sugar, baking powder, baking soda, and salt. Run the mixer briefly on low speed to blend the dry ingredients.

2. In a separate bowl, whisk together the orange juice, water, and eggs. Stir in the melted butter. With the mixer set on low speed, gradually pour the egg mixture into the dry ingredients. Beat until well moistened. Stir in the apricots and walnuts.

3. Pour into the prepared pan and bake for 50 minutes to 1 hour, covering the loaf with aluminum foil during the last 10 minutes if necessary to prevent overbrowning. When a wooden pick inserted into the center comes out clean, transfer the bread to a cooling rack. Let stand for 10 minutes, then turn out. Cool completely before slicing. ❖

Apricot Whole Wheat Bread

MAKES ONE 9x5-INCH LOAF

A spicy whole wheat loaf scented with honey and packed with chunks of dried apricot.

2½ cups whole wheat flour, scoop measured
3 teaspoons baking powder
¾ teaspoon salt
1 teaspoon cinnamon
½ teaspoon nutmeg
½ cup milk
½ cup honey
2 large eggs
2 tablespoons vegetable oil
1 cup coarsely chopped dried apricots
½ cup coarsely chopped walnuts

1. Preheat the oven to 350°F. Generously grease a 9x5-inch loaf pan. In the bowl of an electric mixer, combine the flour, baking powder, salt, cinnamon, and nutmeg. Run the mixer briefly on low speed to blend the dry ingredients.

2. In a separate bowl, whisk together the milk, honey, eggs, and oil. With the mixer set on low speed, gradually pour the egg mixture into the dry ingredients. Beat until well moistened. Stir in the apricots and walnuts.

3. Pour into the prepared pan and bake for 50 minutes to 1 hour, covering the loaf with aluminum foil during the last 10 minutes if necessary to prevent overbrowning. When a wooden pick inserted into the center comes out clean, transfer the bread to a cooling rack. Let stand for 10 minutes, then turn out. Cool completely before slicing. ❖

Bran Banana Loaf

MAKES ONE 9x5-INCH LOAF

Banana quick bread has long been a New England favorite for breakfast, lunch, or tea. In this recipe, wheat bran adds its nutritious attributes and grainy texture.

1¼ cups all-purpose flour, scoop measured
½ cup light brown sugar

1 cup unprocessed wheat bran
1 teaspoon baking powder
1 teaspoon baking soda
½ teaspoon salt
¼ cup sour cream
2 large eggs
¼ cup vegetable oil
3 ripe bananas, mashed
½ cup raisins

1. Preheat the oven to 350°F. Generously grease a 9x5-inch loaf pan. Sift the flour and sugar into the bowl of an electric mixer. Add the bran, baking powder, baking soda, and salt. Run the mixer briefly on low speed to blend the dry ingredients.

2. In a separate bowl, whisk together the sour cream, eggs, and oil. Stir in the mashed banana. With the mixer set on low speed, gradually pour the egg mixture into the dry ingredients. Beat until well moistened. Stir in the raisins.

3. Pour into the prepared pan and bake for 50 minutes to 1 hour, covering the loaf with aluminum foil during the last 10 minutes if necessary to prevent overbrowning. When a wooden pick inserted into the center comes out clean, transfer the bread to a cooling rack. Let stand for 10 minutes, then turn out. Cool completely before slicing. ❖

Banana Walnut Bread

MAKES ONE 9x5-INCH LOAF

This classic favorite is at its best when made with soft, extremely ripe bananas. Let them sit on the counter until the skin develops black spots and the aroma of banana is intense.

2 cups all-purpose flour, scoop measured
1 teaspoon baking soda
½ teaspoon salt
½ cup solid vegetable shortening
1 cup sugar
2 large eggs
3 ripe bananas, sliced thin
½ cup coarsely chopped walnuts

1. Preheat the oven to 350°F. Generously grease a 9x5-inch loaf pan. In a large mixing bowl, combine the flour, baking soda, and salt. Whisk to blend thoroughly.

2. In the bowl of an electric mixer, combine the shortening and sugar. Beat at high speed until light and fluffy. Beat in the eggs, one at a time. Add the bananas and beat until the mixture is smooth. With the mixer on low speed, sprinkle in the dry ingredients. Beat until well moistened. Stir in the walnuts.

3. Pour into the prepared pan and bake for 50 minutes to 1 hour, covering the loaf with aluminum foil during the last 10 minutes if necessary to prevent overbrowning. When a wooden pick inserted into the center comes out clean, transfer the bread to a cooling rack. Let stand for 10 minutes, then turn out. Cool completely before slicing. ❖

Herman Starter Banana Bread

MAKES ONE 9x5-INCH LOAF

Banana bread made with sourdough starter possesses an elusive flavor and a tender crumb.

2¼ cups all-purpose flour, scoop measured
½ cup light brown sugar
¼ cup granulated sugar
2 teaspoons baking powder
½ teaspoon baking soda
½ teaspoon salt
½ teaspoon cinnamon
¼ teaspoon nutmeg
1 cup Herman sourdough starter (p. 49), at
   room temperature
3 ripe bananas, sliced thin
1 large egg
⅓ cup vegetable oil
1 teaspoon vanilla extract
1 teaspoon finely grated lemon zest
1 cup coarsely chopped walnuts

1. Preheat the oven to 350°F. Generously grease a 9x5-inch loaf pan. Sift the flour and brown sugar into a large mixing bowl.

Add the granulated sugar, baking powder, baking soda, salt, cinnamon, and nutmeg. Whisk to blend thoroughly.

2. In the bowl of an electric mixer, combine the sourdough starter and bananas. Beat until the bananas are broken up. Add the egg and oil. Blend in the vanilla and lemon zest. With the mixer on low speed, sprinkle in the dry ingredients. Beat until well moistened. Stir in the walnuts.

3. Pour into the prepared pan and bake for 50 minutes to 1 hour, covering the loaf with aluminum foil during the last 10 minutes if necessary to prevent overbrowning. When a wooden pick inserted into the center comes out clean, transfer the bread to a cooling rack. Let stand for 10 minutes, then turn out. Cool completely before slicing. ❖

Banana Chocolate Bread

MAKES ONE 9x5-INCH LOAF

Semisweet chips melt to form tiny pockets of chocolate in this rich banana loaf. Serve for breakfast as a special treat — it tastes marvelous with coffee.

2½ cups all-purpose flour, scoop measured
1 teaspoon baking powder
1 teaspoon baking soda
½ teaspoon salt
1 large package (8 ounces) cream cheese, softened
¼ cup butter or margarine, softened
1 cup light brown sugar
1 large egg
3 ripe bananas, sliced thin
1 cup semisweet chocolate chips

1. Preheat the oven to 350°F. Generously grease a 9x5-inch loaf pan. In a large mixing bowl, combine the flour, baking powder, baking soda, and salt. Whisk to blend the dry ingredients thoroughly.

2. In the bowl of an electric mixer, combine the cream cheese and butter. Beat at high speed until light and fluffy. Gradually beat in the sugar. Add the egg and beat well.

Add the bananas and beat until the mixture is smooth. With the mixer on low speed, sprinkle in the dry ingredients. Beat until well moistened. Stir in the chocolate chips.

3. Pour into the prepared pan and bake for 50 minutes to 1 hour, covering the loaf with aluminum foil during the last 10 minutes if necessary to prevent overbrowning. When a wooden pick inserted into the center comes out clean, transfer the bread to a cooling rack. Let stand for 10 minutes, then turn out. Cool completely before slicing. ❖

Beach Plum Bread

MAKES ONE 9x5-INCH LOAF

Beach plums are an old Cape Cod favorite. Purple and about the size of a large cherry, they are shaped like common plums. Beach plums are a rare treat, though, because the location of bushes on which they grow is kept secret by most Cape Codders. If you are lucky enough to be given some, try them in this tasty loaf.

2 cups all-purpose flour, scoop measured
¾ cup sugar
2 teaspoons baking powder
½ teaspoon baking soda
¾ teaspoon salt
¾ cup freshly squeezed orange juice
2 large eggs
¼ cup butter or margarine, melted
1 cup coarsely chopped pitted beach plums
½ cup coarsely chopped walnuts

1. Preheat the oven to 350°F. Generously grease a 9x5-inch loaf pan. In the bowl of an electric mixer, combine the flour, sugar, baking powder, baking soda, and salt. Run the mixer briefly on low speed to blend the dry ingredients.

2. In a separate bowl, whisk together the orange juice, eggs, and melted butter. With the mixer set on low speed, gradually pour the egg mixture into the dry ingredients. Beat until well moistened. Stir in the beach plums and walnuts.

3. Pour into the prepared pan and bake for 50 minutes to 1 hour, covering the loaf with aluminum foil during the last 10 minutes if necessary to prevent overbrowning. When a wooden pick inserted into the center comes out clean, transfer the bread to a cooling rack. Let stand for 10 minutes, then turn out. Cool completely before slicing. ❖

Easy Beer Bread

MAKES ONE 9x5-INCH LOAF

This wonderful loaf can be put together without any fuss. The beer adds a yeasty aroma and flavor that makes this bread an excellent partner for hot soup.

2¼ cups all-purpose flour, scoop measured
¼ cup sugar
3 teaspoons baking powder
1 teaspoon salt
1½ cups beer (one 12-ounce bottle)
1 tablespoon caraway seeds
1 tablespoon butter or margarine, melted

1. Preheat the oven to 375°F. Generously grease a 9x5-inch loaf pan. In the bowl of an electric mixer, combine the flour, sugar, baking powder, and salt. Run the mixer briefly on low speed to blend the dry ingredients thoroughly.

2. With the mixer set on low speed, gradually pour in the beer. Beat until well moistened. Stir in the caraway seeds.

3. Pour into the prepared pan and bake for 35 to 45 minutes, or until the surface is nicely browned. When a wooden pick inserted into the center comes out clean, transfer the bread to a cooling rack. Brush the top with the melted butter. Let stand for 10 minutes, then turn out. Serve hot or complete cooling on the rack. ❖

Lemon Blueberry Bread

MAKES ONE 9x5-INCH LOAF

Cut t⁻'s bread into thick slices and wrap it up to take on a Fourth of July picnic.

2 cups all-purpose flour, scoop measured
2 teaspoons baking powder
½ teaspoon baking soda
½ teaspoon salt
½ teaspoon mace
½ cup butter or margarine, softened
1 cup sugar
1 large egg
1 tablespoon finely grated lemon zest
1 tablespoon freshly squeezed lemon juice
1 teaspoon vanilla extract
1 cup milk
1 cup fresh blueberries, rinsed and gently patted dry

1. Preheat the oven to 350°F. Generously grease a 9x5-inch loaf pan. In a large mixing bowl, combine the flour, baking powder, baking soda, salt, and mace. Whisk to blend thoroughly.

2. In the bowl of an electric mixer, combine the butter and sugar. Beat at high speed until light and fluffy. Beat in the egg. Blend in the lemon zest, lemon juice, and vanilla. With the mixer on low speed, sprinkle in the dry ingredients, alternating with the milk. Beat until well moistened. Stir in the blueberries.

3. Pour into the prepared pan and bake for 50 minutes to 1 hour, covering the loaf with aluminum foil during the last 10 minutes if necessary to prevent overbrowning. When a wooden pick inserted into the center comes out clean, transfer the bread to a cooling rack. Let stand for 10 minutes, then turn out. Cool completely before slicing. ❖

Bran Soda Bread

MAKES 1 ROUND LOAF

St. Patrick's Day is celebrated with great enthusiasm in New England, and the holiday would not be complete without soda bread. This version contains wheat bran, which contributes a certain coarseness, much like that found in a true Irish loaf.

1¾ cups all-purpose flour, scoop measured
½ cup unprocessed wheat bran
1 teaspoon baking powder
1 teaspoon baking soda
½ teaspoon salt
4 tablespoons butter or margarine, cut into small pieces
½ cup raisins
1 cup buttermilk
2 tablespoons molasses

1. Preheat the oven to 375°F. Lightly grease a baking sheet without sides. Combine the flour, wheat bran, baking powder, baking soda, and salt in a large mixing bowl. Whisk to blend thoroughly. Add the butter and cut in with a knife until the mixture is crumbly. Add the raisins and toss to combine.

2. In a small bowl, whisk together the buttermilk and molasses. Make a well in the dry ingredients. Pour in the buttermilk mixture and toss with a fork until the dough holds together. Gather the dough into a ball and roll it around the inside of the bowl to pick up any stray particles. Transfer to a lightly floured surface and knead 60 times, sifting on flour if necessary to prevent sticking. Pat the dough into a 9-inch round. Score the round into quarters with the dull edge of a floured chef's knife. Make the marks about 1½ inches deep. Transfer the round to the prepared baking sheet and place in the preheated oven. Bake for 25 to 30 minutes, or until the surface is lightly browned. Transfer to a wire rack to cool. ❖

Herman Starter Bran Bread

MAKES ONE 9x5-INCH LOAF

Applesauce is the secret ingredient in this full-bodied bread. Serve for breakfast with plenty of whipped butter.

1 cup whole wheat flour, scoop measured
½ cup all-purpose flour, scoop measured
⅔ cup unprocessed wheat bran
¾ cup sugar
2 teaspoons baking powder
½ teaspoon baking soda
½ teaspoon salt
1 cup Herman sourdough starter (p. 49), at room temperature
1 cup applesauce
1 large egg
⅓ cup vegetable oil

1. Preheat the oven to 350°F. Generously grease a 9x5-inch loaf pan. In a large mixing bowl, combine the whole wheat flour, all-purpose flour, wheat bran, sugar, baking powder, baking soda, and salt. Whisk to blend thoroughly.

2. In the bowl of an electric mixer, combine the sourdough starter and applesauce. Blend well. Beat in the egg and oil. With the mixer on low speed, sprinkle in the dry ingredients. Beat until well moistened.

3. Pour into the prepared pan and bake for 50 minutes to 1 hour, covering the loaf with aluminum foil during the last 10 minutes if necessary to prevent overbrowning. When a wooden pick inserted into the center comes out clean, transfer the bread to a cooling rack. Let stand for 10 minutes, then turn out. Cool completely before slicing. ❖

Quick Brown Bread

MAKES ONE 9x5-INCH LOAF

Graham flour is unsifted whole wheat flour that has a coarser texture than regular whole wheat flour. It is named after Reverend Sylvester Graham, a Connecticut parson, who preached that wholesome brown bread and the Bible were the way to salvation. If you can't find graham flour in a health-food store, substitute regular whole wheat flour.

1½ cups graham flour, scoop measured
½ cup all-purpose flour, scoop measured
⅓ cup yellow cornmeal
¼ cup sugar
1 teaspoon baking powder

1 teaspoon baking soda
1 teaspoon salt
1 cup milk
2 large eggs
¼ cup molasses
¼ cup vegetable oil

1. Preheat the oven to 350°F. Generously grease a 9x5-inch loaf pan. In the bowl of an electric mixer, combine the graham flour, all-purpose flour, cornmeal, sugar, baking powder, baking soda, and salt. Run the mixer briefly on low speed to blend the dry ingredients.

2. In a separate bowl, whisk together the milk and eggs. Whisk in the molasses and oil. With the mixer set on low speed, gradually pour the egg mixture into the dry ingredients. Beat until well moistened.

3. Pour into the prepared pan and bake for 50 minutes to 1 hour, covering the loaf with aluminum foil during the last 10 minutes if necessary to prevent overbrowning. When a wooden pick inserted into the center comes out clean, transfer the bread to a cooling rack. Let stand for 10 minutes, then turn out. Cool completely before slicing. ❖

Buckwheat Buttermilk Bread

MAKES ONE 9x5-INCH LOAF

As this loaf bakes, the aroma of buckwheat reminds me of morning in New England. Hearty, full-bodied, and a "breakfast that'll do ya."

1 cup all-purpose flour, scoop measured
⅓ cup light brown sugar
1½ cups buckwheat flour, scoop measured
1 teaspoon baking powder
1 teaspoon baking soda
¾ teaspoon salt
1 teaspoon cinnamon
1 cup buttermilk
2 large eggs
¼ cup butter or margarine, melted
½ cup coarsely chopped walnuts

1. Preheat the oven to 350°F. Generously grease a 9x5-inch loaf pan. Sift the all-pur-

pose flour and the sugar into the bowl of an electric mixer. Add the buckwheat flour, baking powder, baking soda, salt, and cinnamon. Run the mixer briefly on low speed to blend the dry ingredients.

2. In a separate bowl, whisk together the buttermilk, eggs, and melted butter. With the mixer on low speed, gradually pour the egg mixture into the dry ingredients. Beat until well moistened. Stir in the walnuts.

3. Pour into the prepared pan and bake for 50 minutes to 1 hour, covering the loaf with aluminum foil during the last 10 minutes if necessary to prevent overbrowning. When a wooden pick inserted into the center comes out clean, transfer the bread to a cooling rack. Let stand for 10 minutes, then turn out. Cool completely before slicing. ❖

Buckwheat Raisin Bread

MAKES ONE 9x5-INCH LOAF

Studded with golden raisins, this honey-flavored buckwheat loaf is extra special. To find buckwheat flour, look in health-food stores and specialty-food shops.

1¼ cups all-purpose flour, scoop measured
1 cup buckwheat flour, scoop measured
2 tablespoons wheat germ
1½ teaspoons baking powder
1 teaspoon baking soda
¾ teaspoon salt
1 cup milk
1 large egg
4 tablespoons honey
¼ cup butter or margarine, melted
½ cup golden raisins.

1. Preheat the oven to 350°F. Generously grease a 9x5-inch loaf pan. In the bowl of an electric mixer, combine the all-purpose flour, buckwheat flour, wheat germ, baking powder, baking soda, and salt. Run the mixer briefly on low speed to blend the dry ingredients.

2. In a separate bowl, whisk together the milk, egg, honey, and melted butter. With the mixer on low speed, gradually pour the

egg mixture into the dry ingredients. Beat until well moistened. Stir in the raisins.

3. Pour into the prepared pan and bake for 50 minutes to 1 hour, covering the loaf with aluminum foil during the last 10 minutes if necessary to prevent overbrowning. When a wooden pick inserted into the center comes out clean, transfer the bread to a cooling rack. Let stand for 10 minutes, then turn out. Cool completely before slicing. ❖

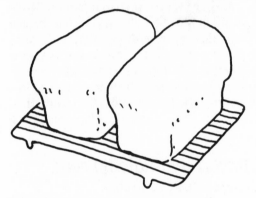

Cardamom Candied Fruit Bread

MAKES ONE 9x5-INCH LOAF

A colorful, festive bread to give as a gift at Christmastime.

2 cups all-purpose flour, scoop measured
½ cup granulated sugar
½ cup light brown sugar
3 teaspoons baking powder
½ teaspoon salt
½ teaspoon ground cardamom
⅔ cup milk
2 large eggs
3 tablespoons butter or margarine, melted
1 cup finely chopped mixed candied fruit

1. Preheat the oven to 350°F. Generously grease a 9x5-inch loaf pan. Sift the flour, granulated sugar, and brown sugar into the bowl of an electric mixer. Add the baking powder, salt, and cardamom. Run the mixer briefly on low speed to blend the dry ingredients thoroughly.

2. In a separate bowl, whisk together the milk, the eggs, and the melted butter. With the mixer set on low speed, gradually pour the egg mixture into the dry ingredients. Beat until well moistened. Stir in the candied fruit.

3. Pour into the prepared pan and bake for 50 minutes to 1 hour, covering the loaf with aluminum foil during the last 10 minutes if necessary to prevent overbrowning. When a wooden pick inserted into the center comes out clean, transfer the bread to a cooling rack. Let stand for 10 minutes, then turn out. Cool completely before slicing. ❖

Carrot Date Bread

MAKES ONE 9x5-INCH LOAF

Creaming the shortening and sugar together produces a cakelike consistency for this delicious bread. Serve plain or buttered for a wholesome snack.

2 cups all-purpose flour, scoop measured
3 teaspoons baking powder
¾ teaspoon salt
⅓ cup solid vegetable shortening
⅔ cup sugar
2 large eggs
1 teaspoon vanilla extract
1 cup milk
1 cup finely grated carrot
¾ cup coarsely chopped dates

1. Preheat the oven to 350°F. Generously grease a 9x5-inch loaf pan. In a large mixing bowl, combine the flour, baking powder, and salt. Whisk to blend thoroughly.

2. In the bowl of an electric mixer, combine the shortening and sugar. Beat at high speed until light and fluffy. Beat in the eggs, one at a time. Blend in the vanilla. With the mixer on low speed, sprinkle in the dry ingredients, alternating with the milk. Beat until well moistened. Stir in the carrot and dates.

3. Pour into the prepared pan and bake for 50 minutes to 1 hour, covering the loaf with aluminum foil during the last 10 minutes if necessary to prevent overbrowning. When a wooden pick inserted into the cen-

ter comes out clean, transfer the bread to a cooling rack. Let stand for 10 minutes, then turn out. Cool completely before slicing. ❖

Carrot and Walnut Loaf

MAKES ONE 9x5-INCH LOAF

Like its cousin, carrot cake, this carrot and walnut bread is a standing favorite with New England cooks. Try it spread with whipped cream cheese.

2 cups all-purpose flour, scoop measured
3 teaspoons baking powder
¾ teaspoon salt
¾ cup sugar
½ cup vegetable oil
2 large eggs
¼ cup milk
1 tablespoon finely grated lemon zest
1 cup finely grated carrot
¾ cup coarsely chopped walnuts

1. Preheat the oven to 350°F. Generously grease a 9x5-inch loaf pan. In a large mixing bowl, combine the flour, baking powder, and salt. Whisk to blend thoroughly.

2. In the bowl of an electric mixer, combine the sugar, oil, and eggs. Beat until slightly thickened. Blend in the milk and lemon zest. With the mixer on low speed, sprinkle in the dry ingredients. Beat until well moistened. Stir in the carrot and walnuts.

3. Pour into the prepared pan and bake for 50 minutes to 1 hour, covering the loaf with aluminum foil during the last 10 minutes if necessary to prevent overbrowning. When a wooden pick inserted into the center comes out clean, transfer the bread to a cooling rack. Let stand for 10 minutes, then turn out. Cool completely before slicing. ❖

Whole Wheat Carrot Bread

MAKES ONE 9x5-INCH LOAF

Whole wheat flour creates a nourishing, coarsely textured carrot loaf.

2½ cups whole wheat flour, scoop measured
1 cup sugar
2 teaspoons baking powder
½ teaspoon baking soda
½ teaspoon salt
1 teaspoon cinnamon
½ teaspoon nutmeg
½ cup milk
2 large eggs
¼ cup vegetable oil
1½ cups finely grated carrot

1. Preheat the oven to 350°F. Generously grease a 9x5-inch loaf pan. In the bowl of an electric mixer, combine the flour, sugar, baking powder, baking soda, salt, cinnamon, and nutmeg. Run the mixer briefly on low speed to blend the dry ingredients.

2. In a separate bowl, whisk together the milk, eggs, and oil. With the mixer set on low speed, gradually pour the egg mixture into the dry ingredients. Beat until well moistened. Stir in the carrot.

3. Pour into the prepared pan and bake for 50 minutes to 1 hour, covering the loaf with aluminum foil during the last 10 minutes if necessary to prevent overbrowning. When a wooden pick inserted into the center comes out clean, transfer the bread to a cooling rack. Let stand for 10 minutes, then turn out. Cool completely before slicing. ❖

Cheddar Dill Bread

MAKES ONE 9x5-INCH LOAF

Fresh dill leaves contribute enticing flavor to this savory loaf. This is a summer bread to enjoy in thin slices with cold shrimp salad.

2 cups all-purpose flour, scoop measured
1 tablespoon sugar
3 teaspoons baking powder
¾ teaspoon salt
½ teaspoon dry mustard
1 cup milk
1 large egg
¼ cup vegetable oil
1½ cups shredded Cheddar cheese
1 tablespoon chopped fresh dill leaves

1. Preheat the oven to 350°F. Generously grease a 9x5-inch loaf pan. In the bowl of an electric mixer, combine the flour, sugar, baking powder, salt, and dry mustard. Run the mixer briefly on low speed to blend the dry ingredients.

2. In a separate bowl, whisk together the milk, egg, and oil. With the mixer set on low speed, gradually pour the egg mixture into the dry ingredients. Beat until well moistened. Stir in the cheese and dill.

3. Pour into the prepared pan and bake for 50 minutes to 1 hour, covering the loaf with aluminum foil during the last 10 minutes if necessary to prevent overbrowning. When a wooden pick inserted into the center comes out clean, transfer the bread to a cooling rack. Let stand for 10 minutes, then turn out. Cool completely before slicing. ❖

Chocolate Walnut Bread

MAKES ONE 9x5-INCH LOAF

Chocolate lovers dote on warm slices of this bread for breakfast. Others prefer to savor it as an afternoon snack.

1 cup milk
1 tablespoon vinegar
2½ cups all-purpose flour, scoop measured
1 cup unsweetened cocoa
1 teaspoon baking soda
¾ teaspoon salt
¼ cup butter or margarine, softened
1 small package (3 ounces) cream cheese, softened
1 cup sugar
2 large eggs
1 teaspoon vanilla extract
½ cup coarsely chopped walnuts

1. Combine the milk and vinegar in a glass measuring cup. Set aside for 10 minutes to sour and thicken slightly.

2. Preheat the oven to 350°F. Generously grease a 9x5-inch loaf pan. In a large mixing bowl, combine the flour, cocoa, baking soda, and salt. Whisk to blend thoroughly.

3. In the bowl of an electric mixer, combine the butter and cream cheese. Beat at high speed until light and fluffy. Gradually sprinkle in the sugar. Beat in the eggs one at a time. Blend in the vanilla. With the mixer on low speed, sprinkle in the dry ingredients, alternating with the sour milk. Beat until well moistened. Stir in the walnuts.

4. Pour into the prepared pan and bake for 50 minutes to 1 hour, covering the loaf with aluminum foil during the last 10 minutes if necessary to prevent overbrowning. When a wooden pick inserted into the center comes out clean, transfer the bread to a cooling rack. Let stand for 10 minutes, then turn out. Cool completely before slicing. ❖

Chorizo Bread

MAKES ONE 9x5-INCH LOAF

Bits of spicy Portuguese sausage spark this flavorful bread. Serve warm with soup or slice thinly and serve with goat cheese as an appetizer. Pepperoni may be substituted for the chorizo if you wish.

6 ounces dry chorizo sausage
1 roasted red bell pepper, fresh or canned
2½ cups all-purpose flour, scoop measured
3 teaspoons baking powder
½ teaspoon salt
1 large package (8 ounces) cream cheese, softened
¼ cup butter or margarine, softened
2 tablespoons sugar
2 large eggs
¾ cup milk
¼ cup freshly grated Parmesan cheese

1. Remove the casing from the sausage and chop coarsely. Peel the roasted pepper if it is fresh. Pat the pepper dry and then chop coarsely. Set aside.

2. Preheat the oven to 350°F. Generously grease a 9x5-inch loaf pan. In a large mixing bowl, combine the flour, baking powder, and salt. Whisk to blend thoroughly.

3. In the bowl of an electric mixer, combine the cream cheese and butter. Beat at

high speed until light and fluffy. Gradually beat in the sugar. Beat the eggs in one at a time. With the mixer on low speed, sprinkle in the dry ingredients, alternating with the milk. Beat until well moistened. Blend in the cheese. Add the sausage and red pepper, and stir to combine.

4. Pour into the prepared pan and bake for 50 minutes to 1 hour, covering the loaf with aluminum foil during the last 10 minutes if necessary to prevent overbrowning. When a wooden pick inserted into the center comes out clean, transfer the bread to a cooling rack. Let stand for 10 minutes, then turn out. Serve warm or complete cooling on the rack.   ❖

Apple Corn Bread

MAKES ONE 8-INCH SQUARE LOAF

Squares of apple-flecked corn bread make a homey accompaniment to roast pork or baked ham.

1 cup yellow cornmeal
1 cup all-purpose flour, scoop measured
¼ cup sugar
1 teaspoon baking powder
1 teaspoon baking soda
¾ teaspoon salt
1 cup buttermilk
1 large egg
¼ cup vegetable oil
1 cup peeled, cored, and coarsely chopped
    tart apple

1. Preheat the oven to 375°F. Generously grease an 8-inch square baking pan. In the bowl of an electric mixer, combine the cornmeal, flour, sugar, baking powder, baking soda, and salt. Run the mixer briefly on low speed to blend the dry ingredients.

2. In a separate bowl, whisk together the buttermilk, egg, and oil. With the mixer set on low speed, gradually pour the egg mixture into the dry ingredients. Beat until well moistened. Stir in the apple.

3. Pour into the prepared pan and bake for 35 to 40 minutes, or until lightly browned. When a wooden pick inserted into the center comes out clean, transfer the bread to a cooling rack. Let stand for 10 minutes. Cut into squares and serve hot, or complete cooling on the rack.   ❖

Herbed Corn Bread

MAKES ONE 8-INCH SQUARE LOAF

This bread is delicious served hot from the oven. It can also be used to make your own corn bread stuffing. Allow the bread to cool, then crumble coarsely and scatter over a jelly-roll pan. Let the crumbs stand overnight to dry, then proceed with your favorite stuffing recipe.

1¼ cups yellow cornmeal
¾ cup all-purpose flour, scoop measured
2 teaspoons baking powder
½ teaspoon baking soda
1 teaspoon salt
1 teaspoon dried sage
½ teaspoon dried marjoram
½ teaspoon dried thyme
1 cup buttermilk
2 large eggs
¼ cup butter or margarine, melted
2 tablespoons finely chopped fresh parsley

1. Preheat the oven to 350°F. Generously grease an 8-inch square baking pan. In the bowl of an electric mixer, combine the cornmeal, flour, baking powder, baking soda, and salt. Add the sage, marjoram, and thyme. Run the mixer briefly on low speed to blend the dry ingredients.

2. In a separate bowl, whisk together the buttermilk, eggs, and melted butter. With the mixer set on low speed, gradually pour the egg mixture into the dry ingredients. Beat until well moistened, then stir in the parsley.

3. Pour into the prepared pan and bake for 35 to 40 minutes, or until lightly browned. When a wooden pick inserted into the center comes out clean, transfer the bread to a cooling rack. Let stand for 10 minutes. Cut into squares and serve hot, or complete cooling on the rack.   ❖

Pecan Corn Bread

MAKES ONE 8-INCH SQUARE LOAF

Offer this savory corn bread with roast turkey or game, and be sure to pass a generous bowl of whipped butter.

1 cup yellow cornmeal
1 cup all-purpose flour, scoop measured
2 tablespoons sugar
3 teaspoons baking powder
1 teaspoon salt
1 cup milk
1 large egg
¼ cup butter or margarine, melted
1 cup pecans, lightly toasted then coarsely
   chopped

1. Preheat the oven to 375°F. Generously grease an 8-inch square baking pan. In the bowl of an electric mixer, combine the cornmeal, flour, sugar, baking powder, and salt. Run the mixer briefly on low speed to blend the dry ingredients.

2. In a separate bowl, whisk together the milk, egg, and melted butter. With the mixer set on low speed, gradually pour the egg mixture into the dry ingredients. Beat until well moistened. Stir in the pecans.

3. Pour into the prepared pan and bake for 35 to 40 minutes, or until lightly browned. When a wooden pick inserted into the center comes out clean, transfer the bread to a cooling rack. Let stand for 10 minutes. Cut into squares and serve hot, or complete cooling on the rack.   ❖

Cranberry Bread

MAKES ONE 9x5-INCH LOAF

What could be more quintessentially New England than fresh cranberry bread? In this recipe freshly squeezed orange juice provides a citrusy counterpoint to the tart red berries.

2 cups all-purpose flour, scoop measured
1 cup sugar
2 teaspoons baking powder
½ teaspoon baking soda
¾ teaspoon salt
¾ cup freshly squeezed orange juice
2 large eggs
¼ cup butter or margarine, melted
1 tablespoon finely grated orange zest
1 cup coarsely chopped fresh cranberries
½ cup coarsely chopped walnuts

1. Preheat the oven to 350°F. Generously grease a 9x5-inch loaf pan. In the bowl of an electric mixer, combine the flour, sugar, baking powder, baking soda, and salt. Run the mixer briefly on low speed to blend the dry ingredients.

2. In a separate bowl, whisk together the orange juice, eggs, and melted butter. With the mixer set on low speed, gradually pour the egg mixture into the dry ingredients. Beat until well moistened. Blend in the orange zest. Add the cranberries and walnuts, and stir to combine.

3. Pour into the prepared pan and bake for 50 minutes to 1 hour, covering the loaf with aluminum foil during the last 10 minutes if necessary to prevent overbrowning. When a wooden pick inserted into the center comes out clean, transfer the bread to a cooling rack. Let stand for 10 minutes, then turn out. Cool completely before slicing.   ❖

Cranberry Banana Bread

MAKES ONE 8-INCH SQUARE LOAF

Steaming squares of this aromatic bread are a welcome snack for weary leaf rakers. Offer cups of warm cider or cocoa alongside.

2 cups all-purpose flour, scoop measured
½ cup sugar
2 teaspoons baking powder
½ teaspoon baking soda
¾ teaspoon salt
¾ cup milk
1 large egg
¼ cup vegetable oil
2 ripe bananas, mashed
1 cup fresh cranberries, finely chopped

1. Preheat the oven to 375°F. Generously grease an 8-inch baking pan. In the bowl of an electric mixer, combine the flour, sugar, baking powder, baking soda, and salt. Run the mixer briefly on low speed to blend the dry ingredients.

2. In a separate bowl, whisk together the milk, egg, and oil. Stir in the mashed banana. With the mixer set on low speed, gradually pour the egg mixture into the dry ingredients. Beat until well moistened. Stir in the cranberries.

3. Pour into the prepared pan and bake for 35 to 40 minutes, or until lightly browned. When a wooden pick inserted into the center comes out clean, transfer the bread to a cooling rack. Let stand for 10 minutes. Cut into squares and serve hot, or complete cooling on the rack.   ❖

Sour Cream Cranberry Bread

MAKES ONE 9x5-INCH LOAF

Sour cream lends a sophisticated air to this almond-flavored cranberry loaf. A wonderful breakfast bread or teatime treat.

2 cups all-purpose flour, scoop measured
1 teaspoon baking powder
1 teaspoon baking soda
¾ teaspoon salt
½ cup solid vegetable shortening
1 cup sugar
2 large eggs
½ teaspoon almond extract
1 cup sour cream
1 cup whole-berry cranberry sauce
½ cup coarsely chopped walnuts

1. Preheat the oven to 350°F. Generously grease a 9x5-inch loaf pan. In a large mixing bowl, combine the flour, baking powder, baking soda, and salt. Whisk to blend the dry ingredients thoroughly.

2. In the bowl of an electric mixer, combine the shortening and sugar. Beat at high speed until light and fluffy. Beat in the eggs, one at a time. Blend in the almond extract.

With the mixer on low speed, sprinkle in the dry ingredients, alternating with the sour cream. Beat until well moistened. Stir in the cranberry sauce and walnuts.

3. Pour into the prepared pan and bake for 50 minutes to 1 hour, covering the loaf with aluminum foil during the last 10 minutes if necessary to prevent overbrowning. When a wooden pick inserted into the center comes out clean, transfer the bread to a cooling rack. Let stand for 10 minutes, then turn out. Cool completely before slicing.   ❖

Fig Loaf

MAKES ONE 9x5-INCH LOAF

Tiny bits of moist fig dot this tender loaf. Serve thinly sliced with fruit salad or with soft unripened goat cheese.

2 cups all-purpose flour, scoop measured
3 teaspoons baking powder
½ teaspoon salt
½ teaspoon allspice
½ cup solid vegetable shortening
1 cup sugar
2 large eggs
¼ cup dark rum
½ cup milk
8 dried Calimyrna figs, coarsely chopped

1. Preheat the oven to 350°F. Generously grease a 9x5-inch loaf pan. In a large mixing bowl, combine the flour, baking powder, salt, and allspice. Whisk to blend the dry ingredients thoroughly.

2. In the bowl of an electric mixer, combine the shortening and sugar. Beat at high speed until light and fluffy. Beat in the eggs, one at a time. Blend in the rum. With the mixer on low speed, sprinkle in the dry ingredients, alternating with the milk. Beat until well moistened. Stir in the figs.

3. Pour into the prepared pan and bake for 50 minutes to 1 hour, covering the loaf with aluminum foil during the last 10 minutes if necessary to prevent overbrowning. When a wooden pick inserted into the cen-

ter comes out clean, transfer the bread to a cooling rack. Let stand for 10 minutes, then turn out. Cool completely before slicing. ❖

Grape-Nuts Bread

MAKES ONE 9x5-INCH LOAF

This cereal-based bread has been a staple on New England tables since Hector was a pup. And that was some time ago.

1¼ cups Grape-Nuts cereal
1 cup buttermilk
1¼ cups all-purpose flour, scoop measured
⅓ cup sugar
2 teaspoons baking powder
½ teaspoon baking soda
½ teaspoon salt
1 large egg, beaten
¼ cup vegetable oil
½ cup raisins

1. Preheat the oven to 350°F. Generously grease a 9x5-inch loaf pan. Combine the Grape-Nuts and buttermilk in a mixing bowl and set aside for 10 minutes to soften.

2. In the bowl of an electric mixer, combine the flour, sugar, baking powder, baking soda, and salt. Run the mixer briefly on low speed to blend the dry ingredients.

3. Stir the beaten egg and vegetable oil into the softened Grape-Nuts. With the mixer set on low speed, gradually pour the egg mixture into the dry ingredients. Beat until well moistened. Stir in the raisins.

4. Pour into the prepared pan and bake for 50 minutes to 1 hour, covering the loaf with aluminum foil during the last 10 min-

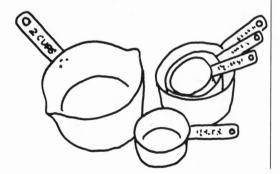

utes if necessary to prevent overbrowning. When a wooden pick inserted into the center comes out clean, transfer the bread to a cooling rack. Let stand for 10 minutes, then turn out. Cool completely before slicing. ❖

Maple Walnut Bread

MAKES ONE 9x5-INCH LOAF

Maple syrup and walnuts have been popular flavor partners in New England for generations. Here they appear in an easy-to-make quick bread your family will adore.

2 cups all-purpose flour, scoop measured
2 teaspoons baking powder
½ teaspoon baking soda
½ teaspoon salt
½ cup butter or margarine, softened
¼ cup light brown sugar
¼ cup granulated sugar
2 large eggs
½ cup pure maple syrup
¼ cup milk
1 cup coarsely chopped walnuts

1. Preheat the oven to 350°F. Generously grease a 9x5-inch loaf pan. In a large mixing bowl, combine the flour, baking powder, baking soda, and salt. Whisk to blend the dry ingredients thoroughly.

2. In the bowl of an electric mixer, combine the butter, brown sugar, and granulated sugar. Beat at high speed until light and fluffy. Beat in the eggs, one at a time. Blend in the maple syrup. With the mixer on low speed, sprinkle in the dry ingredients, alternating with the milk. Beat until well moistened. Stir in the walnuts.

3. Pour into the prepared pan and bake for 50 minutes to 1 hour, covering the loaf with aluminum foil during the last 10 minutes if necessary to prevent overbrowning. When a wooden pick inserted into the center comes out clean, transfer the bread to a cooling rack. Let stand for 10 minutes, then turn out. Cool completely before slicing. ❖

Mincemeat Bread

MAKES ONE 9x5-INCH LOAF

When you smell the wonderful aroma of this bread, all those warm memories of childhood Thanksgivings will come back to you.

1 cup all-purpose flour, scoop measured
⅔ cup light brown sugar
1 cup whole wheat flour, scoop measured
2 teaspoons baking powder
½ teaspoon baking soda
¾ teaspoon salt
½ cup sour cream
2 large eggs
¼ cup butter or margarine, melted
1 cup prepared mincemeat

1. Preheat the oven to 350°F. Generously grease a 9x5-inch loaf pan. Sift the all-purpose flour and sugar into the bowl of an electric mixer. Add the whole wheat flour, baking powder, baking soda, and salt. Run the mixer briefly on low speed to blend the dry ingredients.

2. In a separate bowl, whisk together the sour cream, eggs, and melted butter. Stir in the mincemeat. With the mixer set on low speed, gradually pour the egg mixture into the dry ingredients. Beat until thoroughly moistened.

3. Pour into the prepared pan and bake for 50 minutes to 1 hour, covering the loaf with aluminum foil during the last 10 minutes if necessary to prevent overbrowning. When a wooden pick inserted into the center comes out clean, transfer the bread to a cooling rack. Let stand for 10 minutes, then turn out. Cool completely before slicing. ❖

Molasses Bread

MAKES ONE 9x5-INCH LOAF

A spicy, deep-flavored loaf that's just the thing to serve with baked beans and ham.

2½ cups all-purpose flour, scoop measured
1½ teaspoons baking soda
¾ teaspoon salt
1 teaspoon allspice
½ teaspoon ground ginger
½ cup solid vegetable shortening
½ cup light brown sugar
1 large egg
1 cup molasses
½ cup milk

1. Preheat the oven to 350°F. Generously grease a 9x5-inch loaf pan. In a large mixing bowl, combine the flour, baking soda, salt, allspice, and ginger. Whisk to blend thoroughly.

2. In the bowl of an electric mixer, combine the shortening and sugar. Beat at high speed until light and fluffy. Beat in the egg. Blend in the molasses. With the mixer on low speed, sprinkle in the dry ingredients, alternating with the milk. Beat until well moistened.

3. Pour into the prepared pan and bake for 50 minutes to 1 hour, covering the loaf with aluminum foil during the last 10 minutes if necessary to prevent overbrowning. When a wooden pick inserted into the center comes out clean, transfer the bread to a cooling rack. Let stand for 10 minutes, then turn out. Cool completely before slicing. ❖

Oatmeal Buttermilk Bread

MAKES ONE 9x5-INCH LOAF

The mellow flavor of honey caresses this cinnamon-oatmeal loaf. This bread is marvelous toasted.

1½ cups all-purpose flour, scoop measured
¾ cup quick-cooking rolled oats
1 teaspoon baking powder
1 teaspoon baking soda
½ teaspoon salt
½ teaspoon cinnamon
¼ cup butter or margarine, softened
¼ cup sugar
¼ cup honey
2 large eggs
⅔ cup buttermilk
½ cup raisins

1. Preheat the oven to 350°F. Generously grease a 9x5-inch loaf pan. In a large mixing bowl, combine the flour, oats, baking powder, baking soda, salt, and cinnamon. Whisk to blend thoroughly.

2. In the bowl of an electric mixer, combine the butter, sugar, and honey. Beat at high speed until light and fluffy. Beat in the eggs, one at a time. With the mixer on low speed, sprinkle in the dry ingredients, alternating with the buttermilk. Stir in the raisins.

3. Pour into the prepared pan and bake for 50 minutes to 1 hour, covering the loaf with aluminum foil during the last 10 minutes if necessary to prevent overbrowning. When a wooden pick inserted into the center comes out clean, transfer the bread to a cooling rack. Let stand for 10 minutes, then turn out. Cool completely before slicing. ❖

Oatmeal Raisin Bread

MAKES ONE 9x5-INCH LOAF

A traditional oatmeal loaf, studded with raisins. Serve generously sliced for breakfast or with soup.

1¼ cups all-purpose flour, scoop measured
1¼ cups quick-cooking rolled oats
2 tablespoons sugar
1 teaspoon baking powder
1 teaspoon baking soda
¾ teaspoon salt
1 cup buttermilk
1 large egg
¼ cup butter or margarine, melted
⅓ cup honey
½ cup raisins

1. Preheat the oven to 350°F. Generously grease a 9x5-inch loaf pan. In the bowl of an electric mixer, combine the flour, oats, sugar, baking powder, baking soda, and salt. Run the mixer briefly on low speed to blend the dry ingredients.

2. In a separate bowl, whisk together the buttermilk, egg, and melted butter. Stir in the honey. With the mixer set on low speed,

gradually pour the egg mixture into the dry ingredients. Beat until well moistened. Stir in the raisins.

3. Pour into the prepared pan and bake for 50 minutes to 1 hour, covering the loaf with aluminum foil during the last 10 minutes if necessary to prevent overbrowning. When a wooden pick inserted into the center comes out clean, transfer the bread to a cooling rack. Let stand for 10 minutes, then turn out. Cool completely before slicing. ❖

Olive Bread

MAKES ONE 9x5-INCH LOAF

Green olives stuffed with red pimientos lend festive color to this delightful bread. Spread thin slices with softened cream cheese to create tiny sandwiches and offer as an appetizer.

2½ cups all-purpose flour, scoop measured
¼ cup sugar
3 teaspoons baking powder
¾ teaspoon salt
1 cup milk
1 large egg
¼ cup butter or margarine, melted
1 cup pimiento-stuffed green olives, sliced

1. Preheat the oven to 350°F. Generously grease a 9x5-inch loaf pan. In the bowl of an electric mixer, combine the flour, sugar, baking powder, and salt. Run the mixer briefly on low speed to blend the dry ingredients thoroughly.

2. In a separate bowl, whisk together the milk, egg, and melted butter. With the mixer set on low speed, gradually pour the egg mixture into the dry ingredients. Beat until well moistened. Stir in the olives.

3. Pour into the prepared pan and bake for 50 minutes to 1 hour, covering the loaf with aluminum foil during the last 10 minutes if necessary to prevent overbrowning. When a wooden pick inserted into the center comes out clean, transfer the bread to a cooling rack. Let stand for 10 minutes, then turn out. Cool completely before slicing. ❖

Orange and Date Loaf

MAKES ONE 9x5-INCH LOAF

The entire orange, flesh and all, is used to create this moist, tender bread. Offer with whipped butter or cream cheese.

1 large orange
½ cup sugar
2 large eggs
¼ cup milk
¼ cup vegetable oil
2½ cups all-purpose flour, scoop measured
2 teaspoons baking powder
½ teaspoon baking soda
½ teaspoon salt
⅔ cup coarsely chopped dates

1. Preheat the oven to 350°F. Generously grease a 9x5-inch loaf pan. Remove the orange zest with a swivel-blade peeler and drop into the container of a processor or blender. Remove the white pithy membrane from the orange and discard. Cut the orange in half and pry out any seeds. Break the halves into segments and drop into the processor bowl. Add the sugar and whirl until coarsely chopped. Add the eggs, milk, and oil, and process briefly to blend.

2. In the bowl of an electric mixer, combine the flour, baking powder, baking soda, and salt. Run the mixer briefly on low speed to blend the dry ingredients. With the mixer set on low speed, gradually pour the orange mixture into the dry ingredients. Beat until well moistened. Stir in the dates.

3. Pour into the prepared pan and bake for 50 minutes to 1 hour, covering the loaf

with aluminum foil during the last 10 minutes if necessary to prevent overbrowning. When a wooden pick inserted into the center comes out clean, transfer the bread to a cooling rack. Let stand for 10 minutes, then turn out. Cool completely before slicing. ❖

Orange Oatmeal Bread

MAKES ONE 9x5-INCH LOAF

Perfumed with cinnamon, this nutritious oatmeal loaf makes a welcome bedtime snack. Serve with a glass of warm milk for sweet dreams.

1 large orange
¾ cup sugar
2 large eggs
⅓ cup milk
2 tablespoons butter or margarine, melted
1½ cups all-purpose flour, scoop measured
1 cup quick-cooking rolled oats
2 teaspoons baking powder
½ teaspoon baking soda
½ teaspoon salt
½ teaspoon cinnamon

1. Preheat the oven to 350°F. Generously grease a 9x5-inch loaf pan. Remove the orange zest with a swivel-blade peeler and drop into the container of a processor or blender. Remove the white pithy membrane from the orange and discard. Cut the orange in half and pry out any seeds. Break the halves into segments and drop into the processor bowl. Add the sugar and whirl until coarsely chopped. Add the eggs, milk, and melted butter, and process briefly to blend.

2. In the bowl of an electric mixer, combine the flour, oats, baking powder, baking soda, salt, and cinnamon. Run the mixer briefly on low speed to blend the dry ingredients. With the mixer set on low speed, gradually pour the orange mixture into the dry ingredients. Beat until well moistened.

3. Pour into the prepared pan and bake for 50 minutes to 1 hour, covering the loaf with aluminum foil during the last 10 min-

utes if necessary to prevent overbrowning. When a wooden pick inserted into the center comes out clean, transfer the bread to a cooling rack. Let stand for 10 minutes, then turn out. Cool completely before slicing. ❖

Candied Orange Bread

MAKES ONE 9x5-INCH LOAF

Small chunks of candied orange provide bursts of flavor. This is an especially nice loaf to have on hand for the Christmas holidays.

2 cups all-purpose flour, scoop measured
2 teaspoons baking powder
½ teaspoon baking soda
¾ teaspoon salt
½ cup butter or margarine, softened
1 cup sugar
2 large eggs
½ cup buttermilk
12 ounces candied orange slices, coarsely chopped
½ cup shredded coconut
½ cup coarsely chopped walnuts

1. Preheat the oven to 350°F. Generously grease a 9x5-inch loaf pan. In a large mixing bowl, combine the flour, baking powder, baking soda, and salt. Whisk to blend the dry ingredients thoroughly.

2. In the bowl of an electric mixer, combine the butter and sugar. Beat at high speed until light and fluffy. Beat in the eggs, one at a time. With the mixer on low speed, sprinkle in the dry ingredients, alternating with the buttermilk. Beat until well moistened. Stir in the candied orange, coconut, and walnuts.

3. Pour into the prepared pan and bake for 50 minutes to 1 hour, covering the loaf with aluminum foil during the last 10 minutes if necessary to prevent overbrowning. When a wooden pick inserted into the center comes out clean, transfer the bread to a cooling rack. Let stand for 10 minutes, then turn out. Cool completely before slicing. ❖

Granola Peach Bread

MAKES ONE 9x5-INCH LOAF

Fresh peaches are puréed and then blended with crushed granola to produce a hearty, nutritious loaf.

3 large fresh peaches, peeled, pitted, and sliced
1½ cups all-purpose flour, scoop measured
⅔ cup crushed granola cereal
2 teaspoons baking powder
½ teaspoon baking soda
¾ teaspoon salt
⅓ cup butter or margarine, softened
⅔ cup sugar
2 large eggs
1 teaspoon almond extract
½ cup sour cream

1. Drop the peach slices into the container of a blender or processor and whirl to a coarse purée. Do not overprocess. Set aside.

2. Preheat the oven to 350°F. Generously grease a 9x5-inch loaf pan. In a large mixing bowl, combine the flour, granola, baking powder, baking soda, and salt. Whisk to blend thoroughly.

3. In the bowl of an electric mixer, combine the butter and sugar. Beat at high speed until light and fluffy. Beat in the eggs, one at a time. Blend in the almond extract. With the mixer on low speed, sprinkle in the dry ingredients, alternating with the sour cream. Stir in the puréed peaches and beat until well moistened.

4. Pour into the prepared pan and bake for 50 minutes to 1 hour, covering the loaf

with aluminum foil during the last 10 minutes if necessary to prevent overbrowning. When a wooden pick inserted into the center comes out clean, transfer the bread to a cooling rack. Let stand for 10 minutes, then turn out. Cool completely before slicing. ❖

Peanut Butter Whole Wheat Bread

MAKES ONE 9x5-INCH LOAF

Not only is this bread wholesome, it is absolutely irresistible. Your kids will beg you to make more.

1¼ cups whole wheat flour, scoop measured
1 cup all-purpose flour, scoop measured
2 teaspoons baking powder
½ teaspoon baking soda
¾ teaspoon salt
½ cup smooth peanut butter
⅓ cup solid vegetable shortening
½ cup sugar
1 large egg
½ cup buttermilk
½ cup coarsely chopped dry-roasted peanuts

1. Preheat the oven to 350°F. Generously grease a 9x5-inch loaf pan. In a large mixing bowl, combine the whole wheat flour, all-purpose flour, baking powder, baking soda, and salt. Whisk to blend thoroughly.

2. In the bowl of an electric mixer, combine the peanut butter and shortening. Beat at high speed until light and fluffy. Sprinkle in the sugar. Beat in the egg. With the mixer on low speed, sprinkle in the dry ingredients, alternating with the buttermilk. Beat until well moistened. Stir in the peanuts.

3. Pour into the prepared pan and bake for 50 minutes to 1 hour, covering the loaf with aluminum foil during the last 10 minutes if necessary to prevent overbrowning. When a wooden pick inserted into the center comes out clean, transfer the bread to a cooling rack. Let stand for 10 minutes, then turn out. Cool completely before slicing. ❖

Pear Pecan Bread

MAKES ONE 9x5-INCH LOAF

A lovely fall bread to celebrate the harvest of native pears. Serve thinly sliced, spread with unsalted butter.

2 cups all-purpose flour, scoop measured
2 teaspoons baking powder
½ teaspoon baking soda
¾ teaspoon salt
½ teaspoon nutmeg
½ cup butter or margarine, softened
1 cup sugar
2 large eggs
1 teaspoon vanilla extract
½ cup unflavored yogurt
1 cup coarsely chopped fresh pears
½ cup coarsely chopped pecans

1. Preheat the oven to 350°F. Generously grease a 9x5-inch loaf pan. In a large mixing bowl, combine the flour, baking powder, baking soda, salt, and nutmeg. Whisk to blend thoroughly.

2. In the bowl of an electric mixer, combine the butter and sugar. Beat at high speed until light and fluffy. Beat in the eggs, one at a time. Blend in the vanilla. With the mixer on low speed, sprinkle in the dry ingredients, alternating with the yogurt. Beat until well moistened. Stir in the pears and pecans.

3. Pour into the prepared pan and bake for 50 minutes to 1 hour, covering the loaf with aluminum foil during the last 10 minutes if necessary to prevent overbrowning. When a wooden pick inserted into the center comes out clean, transfer the bread to a cooling rack. Let stand for 10 minutes, then turn out. Cool completely before slicing. ❖

Pineapple Yogurt Bread

MAKES ONE 9x5-INCH LOAF

Yogurt imparts tangy moistness to this whole wheat loaf, which is loaded with bits of pineapple.

1 cup canned pineapple chunks
1 cup whole wheat flour, scoop measured
1 cup all-purpose flour, scoop measured
½ cup sugar
2 tablespoons wheat germ
2 teaspoons baking powder
½ teaspoon baking soda
¾ teaspoon salt
1 cup unflavored yogurt
2 large eggs
⅓ cup honey
3 tablespoons butter or margarine, melted
½ cup coarsely chopped walnuts

1. Coarsely chop the pineapple and set it aside to drain in a sieve.

2. Preheat the oven to 350°F. Generously grease a 9x5-inch loaf pan. In the bowl of an electric mixer, combine the whole wheat flour, all-purpose flour, sugar, wheat germ, baking powder, baking soda, and salt. Run the mixer briefly on low speed to blend the dry ingredients.

3. In a separate bowl, whisk together the yogurt, eggs, honey, and melted butter. With the mixer set on low speed, gradually pour the egg mixture into the dry ingredients. Beat until well moistened. Stir in the pineapple and walnuts.

4. Pour into the prepared pan and bake for 50 minutes to 1 hour, covering the loaf with aluminum foil during the last 10 minutes if necessary to prevent overbrowning. When a wooden pick inserted into the center comes out clean, transfer the bread to a cooling rack. Let stand for 10 minutes, then turn out. Cool completely before slicing. ❖

Pistachio Lemon Loaf

MAKES ONE 9x5-INCH LOAF

A smattering of pistachio nuts accents this lemon-flavored bread. Serve thinly sliced with cream cheese that has been whipped with a generous amount of lemon curd.

2 cups all-purpose flour, scoop measured
2 teaspoons baking powder

½ teaspoon baking soda
¾ teaspoon salt
⅓ cup butter or margarine, softened
⅔ cup sugar
2 large eggs
1 tablespoon finely grated lemon zest
1 cup lemon-flavored yogurt
½ cup coarsely chopped pistachio nuts

1. Preheat the oven to 350°F. Generously grease a 9x5-inch loaf pan. In a large mixing bowl, combine the flour, baking powder, baking soda, and salt. Whisk to blend the dry ingredients thoroughly.

2. In the bowl of an electric mixer, combine the butter and sugar. Beat at high speed until light and fluffy. Beat in the eggs, one at a time. Blend in the lemon zest. With the mixer on low speed, sprinkle in the dry ingredients, alternating with the yogurt. Beat until well moistened. Stir in the pistachio nuts.

3. Pour into the prepared pan and bake for 50 minutes to 1 hour, covering the loaf with aluminum foil during the last 10 minutes if necessary to prevent overbrowning. When a wooden pick inserted into the center comes out clean, transfer the bread to a cooling rack. Let stand for 10 minutes, then turn out. Cool completely before slicing. ❖

Poppy Seed Loaf

MAKES ONE 9x5-INCH LOAF

Poppy seeds are traditionally a favorite ethnic flavoring. Here they add interest to a sour cream quick bread.

2¼ cups all-purpose flour, scoop measured
2 teaspoons baking powder
½ teaspoon baking soda
¾ teaspoon salt
½ teaspoon nutmeg
½ cup butter or margarine, softened
1 cup sugar
2 large eggs
1 tablespoon freshly squeezed lemon juice
1 tablespoon finely grated lemon zest
1¼ cups sour cream
⅓ cup poppy seeds

1. Preheat the oven to 350°F. Generously grease a 9x5-inch loaf pan. In a large mixing bowl, combine the flour, baking powder, baking soda, salt, and nutmeg. Whisk to blend thoroughly.

2. In the bowl of an electric mixer, combine the butter and sugar. Beat at high speed until light and fluffy. Beat in the eggs, one at a time. Blend in the lemon juice and lemon zest. With the mixer on low speed, sprinkle in the dry ingredients, alternating with the sour cream. Beat until well moistened. Stir in the poppy seeds.

3. Pour into the prepared pan and bake for 50 minutes to 1 hour, covering the loaf with aluminum foil during the last 10 minutes if necessary to prevent overbrowning. When a wooden pick inserted into the center comes out clean, transfer the bread to a cooling rack. Let stand for 10 minutes, then turn out. Cool completely before slicing. ❖

Walnut Prune Bread

MAKES ONE 9x5-INCH LOAF

In spite of their dreary reputation, prunes take on a bit of glamour in this delicious bread. Serve warm with a glass of cold milk or a cup of tea.

1 package (12 ounces) pitted prunes, coarsely chopped
1⅓ cups cold water
1 cup sugar
¼ cup butter or margarine
2 cups all-purpose flour, scoop measured
3 teaspoons baking powder
¾ teaspoon salt
¾ teaspoon cinnamon
½ teaspoon nutmeg
1 large egg, beaten
1 teaspoon vanilla extract
½ cup chopped walnuts

1. Combine the prunes, water, sugar, and butter in a wide saucepan. Bring to a boil, then remove from the heat and let stand for 30 minutes.

2. Preheat the oven to 350°F. Generously grease a 9x5-inch loaf pan. In the bowl of an electric mixer, combine the flour, baking powder, salt, cinnamon, and nutmeg. Run the mixer briefly on low speed to blend the dry ingredients.

3. With the mixer set on low speed, gradually pour the prune mixture into the dry ingredients. Beat until well moistened. Blend in the beaten egg and vanilla. Stir in the walnuts.

4. Pour into the prepared pan and bake for 50 minutes to 1 hour, covering the loaf with aluminum foil during the last 10 minutes if necessary to prevent overbrowning. When a wooden pick inserted into the center comes out clean, transfer the bread to a cooling rack. Let stand for 10 minutes, then turn out. Cool completely before slicing. ❖

Pumpkin Cider Bread

MAKES ONE 9x5-INCH LOAF

Apple cider is reduced to increase its flavor intensity for this spicy pumpkin loaf.

1 cup apple cider
2 cups all-purpose flour, scoop measured
¾ cup light brown sugar
2 teaspoons baking powder
½ teaspoon baking soda
¾ teaspoon salt
½ teaspoon cinnamon
¼ teaspoon nutmeg
¼ teaspoon allspice
2 large eggs
¼ cup vegetable oil
1 cup pumpkin purée
1 tablespoon finely grated orange zest
½ cup coarsely chopped walnuts

1. In a nonreactive saucepan, boil the cider gently until it is reduced to ¼ cup. Set aside.

2. Preheat the oven to 350°F. Generously grease a 9x5-inch loaf pan. Sift the flour and sugar into the bowl of an electric mixer. Add the baking powder, baking soda, salt,

cinnamon, nutmeg, and allspice. Run the mixer briefly on low speed to blend the dry ingredients.

3. In a separate bowl, whisk together the eggs, vegetable oil, and pumpkin purée. Blend in the reduced cider and orange zest. With the mixer set on low speed, gradually pour the egg mixture into the dry ingredients. Beat until well moistened. Stir in the walnuts.

4. Pour into the prepared pan and bake for 50 minutes to 1 hour, covering the loaf with aluminum foil during the last 10 minutes if necessary to prevent overbrowning. When a wooden pick inserted into the center comes out clean, transfer the bread to a cooling rack. Let stand for 10 minutes, then turn out. Cool completely before slicing. ❖

Pumpkin Corn Bread

MAKES ONE 9-INCH SQUARE LOAF

The crunch of yellow cornmeal adds textural interest to this satisfying pumpkin bread. For a slightly different twist, present generous squares with a traditional turkey dinner.

½ cup all-purpose flour, scoop measured
½ cup light brown sugar
1 cup yellow cornmeal
½ cup whole wheat flour, scoop measured
3 teaspoons baking powder
¾ teaspoon salt
½ teaspoon cinnamon
½ teaspoon nutmeg
½ teaspoon ground cloves
1 large egg
¼ cup vegetable oil
1 cup pumpkin purée

1. Preheat the oven to 350°F. Generously grease a 9-inch square baking pan. Sift the all-purpose flour and sugar into the bowl of an electric mixer. Add the cornmeal, whole wheat flour, baking powder, salt, cinnamon, nutmeg, and cloves. Run the mixer briefly on low speed to blend the dry ingredients thoroughly.

2. In a separate bowl, whisk together the egg and oil. Stir in the pumpkin purée. With the mixer set on low speed, gradually pour the egg mixture into the dry ingredients. Beat until well moistened.

3. Pour into the prepared pan and bake for 35 to 40 minutes, or until the surface is lightly browned. When a wooden pick inserted into the center comes out clean, transfer the bread to a cooling rack. Let stand for about 10 minutes. Cut into squares and serve hot, or complete cooling on the rack. ❖

Pumpkin Pecan Bread

MAKES ONE 9x5-INCH LOAF

The all-American taste of pecans has a natural kinship with pumpkin. Here the two combine to form a satisfying quick bread.

2 cups all-purpose flour, scoop measured
½ cup light brown sugar
3 teaspoons baking powder
¾ teaspoon salt
½ teaspoon cinnamon
¼ cup milk
2 large eggs
1 cup pumpkin purée
¼ cup butter or margarine, melted
¾ cup coarsely chopped pecans

1. Preheat the oven to 350°F. Generously grease a 9x5-inch loaf pan. Sift the flour and sugar into the bowl of an electric mixer. Add the baking powder, salt, and cinnamon. Run the mixer briefly on low speed to blend the dry ingredients.

2. In a separate bowl, whisk together the milk, eggs, pumpkin purée, and melted butter. With the mixer set on low speed, gradually pour the egg mixture into the dry ingredients. Beat until well moistened. Stir in the pecans.

3. Pour into the prepared pan and bake for 50 minutes to 1 hour, covering the loaf with aluminum foil during the last 10 min-

utes if necessary to prevent overbrowning. When a wooden pick inserted into the center comes out clean, transfer the bread to a cooling rack. Let stand for 10 minutes, then turn out. Cool completely before slicing. ❖

Pumpkin Whole Wheat Bread

MAKES ONE 9x5-INCH LOAF

Pumpkin bread is a classic New England treat, almost always baked in the fall. Enjoy the fragrance of this loaf as it fills the house with the scent of cinnamon and cloves.

1¼ cups whole wheat flour, scoop measured
1 cup all-purpose flour, scoop measured
2 teaspoons baking powder
½ teaspoon baking soda
¾ teaspoon salt
½ teaspoon cinnamon
½ teaspoon ground cloves
⅓ cup solid vegetable shortening
⅔ cup sugar
2 large eggs
1 cup pumpkin purée
⅓ cup milk
½ cup coarsely chopped walnuts

1. Preheat the oven to 350°F. Generously grease a 9x5-inch loaf pan. In a large mixing bowl, combine the whole wheat flour, all-purpose flour, baking powder, baking soda, and salt. Add the cinnamon and cloves. Whisk to blend thoroughly.

2. In the bowl of an electric mixer, combine the shortening and sugar. Beat at high speed until light and fluffy. Beat in the eggs, one at a time. Blend in the pumpkin purée. With the mixer on low speed, sprinkle in the dry ingredients, alternating with the milk. Beat until well moistened. Stir in the walnuts.

3. Pour into the prepared pan and bake for 50 minutes to 1 hour, covering the loaf with aluminum foil during the last 10 minutes if necessary to prevent overbrowning. When a wooden pick inserted into the center comes out clean, transfer the bread to a cooling rack. Let stand for 10 minutes, then turn out. Cool completely before slicing. ❖

Raspberry Almond Loaf

MAKES ONE 9x5-INCH LOAF

Bright bits of fresh raspberry dot this delicate almond-scented bread, a particular favorite of mine. I like to eat it plain, but a touch of whipped, unsalted butter would be an elegant complement.

2 cups all-purpose flour, scoop measured
2 teaspoons baking powder
½ teaspoon baking soda
¾ teaspoon salt
½ cup butter or margarine, softened
1 cup sugar
2 large eggs
1 teaspoon almond extract
¾ cup sour cream
½ cup slivered almonds, toasted
1 cup fresh raspberries, rinsed and gently
   patted dry

1. Preheat the oven to 350°F. Generously grease a 9x5-inch loaf pan. In a large mixing bowl, combine the flour, baking powder, baking soda, and salt. Whisk to blend the dry ingredients thoroughly.

2. In the bowl of an electric mixer, combine the butter and sugar. Beat at high speed until light and fluffy. Beat in the eggs, one at a time. Blend in the almond extract. With the mixer on low speed, sprinkle in the dry ingredients, alternating with the

sour cream. Beat until well moistened. Stir in the almonds and raspberries.

3. Pour into the prepared pan and bake for 50 minutes to 1 hour, covering the loaf with aluminum foil during the last 10 minutes if necessary to prevent overbrowning. When a wooden pick inserted into the center comes out clean, transfer the bread to a cooling rack. Let stand for 10 minutes, then turn out. Cool completely before slicing. ❖

Rhubarb Spice Bread

MAKES ONE 9x5-INCH LOAF

A sweet loaf studded with bits of tart rhubarb. Classic "apple pie" spices underscore the rhubarb taste.

1 cup milk
1 tablespoon freshly squeezed lemon juice
2 cups all-purpose flour, scoop measured
1 cup sugar
1 teaspoon baking soda
¾ teaspoon salt
1 teaspoon cinnamon
½ teaspoon nutmeg
¼ teaspoon ground cloves
2 large eggs
¼ cup butter or margarine, melted
1 cup finely chopped rhubarb

1. Combine the milk and lemon juice in a glass measuring cup. Set aside for 10 minutes to sour and thicken slightly.

2. Preheat the oven to 350°F. Generously grease a 9x5-inch loaf pan. In the bowl of an electric mixer, combine the flour, sugar, baking soda, salt, cinnamon, nutmeg, and cloves. Run the mixer briefly on low speed to blend the dry ingredients.

3. In a separate bowl, whisk together the sour milk, eggs, and melted butter. With the mixer set on low speed, gradually pour the egg mixture into the dry ingredients. Beat until thoroughly moistened. Stir in the rhubarb.

4. Pour into the prepared pan and bake for 50 minutes to 1 hour, covering the loaf with aluminum foil during the last 10 min-

utes if necessary to prevent overbrowning. When a wooden pick inserted into the center comes out clean, transfer the bread to a cooling rack. Let stand for 10 minutes, then turn out. Cool completely before slicing. ❖

Rhubarb Walnut Bread

MAKES ONE 9x5-INCH LOAF

One of the first spring plants to appear in New England gardens is tart rhubarb. It is a popular vegetable in the region and is often prepared in combination with fresh strawberries. Here the stalks are finely chopped and added to an attractive bread, crusted with cinnamon sugar.

1 cup milk
1 tablespoon freshly squeezed lemon juice
2 cups all-purpose flour, scoop measured
½ cup light brown sugar
½ cup granulated sugar
1 teaspoon baking soda
¾ teaspoon salt
2 large eggs
¼ cup vegetable oil
1 teaspoon vanilla extract
1 cup finely chopped rhubarb
½ cup coarsely chopped walnuts
2 tablespoons granulated sugar, blended with
　1 teaspoon cinnamon

1. Combine the milk and lemon juice in a glass measuring cup. Set aside for 10 minutes to sour and thicken slightly.

2. Preheat the oven to 350°F. Generously grease a 9x5-inch loaf pan. Sift the flour and brown sugar into the bowl of an electric mixer. Add the granulated sugar, baking soda, and salt. Run the mixer briefly on low speed to blend the dry ingredients.

3. In a separate bowl, whisk together the eggs and oil. Blend in the sour milk and vanilla. With the mixer set on low speed, gradually pour the egg mixture into the dry ingredients. Beat until well moistened. Stir in the rhubarb and walnuts.

4. Pour into the prepared pan. Sprinkle the surface with the cinnamon sugar, and

bake for 50 minutes to 1 hour, or until the surface is crusted and nicely browned. When a wooden pick inserted into the center comes out clean, transfer the bread to a cooling rack. Let stand for 10 minutes, then turn out. Cool completely before slicing. ❖

Honey-Spiced Rye Bread

MAKES ONE 9x5-INCH LOAF

With a few exceptions, quick breads aren't usually used for sandwiches because their texture is too crumbly. This particular bread, however, makes lovely sandwiches when filled with homemade ham salad.

1½ cups rye flour, scoop measured
1 cup all-purpose flour, scoop measured
2 tablespoons sugar
2 teaspoons baking powder
½ teaspoon baking soda
½ teaspoon salt
1 teaspoon cinnamon
½ teaspoon nutmeg
½ teaspoon allspice
⅔ cup milk
⅓ cup honey
2 large eggs
3 tablespoons vegetable oil
2 tablespoons freshly squeezed lemon juice
½ cup coarsely chopped almonds

1. Preheat the oven to 350°F. Generously grease a 9x5-inch loaf pan. In the bowl of an electric mixer, combine the rye flour, all-purpose flour, baking powder, baking soda, and salt. Add the cinnamon, nutmeg, and allspice. Run the mixer briefly on low speed to blend the dry ingredients.

2. In a separate bowl, whisk together the milk, honey, eggs, and oil. Blend in the lemon juice. With the mixer set on low speed, gradually pour the egg mixture into the dry ingredients. Beat until well moistened. Stir in the almonds.

3. Pour into the prepared pan and bake for 50 minutes to 1 hour, covering the loaf

with aluminum foil during the last 10 minutes if necessary to prevent overbrowning. When a wooden pick inserted into the center comes out clean, transfer the bread to a cooling rack. Let stand for 10 minutes, then turn out. Cool completely before slicing. ❖

Molasses Rye Quick Bread

MAKES ONE 9x5-INCH LOAF

A substantial, wholesome loaf that is easy and quick to prepare. Serve warm with a hearty stew or chili.

1½ cups rye flour, scoop measured
1 cup all-purpose flour, scoop measured
1 teaspoon baking soda
¾ teaspoon salt
⅔ cup buttermilk
2 large eggs
⅓ cup molasses
3 tablespoons butter or margarine, melted
2 teaspoons caraway seeds

1. Preheat the oven to 350°F. Generously grease a 9x5-inch loaf pan. In the bowl of an electric mixer, combine the rye flour, all-purpose flour, baking soda, and salt. Run the mixer briefly on low speed to blend the dry ingredients.

2. In a separate bowl, whisk together the buttermilk, eggs, molasses, and melted butter. With the mixer set on low speed, gradually pour the egg mixture into the dry ingredients. Beat until well moistened. Stir in the caraway seeds.

3. Pour into the prepared pan and bake for 50 minutes to 1 hour, covering the loaf with aluminum foil during the last 10 minutes if necessary to prevent overbrowning. When a wooden pick inserted into the center comes out clean, transfer the bread to a cooling rack. Let stand for 10 minutes, then turn out. Cool completely before slicing. To serve warm, wrap several slices in aluminum foil and heat in a 400°F. oven for 5 to 8 minutes. ❖

Raisin Rye Bread

MAKES ONE 9x5-INCH LOAF

Scented with ginger, this raisin-dotted loaf is just the thing for a picnic supper of cold sliced ham.

1¼ cups rye flour, scoop measured
1 cup all-purpose flour, scoop measured
2 tablespoons sugar
2 teaspoons baking powder
½ teaspoon baking soda
¾ teaspoon salt
½ teaspoon cinnamon
½ teaspoon ground ginger
1 cup milk
1 large egg
⅓ cup honey
¼ cup vegetable oil
½ cup raisins

1. Preheat the oven to 350°F. Generously grease a 9x5-inch loaf pan. In the bowl of an electric mixer, combine the rye flour, all-purpose flour, sugar, baking powder, baking soda, and salt. Add the cinnamon and ginger. Run the mixer briefly on low speed to blend the dry ingredients.

2. In a separate bowl, whisk together the milk, egg, honey, and oil. With the mixer set on low speed, gradually pour the egg mixture into the dry ingredients. Beat until well moistened. Stir in the raisins.

3. Pour into the prepared pan and bake for 50 minutes to 1 hour, covering the loaf with aluminum foil during the last 10 minutes if necessary to prevent overbrowning. When a wooden pick inserted into the center comes out clean, transfer the bread to a cooling rack. Let stand for 10 minutes, then turn out. Cool completely before slicing. ❖

Irish Soda Bread

MAKES 1 ROUND LOAF

This is the classic buttermilk soda bread with the familiar crumbly texture. The only deviation is the inclusion of golden raisins, which are a luxurious touch.

2 cups all-purpose flour, scoop measured
2 tablespoons sugar
1 teaspoon baking powder
1 teaspoon baking soda
¾ teaspoon salt
4 tablespoons butter or margarine, cut into small pieces
½ cup golden raisins
1 cup buttermilk

1. Preheat the oven to 375°F. Lightly grease a baking sheet without sides. Combine the flour, sugar, baking powder, baking soda, and salt in a large mixing bowl. Whisk to blend thoroughly. Add the butter and cut in with a knife until the mixture is crumbly, then add the raisins and toss to combine.

2. Make a well in the dry ingredients. Pour in the buttermilk and toss with a fork until the dough holds together. Gather the dough into a ball and roll it around the inside of the bowl to pick up any stray particles. Transfer to a lightly floured surface and knead 60 times, sifting on flour if necessary to prevent sticking. Pat the dough into a 9-inch round. Score the round into quarters with the dull edge of a floured chef's knife. Make the marks about 1½ inches deep. Transfer the round to the prepared baking sheet and place in the preheated oven. Bake for 25 to 30 minutes, or until lightly browned. Transfer to a wire rack to cool. ❖

Squash Rum Bread

MAKES ONE 9x5-INCH LOAF

Rum was the secret ingredient in many old New England recipes. It is said that even the most straight-laced cook would add a dash of the flavorful liquor, which was locally distilled from molasses.

2 cups all-purpose flour, scoop measured
2 teaspoons baking powder
½ teaspoon baking soda
½ teaspoon salt
1 teaspoon cinnamon

½ teaspoon ground cloves
½ teaspoon ground ginger
½ cup butter or margarine, softened
1 cup sugar
2 large eggs
¼ cup dark rum
1 teaspoon vanilla extract
1 cup puréed acorn or butternut squash
½ cup coarsely chopped walnuts
½ cup golden raisins

1. Preheat the oven to 350°F. Generously grease a 9x5-inch loaf pan. In a large mixing bowl, combine the flour, baking powder, baking soda, and salt. Add the cinnamon, cloves, and ginger. Whisk to blend the dry ingredients thoroughly.

2. In the bowl of an electric mixer, combine the butter and sugar. Beat at high speed until light and fluffy. Beat in the eggs, one at a time. Blend in the rum and vanilla. Gradually beat in the squash purée. With the mixer on low speed, sprinkle in the dry ingredients. Beat until well moistened. Stir in the walnuts and raisins.

3. Pour into the prepared pan and bake for 50 minutes to 1 hour, covering the loaf with aluminum foil during the last 10 minutes if necessary to prevent overbrowning. When a wooden pick inserted into the center comes out clean, transfer the bread to a cooling rack. Let stand for 10 minutes, then turn out. Cool completely before slicing. ❖

Herman Starter Squash Bread

MAKES ONE 9x5-INCH LOAF

A tangy sourdough loaf, packed with nutritious winter squash. This homey bread is wonderful with roast chicken or pork.

1 cup all-purpose flour, scoop measured
½ cup whole wheat flour, scoop measured
½ cup sugar
2 teaspoons baking powder
½ teaspoon baking soda
¾ teaspoon salt
½ teaspoon cinnamon

¼ teaspoon nutmeg
¼ teaspoon ground ginger
1 cup Herman sourdough starter (p. 49), at room temperature
1 cup puréed acorn or butternut squash
1 large egg, beaten
¼ cup vegetable oil
½ cup coarsely chopped walnuts
½ cup raisins

1. Preheat the oven to 350°F. Generously grease a 9x5-inch loaf pan. In a large mixing bowl, combine the all-purpose flour, whole wheat flour, sugar, baking powder, baking soda, and salt. Add the cinnamon, nutmeg, and ginger. Whisk to blend the dry ingredients thoroughly.

2. Measure the sourdough starter into the bowl of an electric mixer. Blend in the squash purée, beaten egg, and vegetable oil. With the mixer on low speed, sprinkle in the dry ingredients. Beat until well moistened. Stir in the walnuts and raisins.

3. Pour into the prepared pan and bake for 50 minutes to 1 hour, covering the loaf with aluminum foil during the last 10 minutes if necessary to prevent overbrowning. When a wooden pick inserted into the center comes out clean, transfer the bread to a cooling rack. Let stand for 10 minutes, then turn out. Cool completely before slicing. ❖

Strawberry Whole Wheat Bread

MAKES ONE 9x5-INCH LOAF

If you want to start a fight, just say you think the best strawberries come from California. Any New Englander knows better. The cool northeastern soil produces exceptionally succulent berries. In this recipe, bits of fresh strawberry enliven a whole wheat loaf.

1¼ cups whole wheat flour, scoop measured
1 cup all-purpose flour, scoop measured
¼ cup wheat germ
3 teaspoons baking powder
¾ teaspoon salt

¼ teaspoon nutmeg
⅓ cup butter or margarine, softened
⅔ cup sugar
2 large eggs
¾ cup milk
1 cup coarsely chopped firm strawberries

1. Preheat the oven to 350°F. Generously grease a 9x5-inch loaf pan. In a large mixing bowl, combine the whole wheat flour, all-purpose flour, wheat germ, baking powder, salt, and nutmeg. Whisk to blend the dry ingredients thoroughly.

2. In the bowl of an electric mixer, combine the butter and sugar. Beat at high speed until light and fluffy. Beat in the eggs, one at a time. With the mixer on low speed, sprinkle in the dry ingredients, alternating with the milk. Beat until well moistened. Stir in the strawberries.

3. Pour into the prepared pan and bake for 50 minutes to 1 hour, covering the loaf with aluminum foil during the last 10 minutes if necessary to prevent overbrowning. When a wooden pick inserted into the center comes out clean, transfer the bread to a cooling rack. Let stand for 10 minutes, then turn out. Cool completely before slicing. ❖

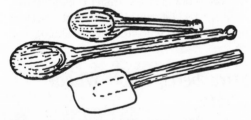

Sweet Potato Bread

MAKES ONE 9x5-INCH LOAF

It is essential that the sweet potatoes for this bread be baked, rather than boiled or steamed. In that way, it is possible to create a purée that is exceptionally low in moisture. Baked, puréed sweet potato freezes well, so you can keep a ready supply on hand for use as an ingredient.

2 cups all-purpose flour, scoop measured
½ cup light brown sugar
3 teaspoons baking powder

¾ teaspoon salt
¼ cup milk
2 large eggs
¼ cup butter or margarine, melted
2 tablespoons honey
¾ cup puréed sweet potato
½ cup coarsely chopped walnuts

1. Preheat the oven to 350°F. Generously grease a 9x5-inch loaf pan. Sift the flour and sugar into the bowl of an electric mixer. Add the baking powder and salt. Run the mixer briefly on low speed to blend the dry ingredients.

2. In a separate bowl, whisk together the milk, eggs, melted butter, and honey. Stir in the sweet potato purée. With the mixer set on low speed, gradually pour the egg mixture into the dry ingredients. Beat until well moistened. Stir in the walnuts.

3. Pour into the prepared pan and bake for 50 minutes to 1 hour, covering the loaf with aluminum foil during the last 10 minutes if necessary to prevent overbrowning. When a wooden pick inserted into the center comes out clean, transfer the bread to a cooling rack. Let stand for 10 minutes, then turn out. Cool completely before slicing. ❖

Tangerine Bread

MAKES ONE 9x5-INCH LOAF

I remember tangerines as a special Christmas treat. At whatever time of year you can find them, their intense flavor produces a spectacular bread.

2 cups all-purpose flour, scoop measured
1 cup sugar
2 teaspoons baking powder
½ teaspoon baking soda
½ teaspoon salt
⅔ cup freshly squeezed tangerine juice
2 large eggs
3 tablespoons butter or margarine, melted
1 tablespoon finely grated tangerine zest
½ cup coarsely chopped walnuts

1. Preheat the oven to 350°F. Generously grease a 9x5-inch loaf pan. In the bowl of an electric mixer, combine the flour, sugar,

baking powder, baking soda, and salt. Run the mixer briefly on low speed to blend the dry ingredients.

2. In a separate bowl, whisk together the tangerine juice, eggs, and melted butter. Stir in the tangerine zest. With the mixer set on low speed, gradually pour the egg mixture into the dry ingredients. Beat until well moistened. Stir in the walnuts.

3. Pour into the prepared pan and bake for 50 minutes to 1 hour, covering the loaf with aluminum foil during the last 10 minutes if necessary to prevent overbrowning. When a wooden pick inserted into the center comes out clean, transfer the bread to a cooling rack. Let stand for 10 minutes, then turn out. Cool completely before slicing. ❖

Black Walnut Bread

MAKES ONE 9x5-INCH LOAF

Native black walnuts were once a common ingredient in baked goods but have now become quite scarce. If you are fortunate enough to locate some, try them in this moist, tender quick bread.

2¼ cups all-purpose flour, scoop measured
3 teaspoons baking powder
¾ teaspoon salt
½ cup butter or margarine, softened
1 cup sugar
2 large eggs
1 teaspoon vanilla extract
⅔ cup milk
1 cup finely chopped black walnuts

1. Preheat the oven to 350°F. Generously grease a 9x5-inch loaf pan. In a large mixing bowl, combine the flour, baking powder, and salt. Whisk to blend thoroughly.

2. In the bowl of an electric mixer, combine the butter and sugar. Beat at high speed until light and fluffy. Beat in the eggs, one at a time. Blend in the vanilla. With the mixer on low speed, sprinkle in the dry ingredients, alternating with the milk. Beat until well moistened. Stir in the walnuts.

3. Pour into the prepared pan and bake for 50 minutes to 1 hour, covering the loaf with aluminum foil during the last 10 minutes if necessary to prevent overbrowning. When a wooden pick inserted into the center comes out clean, transfer the bread to a cooling rack. Let stand for 10 minutes, then turn out. Cool completely before slicing. ❖

Wheat Germ Cheddar Cheese Bread

MAKES ONE 9x5-INCH LOAF

Bolstered by crunchy wheat germ, this cheese-filled loaf is tasty and nutritious. Try thin slices with cold corned beef.

1¾ cups all-purpose flour, scoop measured
2 tablespoons light brown sugar
¾ cup wheat germ, plus 1 tablespoon
3 teaspoons baking powder
¾ teaspoon salt
1 cup milk
2 large eggs
¼ cup vegetable oil
1 cup shredded sharp Cheddar cheese

1. Preheat the oven to 350°F. Generously grease a 9x5-inch loaf pan. Sift the flour and sugar into the bowl of an electric mixer. Add ¾ cup of the wheat germ, the baking powder, and the salt. Run the mixer briefly on low speed to blend the dry ingredients.

2. In a separate bowl, whisk together the milk, eggs, and oil. With the mixer set on low speed, gradually pour the egg mixture into the dry ingredients. Beat until well moistened. Blend in the cheese.

3. Pour into the prepared pan and sprinkle the surface with the remaining tablespoon of wheat germ. Bake for 50 minutes to 1 hour, covering the loaf with aluminum foil during the last 10 minutes if necessary to prevent overbrowning. When a wooden pick inserted into the center comes out clean, transfer the bread to a cooling rack. Let stand for 10 minutes, then turn out. Cool completely before slicing. ❖

Whole Wheat Apricot Bread

MAKES ONE 9x5-INCH LOAF

Coarsely chopped dried apricots lend bright flavor to this whole wheat quick bread. This is delicious toasted and spread with cream cheese.

2 cups whole wheat flour, scoop measured
⅓ cup wheat germ
¼ cup light brown sugar
3 teaspoons baking powder
¾ teaspoon salt
1 cup milk
1 large egg
2 tablespoons vegetable oil
¾ cup coarsely chopped dried apricots

1. Preheat the oven to 350°F. Generously grease a 9x5-inch loaf pan. In the bowl of an electric mixer, combine the flour, wheat germ, sugar, baking powder, and salt. Run the mixer briefly on low speed to blend the dry ingredients.

2. In a separate bowl, whisk together the milk, egg, and oil. With the mixer set on low speed, gradually pour the egg mixture into the dry ingredients. Beat until well moistened. Stir in the apricots.

3. Pour into the prepared pan and bake for 50 minutes to 1 hour, covering the loaf with aluminum foil during the last 10 minutes if necessary to prevent overbrowning. When a wooden pick inserted into the center comes out clean, transfer the bread to a cooling rack. Let stand for 10 minutes, then turn out. Cool completely before slicing. ❖

Whole Wheat Cornmeal Bread

MAKES ONE 9x5-INCH LOAF

Golden raisins dot this lovely quick bread. Serve generous slices with a hearty casserole or beef stew.

1 cup milk
1 tablespoon freshly squeezed lemon juice
1 cup whole wheat flour, scoop measured
½ cup yellow cornmeal
½ cup all-purpose flour, scoop measured
2 tablespoons sugar
1 teaspoon baking powder
1 teaspoon baking soda
¾ teaspoon salt
1 large egg
2 tablespoons molasses
½ cup golden raisins

1. In a glass measuring cup, combine the milk and lemon juice. Set aside for 10 minutes to sour and thicken slightly.

2. Preheat the oven to 350°F. Generously grease a 9x5-inch loaf pan. In the bowl of an electric mixer, combine the whole wheat flour, cornmeal, all-purpose flour, sugar, baking powder, baking soda, and salt. Run the mixer briefly on low speed to blend the dry ingredients.

3. In a separate bowl, whisk together the sour milk, egg, and molasses. With the mixer set on low speed, gradually pour the egg mixture into the dry ingredients. Beat until well moistened. Stir in the raisins.

4. Pour into the prepared pan and bake for 50 minutes to 1 hour, covering the loaf with aluminum foil during the last 10 minutes if necessary to prevent overbrowning. When a wooden pick inserted into the center comes out clean, transfer the bread to a cooling rack. Let stand for 10 minutes, then turn out. Cool completely before slicing. ❖

Yogurt Raisin Bread

MAKES ONE 9x5-INCH LOAF

Unflavored yogurt produces quick bread with a tender crumb and a moist consistency. This makes an excellent breakfast bread, either toasted or plain.

1 large egg
¼ cup vegetable oil
1 cup unflavored yogurt
¾ cup raisins
¼ cup 100% bran cereal (not flakes)
1 cup all-purpose flour, scoop measured
⅔ cup dark brown sugar

1 cup whole wheat flour, scoop measured
1 teaspoon baking powder
1 teaspoon baking soda
¾ teaspoon salt
½ teaspoon cinnamon

1. In a large mixing bowl, whisk the egg and oil together. Stir in the yogurt. Add the raisins and bran, and set aside for 10 minutes to soften. Preheat the oven to 350°F. Generously grease a 9x5-inch loaf pan.

2. Sift the all-purpose flour and sugar into the bowl of an electric mixer. Add the whole wheat flour, baking powder, baking soda, salt, and cinnamon. Run the mixer briefly on low speed to blend the dry ingredients. With the mixer set on low speed, gradually pour the egg mixture into the dry ingredients. Beat until well moistened.

3. Pour into the prepared pan and bake for 50 minutes to 1 hour, covering the loaf with aluminum foil during the last 10 minutes if necessary to prevent overbrowning. When a wooden pick inserted into the center comes out clean, transfer the bread to a cooling rack. Let stand for 10 minutes, then turn out. Cool completely before slicing. ❖

Zucchini Carrot Bread

MAKES ONE 9x5-INCH LOAF

New England gardeners invariably find themselves with too much zucchini squash, and quick breads are one of the most popular ways to use them up. In this recipe, shredded zucchini and shredded carrot combine to create a simple yet captivating loaf.

2 cups all-purpose flour, scoop measured
½ cup light brown sugar
1 teaspoon baking powder
1 teaspoon baking soda
¾ teaspoon salt
1 teaspoon cinnamon
½ teaspoon nutmeg
¼ teaspoon allspice
1 cup buttermilk
2 large eggs

¼ cup vegetable oil
¾ cup shredded, unpeeled zucchini
¾ cup shredded carrot
½ cup coarsely chopped walnuts

1. Preheat the oven to 350°F. Generously grease a 9x5-inch loaf pan. Sift the flour and sugar into the bowl of an electric mixer. Add the baking powder, baking soda, salt, cinnamon, nutmeg, and allspice. Run the mixer briefly on low speed to blend the dry ingredients.

2. In a separate bowl, whisk together the buttermilk, eggs, and oil. With the mixer set on low speed, gradually pour the egg mixture into the dry ingredients. Beat until well moistened. Blend in the zucchini and carrot. Stir in the walnuts.

3. Pour into the prepared pan and bake for 50 minutes to 1 hour, covering the loaf with aluminum foil during the last 10 minutes if necessary to prevent overbrowning. When a wooden pick inserted into the center comes out clean, transfer the bread to a cooling rack. Let stand for 10 minutes, then turn out. Cool completely before slicing. ❖

Pineapple Zucchini Bread

MAKES ONE 9x5-INCH LOAF

Crushed pineapple contributes lively flavor to this zucchini loaf. Slice thinly and serve with chilled fruit salad.

2 cups all-purpose flour, scoop measured
¾ cup light brown sugar
1 cup quick-cooking rolled oats
3 teaspoons baking powder
1 teaspoon cinnamon
¾ teaspoon salt
¼ cup milk
2 large eggs
½ cup vegetable oil
1 can (8 ounces) crushed pineapple,
    undrained
1½ cups shredded, unpeeled zucchini

1. Preheat the oven to 350°F. Generously grease a 9x5-inch loaf pan. Sift the flour and sugar into the bowl of an electric mixer.

Add the oats, baking powder, cinnamon, and salt. Run the mixer briefly on low speed to blend the dry ingredients.

2. In a separate bowl, whisk together the milk, eggs, and oil. Stir in the pineapple, juice and all. With the mixer set on low speed, gradually pour the egg mixture into the dry ingredients. Beat until well moistened. Stir in the zucchini.

3. Pour into the prepared pan and bake for 50 minutes to 1 hour, covering the loaf with aluminum foil during the last 10 minutes if necessary to prevent overbrowning. When a wooden pick inserted into the center comes out clean, transfer the bread to a cooling rack. Let stand for 10 minutes, then turn out. Cool completely before slicing. ❖

Zucchini Corn Bread

MAKES ONE 8-INCH SQUARE LOAF

Squares of hot zucchini corn bread are an outstanding accompaniment to home-made tomato soup. Since zucchini and fresh tomatoes are harvested at the same time, it is possible to buy tomatoes enough for soup at a reasonable price.

1 cup all-purpose flour, scoop measured
1 cup yellow cornmeal
3 teaspoons baking powder
¾ teaspoon salt
1 cup milk
1 large egg
¼ cup butter or margarine, melted
⅓ cup freshly grated Parmesan cheese
1½ cups shredded, unpeeled zucchini

1. Preheat the oven to 375°F. Generously grease an 8-inch square baking pan. In the bowl of an electric mixer, combine the flour, cornmeal, baking powder, and salt. Run the mixer briefly on low speed to blend the dry ingredients.

2. In a separate bowl, whisk together the milk, egg, and melted butter. Stir in the cheese. With the mixer set on low speed, gradually pour the egg mixture into the dry ingredients. Beat until well moistened. Stir in the zucchini.

3. Pour into the prepared pan and bake for 35 to 40 minutes, or until lightly browned. When a wooden pick inserted into the center comes out clean, transfer the bread to a cooling rack. Let stand for 10 minutes. Cut into squares and serve hot, or complete cooling on the rack. ❖

❖ Tea Loaves, Crumpets, and Scones ❖

SAY WHAT you will about New England, it has always maintained a civilized air. For example, there's afternoon tea. Since before the days of the American Revolution, women have paused late in the day for a refreshing cup of hot tea. Those of high social station indulged in fancy cakes and sterling silver tea sets, while women of lower rank made do with toast and a pottery pot, but regardless of wealth or social status afternoon tea was long a common practice among Yankee housewives. Today, with some newly published cookbooks devoted entirely to the subject of afternoon tea, it appears that this traditional ceremony is enjoying a well-deserved revival.

The serving of afternoon tea was a ritual transplanted from England, and so it is not surprising that the breads offered alongside reflect that heritage. Tea loaves, crumpets, and scones are all classic choices. Tea loaves are finely textured and rather sweet. They are thinly sliced and served at room temperature accompanied by whipped butter or cream cheese. Crumpets, which are toasted and served hot, are eaten with butter, jam, or preserves. Scones also are customarily served warm with butter and jam, but for special occasions they may be presented with clotted cream or lemon curd.

Tea loaves are nearly identical to quick breads and are prepared in much the same way. The only difference is that tea loaves usually contain a higher proportion of shortening and sugar, which tends to produce a richer flavor and more cakelike crumb. Also, tea loaves are frequently baked in smaller pans to give them a more elegant appearance.

Scones are similar to biscuits in that they have a flaky, crumbly texture. But they are a great deal richer than biscuits because they are made with eggs and, quite often, cream. Scones may be formed into circles, triangles, or small diamonds. The most familiar shape, however, is the traditional wedge, created by dividing a circle of dough into pie-shaped portions of equal size. Wedge-shaped scones may be baked as a scored round, or the segments may be separated and placed on the baking sheet apart from one another. The first method produces soft-sided scones; the latter results in scones with a uniform crust.

Crumpets, unlike tea loaves and scones, have no related counterparts with which they closely compare; they are unique unto themselves. Crumpets are round and about the diameter of an English muffin, yet they resemble pancakes in thickness and texture. Like an English muffin, they are full of tiny holes. They possess a chewy consistency with a hint of sourdough taste. Straight from the griddle, crumpets seem slightly undercooked, so it is customary to toast them, unsplit, before serving.

Tea loaves, crumpets, and scones store well and freeze successfully, and all three make welcome gifts. Don't hesitate to prepare several batches ahead and freeze them in sealed plastic storage bags. Defrost at room temperature inside the sealed bag. To serve crumpets hot, toast as usual. Scones may be warmed by wrapping them in aluminum foil and placing them in a preheated 375°F. oven for 5 minutes. Open the foil and fold it back, exposing the surface. Then heat the scones for 3 to 5 minutes more, or until the crust is slightly crisp.

Almond Shortbread

MAKES 16 WEDGES

Shortbread is a rich, crumbly delicacy that might best be described as a cross between butter cookies and scones. Traditionally served in wedges, it is wonderful warm from the oven.

1 cup butter (do not substitute margarine), softened
1 cup sifted confectioners' sugar
1 teaspoon almond extract
½ teaspoon salt
½ cup toasted almonds, very finely chopped
2 cups all-purpose flour, scoop measured, sifted

1. Preheat the oven to 325°F. Generously butter two 9-inch pie pans. In the bowl of an electric mixer, combine the butter and sugar, and beat at high speed until light and fluffy. Beat in the almond extract and salt. Stir in the almonds and flour with swift, gentle strokes. Divide into 2 equal portions and press into the prepared pans.

2. Run a knife around the edge of the dough to separate it from the pan. Then scallop the edge of the dough with your fingers or a knife. Mark off 8 wedges by scoring with a knife and prick the surface with the tines of a fork. Bake for 25 to 30 minutes, or until the edges are lightly browned. Cool for 5 minutes on a rack and serve while still warm.   ❖

Applesauce Tea Loaf

MAKES TWO 5x3-INCH LOAVES OR
ONE 9x5-INCH LOAF

A spicy loaf with a hint of apple flavor. Slice thinly and serve with whipped unsalted butter.

2 cups all-purpose flour, scoop measured
2 teaspoons baking powder
½ teaspoon baking soda
½ teaspoon cinnamon
½ teaspoon salt
½ cup butter or margarine, softened

1 cup sugar
2 large eggs
1 cup applesauce

1. Preheat the oven to 350°F. Generously grease 1 or 2 loaf pans. In a large mixing bowl, combine the flour, baking powder, baking soda, cinnamon, and salt. Whisk to blend thoroughly.

2. In the bowl of an electric mixer, combine the butter and sugar, and beat at high speed until light and fluffy. Beat in the eggs, one at a time. With the mixer on low speed, sprinkle in the dry ingredients, alternating with the applesauce. Beat until thoroughly moistened.

3. Pour into the prepared pans and bake for 45 minutes to 1 hour, covering the loaves with aluminum foil during the last 10 minutes if necessary to prevent over-browning. When a wooden pick inserted into the center comes out clean, transfer the bread to a cooling rack. Let stand for 10 minutes, then turn out. Cool completely before slicing.   ❖

Apricot Almond Tea Loaf

MAKES TWO 5x3-INCH LOAVES OR
ONE 9x5-INCH LOAF

Amaretto liqueur contributes its silky almond flavor to this apricot-studded loaf.

2 cups all-purpose flour, scoop measured
3 teaspoons baking powder
½ teaspoon salt
½ cup butter or margarine, softened
1 cup sugar
2 large eggs
3 tablespoons amaretto liqueur
⅔ cup milk
½ cup coarsely chopped dried apricots

1. Preheat the oven to 350°F. Generously grease 1 or 2 loaf pans. In a large mixing bowl, combine the flour, baking powder, and salt. Whisk to blend thoroughly.

2. In the bowl of an electric mixer, combine the butter and sugar, and beat at high speed until light and fluffy. Beat in the eggs,

one at a time. Add the amaretto and blend well. With the mixer on low speed, sprinkle in the dry ingredients, alternating with the milk. Beat until thoroughly moistened. Stir in the apricots.

3. Pour into the prepared pans and bake for 45 minutes to 1 hour, covering the loaves with aluminum foil during the last 10 minutes if necessary to prevent over-browning. When a wooden pick inserted into the center comes out clean, transfer the bread to a cooling rack. Let stand for 10 minutes, then turn out. Cool completely before slicing.   ❖

Banana Orange Tea Loaf

MAKES TWO 5x3-INCH LOAVES OR
ONE 9x5-INCH LOAF

Orange marmalade is the secret ingredient in this remarkable banana loaf.

1 cup all-purpose flour, scoop measured
½ cup whole wheat flour, scoop measured
½ cup wheat bran
1 teaspoon baking soda
½ teaspoon salt
½ cup solid vegetable shortening
1 cup sugar
2 large eggs
3 very ripe bananas, sliced thin
¼ cup orange marmalade
½ cup coarsely chopped pecans

1. Preheat the oven to 350°F. Generously grease 1 or 2 loaf pans. In a large mixing bowl, combine the all-purpose flour, whole wheat flour, wheat bran, baking soda, and salt. Whisk to blend thoroughly.

2. In the bowl of an electric mixer, combine the shortening and sugar, and beat at high speed until light and fluffy. Beat in the eggs, one at a time. Add the bananas and marmalade, and beat until almost smooth. With the mixer on low speed, sprinkle in the dry ingredients. Beat until thoroughly moistened. Stir in the pecans.

3. Pour into the prepared pans and bake for 45 minutes to 1 hour, covering the

loaves with aluminum foil during the last 10 minutes if necessary to prevent over-browning. When a wooden pick inserted into the center comes out clean, transfer the bread to a cooling rack. Let stand for 10 minutes, then turn out. Cool completely before slicing.   ❖

Spiced Carrot Tea Loaf

MAKES TWO 5x3-INCH LOAVES OR
ONE 9x5-INCH LOAF

Whipped cream cheese flavored with a few drops of freshly squeezed lemon juice makes the perfect spread for this carrot loaf.

2 cups all-purpose flour, scoop measured
3 teaspoons baking powder
½ teaspoon baking soda
¾ teaspoon salt
½ teaspoon cinnamon
¼ teaspoon allspice
½ cup butter or margarine, softened
¾ cup sugar
2 large eggs
1 teaspoon vanilla extract
¾ cup milk
1 cup grated raw carrot

1. Preheat the oven to 350°F. Generously grease 1 or 2 loaf pans. In a large mixing bowl, combine the flour, baking powder, baking soda, salt, cinnamon, and allspice. Whisk to blend thoroughly.

2. In the bowl of an electric mixer, combine the butter and sugar, and beat at high speed until light and fluffy. Beat in the eggs, one at a time. Add the vanilla and blend well. With the mixer on low speed, sprinkle in the dry ingredients, alternating with the milk. Beat until thoroughly moistened. Stir in the carrot.

3. Pour into the prepared pans and bake for 45 minutes to 1 hour, covering the loaves with aluminum foil during the last 10 minutes if necessary to prevent over-browning. When a wooden pick inserted into the center comes out clean, transfer the bread to a cooling rack. Let stand for 10 minutes, then turn out. Cool completely before slicing.   ❖

Cinnamon Wedges

MAKES 12

Offer these warm, spicy wedges with tea or hot chocolate. If you're not counting calories, a dollop of whipped cream to one side is an irresistible flourish.

1¼ cups all-purpose flour, scoop measured
¾ cup whole wheat flour, scoop measured
¼ cup sugar, plus 2 tablespoons
2 teaspoons baking powder
½ teaspoon baking soda
½ teaspoon salt
4 tablespoons butter or margarine, cut into
    small pieces, plus 2 tablespoons
½ cup raisins
1 cup unflavored yogurt
1½ teaspoons cinnamon

1. Preheat the oven to 425°F. Generously grease a baking sheet without sides. Combine the all-purpose flour, the whole wheat flour, ¼ cup of the sugar, the baking powder, the baking soda, and the salt in a large mixing bowl. Whisk to blend thoroughly. Add 4 tablespoons of the butter and cut in with a knife until the mixture is crumbly. Stir in the raisins.

2. Make a well in the dry ingredients and pour in the yogurt. Toss with a fork until the dough holds together. Gather the dough into a ball and roll it around the inside of the bowl to pick up any stray particles. Transfer to a lightly floured surface and knead 20 to 25 times, sifting on flour if necessary to prevent sticking. Pat into a circle. Transfer to the prepared baking sheet and press the dough into a ¼-inch-thick round. Bake for 10 minutes. Meanwhile, melt the remaining 2 tablespoons butter in a small saucepan. Add the remaining 2 tablespoons of sugar and the cinnamon. Stir until the sugar is melted. Brush over the surface of the hot dough, then return to the oven for 8 to

10 minutes, or until well browned. Cool on a rack for 5 minutes. Cut into wedges and serve warm. ❖

Gingerbread

MAKES ONE 8-INCH SQUARE

Boiling water is an unexpected ingredient in this light, moist gingerbread. Serve warm, cut into squares, or slice thinly at room temperature and spread with whipped butter.

2 cups all-purpose flour, scoop measured
1 teaspoon baking soda
½ teaspoon salt
1 teaspoon ground ginger
½ cup sugar
½ cup vegetable oil
½ cup molasses
1 large egg
¾ cup boiling water

1. Preheat the oven to 350°F. Generously grease an 8-inch square baking pan. In the bowl of an electric mixer, combine the flour, baking soda, salt, and ginger. Run the mixer briefly on low speed to blend the dry ingredients thoroughly.

2. In a separate bowl, whisk together the sugar, oil, molasses, and egg. Stir in the boiling water. With the mixer set at low speed, gradually pour the egg mixture into the dry ingredients. Beat until thoroughly moistened.

3. Pour into the prepared pan and bake for 40 to 45 minutes, or until a wooden pick inserted into the center comes out clean. Serve straight from the oven or allow to cool on a rack. ❖

Pumpkin Gingerbread

MAKES ONE 9-INCH SQUARE

Dusted with confectioners' sugar, a square of pumpkin gingerbread makes a delightful teatime sweet.

⅓ cup milk
½ cup molasses

2 cups 100% bran cereal flakes
1¾ cups all-purpose flour
1 teaspoon baking powder
1 teaspoon baking soda
½ teaspoon salt
1 teaspoon ground ginger
1 teaspoon cinnamon
¼ teaspoon ground cloves
½ cup solid vegetable shortening
½ cup sugar
1 large egg
1 cup pumpkin purée

1. Preheat the oven to 350°F. Generously grease a 9-inch square baking pan. Combine the milk, molasses, and bran flakes in a large bowl and set aside to soften the bran. In a separate bowl, combine the flour, baking powder, baking soda, salt, ginger, cinnamon, and cloves. Whisk to blend the dry ingredients thoroughly.

2. In the bowl of an electric mixer, combine the shortening and sugar, and beat at high speed until light and fluffy. Beat in the egg. With the mixer on low speed, blend in the softened bran mixture. Gradually sprinkle in the dry ingredients, alternating with the pumpkin purée. Beat until thoroughly moistened.

3. Pour into the prepared pan and bake for 40 to 45 minutes, or until a wooden pick inserted into the center comes out clean. Transfer to a cooling rack. Let stand for 10 minutes, then turn out to complete cooling. Dust with confectioners' sugar, using a lace paper doily to create a decorative pattern if you wish. ❖

Lemon Tea Bread

MAKES ONE 9x5-INCH LOAF

This lemony yeast loaf makes a delicious tea bread. Toast thin slices and spread them with whipped cream cheese blended with a small amount of freshly grated gingerroot.

½ cup milk
¼ cup sugar
¼ cup butter or margarine

½ teaspoon salt

1 package dry yeast, dissolved in ¼ cup warm
water

1 large egg, plus 2 egg yolks, beaten

2 teaspoons finely grated lemon zest

¾ teaspoon lemon extract

3 to 3½ cups bread flour, scoop measured

1. In a wide saucepan, combine the milk, sugar, butter, and salt. Place over medium heat and stir until the butter is melted. Transfer to a large mixing bowl.

2. When the mixture is barely warm to the touch, stir in the dissolved yeast. Add the beaten egg, lemon zest, and lemon extract. Add 1 cup of the flour and beat with a wooden spoon until smooth. Stir in enough of the remaining flour to form a stiff dough. Turn out onto a floured surface and knead, working in as much additional flour as necessary to form a smooth, resilient dough. Transfer to a greased bowl and cover with a clean kitchen towel. Set aside to rise until double in bulk.

3. Generously grease a 9x5-inch loaf pan. Punch the dough down, then turn it out onto a floured surface. Shape it into a loaf and place it in the prepared pan. Cover and set aside to rise. When double in bulk, bake in a preheated 375°F. oven for 35 to 40 minutes, or until nicely browned. Cool on a rack for 5 minutes, then turn out.   ❖

Glazed Lemon Tea Loaf

MAKES ONE 9x5-INCH LOAF

A mixture of freshly squeezed lemon juice and confectioners' sugar glazes the top of this sassy loaf.

2 cups all-purpose flour, scoop measured

2 teaspoons baking powder

½ teaspoon baking soda

½ teaspoon salt

½ cup solid vegetable shortening

1 cup sugar

2 large eggs

1 tablespoon finely grated lemon zest

4 tablespoons freshly squeezed lemon juice

½ cup milk

½ cup coarsely chopped walnuts

3 tablespoons butter or margarine

⅓ cup confectioners' sugar

1. Preheat the oven to 350°F. Generously grease a 9x5-inch loaf pan. In a large mixing bowl, combine the flour, baking powder, baking soda, and salt. Whisk to blend the dry ingredients thoroughly.

2. In the bowl of an electric mixer, combine the shortening and sugar, and beat at high speed until light and fluffy. Beat in the eggs, one at a time. Add the lemon zest and 2 tablespoons of the lemon juice and blend well. With the mixer on low speed, sprinkle in the dry ingredients, alternating with the milk. Beat until thoroughly moistened. Stir in the walnuts.

3. Pour into the prepared pan and bake for 50 minutes to 1 hour, covering the loaf during the last 10 minutes if necessary to prevent overbrowning. When a wooden pick inserted into the center comes out clean, transfer the bread to a cooling rack. Let stand for 10 minutes.

4. Meanwhile, combine the butter, confectioners' sugar, and remaining 2 tablespoons lemon juice in a small saucepan. Heat until the mixture bubbles vigorously. Brush over the warm loaf and let stand until completely cooled. Turn out and wrap in aluminum foil for at least 24 hours before serving.   ❖

Marsala Date Tea Loaf

MAKES TWO 5x3-INCH LOAVES OR
ONE 9x5-INCH LOAF

Marsala wine flavors this delicate tea bread. Serve plain or spread lightly with unsalted butter.

2 cups all-purpose flour, scoop measured

1 cup sugar

2 teaspoons baking powder

½ teaspoon baking soda

¾ teaspoon salt

¼ cup milk

2 large eggs
½ cup Marsala wine
¼ cup vegetable oil
1 cup coarsely chopped dates
½ cup coarsely chopped walnuts

1. Preheat the oven to 350°F. Generously grease 1 or 2 loaf pans. In the bowl of an electric mixer, combine the flour, sugar, baking powder, baking soda, and salt. Run the mixer briefly on low speed to blend the dry ingredients.

2. In a separate bowl, whisk together the milk, eggs, Marsala, and oil. With the mixer set on low speed, gradually pour the egg mixture into the dry ingredients. Beat until thoroughly moistened. Stir in the dates and walnuts.

3. Pour into the prepared pans and bake for 45 minutes to 1 hour, covering the loaves with aluminum foil during the last 10 minutes if necessary to prevent over-browning. When a wooden pick inserted into the center comes out clean, transfer the bread to a cooling rack. Let stand for 10 minutes, then turn out. Cool completely before slicing.   ❖

Orange Cardamom Loaf

MAKES TWO 5x3-INCH LOAVES OR
ONE 9x5-INCH LOAF

The classic flavor of cardamom is a welcome companion to a cup of hot tea. Serve sandwiched with whipped cream cheese.

2 cups all-purpose flour, scoop measured
1 cup sugar
2 teaspoons baking powder
½ teaspoon baking soda
½ teaspoon salt
½ teaspoon ground cardamom
⅔ cup freshly squeezed orange juice
2 large eggs
3 tablespoons butter or margarine, melted
1 tablespoon finely grated orange zest

1. Preheat the oven to 350°F. Generously grease 1 or 2 loaf pans. In the bowl of an electric mixer, combine the flour, sugar, baking powder, baking soda, salt, and cardamom. Run the mixer briefly on low speed to blend the dry ingredients.

2. In a separate bowl, whisk together the orange juice, eggs, and melted butter. Stir in the orange zest. With the mixer set on low speed, gradually pour the egg mixture into the dry ingredients. Beat until thoroughly moistened.

3. Pour into the prepared pans and bake for 45 minutes to 1 hour, covering the loaves with aluminum foil during the last 10 minutes if necessary to prevent over-browning. When a wooden pick inserted into the center comes out clean, transfer the bread to a cooling rack. Let stand for 10 minutes, then turn out. Cool completely before slicing.   ❖

Pear Cider Tea Loaf

MAKES TWO 5x3-INCH LOAVES OR
ONE 9x5-INCH LOAF

Cider made from pears possesses a startlingly true pear flavor. The best place to find it is at a farm stand or cider mill. Here it combines with a touch of mace to create an exceptional bread.

2 cups all-purpose flour, scoop measured
⅔ cup sugar
1½ teaspoons baking powder
½ teaspoon baking soda
¾ teaspoon salt
½ teaspoon mace
1 cup pear cider
2 large eggs
¼ cup butter or margarine, melted
½ cup coarsely chopped pecans

1. Preheat the oven to 350°F. Generously grease 1 or 2 loaf pans. In the bowl of an electric mixer, combine the flour, sugar, baking powder, baking soda, salt, and mace. Run the mixer briefly on low speed to blend the dry ingredients.

2. In a separate bowl, whisk together the cider, the eggs, and the melted butter. With the mixer set at low speed, gradually pour the egg mixture into the dry ingredients. Beat until thoroughly moistened. Stir in the pecans.

3. Pour into the prepared pans and bake for 45 minutes to 1 hour, covering the loaves with aluminum foil during the last 10 minutes if necessary to prevent over-browning. When a wooden pick inserted into the center comes out clean, transfer the bread to a cooling rack. Let stand for 10 minutes, then turn out. Cool completely before slicing.   ❖

Pineapple Tea Loaf

MAKES TWO 5x3-INCH LOAVES OR
ONE 9x5-INCH LOAF

An elegant loaf to offer not only with tea, but also with an afternoon glass of sherry.

2 cups all-purpose flour, scoop measured
1 teaspoon baking soda
½ teaspoon salt
½ cup cream cheese, softened
1 cup sugar
1 large egg
1 teaspoon vanilla extract
½ cup sour cream
¾ cup canned crushed pineapple, drained

1. Preheat the oven to 350°F. Generously grease 1 or 2 loaf pans. In a large mixing bowl, combine the flour, baking soda, and salt. Whisk to blend thoroughly.

2. In the bowl of an electric mixer, combine the cream cheese and sugar, and beat at high speed until light and fluffy. Beat in the egg. Add the vanilla and blend well. With the mixer on low speed, sprinkle in

the dry ingredients, alternating with the sour cream. Beat until thoroughly moistened. Stir in the pineapple.

3. Pour into the prepared pans and bake for 45 minutes to 1 hour, covering the loaves with aluminum foil during the last 10 minutes if necessary to prevent over-browning. When a wooden pick inserted into the center comes out clean, transfer the bread to a cooling rack. Let stand for 10 minutes, then turn out. Cool completely before slicing.   ❖

Pumpkin Almond Tea Loaf

MAKES TWO 5x3-INCH LOAVES OR
ONE 9x5-INCH LOAF

Entertaining a special friend? Splurge on a jar of clotted cream to spread on slices of this delicious tea loaf.

2 cups all-purpose flour, scoop measured
2 teaspoons baking powder
½ teaspoon baking soda
½ teaspoon salt
½ teaspoon cinnamon
¼ teaspoon ground cloves
½ cup butter or margarine, softened
1 cup sugar
2 large eggs
1 cup pumpkin purée
1 cup slivered almonds

1. Preheat the oven to 350°F. Generously grease 1 or 2 loaf pans. In a large mixing bowl, combine the flour, baking powder, baking soda, salt, cinnamon, and cloves. Whisk to blend thoroughly.

2. In the bowl of an electric mixer, combine the butter and sugar, and beat at high speed until light and fluffy. Beat in the eggs, one at a time. With the mixer on low speed, sprinkle in the dry ingredients, alternating with the pumpkin purée. Beat until thoroughly moistened. Stir in the almonds.

3. Pour into the prepared pans and bake for 45 minutes to 1 hour, covering the loaves with aluminum foil during the last 10 minutes if necessary to prevent over-

browning. When a wooden pick inserted into the center comes out clean, transfer the bread to a cooling rack. Let stand for 10 minutes, then turn out. Cool completely before slicing. ❖

Shortbread

MAKES 8 WEDGES

Lightly browned triangles of shortbread are buttery rich and therefore usually eaten plain. For an extravagant treat, serve them with whipped cream dusted with cinnamon.

1 cup butter (do not substitute margarine), softened
½ cup sugar
1 teaspoon vanilla extract
½ teaspoon salt
2½ cups all-purpose flour, scoop measured, sifted

1. Preheat the oven to 325°F. Generously butter an 8-inch square baking pan. In the bowl of an electric mixer, combine the butter and sugar, and beat at high speed until light and fluffy. Beat in the vanilla and salt. Stir in the flour with swift, gentle strokes.

2. Press the dough into the prepared pan. Using the tines of a fork, score the dough in half across the pan. Then mark off in trian-

To make shortbread wedges, score the dough in half across the pan, using the tines of a fork. Then mark off in triangles, 4 to each half of the dough.

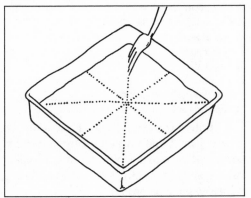

gles, 4 to each half of the dough. (See illustration.) Bake for 25 to 30 minutes, or until the edges are lightly browned. Cool for 5 minutes on a rack and serve while still warm. ❖

Spiced Tea Loaf

MAKES TWO 5x3-INCH LOAVES OR
ONE 9x5-INCH LOAF

Hot lemonade is a lovely old-fashioned beverage that may be served in place of tea. Prepare your favorite lemonade recipe using boiling water, then pour into glass cups and serve with slices of this spicy bread.

2 cups all-purpose flour, scoop measured
3 teaspoons baking powder
¾ teaspoon salt
½ teaspoon cinnamon
¼ teaspoon nutmeg
⅛ teaspoon ground cloves
½ cup butter or margarine, softened
1 cup sugar
2 large eggs
1 teaspoon vanilla extract
¾ cup milk

1. Preheat the oven to 350°F. Generously grease 1 or 2 loaf pans. In a large mixing bowl, combine the flour, baking powder, salt, cinnamon, nutmeg, and cloves. Whisk to blend thoroughly.

2. In the bowl of an electric mixer, combine the butter and sugar, and beat at high speed until light and fluffy. Beat in the eggs, one at a time. Add the vanilla and blend well. With the mixer on low speed, sprinkle in the dry ingredients, alternating with the milk. Beat until thoroughly moistened.

3. Pour into the prepared pans and bake for 45 minutes to 1 hour, covering the loaves with aluminum foil during the last 10 minutes if necessary to prevent overbrowning. When a wooden pick inserted into the center comes out clean, transfer the bread to a cooling rack. Let stand for 10 minutes, then turn out. Cool completely before slicing. ❖

Sweet Potato Tea Loaf

MAKES ONE 9x5-INCH LOAF

Bourbon lends its lusty flavor to this otherwise demure tea loaf.

2 cups all-purpose flour, scoop measured
3 teaspoons baking powder
¾ teaspoon salt
½ cup butter or margarine, softened
½ cup light brown sugar
½ cup granulated sugar
2 large eggs
3 tablespoons bourbon
¾ cup sweet potato purée
½ cup raisins

1. Preheat the oven to 350°F. Generously grease a 9x5-inch loaf pan. In a large mixing bowl, combine the flour, baking powder, and salt. Whisk to blend thoroughly.

2. In the bowl of an electric mixer, combine the butter, brown sugar, and granulated sugar, and beat at high speed until light and fluffy. Beat in the eggs, one at a time. Add the bourbon and blend well. With the mixer on low speed, sprinkle in the dry ingredients, alternating with the sweet potato purée. Beat until thoroughly moistened. Stir in the raisins.

3. Pour into the prepared pan and bake for 50 minutes to 1 hour, covering the loaf with aluminum foil during the last 10 minutes if necessary to prevent overbrowning. When a wooden pick inserted into the center comes out clean, transfer the bread to a cooling rack. Let stand for 10 minutes, then turn out. Cool completely before slicing. ❖

Tea Puffs

MAKES 36

Similar to small muffins, these tiny puffs are baked in miniature 1½-inch muffin cups. Serve with jam or lemon curd.

2 cups all-purpose flour, scoop measured
¼ cup sugar
3 teaspoons baking powder
½ teaspoon salt
1 cup milk
1 large egg
¼ cup butter or margarine, melted

1. Preheat the oven to 400°F. Generously butter 36 small muffin cups. In the bowl of an electric mixer, combine the flour, sugar, baking powder, and salt. Run the mixer briefly on low speed to blend the dry ingredients thoroughly.

2. In a separate bowl, whisk together the milk, egg, and melted butter. With the mixer set at low speed, gradually pour the egg mixture into the dry ingredients. Beat until thoroughly moistened.

3. Drop the batter by scant tablespoonfuls into the prepared muffin cups. Bake for 12 to 15 minutes, or until a wooden pick inserted into the center comes out clean. Transfer to a cooling rack for 5 minutes, then turn the puffs out of the pan and serve immediately. ❖

Zucchini Date Nut Tea Loaf

MAKES TWO 5x3-INCH LOAVES OR
ONE 9x5-INCH LOAF

A slightly different variation of classic date nut loaf. Sandwich with whipped cream cheese.

2 cups all-purpose flour, scoop measured
2 teaspoons baking powder
½ teaspoon baking soda
½ teaspoon salt
½ teaspoon cinnamon
¼ teaspoon allspice
½ cup solid vegetable shortening
½ cup sugar
2 large eggs
¾ cup milk
1 cup grated unpeeled zucchini
½ cup coarsely chopped dates
½ cup coarsely chopped walnuts

1. Preheat the oven to 350°F. Generously grease 1 or 2 loaf pans. In a large mixing bowl, combine the flour, baking powder, baking soda, salt, cinnamon, and allspice. Whisk to blend thoroughly.

2. In the bowl of an electric mixer, combine the shortening and sugar, and beat at high speed until light and fluffy. Beat in the eggs, one at a time. With the mixer on low speed, sprinkle in the dry ingredients, alternating with the milk. Beat until thoroughly moistened. Stir in the zucchini, dates, and walnuts.

3. Pour into the prepared pans and bake for 45 minutes to 1 hour, covering the loaves with aluminum foil during the last 10 minutes if necessary to prevent over-browning. When a wooden pick inserted into the center comes out clean, transfer the bread to a cooling rack. Let stand for 10 minutes, then turn out. Cool completely before slicing.   ❖

Tea Crumpets

MAKES 10

Crumpets might best be described as a cross between a pancake and an English muffin. They are customarily served toasted, without being split, and are a traditional accompaniment to tea.

½ cup warm water
1 package dry yeast
1 teaspoon sugar
1 cup milk
2 tablespoons butter or margarine
½ teaspoon salt
2 cups all-purpose flour, scoop measured
½ teaspoon baking soda
1 tablespoon tepid water

1. In a large mixing bowl, combine the warm water and yeast. Add the sugar and stir to dissolve the yeast. Set aside.

2. In a small saucepan, heat ½ cup of the milk and the butter until the butter melts. Remove from the heat and stir in the salt and the remaining ½ cup milk. Set aside to cool to room temperature.

3. Add the cooled milk to the dissolved yeast and stir to blend. Mix in the flour with a wooden spoon. The batter will be very lumpy. Cover the bowl with plastic wrap and secure with an elastic band. Set aside

to rise for 1½ hours, or until the bubbling action slows and the mixture begins to collapse on itself.

4. Place 4 crumpet rings on a griddle, allowing the sides to touch. Set over medium heat and lightly grease all surfaces by spraying with vegetable oil. Meanwhile, dissolve the baking soda in the tepid water. Add to the batter and stir to blend. The batter will be moist and ropy. When the griddle is hot, take up by scant ¼ cups and pour into the crumpet rings. Spread to the sides with the back of a spoon. As the batter begins to set, carefully turn the rings around to ensure even cooking. When the surface of the crumpets is covered with holes and no longer looks wet (about 3 minutes), remove the rings with a pair of kitchen tongs. Turn the crumpets over and continue cooking for about 1 minute, or until the surface is lightly browned. Repeat with the remaining batter, spraying the griddle and crumpet rings before each batch. Transfer the cooked crumpets to a cooling rack. Toast before serving.   ❖

Apple Crumpets

MAKES 10

Apple juice and a touch of cinnamon create the unique flavor of these crumpets. Toast and serve with whipped butter.

½ cup warm water
1 package dry yeast
1 teaspoon sugar
⅔ cup apple juice
⅓ cup milk
2 tablespoons butter or margarine, melted
½ teaspoon cinnamon
½ teaspoon salt
1 cup all-purpose flour, scoop measured
1 cup whole wheat flour, scoop measured
½ teaspoon baking soda
2 tablespoons tepid water

1. In a large mixing bowl, combine the warm water and yeast. Add the sugar and stir to dissolve the yeast. Set aside.

2. In a small bowl, combine the apple juice, milk, melted butter, cinnamon, and salt. Whisk to combine, then stir into the dissolved yeast.

3. Add the all-purpose flour and whole wheat flour and mix in with a wooden spoon. The batter will be very lumpy. Cover the bowl with plastic wrap and secure with an elastic band. Set aside to rise for 1½ hours, or until the bubbling action slows and the mixture begins to collapse on itself.

4. Place 4 crumpet rings on a griddle, allowing the sides to touch. Set over medium heat and lightly grease all surfaces by spraying with vegetable oil. Meanwhile, dissolve the baking soda in the tepid water. Add to the batter and stir to blend. The batter will be moist and ropy. When the griddle is hot, take up by scant ¼ cups and pour into the crumpet rings. Spread to the sides with the back of a spoon. As the batter begins to set, carefully turn the rings around to ensure even cooking. When the surface of the crumpets is covered with holes and no longer looks wet (about 3 minutes), remove the rings with a pair of kitchen tongs. Turn the crumpets over and continue cooking for about 1 minute, or until the surface is lightly browned. Repeat with the remaining batter, spraying the griddle and crumpet rings before each batch. Transfer the cooked crumpets to a cooling rack. Toast before serving.   ❖

Buttermilk Crumpets

MAKES 10

Crumpets can be frozen successfully. Place them in a plastic bag secured with a wire twist and store in the freezer for up to 3 months. This enables you to defrost 2 or 3 at a time and keep some on hand for unexpected guests.

⅓ cup warm water
1 package dry yeast
1 teaspoon sugar

1 cup buttermilk
2 tablespoons butter or margarine, melted
½ teaspoon salt
1⅔ cups all-purpose flour, scoop measured
½ teaspoon baking soda
3 tablespoons tepid water

1. In a large mixing bowl, combine the warm water and yeast. Add the sugar and stir to dissolve the yeast. Set aside.

2. In a small bowl, combine the buttermilk, melted butter, and salt. Whisk to combine, then stir into the dissolved yeast.

3. Add the flour and mix with a wooden spoon. The batter will be very lumpy. Cover the bowl with plastic wrap and secure with an elastic band. Set aside to rise for 1½ hours, or until the bubbling action slows and the mixture begins to collapse on itself.

4. Place 4 crumpet rings on a griddle, allowing the sides to touch. Set over medium heat and lightly grease all surfaces by spraying with vegetable oil. Meanwhile, dissolve the baking soda in the tepid water. Add to the batter and stir to blend. The batter will be moist and ropy. When the griddle is hot, take up by scant ¼ cups and pour into the crumpet rings. Spread to the sides with the back of a spoon. As the batter begins to set, carefully turn the rings around to ensure even cooking. When the surface of the crumpets is covered with holes and no longer looks wet (about 3 minutes), remove the rings with a pair of kitchen tongs. Turn the crumpets over and continue cooking for about 1 minute, or until the surface is lightly browned. Repeat with the remaining batter, spraying the griddle and crumpet rings before each batch. Transfer the cooked crumpets to a cooling rack. Toast before serving.   ❖

Orange Crumpets

MAKES 10

Toast these orange-scented crumpets and serve with clotted cream.

⅓ cup warm water
1 package dry yeast
1 teaspoon sugar
⅔ cup freshly squeezed orange juice
⅓ cup milk
2 tablespoons butter or margarine, melted
1 tablespoon finely grated orange zest
½ teaspoon salt
1⅔ cups all-purpose flour, scoop measured
½ teaspoon baking soda
1 tablespoon tepid water

1. In a large mixing bowl, combine the warm water and yeast. Add the sugar and stir to dissolve the yeast. Set aside.

2. In a small bowl, combine the orange juice, milk, melted butter, orange zest, and salt. Whisk to combine, then stir into the dissolved yeast.

3. Add the flour and mix in with a wooden spoon. The batter will be very lumpy. Cover the bowl with plastic wrap and secure with an elastic band. Set aside to rise for 1½ hours, or until the bubbling action slows and the mixture begins to collapse on itself.

4. Place 4 crumpet rings on a griddle, allowing the sides to touch. Set over medium heat and lightly grease all surfaces by spraying with vegetable oil. Meanwhile, dissolve the baking soda in the tepid water. Add to the batter and stir to blend. The batter will be moist and ropy. When the griddle is hot, take up by scant ¼ cups and pour into the crumpet rings. Spread to the sides with the back of a spoon. As the batter begins to set, carefully turn the rings around to ensure even cooking. When the surface of the crumpets is covered with holes and no longer looks wet (about 3 minutes), remove the rings with a pair of kitchen tongs. Turn the crumpets over and continue cooking for about 1 minute, or until the surface is lightly browned. Repeat with the remaining batter, spraying the griddle and crumpet rings before each batch. Transfer the cooked crumpets to a cooling rack. Toast before serving.   ❖

Spiced Crumpets

MAKES 10

Cream cheese whipped with a generous spoonful of ginger marmalade makes a compatible spread for these crumpets.

½ cup warm water
1 package dry yeast
1 tablespoon molasses
1 cup milk
2 tablespoons butter or margarine
½ teaspoon salt
½ teaspoon cinnamon
¼ teaspoon ground cloves
2 cups all-purpose flour, scoop measured
½ teaspoon baking soda
2 tablespoons tepid water

1. In a large mixing bowl, combine the warm water and yeast. Add the molasses and stir to dissolve the yeast. Set aside.

2. In a small saucepan, heat ½ cup of the milk and the butter until the butter melts. Remove from the heat and stir in the salt, cinnamon, cloves, and remaining ½ cup milk. Set aside to cool to room temperature.

3. Add the cooled milk to the dissolved yeast and stir to blend. Mix in the flour with a wooden spoon. The batter will be very lumpy. Cover the bowl with plastic wrap and secure with an elastic band. Set aside to rise for 1½ hours, or until the bubbling action slows and the mixture begins to collapse on itself.

4. Place 4 crumpet rings on a griddle, allowing the sides to touch. Set over medium heat and lightly grease all surfaces by spraying with vegetable oil. Meanwhile, dissolve the baking soda in the tepid water. Add to the batter and stir to blend. The batter will be moist and ropy. When the griddle is hot, take up by scant ¼ cups and pour into the crumpet rings. Spread to the sides

with the back of a spoon. As the batter begins to set, carefully turn the rings around to ensure even cooking. When the surface of the crumpets is covered with holes and no longer looks wet (about 3 minutes), remove the rings with a pair of kitchen tongs. Turn the crumpets over and continue cooking for about 1 minute, or until the surface is lightly browned. Repeat with the remaining batter, spraying the griddle and crumpet rings before each batch. Transfer the cooked crumpets to a cooling rack. Toast before serving.   ❖

Whole Wheat Crumpets

MAKES 10

These are hearty crumpets — perhaps as suitable for breakfast as for tea.

½ cup warm water
1 package dry yeast
1 tablespoon honey
1 cup milk
2 tablespoons butter or margarine
½ teaspoon salt
1 cup all-purpose flour, scoop measured
1 cup whole wheat flour, scoop measured
½ teaspoon baking soda
2 tablespoons tepid water

1. In a large mixing bowl, combine the warm water and yeast. Add the honey and stir to dissolve the yeast. Set aside.

2. In a small saucepan, heat ½ cup of the milk and the butter until the butter melts. Remove from the heat and stir in the salt and the remaining ½ cup milk. Set aside to cool to room temperature.

3. Add the cooled milk to the dissolved yeast and stir to blend. Mix in the all-purpose flour and whole wheat flour with a wooden spoon. The batter will be very lumpy. Cover the bowl with plastic wrap and secure with an elastic band. Set aside to rise for 1½ hours, or until the bubbling action slows and the mixture begins to collapse on itself.

4. Place 4 crumpet rings on a griddle, allowing the sides to touch. Set over medium heat and lightly grease all surfaces by spraying with vegetable oil. Meanwhile, dissolve the baking soda in the tepid water. Add to the batter and stir to blend. The batter will be moist and ropy. When the griddle is hot, take up by scant ¼ cups and pour into the crumpet rings. Spread to the sides with the back of a spoon. As the batter begins to set, carefully turn the rings around to ensure even cooking. When the surface of the crumpets is covered with holes and no longer looks wet (about 3 minutes), remove the rings with a pair of kitchen tongs. Turn the crumpets over and continue cooking for about 1 minute, or until the surface is lightly browned. Repeat with the remaining batter, spraying the griddle and crumpet rings before each batch. Transfer the cooked crumpets to a cooling rack. Toast before serving.   ❖

Baked Crumpets

MAKES 18

Dainty cakes baked in muffin tins, these crumpets need no toasting. Simply split and serve with jam.

½ cup warm water
1 package dry yeast
1 teaspoon sugar
1½ cups milk
2 tablespoons butter or margarine
¾ teaspoon salt
2 large eggs
3 cups all-purpose flour, scoop measured

1. In a large mixing bowl, combine the warm water and yeast. Add the sugar and stir to dissolve the yeast. Set aside.

2. In a small saucepan, heat ½ cup of the milk and the butter until the butter melts. Remove from the heat and stir in the salt and the remaining 1 cup milk. Whisk the eggs in a small bowl, then add to the milk mixture. Stir into the dissolved yeast and

blend well. Mix in the flour with a wooden spoon. The batter will be very lumpy. Cover the bowl with plastic wrap and secure with an elastic band. Set aside for 30 minutes.

3. Preheat the oven to 400°F. Generously grease 18 muffin cups. Stir the batter down and spoon into the prepared cups, filling them only half full. Bake for 15 to 20 minutes, or until puffed and golden. Serve immediately or cool on a rack.   ❖

Apricot Bran Scones

MAKES 12

Dried fruits of all kinds have been a traditional ingredient in New England baking for generations. Here, bits of dried apricot enliven bran-flavored scones.

2 cups all-purpose flour, scoop measured
¼ cup sugar
3 teaspoons baking powder
¾ teaspoon salt
3 tablespoons butter or margarine, cut into
   small pieces
3 tablespoons solid vegetable shortening
2 cups 100% bran cereal flakes
½ cup coarsely chopped dried apricots
2 large eggs
1 cup milk

1. Preheat the oven to 425°F. Lightly grease a baking sheet without sides. Combine the flour, sugar, baking powder, and salt in a large mixing bowl. Whisk to blend thoroughly. Add the butter and shortening, and cut in with a knife until the mixture is crumbly. Add the bran and apricots, and toss to combine.

2. In a separate bowl, whisk together the eggs and milk. Make a well in the dry ingredients. Pour in the egg mixture and toss with a fork until the dough holds together. Gather the dough into a ball and roll it around the inside of the bowl to pick up any stray particles. Transfer to a lightly floured surface and knead 20 to 25 times, sifting on flour if necessary to prevent sticking.

3. Divide the dough into 2 equal portions. Pat each portion into a 6½-inch round. Transfer the rounds to the prepared baking sheet, placing them well apart. Score each round into 6 wedges with the dull edge of a floured chef's knife. Make the marks deep, but do not cut all the way through. Bake in the preheated oven for 12 to 15 minutes, or until lightly browned. Using a metal spatula, transfer the rounds to a cooling rack. Allow to cool for 10 minutes, then separate into wedges with the tines of a fork. Serve warm or complete cooling on the rack.   ❖

Blueberry Scones

MAKES 12

The best blueberries to use are the tiny wild berries from Maine. If you are unable to obtain them fresh, they are available frozen and in cans.

3 cups all-purpose flour, scoop measured
½ cup sugar
3 teaspoons baking powder
¾ teaspoon salt
½ teaspoon mace
6 tablespoons butter or margarine, cut into
   small pieces
2 large eggs
1 cup milk
1 cup small fresh blueberries, rinsed and
   gently patted dry

1. Preheat the oven to 425°F. Lightly grease a baking sheet without sides. Combine the flour, sugar, baking powder, salt, and mace in a large mixing bowl. Whisk to blend thoroughly. Add the butter and cut in with a knife until the mixture is crumbly.

2. In a separate bowl, whisk together the eggs and milk. Make a well in the dry ingredients. Pour in the egg mixture and toss with a fork until the dough just begins to hold together. Scatter the blueberries over the dough and continue to mix gently. Gather the dough into a ball and roll it around the inside of the bowl to pick up any stray particles. Transfer to a lightly floured sur-

face and knead 20 to 25 times with very soft strokes so as not to break the blueberries. Sift on flour if necessary to prevent sticking.

3. Divide the dough into 2 equal portions. Pat each portion into a 6½-inch round. Transfer the rounds to the prepared baking sheet, placing them well apart. Score each round into 6 wedges with the dull edge of a floured chef's knife. Make the marks deep, but do not cut all the way through. Brush the surface with melted butter. Bake in the preheated oven for 12 to 15 minutes, or until lightly browned. Using a metal spatula, transfer the rounds to a cooling rack. Allow to cool for 10 minutes, then separate into wedges with the tines of a fork. Serve warm or complete cooling on the rack. ❖

Buttermilk Scones

MAKES 12

The flavor of buttermilk is enhanced by serving these scones hot from the oven. Ginger marmalade makes a companionable spread.

3 cups all-purpose flour, scoop measured
¼ cup sugar
2 teaspoons baking powder
¾ teaspoon baking soda
¾ teaspoon salt
6 tablespoons butter or margarine, cut into
   small pieces
2 large eggs
1 cup buttermilk
2 tablespoons milk
¼ teaspoon cinnamon, mixed with 2
   tablespoons sugar

1. Preheat the oven to 425°F. Lightly grease a baking sheet without sides. Combine the flour, sugar, baking powder, baking soda, and salt in a large mixing bowl. Whisk to blend thoroughly. Add the butter and cut in with a knife until the mixture is crumbly.

2. In a separate bowl, whisk together the eggs and buttermilk. Make a well in the dry

ingredients. Pour in the egg mixture and toss with a fork until the dough holds together. Gather the dough into a ball and roll it around the inside of the bowl to pick up any stray particles. Transfer to a lightly floured surface and knead 20 to 25 times, sifting on flour if necessary to prevent sticking.

3. Divide the dough into 2 equal portions. Pat each portion into a 6½-inch round. Transfer the rounds to the prepared baking sheet, placing them well apart. Score each round into 6 wedges with the dull edge of a floured chef's knife. Make the marks deep, but do not cut all the way through. Brush the surface with the milk and sprinkle on the cinnamon sugar. Bake in the preheated oven for 12 to 15 minutes, or until lightly browned. Using a metal spatula, transfer the rounds to a cooling rack. Allow to cool for 10 minutes, then separate into wedges with the tines of a fork. Serve warm or complete cooling on the rack. ❖

Cheddar Cheese Scones

MAKES 16

Sparked with dry mustard, these savory scones may be served with cold meats, fruit, or seafood salad.

3 cups all-purpose flour, scoop measured
1 tablespoon sugar
3 teaspoons baking powder
¾ teaspoon salt
1 teaspoon dry mustard
Generous sprinkling of paprika
3 tablespoons butter or margarine, cut into
   small pieces

3 tablespoons solid vegetable shortening
1 cup shredded Cheddar cheese
2 large eggs
1 cup milk

1. Preheat the oven to 425°F. Lightly grease a baking sheet without sides. Combine the flour, sugar, baking powder, salt, mustard, and paprika in a large mixing bowl. Whisk to blend thoroughly. Add the butter and shortening, and cut in with a knife until the mixture is crumbly. Add the cheese and toss to combine.

2. In a separate bowl, whisk together the eggs and milk. Make a well in the dry ingredients. Pour in the egg mixture and toss with a fork until the dough holds together. Gather the dough into a ball and roll it around the inside of the bowl to pick up any stray particles. Transfer to a lightly floured surface and knead 20 to 25 times, sifting on flour if necessary to prevent sticking.

3. Divide the dough into 2 equal portions. Pat each portion into an 8-inch round. Transfer the rounds to the prepared baking sheet, placing them well apart. Score each round into 8 wedges with the dull edge of a floured chef's knife. Make the marks deep, but do not cut all the way through. Bake in the preheated oven for 12 to 15 minutes, or until lightly browned. Using a metal spatula, transfer the rounds to a cooling rack. Allow to cool for 10 minutes, then separate into wedges with the tines of a fork. Serve warm or complete cooling on the rack. ❖

Cornstarch Scones

MAKES 12

Cornstarch gives these scones an exceptionally light texture. They are elegant when served with clotted cream.

2¼ cups all-purpose flour, scoop measured
¾ cup cornstarch
¼ cup sugar
3 teaspoons baking powder
¾ teaspoon salt

6 tablespoons butter or margarine, cut into
    small pieces
2 large eggs
1 cup milk

1. Preheat the oven to 425°F. Lightly grease a baking sheet without sides. Sift the flour and cornstarch into a large mixing bowl. Add the sugar, baking powder, and salt. Whisk to blend thoroughly. Add the butter and cut in with a knife until the mixture is crumbly.

2. In a separate bowl, whisk together the eggs and milk. Make a well in the dry ingredients. Pour in the egg mixture and toss with a fork until the dough holds together. Gather the dough into a ball and roll it around the inside of the bowl to pick up any stray particles. Transfer to a lightly floured surface and knead 20 to 25 times, sifting on flour if necessary to prevent sticking.

3. Divide the dough into 2 equal portions. Pat each portion into a 6½-inch round. Transfer the rounds to the prepared baking sheet, placing them well apart. Score each round into 6 wedges with the dull edge of a floured chef's knife. Make the marks deep, but do not cut all the way through. Bake in the preheated oven for 12 to 15 minutes, or until lightly browned. Using a metal spatula, transfer the rounds to a cooling rack. Allow to cool for 10 minutes, then separate into wedges with the tines of a fork. Serve warm or complete cooling on the rack. ❖

Rich Cream Scones

MAKES 12

You can actually taste the richness of cream coming through when you bite into one of these silken scones. Golden raisins add an understated flourish.

3 cups all-purpose flour, scoop measured
½ cup sugar
3 teaspoons baking powder
¾ teaspoon salt
6 tablespoons butter or margarine, cut into
    small pieces

½ cup golden raisins
2 large eggs
1 cup medium or whipping cream

1. Preheat the oven to 425°F. Lightly grease a baking sheet without sides. Combine the flour, sugar, baking powder, and salt in a large mixing bowl. Whisk to blend thoroughly. Add the butter and cut in with a knife until the mixture is crumbly. Add the raisins and toss to combine.

2. In a separate bowl, whisk together the eggs and cream. Make a well in the dry ingredients. Pour in the egg mixture and toss with a fork until the dough holds together. Gather the dough into a ball and roll it around the inside of the bowl to pick up any stray particles. Transfer to a lightly floured surface and knead 20 to 25 times, sifting on flour if necessary to prevent sticking.

3. Divide the dough into 2 equal portions. Pat each portion into a 6½-inch round. Transfer the rounds to the prepared baking sheet, placing them well apart. Score each round into 6 wedges with the dull edge of a floured chef's knife. Make the marks deep, but do not cut all the way through. Bake in the preheated oven for 12 to 15 minutes, or until lightly browned. Using a metal spatula, transfer the rounds to a cooling rack. Allow to cool for 10 minutes, then separate into wedges with the tines of a fork. Serve warm or complete cooling on the rack.   ❖

Currant-Filled Scones

MAKES 12

Sometimes called "Eccles cakes," these rich scones are shaped by cutting the dough into squares, then pinching the edges over a filling of butter and dried currants.

3 cups all-purpose flour, scoop measured
¼ cup sugar
3 teaspoons baking powder
¾ teaspoon salt

6 tablespoons butter or margarine, melted
    and cooled
2 large eggs
1 cup medium or whipping cream
½ cup dried currants
Additional butter for filling
¼ teaspoon cinnamon, mixed with 2
    tablespoons sugar

1. Preheat the oven to 425°F. Lightly grease a baking sheet without sides. Combine the flour, sugar, baking powder, and salt in a large mixing bowl. Whisk to blend thoroughly.

2. In a separate bowl, whisk together the butter, eggs, and cream. Make a well in the dry ingredients. Pour in the egg mixture and toss with a fork until the dough holds together. Gather the dough into a ball and roll it around the inside of the bowl to pick up any stray particles. Transfer to a lightly floured surface and knead 20 to 25 times, sifting on flour if necessary to prevent sticking.

To make Currant-Filled Scones, cut the dough into 4-inch squares and place the filling in the center of each square. Bring adjacent points of the square together, pinching the dough to form a seam.

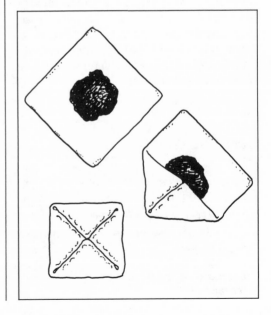

3. Roll the dough into a 12x16-inch rectangle. Trim the edges to square off the rectangle. Lift the dough to loosen it from the work surface. Using a pastry wheel, cut the rectangle into twelve 4-inch squares. Place a few currants and a dab of butter in the center of each square. Bring adjacent points of the square together, pinching the dough to form a seam. (See illustration on previous page.) Repeat this process with the remaining squares. (The scones will pull slightly apart during baking to reveal the currants inside.) Brush the tops with cold water and sprinkle on the cinnamon sugar. Transfer to the prepared sheet and bake for 12 to 15 minutes, or until lightly browned. Serve immediately or cool on a rack.   ❖

Drop Scones

MAKES 18

This variation is cooked on a hot griddle rather than in the oven. Serve warm with butter and honey or jam.

2 large eggs
⅓ cup sugar
¼ cup vegetable oil
¾ cup light cream
2 cups all-purpose flour, scoop measured
2 teaspoons baking powder
½ teaspoon salt

1. Combine the eggs and sugar in the large bowl of an electric mixer. Beat until light and pale yellow in color. Blend in the oil and cream.

2. In a separate bowl, combine the flour, baking powder, and salt. Whisk to blend thoroughly. With the mixer set at low speed, gradually sprinkle in the dry ingredients. Beat until thoroughly blended.

3. Place a griddle over medium-high heat. Brush the surface with vegetable oil. When the griddle is hot, drop the batter by generous tablespoonfuls onto the surface. Cook

until bubbles appear on top. When half the bubbles are broken, turn the scones over and brown the other side. Serve immediately or cool on a rack.   ❖

Gingered Cream Scones

MAKES 32

In addition to the traditional wedge, scones may be shaped into rounds, squares, or diamonds. These fresh-ginger scones are cut with a biscuit cutter to create small circles, a delicate way to present teatime treats.

3 cups all-purpose flour, scoop measured
½ cup sugar
3 teaspoons baking powder
¾ teaspoon salt
8 tablespoons butter or margarine
2 tablespoons minced fresh gingerroot
2 large eggs
1 cup medium or whipping cream
2 tablespoons light brown sugar

1. Preheat the oven to 425°F. Lightly grease a baking sheet without sides. Combine the flour, sugar, baking powder, and salt in a large mixing bowl. Whisk to blend thoroughly.

2. Melt 2 tablespoons of the butter in a small saucepan and set aside. Cut the remaining 6 tablespoons butter into small pieces and add to the dry ingredients. Cut in with a knife until the mixture is crumbly. Add the ginger and toss to combine.

3. In a separate bowl, whisk together the eggs and cream. Make a well in the dry ingredients. Pour in the egg mixture and toss with a fork until the dough holds together. Gather the dough into a ball and roll it around the inside of the bowl to pick up any stray particles. Transfer to a lightly floured surface and knead 20 to 25 times, sifting on flour if necessary to prevent sticking. Roll to a ¾-inch thickness and cut with a 1½-inch biscuit cutter. Brush the tops with the reserved melted butter, then sift on the

brown sugar. Transfer to the prepared sheet and bake for 12 to 15 minutes, or until lightly browned. Serve immediately or transfer to a rack to cool.   ❖

Honey Whole Wheat Scones

MAKES 12

Rather substantial scones, these may be split and toasted. Spread with butter or drizzle with warm honey.

1½ cups whole wheat flour, scoop measured
1½ cups all-purpose flour, scoop measured
3 teaspoons baking powder
¾ teaspoon salt
3 tablespoons butter or margarine, cut into small pieces
3 tablespoons solid vegetable shortening
2 large eggs
¼ cup honey
¾ cup milk

1. Preheat the oven to 425°F. Lightly grease a baking sheet without sides. Combine the whole wheat flour, all-purpose flour, baking powder, and salt in a large mixing bowl. Whisk to blend thoroughly. Add the butter and shortening, and cut in with a knife until the mixture is crumbly.

2. In a separate bowl, whisk together the eggs and honey. Stir in the milk. Make a well in the dry ingredients. Pour in the egg mixture and toss with a fork until the dough holds together. Gather the dough into a ball and roll it around the inside of the bowl to pick up any stray particles. Transfer to a lightly floured surface and knead 20 to 25 times, sifting on flour if necessary to prevent sticking.

3. Divide the dough into 2 equal portions. Pat each portion into a 6½-inch round. Transfer the rounds to the prepared baking sheet, placing them well apart. Score each round into 6 wedges with the dull edge of a floured chef's knife. Make the marks deep, but do not cut all the way through. Brush the surface with milk. Bake in the preheat-

ed oven for 12 to 15 minutes, or until lightly browned. Using a metal spatula, transfer the rounds to a cooling rack. Allow to cool for 10 minutes, then separate into wedges with the tines of a fork. Serve warm or complete cooling on the rack.   ❖

Lemon Cream Scones

MAKES 12

The custom of serving afternoon tea is being revived in cities across the United States. Yet the practice never fell out of favor in Boston. For centuries, delicate treats, like these lemon scones, have been offered with cups of tea.

3 cups all-purpose flour, scoop measured
½ cup sugar
3 teaspoons baking powder
¾ teaspoon salt
6 tablespoons butter or margarine, cut into small pieces
2 teaspoons finely grated lemon zest
2 large eggs
¾ cup medium or whipping cream
¼ cup freshly squeezed lemon juice

1. Preheat the oven to 425°F. Lightly grease a baking sheet without sides. Combine the flour, sugar, baking powder, and salt in a large mixing bowl. Whisk to blend thoroughly. Add the butter and cut in with a knife until the mixture is crumbly. Add the lemon zest and toss to combine.

2. In a separate bowl, whisk together the eggs and cream. Stir in the lemon juice. Make a well in the dry ingredients. Pour in the egg mixture and toss with a fork until the dough holds together. Gather the dough into a ball and roll it around the inside of the bowl to pick up any stray particles. Transfer to a lightly floured surface and knead 20 to 25 times, sifting on flour if necessary to prevent sticking.

3. Divide the dough into 2 equal portions. Pat each portion into a 6½-inch round. Transfer the rounds to the prepared baking sheet, placing them well apart. Score each

round into 6 wedges with the dull edge of a floured chef's knife. Make the marks deep, but do not cut all the way through. Bake in the preheated oven for 12 to 15 minutes, or until lightly browned. Using a metal spatula, transfer the rounds to a cooling rack. Allow to cool for 10 minutes, then separate into wedges with the tines of a fork. Serve warm or complete cooling on the rack.   ❖

Maple Walnut Scones

MAKES 16

Finely chopped walnuts fleck these maple-flavored scones. Serve piping hot with soft butter that has been whipped with a small amount of maple syrup.

3 cups all-purpose flour, scoop measured
1 tablespoon sugar
3 teaspoons baking powder
¾ teaspoon salt
¼ teaspoon cinnamon
6 tablespoons butter or margarine, cut into
  small pieces
½ cup finely chopped walnuts
2 large eggs
¾ cup medium or whipping cream
¼ cup pure maple syrup

1. Preheat the oven to 425°F. Lightly grease a baking sheet without sides. Combine the flour, sugar, baking powder, salt, and cinnamon in a large mixing bowl. Whisk to blend thoroughly. Add the butter and cut in with a knife until the mixture is crumbly. Stir in the walnuts.

2. In a separate bowl, whisk together the eggs and cream. Stir in the maple syrup. Make a well in the dry ingredients. Pour in the egg mixture and toss with a fork until the dough holds together. Gather the dough into a ball and roll it around the inside of the bowl to pick up any stray particles. Transfer to a lightly floured surface and

knead 20 to 25 times, sifting on flour if necessary to prevent sticking.

3. Divide the dough into 2 equal portions. Pat each portion into an 8-inch round. Transfer the rounds to the prepared baking sheet, placing them well apart. Score each round into 8 wedges with the dull edge of a floured chef's knife. Make the marks deep, but do not cut all the way through. Bake in the preheated oven for 12 to 15 minutes, or until lightly browned. Using a metal spatula, transfer the rounds to a cooling rack. Allow to cool for 10 minutes, then separate into wedges with the tines of a fork. Serve warm or complete cooling on the rack.   ❖

Molasses Scones

MAKES 12

Molasses lends its upcountry flavor to these spicy scones. A welcome treat with coffee as well as tea.

3 cups all-purpose flour, scoop measured
2 tablespoons sugar
2 teaspoons baking powder
½ teaspoon baking soda
¾ teaspoon salt
½ teaspoon ground ginger
¼ teaspoon cinnamon
¼ teaspoon ground cloves
6 tablespoons butter or margarine, cut into
  small pieces
2 large eggs
¾ cup milk
2 tablespoons molasses

1. Preheat the oven to 425°F. Lightly grease a baking sheet without sides. Combine the flour, sugar, baking powder, baking soda, and salt in a large mixing bowl. Add the ginger, cinnamon, and cloves, and whisk to blend thoroughly. Add the butter and cut in with a knife until the mixture is crumbly.

2. In a separate bowl, whisk together the eggs and milk. Stir in the molasses. Make a well in the dry ingredients. Pour in the egg mixture and toss with a fork until the

dough holds together. Gather the dough into a ball and roll it around the inside of the bowl to pick up any stray particles. Transfer to a lightly floured surface and knead 20 to 25 times, sifting on flour if necessary to prevent sticking.

3. Divide the dough into 2 equal portions. Pat each portion into a 6½-inch round. Transfer the rounds to the prepared baking sheet, placing them well apart. Score each round into 6 wedges with the dull edge of a floured chef's knife. Make the marks deep, but do not cut all the way through. Bake in the preheated oven for 12 to 15 minutes, or until lightly browned. Using a metal spatula, transfer the rounds to a cooling rack. Allow to cool for 10 minutes, then separate into wedges with the tines of a fork. Serve warm or complete cooling on the rack. ❖

Oatmeal Scones

MAKES 16

The old-fashioned character of oats is evident in these rough-textured scones.

2 cups all-purpose flour, scoop measured
2 tablespoons sugar
1½ teaspoons baking powder
½ teaspoon baking soda
¾ teaspoon salt
6 tablespoons butter or margarine, cut into small pieces
1½ cups quick-cooking rolled oats
½ cup raisins
2 large eggs
1 cup buttermilk

1. Preheat the oven to 425°F. Lightly grease a baking sheet without sides. Combine the flour, sugar, baking powder, baking soda, and salt in a large mixing bowl. Whisk to blend thoroughly. Add the butter and cut in with a knife until the mixture is crumbly. Add the oats and raisins, and toss to combine.

2. In a separate bowl, whisk together the eggs and buttermilk. Make a well in the dry ingredients. Pour in the egg mixture and

toss with a fork until the dough holds together. Gather the dough into a ball and roll it around the inside of the bowl to pick up any stray particles. Transfer to a lightly floured surface and knead 20 to 25 times, sifting on flour if necessary to prevent sticking.

3. Divide the dough into 2 equal portions. Pat each portion into an 8-inch round. Transfer the rounds to the prepared baking sheet, placing them well apart. Score each round into 8 wedges with the dull edge of a floured chef's knife. Make the marks deep, but do not cut all the way through. Bake in the preheated oven for 12 to 15 minutes, or until lightly browned. Using a metal spatula, transfer the rounds to a cooling rack. Allow to cool for 10 minutes, then separate into wedges with the tines of a fork. Serve warm or complete cooling on the rack. ❖

Orange Cranberry Scones

MAKES 25

Since colonial times, cranberries have been an integral part of the New England cuisine. Here they dot orange-scented scones — a wonderful addition to the holiday bread basket as well as the tea plate.

3 cups all-purpose flour, scoop measured
½ cup sugar
3 teaspoons baking powder
¾ teaspoon salt
½ teaspoon nutmeg
6 tablespoons butter or margarine, cut into small pieces
1 tablespoon finely grated orange zest
1 cup fresh cranberries, coarsely chopped
2 large eggs
¼ cup freshly squeezed orange juice
¾ cup milk

1. Preheat the oven to 425°F. Lightly grease a baking sheet without sides. Combine the flour, sugar, baking powder, salt, and nutmeg in a large mixing bowl. Whisk to blend thoroughly. Add the butter and cut in with a knife until the mixture is crumbly.

Add the orange zest and cranberries, and toss to combine.

2. In a separate bowl, whisk together the eggs and orange juice. Stir in the milk. Make a well in the dry ingredients. Pour in the egg mixture and toss with a fork until the dough holds together. Gather the dough into a ball and roll it around the inside of the bowl to pick up any stray particles. Transfer to a lightly floured surface and knead 20 to 25 times, sifting on flour if necessary to prevent sticking.

3. Pat the dough into a 10-inch square. Smooth the surface with a rolling pin. Trim the edges with a floured chef's knife, then cut the dough into 5 equal strips. Divide the strips into 5 equal portions to create 25 squares. Transfer to the prepared baking sheet. Bake in the preheated oven for 12 to 15 minutes, or until lightly browned. Serve immediately or cool on a rack.   ❖

Orange Date Scones

MAKES 16

Creaming the butter and sugar produces scones with a tender, cakelike crumb. Serve hot, and split to spread with softened cream cheese.

6 tablespoons butter or margarine, softened
½ cup sugar
2 large eggs
¼ cup milk
3 cups all-purpose flour, scoop measured
2 teaspoons baking powder
½ teaspoon baking soda
¾ teaspoon salt
¾ cup freshly squeezed orange juice
1 tablespoon finely grated orange zest
½ cup coarsely chopped dates

1. Preheat the oven to 425°F. Lightly grease a baking sheet without sides. Combine the butter and sugar in the large bowl of an electric mixer. Beat until light and pale yellow in color. Beat in the eggs, one at a time. Blend in the milk.

2. In a separate bowl, combine the flour, baking powder, baking soda, and salt. Whisk to blend thoroughly. With the mixer set at low speed, gradually sprinkle in the dry ingredients, alternating with the orange juice. Blend in the orange zest and dates.

3. Transfer to a lightly floured surface and knead 20 to 25 times, sifting on flour if necessary to prevent sticking. Divide into 2 equal portions and pat each into an 8-inch round. Cut each round into 8 wedges with a floured chef's knife, then transfer to the prepared baking sheet, placing the wedges well apart from each other. Bake in the preheated oven for 12 to 15 minutes, or until lightly browned. Serve immediately or cool on a rack.   ❖

Potato Scones

MAKES 16

Mashed potato incorporated into scones gives them a homey, comforting taste. Split and serve warm with lemon curd.

2 cups all-purpose flour, scoop measured
¼ cup sugar
3 teaspoons baking powder
1 teaspoon salt
6 tablespoons butter or margarine, cut into small pieces
1 cup cooled mashed potato
2 large eggs
1 cup milk

1. Preheat the oven to 425°F. Lightly grease a baking sheet without sides. Combine the flour, sugar, baking powder, and salt in a large mixing bowl. Whisk to blend thoroughly. Add the butter and cut in with a knife until the mixture is crumbly. Add the mashed potato and again cut in until the mixture is crumbly.

2. In a separate bowl, whisk together the eggs and milk. Make a well in the dry ingredients. Pour in the egg mixture and toss with a fork until the dough holds together. Gather the dough into a ball and roll it

around the inside of the bowl to pick up any stray particles. Transfer to a lightly floured surface and knead 20 to 25 times, sifting on flour if necessary to prevent sticking.

3. Divide the dough into 2 equal portions. Pat each portion into an 8-inch round. Transfer the rounds to the prepared baking sheet, placing them well apart. Score each round into 8 wedges with the dull edge of a floured chef's knife. Make the marks deep, but do not cut all the way through. Bake in the preheated oven for 12 to 15 minutes, or until lightly browned. Using a metal spatula, transfer the rounds to a cooling rack. Allow to cool for 10 minutes, then separate into wedges with the tines of a fork. Serve warm or complete cooling on the rack.   ❖

Sour Cream Scones

MAKES 12

Almond is the elusive flavor in these rich, seductive scones. Serve hot, or split when cool and toast.

3 cups all-purpose flour, scoop measured
¼ cup sugar
2 teaspoons baking powder
½ teaspoon baking soda
¾ teaspoon salt
½ teaspoon cinnamon
6 tablespoons butter or margarine, melted
    and cooled
2 large eggs
1 cup sour cream
1 teaspoon almond extract

1. Preheat the oven to 425°F. Lightly grease a baking sheet without sides. Combine the flour, sugar, baking powder, baking soda, salt, and cinnamon in a large mixing bowl. Whisk to blend thoroughly.

2. In a separate bowl, whisk together the butter, eggs, sour cream, and almond extract. Make a well in the dry ingredients. Pour in the egg mixture and toss with a fork until the dough holds together. Gather the dough into a ball and roll it around the inside of the bowl to pick up any stray parti-

cles. Transfer to a lightly floured surface and knead 20 to 25 times, sifting on flour if necessary to prevent sticking.

3. Divide the dough into 2 equal portions. Pat each portion into a 6½-inch round. Transfer the rounds to the prepared baking sheet, placing them well apart. Score each round into 6 wedges with the dull edge of a floured chef's knife. Make the marks deep, but do not cut all the way through. Brush the surface with milk, then bake in the preheated oven for 12 to 15 minutes, or until lightly browned. Using a metal spatula, transfer the rounds to a cooling rack. Allow to cool for 10 minutes, then separate into wedges with the tines of a fork. Serve warm or complete cooling on the rack.   ❖

Quick Tea Scones

MAKES 12

Melting the butter eliminates the more time-consuming step of cutting it in, so these scones can be made in a matter of minutes.

3 cups all-purpose flour, scoop measured
¼ cup sugar
3 teaspoons baking powder
¾ teaspoon salt
1 teaspoon freshly grated nutmeg
½ cup butter or margarine, melted and cooled
2 large eggs
1 cup medium or whipping cream

1. Preheat the oven to 425°F. Lightly grease a baking sheet without sides. Combine the flour, sugar, baking powder, salt, and nutmeg in a large mixing bowl. Whisk to blend thoroughly.

2. Measure out 2 tablespoons of the melted butter and set aside. Combine the remaining butter and the eggs in a separate bowl. Add the cream and whisk together. Make a well in the dry ingredients. Pour in the egg mixture and toss with a fork until the dough holds together. Gather the dough into a ball and roll it around the inside of

the bowl to pick up any stray particles. Transfer to a lightly floured surface and knead 20 to 25 times, sifting on flour if necessary to prevent sticking.

3. Divide the dough into 2 equal portions. Pat each portion into a 6½-inch round. Transfer the rounds to the prepared baking sheet, placing them well apart. Score each round into 6 wedges with the dull edge of a floured chef's knife. Make the marks deep, but do not cut all the way through. Brush the surface with the reserved butter, then bake in the preheated oven for 12 to 15 minutes, or until lightly browned. Using a metal spatula, transfer the rounds to a cooling rack. Allow to cool for 10 minutes, then separate into wedges with the tines of a fork. Serve warm or complete cooling on the rack.   ❖

Whole Wheat Cinnamon Scones

MAKES 12

Coarsely textured scones to satisfy hearty appetites. Offer fresh from the oven as an afternoon snack with cold milk.

2½ cups whole wheat flour, scoop measured
½ cup wheat germ
¼ cup sugar
3 teaspoons baking powder
¾ teaspoon salt
¾ teaspoon cinnamon

3 tablespoons butter or margarine, cut into
  small pieces
3 tablespoons solid vegetable shortening
2 large eggs
1 cup milk

1. Preheat the oven to 425°F. Lightly grease a baking sheet without sides. Combine the flour, wheat germ, sugar, baking powder, salt, and cinnamon in a large mixing bowl. Whisk to blend thoroughly. Add the butter and shortening, and cut in with a knife until the mixture is crumbly.

2. In a separate bowl, whisk together the eggs and milk. Make a well in the dry ingredients. Pour in the egg mixture and toss with a fork until the dough holds together. Gather the dough into a ball and roll it around the inside of the bowl to pick up any stray particles. Transfer to a lightly floured surface and knead 20 to 25 times, sifting on flour if necessary to prevent sticking.

3. Divide the dough into 2 equal portions. Pat each portion into a 6½-inch round. Transfer the rounds to the prepared baking sheet, placing them well apart. Score each round into 6 wedges with the dull edge of a floured chef's knife. Make the marks deep, but do not cut all the way through. Bake in the preheated oven for 12 to 15 minutes, or until lightly browned. Using a metal spatula, transfer the rounds to a cooling rack. Allow to cool for 10 minutes, then separate into wedges with the tines of a fork. Serve warm or complete cooling on the rack.   ❖

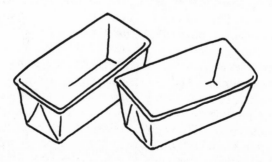

❖ Biscuits ❖

ALONG WITH the ability to make a good pie crust, biscuits have traditionally been considered the true test of a good cook. And although biscuit making may be more closely associated with Southern cuisine, generations of Yankee cooks have prided themselves on their tender, flaky biscuits. After all, what would strawberry shortcake be without the proper foundation?

New England homemakers serve biscuits in other ways, too. Fresh salmon or cod can be combined with a white sauce and spooned over biscuits that have been split in half. Some years back, creamed tuna on a biscuit was a fashionable luncheon dish. And, to add to the list, there's Vermont chicken pie, a well-loved casserole of creamed chicken and vegetables baked with a golden crown of puffy biscuit rounds. Like pie crust, the characteristics of a first-rate biscuit are a light, delicate consistency, rich flavor, and a texture that makes the biscuit flake apart when it is split with a fork. It is not surprising then that pie crust and biscuits are prepared in much the same way: Flour and other dry ingredients are blended together in a large bowl; butter or shortening is cut in until the mixture is crumbly; and a liquid is added until a soft dough forms. The crucial difference is that biscuit dough is kneaded gently and briefly to develop a slight degree of gluten, which contributes body and helps the biscuits to rise with straight sides.

Biscuits are baked in a relatively hot oven, usually at 425°F., to provide a quick rise and produce nicely browned tops. They may be served immediately or cooled on a rack to ensure that the bottom surface doesn't turn soggy.

Contemporary New England cooks make biscuits in a variety of flavors. Cheese biscuits, orange biscuits, maple biscuits, and biscuits sparked with herbs are just a few of the innovations that have replaced plain baking soda biscuits in the bread basket. Then too, biscuits are a remarkably versatile companion. They may be served at breakfast or at any other time of day and are wonderful with soups, salads, and roasted meats.

Biscuits freeze well and reheat easily. To store in the freezer, simply drop cooled biscuits into a plastic freezer bag and secure with a wire twist. Defrost them in the sealed bag, then wrap tightly in aluminum foil. Place in a 375°F. oven for 5 to 8 minutes to warm. Biscuits also may be wrapped in absorbent paper and heated in a microwave oven, but the results are not quite as pleasing as when a conventional oven is used.

Angel Biscuits

MAKES 15

Leavened with yeast, these delicate biscuits are exceptionally light.

2½ cups all-purpose flour, scoop measured
2 tablespoons sugar
2 teaspoons baking powder
¾ teaspoon salt
½ cup solid vegetable shortening
1 cup milk
1 package dry yeast, dissolved in ¼ cup warm water

1. Preheat the oven to 425°F. Lightly grease a baking sheet without sides. Combine the flour, sugar, baking powder, and salt in a large mixing bowl. Whisk to blend

thoroughly. Add the shortening and cut in with a knife until the mixture is crumbly.

2. In a separate bowl, whisk together the milk and dissolved yeast. Make a well in the dry ingredients. Pour in the milk and toss with a fork until the dough holds together. Gather the dough into a ball and roll it around the inside of the bowl to pick up any stray particles. Transfer to a lightly floured surface and knead 20 to 25 times, sifting on flour if necessary to prevent sticking. Without letting the dough rise, pat into a circle, then roll to a ½-inch thickness. Cut out with a 2-inch biscuit cutter and place on the prepared baking sheet. Bake for 12 to 15 minutes, or until nicely browned. Serve immediately or cool on a rack. ❖

Applesauce Biscuits

MAKES 15

Applesauce gives these aromatic biscuits a cakey texture. Warm some in the toaster oven for a healthy after-school snack.

1½ cups all-purpose flour, scoop measured
2 tablespoons brown sugar
½ cup whole wheat flour, scoop measured
1½ teaspoons baking powder
½ teaspoon baking soda
½ teaspoon salt
½ teaspoon cinnamon
¼ teaspoon allspice
¼ cup solid vegetable shortening
⅔ cup applesauce
2 tablespoons milk

1. Preheat the oven to 425°F. Lightly grease a baking sheet without sides. Sift the all-purpose flour and brown sugar into a large mixing bowl. Add the whole wheat flour, baking powder, baking soda, salt, cinnamon, and allspice. Whisk to blend thoroughly. Add the shortening and cut in with a knife until the mixture is crumbly.

2. In a separate bowl, whisk together the applesauce and milk. Make a well in the dry ingredients. Pour in the applesauce mix-

ture and toss with a fork until the dough holds together. Gather the dough into a ball and roll it around the inside of the bowl to pick up any stray particles. Transfer to a lightly floured surface and knead 20 to 25 times, sifting on flour if necessary to prevent sticking. Pat into a circle, then roll to a ¾-inch thickness. Cut out with a 2-inch biscuit cutter and place on the prepared baking sheet. Bake for 12 to 15 minutes, or until nicely browned. Serve immediately or cool on a rack.　　　　❖

Baking Soda Biscuits

MAKES 15

In these days of Lean Cuisine and healthier eating habits, lard has lost its popularity. Yet no other shortening imparts such old-time flavor to biscuits.

2 cups all-purpose flour, scoop measured
1 teaspoon baking soda
¾ teaspoon salt
⅓ cup lard
¾ cup buttermilk

1. Preheat the oven to 425°F. Lightly grease a baking sheet without sides. Combine the flour, baking soda, and salt in a large mixing bowl. Whisk to blend thoroughly. Add the lard and cut in with a knife until the mixture is crumbly.

2. Make a well in the dry ingredients. Pour in the buttermilk and toss with a fork until the dough holds together. Gather the dough into a ball and roll it around the inside of the bowl to pick up any stray particles. Transfer to a lightly floured surface and knead 20 to 25 times, sifting on flour if necessary to prevent sticking. Pat into a circle, then roll to a ¾-inch thickness. Cut out with a 2-inch biscuit cutter and place on the prepared baking sheet. Bake for 12 to 15 minutes, or until nicely browned. Serve immediately or cool on a rack.　　　　❖

Breakfast Biscuits

MAKES 8

These yeast-leavened biscuits are cut extra large. Split and stuff with a sausage patty, a portion of scrambled eggs, and a slice of Cheddar cheese.

2½ cups all-purpose flour, scoop measured
1 tablespoon sugar
1 teaspoon baking soda
¾ teaspoon salt
⅓ cup solid vegetable shortening
1 cup buttermilk
1 large egg
1 package dry yeast, dissolved in ¼ cup warm water

1. In a large mixing bowl, combine the flour, sugar, baking soda, and salt. Add the vegetable shortening and cut in with a knife until the mixture is crumbly.

2. In a separate bowl, whisk together the buttermilk, egg, and dissolved yeast. Make a well in the dry ingredients. Pour in the egg mixture and toss with a fork until the dough holds together. Gather the dough into a ball and roll it around the inside of the bowl to pick up any stray particles. Transfer to a lightly floured surface and knead 20 to 25 times, sifting on flour if necessary to prevent sticking. Roll to a ½-inch thickness. Cover with a clean kitchen towel and let rise 1½ hours.

3. Lightly grease a baking sheet without sides. Cut the dough into 3-inch rounds with a biscuit cutter and place on the prepared baking sheet. Cover and let rise 45 minutes. Bake in a preheated 400°F. oven for 12 to 15 minutes, or until nicely browned. Serve immediately or cool on a rack.　　　　❖

Blueberry Drop Biscuits

MAKES 18

Drop biscuits are a cross between a true biscuit and a muffin. They are quicker to produce than biscuits because they don't need to be rolled out and cut.

2 cups all-purpose flour, scoop measured
2 tablespoons sugar
3 teaspoons baking powder
¾ teaspoon salt
¼ teaspoon freshly grated nutmeg
1 cup milk
¼ cup vegetable oil
1 cup fresh blueberries, rinsed and gently
  patted dry

1. Preheat the oven to 400°F. Lightly grease a baking sheet without sides. Combine the flour, sugar, baking powder, salt, and nutmeg in a large mixing bowl. Whisk to blend thoroughly.

2. In a separate bowl, whisk together the milk and vegetable oil. Make a well in the dry ingredients. Pour in the milk mixture and the blueberries. Toss with a fork until the dough begins to hold together. Take up by generous tablespoonfuls and drop onto the prepared baking sheet. Bake for 15 to 18 minutes, or until nicely browned. Serve immediately or cool on a rack.   ❖

Old-Fashioned Buttermilk Biscuits

MAKES 15

Buttermilk biscuits are a traditional favorite with fried chicken, but they also taste wonderful split, toasted, and sandwiched with baked ham.

2 cups all-purpose flour, scoop measured
2 tablespoons sugar
2 teaspoons baking powder
½ teaspoon baking soda
½ teaspoon salt
4 tablespoons butter or margarine, cut into
  small pieces
¾ cup buttermilk

1. Preheat the oven to 425°F. Lightly grease a baking sheet without sides. Combine the flour, sugar, baking powder, baking

soda, and salt in a large mixing bowl. Whisk to blend thoroughly. Add the butter and cut in with a knife until the mixture is crumbly.

2. Make a well in the dry ingredients. Pour in the buttermilk and toss with a fork until the dough holds together. Gather the dough into a ball and roll it around the inside of the bowl to pick up any stray particles. Transfer to a lightly floured surface and knead 20 to 25 times, sifting on flour if necessary to prevent sticking. Pat into a circle, then roll to a ¾-inch thickness. Cut out with a 2-inch biscuit cutter and place on the prepared baking sheet. Bake for 12 to 15 minutes, or until nicely browned. Serve immediately or cool on a rack.   ❖

Cheddar Biscuits

MAKES 18

Biscuit dough, sprinkled with sharp Cheddar cheese, is rolled up like a jelly roll, then cut into slices. Serve these zesty biscuits with either baked ham or smoked turkey.

2 cups all-purpose flour, scoop measured
3 teaspoons baking powder
¾ teaspoon salt
4 tablespoons butter or margarine, cut into
  small pieces
½ cup milk
1 large egg
¾ cup shredded sharp Cheddar cheese
Paprika

1. Preheat the oven to 425°F. Lightly grease a baking sheet without sides. Combine the flour, baking powder, and salt in a large mixing bowl. Whisk to blend thoroughly. Add the butter and cut in with a knife until the mixture is crumbly.

2. In a separate bowl, whisk together the milk and egg. Make a well in the dry ingredients. Pour in the egg mixture and toss with a fork until the dough holds together.

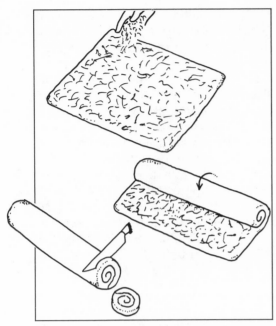

To make Cheddar Biscuits, distribute the filling over the surface of the dough. Roll the dough up like a jelly roll and cut into 18 slices. Place the slices, cut side down, on the prepared baking sheet.

Gather the dough into a ball and roll it around the inside of the bowl to pick up any stray particles. Transfer to a lightly floured surface and knead 20 to 25 times, sifting on flour if necessary to prevent sticking. Pat into a rectangle and roll to a ½-inch thickness. Trim the edges to square off the rectangle. Lift the dough to loosen it from the work surface. Distribute the cheese over the surface and sprinkle on the paprika. Roll the dough up like a jelly roll and cut into 18 slices. Place the slices, cut side down, on the prepared baking sheet. (See illustration.) Bake for 12 to 15 minutes, or until nicely browned. Serve immediately or cool on a rack.   ❖

Zesty Cheese Biscuits

MAKES 36

Tiny appetizer biscuits are enlivened with the sharp taste of Cheddar cheese

spread. Serve whole, or split and stuff with chicken salad to pass with cocktails.

2 cups all-purpose flour, scoop measured
3 teaspoons baking powder
¾ teaspoon salt
½ cup sharp processed cheese spread, such as Wispread
3 tablespoons butter or margarine, cut into small pieces
¾ cup milk

1. Preheat the oven to 425°F. Lightly grease a baking sheet without sides. Combine the flour, baking powder, and salt in a large mixing bowl. Whisk to blend thoroughly. Add the cheese and butter, and cut in with a knife until the mixture is crumbly.
2. Make a well in the dry ingredients. Pour in the milk and toss with a fork until the dough holds together. Gather the dough into a ball and roll it around the inside of the bowl to pick up any stray particles. Transfer to a lightly floured surface and knead 20 to 25 times, sifting on flour if necessary to prevent sticking. Pat into a circle, then roll to a ¾-inch thickness. Cut out with a 1-inch biscuit cutter and place on the prepared baking sheet. Bake for 12 to 15 minutes, or until nicely browned. Serve immediately or cool on a rack.   ❖

Cream Cheese and Bacon Biscuits

MAKES 15

Cream cheese gives these bacon-flecked biscuits a cakey texture.

2 cups all-purpose flour, scoop measured
3 teaspoons baking powder
¾ teaspoon salt
½ cup cream cheese, softened
3 tablespoons butter or margarine, cut into small pieces
6 strips of bacon, cooked, drained, and finely crumbled
¾ cup milk

1. Preheat the oven to 425°F. Lightly grease a baking sheet without sides. Com-

bine the flour, baking powder, and salt in a large mixing bowl. Whisk to blend thoroughly. Add the cream cheese and butter, and cut in with a knife until the mixture is crumbly. Stir in the bacon.

2. Make a well in the dry ingredients. Pour in the milk and toss with a fork until the dough holds together. Gather the dough into a ball and roll it around the inside of the bowl to pick up any stray particles. Transfer to a lightly floured surface and knead 20 to 25 times, sifting on flour if necessary to prevent sticking. Pat into a circle, then roll to a ¾-inch thickness. Cut out with a 2-inch biscuit cutter and place on the prepared baking sheet. Bake for 12 to 15 minutes, or until nicely browned. Serve immediately or cool on a rack.   ❖

Chive Biscuits

MAKES 15

Sour cream is the secret ingredient that makes these biscuits extra tender.

2 cups all-purpose flour, scoop measured
2 teaspoons baking powder
½ teaspoon baking soda
¾ teaspoon salt
4 tablespoons butter or margarine, cut into small pieces
1 tablespoon freeze-dried chives
¾ cup sour cream

1. Preheat the oven to 425°F. Lightly grease a baking sheet without sides. Combine the flour, baking powder, baking soda, and salt in a large mixing bowl. Whisk to blend thoroughly. Add the butter and cut in with a knife until the mixture is crumbly. Stir in the chives.

2. Make a well in the dry ingredients. Pour in the sour cream and toss with a fork until the dough holds together. Gather the dough into a ball and roll it around the inside of the bowl to pick up any stray particles. Transfer to a lightly floured surface and knead 20 to 25 times, sifting on flour if

necessary to prevent sticking. Pat into a circle, then roll to a ¾-inch thickness. Cut out with a 2-inch biscuit cutter and place on the prepared baking sheet. Bake for 12 to 15 minutes, or until nicely browned. Serve immediately or cool on a rack.   ❖

Cinnamon Drop Biscuits

MAKES 18

The combination of buttermilk and cinnamon makes these easy biscuits a breakfast favorite.

2½ cups all-purpose flour, scoop measured
½ cup sugar
1½ teaspoons baking powder
½ teaspoon baking soda
½ teaspoon salt
1 teaspoon cinnamon
¼ cup solid vegetable shortening
1 cup buttermilk

1. Preheat the oven to 400°F. Lightly grease a baking sheet without sides. Combine the flour, sugar, baking powder, baking soda, salt, and cinnamon in a large mixing bowl. Whisk to blend thoroughly. Add the shortening and cut in with a knife until the mixture is crumbly.

2. Make a well in the dry ingredients. Pour in the buttermilk and toss with a fork until the dough begins to hold together. Take up by generous tablespoonfuls and drop onto the prepared baking sheet. Bake for 15 to 18 minutes, or until nicely browned. Serve immediately or cool on a rack.   ❖

Gingerbread Biscuits

MAKES 15

What could be better than warm gingerbread on a snowy afternoon? Split these biscuits and spread with dollops of whipped butter.

2 cups all-purpose flour, scoop measured
¼ cup sugar

1 teaspoon baking soda
½ teaspoon salt
½ teaspoon ground ginger
⅓ cup butter or margarine, cut into small
    pieces
½ cup milk
¼ cup molasses

1. Preheat the oven to 425°F. Lightly grease a baking sheet without sides. Combine the flour, sugar, baking soda, salt, and ginger in a large mixing bowl. Whisk to blend thoroughly. Add the butter and cut in with a knife until the mixture is crumbly. In a separate bowl, whisk together the milk and molasses.

2. Make a well in the dry ingredients. Pour in the molasses mixture and toss with a fork until the dough holds together. Gather the dough into a ball and roll it around the inside of the bowl to pick up any stray particles. Transfer to a lightly floured surface and knead 20 to 25 times, sifting on flour if necessary to prevent sticking. Pat into a circle, then roll to a ¾-inch thickness. Cut out with a 2-inch biscuit cutter and place on the prepared baking sheet. Bake for 12 to 15 minutes, or until nicely browned. Serve immediately or cool on a rack.   ❖

Gorgonzola Biscuits

MAKES 15

Sensational biscuits to serve in place of rolls with roast veal or to accompany a chilled green salad.

2 cups all-purpose flour, scoop measured
3 teaspoons baking powder
½ teaspoon salt
4 tablespoons butter or margarine, cut into
    small pieces
½ cup crumbled Gorgonzola cheese
¾ cup milk

1. Preheat the oven to 425°F. Lightly grease a baking sheet without sides. Combine the flour, baking powder, and salt in a

large mixing bowl. Whisk to blend thoroughly. Add the butter and cut in with a knife until the mixture is crumbly. Stir in the cheese.

2. Make a well in the dry ingredients. Pour in the milk and toss with a fork until the dough holds together. Gather the dough into a ball and roll it around the inside of the bowl to pick up any stray particles. Transfer to a lightly floured surface and knead 20 to 25 times, sifting on flour if necessary to prevent sticking. Pat into a circle, then roll to a ¾-inch thickness. Cut out with a 2-inch biscuit cutter and place on the prepared baking sheet. Bake for 12 to 15 minutes, or until nicely browned. Serve immediately or cool on a rack.   ❖

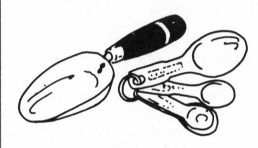

Herbed Biscuits

MAKES 15

These raised biscuits, redolent of herbs, are a terrific complement to hot creamed soup.

2 cups all-purpose flour
2 teaspoons baking powder
¾ teaspoon salt
4 tablespoons butter or margarine, cut into
    small pieces
1 teaspoon dried chervil
1 teaspoon dried thyme
¾ cup milk
1 large egg
1 package dry yeast, dissolved in ¼ cup warm
    water

1. In a large mixing bowl, combine the flour, baking powder, and salt. Whisk to blend thoroughly. Add the butter and cut in

with a knife until the mixture is crumbly. Stir in the chervil and thyme.

2. In a separate bowl, whisk together the milk and egg. Stir in the dissolved yeast. Make a well in the dry ingredients. Pour in the egg mixture and toss with a fork until the dough holds together. Gather the dough into a ball and roll it around the inside of the bowl to pick up any stray particles. Transfer to a lightly floured surface and knead 20 to 25 times, sifting on flour if necessary to prevent sticking. Pat into a circle, then roll to a ½-inch thickness. Cover with a clean kitchen towel and let rise for 1½ hours.

3. Lightly grease a baking sheet without sides. Cut out the dough with a 2-inch biscuit cutter and place on the prepared baking sheet. Cover and let rise for 45 minutes. Bake in a preheated 375°F. oven for 15 to 20 minutes, or until nicely browned. Serve immediately or cool on a rack. ❖

Herman Starter Sourdough Biscuits

MAKES 15

Herman sourdough starter creates biscuits that possess the tangy taste and smell customarily associated with sourdough bread.

1½ cups all-purpose flour, scoop measured
2 tablespoons sugar
2 teaspoons baking powder
½ teaspoon baking soda
½ teaspoon salt
4 tablespoons butter or margarine, cut into small pieces
1 cup Herman sourdough starter (p. 49), at room temperature
¼ cup milk

1. Preheat the oven to 425°F. Lightly grease a baking sheet without sides. Combine the flour, sugar, baking powder, baking soda, and salt in a large mixing bowl. Whisk to blend thoroughly. Add the butter

and cut in with a knife until the mixture is crumbly.

2. In a separate bowl, whisk together the sourdough starter and milk. Make a well in the dry ingredients. Pour in the sourdough mixture and toss with a fork until the dough holds together. Gather the dough into a ball and roll it around the inside of the bowl to pick up any stray particles. Transfer to a lightly floured surface and knead 20 to 25 times, sifting on flour if necessary to prevent sticking. Pat into a circle, then roll to a ¾-inch thickness. Cut out using a 2-inch biscuit cutter and place on the prepared baking sheet. Bake for 12 to 15 minutes, or until nicely browned. Serve immediately or cool on a rack. ❖

Jam-Filled Biscuits

MAKES 15

Packets of tender biscuit dough are filled with jam and fried in deep fat until golden brown.

2⅓ cups all-purpose flour, scoop measured
2 tablespoons sugar
3 teaspoons baking powder
¾ teaspoon salt
⅓ cup solid vegetable shortening
¾ cup milk
1 large egg
½ cup blueberry, strawberry, or raspberry jam
Vegetable oil for deep-frying
Confectioners' sugar

1. In a large mixing bowl, combine the flour, sugar, baking powder, and salt. Whisk to blend thoroughly. Add the shortening and cut in with a knife until the mixture is crumbly.

2. In a separate bowl, whisk together the milk and egg. Make a well in the dry ingredients. Pour in the egg mixture and toss with a fork until the dough holds together. Gather the dough into a ball and roll it around the inside of the bowl to pick up any stray particles. Transfer to a lightly floured

surface and knead 20 to 25 times, sifting on flour if necessary to prevent sticking. Pat into a circle, then roll to a ¼-inch thickness. Cut out with a 2½-inch biscuit cutter. Spoon a dollop of jam on half the rounds. Moisten the edge of each round and top with the remaining rounds of dough. Press to seal with your fingers or the tines of a fork. Heat the oil to 370°F. Transfer 6 biscuits at a time to the hot oil and deep-fry until golden brown. Drain on absorbent paper and dust with sifted confectioners' sugar before serving.   ❖

Lemon Sour Cream Biscuits

MAKES 36

These engaging lemon-scented biscuits are a wonderful addition to a plate of teatime goodies.

2 cups all-purpose flour, scoop measured
2 teaspoons baking powder
½ teaspoon baking soda
½ teaspoon salt
4 tablespoons butter or margarine, cut into
   small pieces
¾ cup sour cream
2 tablespoons freshly squeezed lemon juice
1 teaspoon finely grated lemon zest

1. Preheat the oven to 425°F. Lightly grease a baking sheet without sides. Combine the flour, baking powder, baking soda, and salt in a large mixing bowl. Whisk to blend thoroughly. Add the butter and cut in with a knife until the mixture is crumbly.

2. In a separate bowl, whisk together the sour cream and lemon juice. Stir in the lemon zest. Make a well in the dry ingredients. Pour in the sour cream mixture and toss with a fork until the dough holds together. Gather the dough into a ball and roll it around the inside of the bowl to pick up any stray particles. Transfer to a lightly floured surface and knead 20 to 25 times, sifting on flour if necessary to prevent sticking. Pat into a circle, then roll to a ¾-inch thickness. Cut out with a 1-inch biscuit cutter

and place on the prepared baking sheet. Bake for 12 to 15 minutes, or until nicely browned. Serve immediately or cool on a rack.   ❖

Maine Biscuits

MAKES 15

Traditionally made with water instead of milk, these biscuits are a classic Down East favorite.

2 cups all-purpose flour, scoop measured
3 teaspoons baking powder
1 teaspoon salt
¼ cup solid vegetable shortening
¾ cup cold water
2 tablespoons butter or margarine, melted

1. Preheat the oven to 425°F. Lightly grease a baking sheet without sides. Combine the flour, baking powder, and salt in a large mixing bowl. Whisk to blend thoroughly. Add the shortening and cut in with a knife until the mixture is crumbly.

2. Make a well in the dry ingredients. Pour in the water and toss with a fork until the dough holds together. Gather the dough into a ball and roll it around the inside of the bowl to pick up any stray particles. Transfer to a lightly floured surface and knead 20 to 25 times, sifting on flour if necessary to prevent sticking. Pat into a circle, then roll to a ¾-inch thickness. Cut out with a 2-inch biscuit cutter and place on the prepared baking sheet. Brush the tops with the melted butter and bake for 12 to 15 minutes, or until nicely browned. Serve immediately or cool on a rack.   ❖

Maple Biscuits

MAKES 36

These unique biscuits are shaped into small squares. Serve them as appetizers, stuffed with shaved smoked ham.

2 cups all-purpose flour, scoop measured
3 teaspoons baking powder

¾ teaspoon salt
4 tablespoons butter or margarine, cut into
  small pieces, plus 1 tablespoon
⅔ cup milk
⅓ cup pure maple syrup, plus 2 tablespoons

1. Preheat the oven to 425°F. Lightly grease a baking sheet without sides. Combine the flour, baking powder, and salt in a large mixing bowl. Whisk to blend thoroughly. Add 4 tablespoons of the butter and cut in with a knife until the mixture is crumbly.

2. In a separate bowl, whisk together the milk and ⅓ cup of the maple syrup. Make a well in the dry ingredients. Pour in the maple syrup mixture and toss with a fork until the dough holds together. Gather the dough into a ball and roll it around the inside of the bowl to pick up any stray particles. Transfer to a lightly floured surface and knead 20 to 25 times, sifting on flour if necessary to prevent sticking. Press into a 9-inch square. Trim the edges with a serrated knife. Cut the dough into 6 equal strips. Divide the strips into 6 equal portions to form square biscuits.

3. Transfer the biscuits to the prepared baking sheet. In a small saucepan, heat the remaining tablespoon butter with the remaining 2 tablespoons maple syrup. Stir until the butter is melted, then brush over the tops of the biscuits. Bake for 12 to 15 minutes, or until nicely browned. Split with a fork and stuff to serve immediately, or cool on a rack to use later.   ❖

Mustard Thyme Biscuits

MAKES 24

Form these zesty biscuits into tiny rounds, then serve them as an appetizer stuffed with shaved smoked turkey and alfalfa sprouts.

2 cups all-purpose flour, scoop measured
1 tablespoon dry mustard
3 teaspoons baking powder
½ teaspoon salt
1½ teaspoons dried thyme
⅓ cup butter or margarine, cut into small
  pieces
¾ cup milk

1. Preheat the oven to 425°F. Lightly grease a baking sheet without sides. Combine the flour, mustard, baking powder, and salt in a large mixing bowl. Whisk to blend thoroughly. Stir in the thyme. Add the butter and cut in with a knife until the mixture is crumbly.

2. Make a well in the dry ingredients. Pour in the milk and toss with a fork until the dough holds together. Gather the dough into a ball and roll it around the inside of the bowl to pick up any stray particles. Transfer to a lightly floured surface and knead 20 to 25 times, sifting on flour if necessary to prevent sticking. Pat into a circle, then roll to a ¾-inch thickness. Cut out with a 1½-inch biscuit cutter and place on the prepared baking sheet. Bake for 12 to 15 minutes, or until nicely browned. Serve immediately or cool on a rack.   ❖

Orange Biscuits

MAKES 15

Freshly squeezed orange juice lends a sunny flavor and cheerful color to these flaky biscuits.

2 cups all-purpose flour, scoop measured
¼ cup sugar
2 teaspoons baking powder
½ teaspoon baking soda
½ teaspoon salt
1½ teaspoons finely grated orange zest
⅓ cup butter or margarine, cut into small
  pieces
¾ cup freshly squeezed orange juice

1. Preheat the oven to 425°F. Lightly grease a baking sheet without sides. Combine the flour, sugar, baking powder, baking soda, and salt in a large mixing bowl. Whisk to blend thoroughly. Stir in the or-

ange zest. Add the butter and cut in with a knife until the mixture is crumbly.

2. Make a well in the dry ingredients. Pour in the orange juice and toss with a fork until the dough holds together. Gather the dough into a ball and roll it around the inside of the bowl to pick up any stray particles. Transfer to a lightly floured surface and knead 20 to 25 times, sifting on flour if necessary to prevent sticking. Pat into a circle, then roll to a ¾-inch thickness. Cut out with a 2-inch biscuit cutter and place on the prepared baking sheet. Bake for 12 to 15 minutes, or until nicely browned. Serve immediately or cool on a rack.   ❖

Onion Poppy Seed Biscuits

MAKES 15

These savory, onion-filled biscuits go well with grilled flank steak.

2 cups all-purpose flour, scoop measured
2 tablespoons sugar
3 teaspoons baking powder
¾ teaspoon salt
1 medium onion, grated
1 tablespoon poppy seeds
4 tablespoons butter or margarine, cut into small pieces
⅔ cup milk
1 large egg

1. Preheat the oven to 400°F. Lightly grease a baking sheet without sides. Combine the flour, sugar, baking powder, and salt in a large mixing bowl. Whisk to blend thoroughly. Stir in the onion and poppy seeds. Add the butter and cut in with a knife until the mixture is crumbly.

2. In a separate bowl, whisk together the milk and egg. Make a well in the dry ingredients and pour in the egg mixture. Toss with a fork until the dough holds together. Gather the dough into a ball and roll it around the inside of the bowl to pick up any stray particles. Transfer to a lightly floured surface and knead 20 to 25 times, sifting on flour if necessary to prevent sticking. Pat

into a circle, then roll to a ¾-inch thickness. Cut out with a 2-inch biscuit cutter and place on the prepared baking sheet. Bake for 15 to 18 minutes, or until nicely browned. Serve immediately or cool on a rack.   ❖

Caramelized Onion Biscuits

MAKES 18

Memorable drop biscuits to take on a picnic with cold sliced ham or pork pâté.

2 tablespoons vegetable oil
2 tablespoons butter or margarine, plus 4 tablespoons, cut into small pieces
1 medium onion, finely chopped
1 tablespoon sugar
2 cups all-purpose flour, scoop measured
3 teaspoons baking powder
¾ teaspoon salt
¾ cup milk
1 large egg

1. Heat the oil and 2 tablespoons of the butter in a small saucepan. When the butter is melted, stir in the onion and sugar. Cook, uncovered, over low heat until the onion is golden brown. Remove from the heat and set aside.

2. Preheat the oven to 400°F. Lightly grease a baking sheet without sides. Combine the flour, baking powder, and salt in a large mixing bowl. Whisk to blend thoroughly. Add the remaining 4 tablespoons of butter and cut in with a knife until the mixture is crumbly.

3. In a separate bowl, whisk together the milk and egg. Stir in the onion. Make a well in the dry ingredients. Pour in the egg mixture and toss with a fork until the dough begins to hold together. Take up by generous tablespoonfuls and drop onto the prepared

baking sheet. Bake for 15 to 18 minutes, or until nicely browned. Serve immediately or cool on a rack.   ❖

Peanut Butter Biscuits

MAKES 15

A real treat for peanut butter lovers, these biscuits are very nutritious as well.

2 cups all-purpose flour, scoop measured
1 tablespoon sugar
3 teaspoons baking powder
¾ teaspoon salt
¼ cup smooth peanut butter
2 tablespoons solid vegetable shortening
¾ cup milk

1. Preheat the oven to 425°F. Lightly grease a baking sheet without sides. Combine the flour, sugar, baking powder, and salt in a large mixing bowl. Whisk to blend thoroughly. Add the peanut butter and shortening, and cut in with a knife until the mixture is crumbly.

2. Make a well in the dry ingredients. Pour in the milk and toss with a fork until the dough holds together. Gather the dough into a ball and roll it around the inside of the bowl to pick up any stray particles. Transfer to a lightly floured surface and knead 20 to 25 times, sifting on flour if necessary to prevent sticking. Pat into a circle, then roll to a ¾-inch thickness. Cut out with a 2-inch biscuit cutter and place on the prepared baking sheet. Bake for 12 to 15 minutes, or until nicely browned. Serve immediately or cool on a rack.   ❖

Pinwheel Biscuits

MAKES 18

These old-time favorites are made by rolling biscuit dough into a rectangle, then brushing on melted butter. Rolled up jelly-roll style and cut into slices, this dough produces lovely looking biscuits.

2 cups all-purpose flour, scoop measured
2 tablespoons sugar

3 teaspoons baking powder
¾ teaspoon salt
4 tablespoons butter or margarine, cut into small pieces, plus 2 tablespoons
¾ cup milk

1. Preheat the oven to 425°F. Lightly grease a baking sheet without sides. Combine the flour, sugar, baking powder, and salt in a large mixing bowl. Whisk to blend thoroughly. Add 4 tablespoons of the butter and cut in with a knife until the mixture is crumbly. Melt the remaining 2 tablespoons butter.

2. Make a well in the dry ingredients. Pour in the milk and toss with a fork until the dough holds together. Gather the dough into a ball and roll it around the inside of the bowl to pick up any stray particles. Transfer to a lightly floured surface and knead 20 to 25 times, sifting on flour if necessary to prevent sticking. Pat into a rectangle and roll to a ½-inch thickness. Trim the edges to square off the rectangle. Lift the dough to loosen it from the work surface. Brush the surface with the melted butter. Roll the dough up like a jelly roll and cut into 18 slices. Place the slices, cut side down, on the prepared baking sheet. (See illustration on page 174.) Bake for 12 to 15 minutes, or until nicely browned. Serve immediately or cool on a rack.   ❖

Baked Potato Biscuits

MAKES 18

Feta cheese lends its tangy flavor to these unique biscuits made with mashed baked potato.

1 large potato, baked until tender
2 tablespoons butter or margarine, plus 2 tablespoons, cut into small pieces
1½ cups all-purpose flour, scoop measured
3 teaspoons baking powder
¾ teaspoon salt
½ cup finely crumbled feta cheese
2 tablespoons chopped fresh parsley
⅔ cup milk

1. Cut the hot baked potato in half and scoop out the flesh. Mash with 2 table-spoons of the butter and set aside.

2. Preheat the oven to 425°F. Lightly grease a baking sheet without sides. Com-bine the flour, baking powder, and salt in a large mixing bowl. Whisk to blend thor-oughly. Stir in the feta cheese and parsley. Add the remaining 2 tablespoons butter and cut in with a knife until the mixture is crumbly. Cut in the mashed potato.

3. Make a well in the dry ingredients. Pour in the milk and toss with a fork until the dough holds together. Gather the dough into a ball and roll it around the inside of the bowl to pick up any stray particles. Transfer to a lightly floured surface and knead 20 to 25 times, sifting on flour if nec-essary to prevent sticking. Pat into a circle, then roll to a ¾-inch thickness. Cut out with a 2-inch biscuit cutter and place on the prepared baking sheet. Bake for 12 to 15 minutes, or until nicely browned. Serve immediately or cool on a rack.   ❖

Pumpkin Biscuits

MAKES 15

For a change from standard holiday fare, offer these spicy biscuits as an accompa-niment to roast turkey.

⅓ cup milk
2 tablespoons molasses
½ cup pumpkin purée
2 cups all-purpose flour, scoop measured
2 tablespoons light brown sugar
2 teaspoons baking powder
½ teaspoon baking soda
¾ teaspoon salt
1 teaspoon ground ginger
½ teaspoon cinnamon
¼ teaspoon ground cloves
4 tablespoons butter or margarine, cut into small pieces

1. In a small saucepan, heat the milk and molasses until the molasses liquefies. Stir in the pumpkin purée and set aside.

2. Preheat the oven to 425°F. Lightly grease a baking sheet without sides. Sift the flour, sugar, baking powder, baking soda, salt, ginger, cinnamon, and cloves into a large bowl. Whisk to blend thorough-ly. Add the butter and cut in with a knife until the mixture is crumbly.

3. Make a well in the dry ingredients. Pour in the pumpkin mixture and toss with a fork until the dough holds together. Gath-er the dough into a ball and roll it around the inside of the bowl to pick up any stray particles. Transfer to a lightly floured sur-face and knead 20 to 25 times, sifting on flour if necessary to prevent sticking. Pat into a circle, then roll to a ¾-inch thick-ness. Cut out with a 2-inch biscuit cutter and place on the prepared baking sheet. Bake for 12 to 15 minutes, or until nicely browned. Serve immediately or cool on a rack.   ❖

Rye Biscuits

MAKES 15

These caraway-dotted biscuits are the perfect complement to grilled salmon or a cold shrimp salad.

1 cup rye flour, scoop measured
1 cup all-purpose flour, scoop measured
3 teaspoons baking powder
¾ teaspoon salt
1 tablespoon caraway seeds
⅓ cup solid vegetable shortening
¾ cup medium or whipping cream, plus 2 tablespoons

1. Preheat the oven to 425°F. Lightly grease a baking sheet without sides. Com-bine the rye flour, all-purpose flour, baking powder, and salt. Whisk to blend the dry ingredients thoroughly. Stir in the caraway seeds. Add the shortening and cut in with a knife until the mixture is crumbly.

2. Make a well in the dry ingredients. Pour in ¾ cup of the cream. Toss with a fork until the dough holds together. Gather the dough into a ball and roll it around the in-

side of the bowl to pick up any stray particles. Transfer to a lightly floured surface and knead 20 to 25 times, sifting on flour if necessary to prevent sticking. Pat into a circle, then roll to a ¾-inch thickness. Cut out with a 2-inch biscuit cutter and place on the prepared baking sheet. Brush the tops with the remaining 2 tablespoons cream. Bake for 12 to 15 minutes, or until nicely browned. Serve immediately or cool on a rack. ❖

Toasted Sesame Biscuits

MAKES 36

Offer these tasty biscuits as an appetizer with a wedge of sharp Cheddar cheese.

2 cups all-purpose flour, scoop measured
2 tablespoons sugar
3 teaspoons baking powder
¾ teaspoon salt
½ cup toasted sesame seeds, plus 2 tablespoons
6 tablespoons butter or margarine, cut into small pieces
¾ cup milk
1 egg white, beaten until foamy

1. Preheat the oven to 425°F. Lightly grease a baking sheet without sides. Combine the flour, sugar, baking powder, and salt in a large mixing bowl. Whisk to blend thoroughly. Stir in ½ cup of the sesame seeds. Add the butter and cut in with a knife until the mixture is crumbly.

2. Make a well in the dry ingredients. Pour in the milk and toss with a fork until the dough holds together. Gather the dough into a ball and roll it around the inside of the bowl to pick up any stray particles.

Transfer to a lightly floured surface and knead 20 to 25 times, sifting on flour if necessary to prevent sticking. Pat into a circle, then roll to a ¾-inch thickness. Cut out with a 1-inch biscuit cutter and place on the prepared baking sheet. Brush the tops with the beaten egg white and sprinkle on the remaining 2 tablespoons sesame seeds. Bake for 12 to 15 minutes, or until nicely browned. Serve immediately or cool on a rack. ❖

Shortcake Biscuits

MAKES 12

Split these delectable biscuits and spoon on your favorite berries. Add generous dollops of whipped cream, and you've created old-fashioned shortcake.

2 cups all-purpose flour, scoop measured
¼ cup sugar
3 teaspoons baking powder
¼ teaspoon salt
Generous amount of freshly grated nutmeg
4 tablespoons butter or margarine, cut into small pieces
¾ cup milk

1. Preheat the oven to 425°F. Lightly grease a baking sheet without sides. Combine the flour, sugar, baking powder, and salt in a large mixing bowl. Whisk to blend thoroughly. Stir in the nutmeg. Add the butter and cut in with a knife until the mixture is crumbly.

2. Make a well in the dry ingredients. Pour in the milk and toss with a fork until the dough holds together. Gather the dough into a ball and roll it around the inside of the bowl to pick up any stray particles. Transfer to a lightly floured surface and knead 20 to 25 times, sifting on flour if necessary to prevent sticking. Pat into a circle, then roll to a ¾-inch thickness. Cut out with a 2½-inch biscuit cutter and place on the prepared baking sheet. Bake for 12 to 15 minutes, or until nicely browned. Serve immediately or cool on a rack. ❖

Squash Raisin Biscuits

MAKES 15

Dotted with raisins, these enticing biscuits are ideal for brunch.

2 cups all-purpose flour, scoop measured
½ cup sugar
3 teaspoons baking powder
¾ teaspoon salt
½ teaspoon allspice
4 tablespoons butter or margarine, cut into
   small pieces
½ cup raisins
⅓ cup milk
½ cup puréed winter squash
2 tablespoons pure maple syrup

1. Preheat the oven to 425°F. Lightly grease a baking sheet without sides. Combine the flour, sugar, baking powder, salt, and allspice in a large mixing bowl. Whisk to blend thoroughly. Add the butter and cut in with a knife until the mixture is crumbly. Stir in the raisins.

2. In a separate bowl, whisk together the milk, puréed squash, and maple syrup. Make a well in the dry ingredients. Pour in the squash mixture and toss with a fork until the dough holds together. Gather the dough into a ball and roll it around the inside of the bowl to pick up any stray particles. Transfer to a lightly floured surface and knead 20 to 25 times, sifting on flour if necessary to prevent sticking. Pat into a circle, then roll to a ¾-inch thickness. Cut out with a 2-inch biscuit cutter and place on the prepared baking sheet. Bake for 12 to 15 minutes, or until nicely browned. Serve immediately or cool on a rack.   ❖

Sweet Potato Drop Biscuits

MAKES 18

Sweet potato purée can be frozen in quantity. Bake sweet potatoes until tender, split the skins, and scoop out the flesh. Put through a sieve or food mill and freeze in containers. Defrost and use as needed.

1 cup all-purpose flour, scoop measured
2 tablespoons light brown sugar
3 teaspoons baking powder
¾ teaspoon salt
½ teaspoon cinnamon
¼ teaspoon nutmeg
1 cup whole wheat flour, scoop measured
3 tablespoons butter or margarine, cut into
   small pieces
3 tablespoons solid vegetable shortening
⅓ cup milk
¾ cup mashed baked sweet potato

1. Preheat the oven to 400°F. Lightly grease a baking sheet without sides. Sift the all-purpose flour, sugar, baking powder, salt, cinnamon, and nutmeg into a large bowl. Add the whole wheat flour and whisk to blend thoroughly. Add the butter and vegetable shortening, and cut in with a knife until the mixture is crumbly.

2. In a separate bowl, whisk together the milk and sweet potato. Make a well in the dry ingredients. Pour in the sweet potato mixture and toss with a fork until the dough begins to hold together. Take up by generous tablespoonfuls and drop onto the prepared baking sheet. Bake for 15 to 18 minutes, or until nicely browned. Serve immediately or cool on a rack.   ❖

Tomato Herb Biscuits

MAKES 15

The pizzalike flavor of these biscuits makes them a popular accompaniment to grilled chicken or lamb.

2 cups all-purpose flour, scoop measured
2 tablespoons sugar
3 teaspoons baking powder
¾ teaspoon salt
2 tablespoons freshly grated Parmesan cheese
1 teaspoon dried basil
½ teaspoon dried oregano
4 tablespoons butter or margarine, cut into
   small pieces
½ cup tomato purée
¼ cup water

1. Preheat the oven to 425°F. Lightly grease a baking sheet without sides. Combine the flour, sugar, baking powder, and salt in a large mixing bowl. Whisk to blend thoroughly. Stir in the Parmesan cheese, basil, and oregano. Add the butter and cut in with a knife until the mixture is crumbly.

2. In a separate bowl, whisk together the tomato purée and water. Make a well in the dry ingredients. Pour in the tomato mixture and toss with a fork until the dough holds together. Gather the dough into a ball and roll it around the inside of the bowl to pick up any stray particles. Transfer to a lightly floured surface and knead 20 to 25 times, sifting on flour if necessary to prevent sticking. Pat into a circle, then roll out to a ¾-inch thickness. Cut out with a 2-inch biscuit cutter and place on the prepared baking sheet. Bake for 12 to 15 minutes, or until nicely browned. Serve immediately or cool on a rack.   ❖

Whipped Cream Biscuits

MAKES 15

Made with whipped heavy cream, these captivating biscuits are exceptionally rich, yet light and tender.

2 cups all-purpose flour, scoop measured
¼ cup sugar
3 teaspoons baking powder
½ teaspoon salt
⅓ cup butter or margarine, cut into small
 pieces
1 cup heavy cream, whipped

1. Preheat the oven to 425°F. Lightly grease a baking sheet without sides. Combine the flour, sugar, baking powder, and salt in a large mixing bowl. Whisk to blend thoroughly. Add the butter and cut in with a knife until the mixture is crumbly.

2. Make a well in the dry ingredients. Pour in the whipped cream and toss with a fork until the dough holds together. Gather the dough into a ball and roll it around the inside of the bowl to pick up any stray parti-

cles. Transfer to a lightly floured surface and knead 20 to 25 times, sifting on flour if necessary to prevent sticking. Pat into a circle, then roll to a ¾-inch thickness. Cut out with a 2-inch biscuit cutter and place on the prepared baking sheet. Bake for 12 to 15 minutes, or until nicely browned. Serve immediately or cool on a rack.   ❖

Whole Wheat Biscuits

MAKES 15

Wheat germ gives these handsome biscuits an interesting texture.

1 cup all-purpose flour, scoop measured
1 tablespoon sugar
3 teaspoons baking powder
¾ teaspoon salt
1 cup whole wheat flour, scoop measured
⅓ cup solid vegetable shortening
¼ cup wheat germ, plus 2 tablespoons
1 cup milk
1 egg white, beaten until foamy

1. Preheat the oven to 425°F. Lightly grease a baking sheet without sides. Combine the all-purpose flour, sugar, baking powder, and salt in a large mixing bowl. Add the whole wheat flour and whisk to blend thoroughly. Add the shortening and cut in with a knife until the mixture is crumbly. Stir in ¼ cup of the wheat germ.

2. Make a well in the dry ingredients. Pour in the milk and toss with a fork until the dough holds together. Gather the dough into a ball and roll it around the inside of the bowl to pick up any stray particles. Transfer to a lightly floured surface and knead 20 to 25 times, sifting on flour if necessary to prevent sticking. Pat into a circle, then roll to a ¾-inch thickness. Cut out with a 2-inch biscuit cutter and place on the prepared baking sheet. Brush with the beaten egg white and sprinkle on the remaining 2 tablespoons wheat germ. Bake for 12 to 15 minutes, or until nicely browned. Serve immediately or cool on a rack.   ❖

❖ Pancakes and Waffles ❖

MENTION breakfast in New England, and right away I picture a stack of steaming pancakes. This probably has to do with the fact that pancakes were an integral part of my childhood. My grandmother made them every Sunday, and so did my father. Many things might change in life, but Sunday always meant pancakes.

Other New Englanders seem to share this love. Country inns and bed-and-breakfast places throughout the region regularly offer pancakes as part of the morning meal. And while health experts lament the nutritionally unsound practice of consuming hotcakes dripping in butter and syrup, the custom shows no signs of losing favor.

The very best pancakes are made from fresh batter, cooked immediately and eaten straight from the stove. To guarantee a delicate texture, mix the batter by hand with a wooden spoon. Combine the dry and liquid ingredients in a large bowl and stir until well moistened, but don't overbeat. As with muffins, expect pancake batter to contain a few lumps. They will break down during cooking.

To achieve light, puffy pancakes with a golden brown exterior, it is necessary to grease the griddle and heat it to just the right point before adding the batter. Place a griddle over medium-high heat, then spray or brush the surface with vegetable oil. You may also grease the griddle by wiping it with a piece of fat. My father used to use a slice of salt pork speared on a fork. Salt pork isn't kept in many kitchens today, but if you want to duplicate the faintly smoky flavor that results from this technique, try rubbing the hot griddle with a piece of uncooked bacon.

To test the griddle for hotness, sprinkle a few drops of water onto the surface. When the drops bead up, hop vigorously across the griddle, then evaporate, the surface is at the correct temperature. If the drops fail to bead up, the griddle is too hot; if they fail to hop, the griddle is too cold.

A convenient way to transfer pancake batter from bowl to cooking surface is with one of those measuring cups that is part of a nesting set. One-quarter cup of batter makes a generous-size pancake. You can dip the measuring cup in and scoop out the same portion every time. Consequently, all your pancakes will be an identical size.

As pancake batter stands, it becomes thicker. And since thicker batter produces pancakes with a heavier texture, it is a good idea to check it as you go along. The batter should have a pourable consistency, similar to that of thick heavy cream. To maintain that consistency, stir in a small amount of milk whenever it is needed.

Pancakes should be served as soon as they are cooked, but that is sometimes impractical. For those occasions when you need to prepare a quantity of pancakes ahead of time, you may transfer them to a jelly-roll pan as they come off the griddle. Arrange the pancakes in stacks of 2 or 3 and place the pan in a preheated 325°F. oven for up to 30 minutes. Keep in mind, however, that their quality will suffer.

Waffles are a close cousin to pancakes, except that they are cooked in a decorative grill. The batter is relatively thick, but in most cases it is lightened by folding in whipped egg whites. Waffles should be cooked on a grill that has been greased.

Spray-type vegetable oil is the most efficient way to get the job done because it covers the indentations of the grill evenly yet lightly. To prevent sticking, spray your waffle iron with oil before each batch, even if you have one with a nonstick surface. Then heat the waffle iron until the indicator signals that the surface is hot. Pour on enough batter to cover the grid and close the top.

Like pancakes, waffles are best when eaten as soon as they are cooked, but if necessary they may be kept in a warm oven as described above. Waffles are traditionally served for breakfast with butter and syrup. Contemporary cooks, however, frequently pair them with fresh fruit and light toppings, such as a dollop of yogurt.

In spite of the fact that pancakes and waffles are best when eaten freshly made, it is possible to freeze them with acceptable results. When they are cooked, transfer them to a baking sheet and arrange them in a single layer. Allow them to cool and place them in the freezer without wrapping. Freeze for 6 hours, then transfer to a large plastic freezer bag. Secure with a wire twist and store in the freezer. To serve, remove 2 or 3 pancakes or waffles per person. Defrost slightly and toast, or put them directly into a microwave oven. Heat on medium power for approximately 2 minutes.

Sour Cream Apple Pancakes

MAKES 12 LARGE PANCAKES

Grated apple contributes a wonderful taste and aroma to these pancakes. Serve large ones for breakfast or form into silver-dollar–size cakes as an accompaniment to ham or roast turkey.

1½ cups all-purpose flour, scoop measured
¼ cup sugar
1½ teaspoons baking powder
½ teaspoon baking soda
¾ teaspoon salt
½ teaspoon cinnamon

½ cup milk
2 large eggs
¼ cup butter or margarine, melted
1 teaspoon vanilla extract
1½ cups sour cream
2 medium apples, peeled, cored, and grated

1. Combine the flour, sugar, baking powder, baking soda, salt, and cinnamon in a large mixing bowl. Whisk to blend the dry ingredients thoroughly.

2. In a separate bowl, whisk together the milk, eggs, melted butter, and vanilla. Stir in the sour cream. Make a well in the dry ingredients and pour in the egg mixture. Stir with a wooden spoon until well moistened. The batter will contain some lumps. Mix in the grated apple. Set the batter aside.

3. Place a griddle over medium-high heat. Brush the surface with vegetable oil or rub with a strip of uncooked bacon as the griddle warms. When the griddle is hot, stir the batter, adding more milk if necessary to create a consistency like thick heavy cream. Take up the batter by scant ¼ cups and pour onto the hot griddle. Cook until the bubbles that have formed around the outside edge are broken. Turn the pancakes over and cook the other side. Repeat with the remaining batter. Stir in additional milk as needed to maintain a pourable consistency.   ❖

Applesauce Pancakes

MAKES 12

Serve these spicy pancakes with pork sausage patties and lots of maple syrup.

2 cups all-purpose flour, scoop measured
3 tablespoons sugar
3 teaspoons baking powder
¾ teaspoon salt
1 teaspoon cinnamon
¼ teaspoon allspice
1 cup milk
2 large eggs
2 tablespoons vegetable oil

1 teaspoon vanilla extract
1 cup applesauce

1. Combine the flour, sugar, baking powder, salt, cinnamon, and allspice in a large mixing bowl. Whisk to blend thoroughly.

2. In a separate bowl, whisk together the milk, eggs, oil, and vanilla. Stir in the applesauce. Make a well in the dry ingredients and pour in the egg mixture. Stir with a wooden spoon until well moistened. The batter will contain some lumps. Set the batter aside.

3. Place a griddle over medium-high heat. Brush the surface with vegetable oil or rub with a strip of uncooked bacon as the griddle warms. When the griddle is hot, stir the batter, adding more milk if necessary to create a consistency like thick heavy cream. Take up the batter by scant ¼ cups and pour onto the hot griddle. Cook until the bubbles that have formed around the outside edge are broken. Turn the pancakes over and cook the other side. Repeat with the remaining batter. Stir in additional milk as needed to maintain a pourable consistency.   ❖

Banana Pancakes

MAKES 12

If you like banana bread, be sure to try these wonderful pancakes! The banana flavor is heightened by a small amount of cinnamon.

1½ cups all-purpose flour, scoop measured
2 tablespoons sugar
1½ teaspoons baking powder
½ teaspoon baking soda
½ teaspoon salt
¼ teaspoon cinnamon
1 cup milk
2 large eggs, separated
2 tablespoons butter or margarine, melted
1 cup mashed banana (about 2 large bananas)

1. Combine the flour, sugar, baking powder, baking soda, salt, and cinnamon in a

large mixing bowl. Whisk to blend the dry ingredients thoroughly.

2. In a separate bowl, whisk together the milk, egg yolks, and melted butter. Stir in the mashed banana. Make a well in the dry ingredients and pour in the egg yolk mixture. Stir with a wooden spoon until well moistened. The batter will contain some lumps. Whip the egg whites until soft peaks form, then fold into the batter. Set the batter aside.

3. Place a griddle over medium-high heat. Brush the surface with vegetable oil or rub with a strip of uncooked bacon as the griddle warms. When the griddle is hot, stir the batter, adding more milk if necessary to create a consistency like thick heavy cream. Take up the batter by scant ¼ cups and pour onto the hot griddle. Cook until the bubbles that have formed around the outside edge are broken. Turn the pancakes over and cook the other side. Repeat with the remaining batter. Stir in additional milk as needed to maintain a pourable consistency. ❖

Beer Pancakes

MAKES 12

Present platters of these hearty pancakes for brunch with grilled pork chops and slices of apple sautéed in butter.

2 cups all-purpose flour, scoop measured
2 tablespoons sugar
3 teaspoons baking powder
¾ teaspoon salt
½ teaspoon cinnamon
¼ teaspoon nutmeg
1½ cups beer (one 12-ounce bottle)
3 large eggs
¼ cup butter or margarine, melted

1. Combine the flour, sugar, baking powder, salt, cinnamon, and nutmeg in a large mixing bowl. Whisk to blend thoroughly.

2. In a separate bowl, whisk together the beer, eggs, and melted butter. Make a well in the dry ingredients and pour in the egg mixture. Stir with a wooden spoon until well moistened. The batter will contain some lumps. Set the batter aside.

3. Place a griddle over medium-high heat. Brush the surface with vegetable oil or rub with a strip of uncooked bacon as the griddle warms. When the griddle is hot, stir the batter, adding more beer if necessary to create a consistency like thick heavy cream. Take up the batter by scant ¼ cups and pour onto the hot griddle. Cook until the bubbles that have formed around the outside edge are broken. Turn the pancakes over and cook the other side. Repeat with the remaining batter. Stir in additional beer as needed to maintain a pourable consistency. ❖

Blueberry Oat Pancakes

MAKES 12

Quick-cooking rolled oats are whirled in a blender until fine to form the basis of these tasty blueberry pancakes.

1 cup quick-cooking rolled oats
2 tablespoons light brown sugar
1 cup all-purpose flour, scoop measured
3 teaspoons baking powder
¾ teaspoon salt
2 cups milk
1 large egg
2 tablespoons vegetable oil
1 cup fresh blueberries, rinsed and gently patted dry

1. Place the oats in the container of a blender and whirl until fine. Add the sugar and whirl to blend. Transfer to a large mixing bowl. Add the flour, baking powder, and salt, and whisk to blend thoroughly.

2. In a separate bowl, whisk together the milk, egg, and oil. Make a well in the dry ingredients and pour in the egg mixture. Stir with a wooden spoon until well moistened. The batter will contain some lumps. Stir in the blueberries and set the batter aside.

3. Place a griddle over medium-high heat. Brush the surface with vegetable oil or rub with a strip of uncooked bacon as the griddle warms. When the griddle is hot, stir the batter, adding more milk if necessary to create a consistency like thick heavy cream. Take up the batter by scant ¼ cups and pour onto the hot griddle. Cook until the bubbles that have formed around the outside edge are broken. Turn the pancakes over and cook the other side. Repeat with the remaining batter. Stir in additional milk as needed to maintain a pourable consistency.   ❖

Lemon Blueberry Pancakes

MAKES 12

Scattering the blueberries over the pancakes as they cook guarantees an even distribution of the berries.

1½ cups all-purpose flour, scoop measured
½ cup whole wheat flour, scoop measured
¼ cup sugar
1½ teaspoons baking powder
½ teaspoon baking soda
¾ teaspoon salt
2 cups buttermilk
1 large egg
3 tablespoons butter or margarine, melted
1 tablespoon freshly squeezed lemon juice
1 tablespoon finely grated lemon zest
1 cup fresh blueberries, rinsed and gently
    patted dry

1. Combine the all-purpose flour, whole wheat flour, sugar, baking powder, baking soda, and salt in a large mixing bowl. Whisk to blend thoroughly.

2. In a separate bowl, whisk together the buttermilk, egg, and melted butter. Stir in the lemon juice and lemon zest. Make a well in the dry ingredients and pour in the egg mixture. Stir with a wooden spoon until well moistened. The batter will contain some lumps. Set the batter aside.

3. Place a griddle over medium-high heat. Brush the surface with vegetable oil as the

griddle warms. When the griddle is hot, stir the batter, adding more buttermilk if necessary to create a consistency like thick heavy cream. Take up the batter by scant ¼ cups and pour onto the hot griddle. Scatter a handful of berries over the top. Cook until the bubbles that have formed around the outside edge are broken. Turn the pancakes over and cook the other side. Repeat with the remaining batter. Stir in additional buttermilk as needed to maintain a pourable consistency.   ❖

Buckwheat Pancakes

MAKES 12

Buckwheat flour is an assertively flavored flour ground from the seeds of the buckwheat plant. Long a New England staple, its availability is now generally limited to specialty food shops.

1 cup buckwheat flour, scoop measured
1 cup all-purpose flour, scoop measured
2 tablespoons sugar
2 teaspoons baking powder
½ teaspoon baking soda
¾ teaspoon salt
2 cups buttermilk
2 large eggs, separated
3 tablespoons vegetable oil

1. Combine the buckwheat flour, all-purpose flour, sugar, baking powder, baking soda, and salt in a large mixing bowl. Whisk to blend thoroughly.

2. In a separate bowl, whisk together the buttermilk, egg yolks, and oil. Make a well in the dry ingredients and pour in the egg yolk mixture. Stir with a wooden spoon until well moistened. The batter will contain some lumps. Whip the egg whites until soft peaks form, then fold into the batter. Set the batter aside.

3. Place a griddle over medium-high heat. Brush the surface with vegetable oil or rub with a strip of uncooked bacon as the griddle warms. When the griddle is hot, stir the batter, adding more buttermilk if necessary

to create a consistency like thick heavy cream. Take up the batter by scant ¼ cups and pour onto the hot griddle. Cook until the bubbles that have formed around the outside edge are broken. Turn the pancakes over and cook the other side. Repeat with the remaining batter. Stir in additional buttermilk as needed to maintain a pourable consistency. ❖

Raised Buckwheat Cakes

MAKES 12

Yeast in this pancake batter produces a slightly sour tang as it ferments. For fully developed flavor, allow the batter to stand in the refrigerator overnight.

1 cup buckwheat flour, scoop measured
1 cup all-purpose flour, scoop measured
3 tablespoons sugar
¾ teaspoon salt
2 cups milk
3 large eggs
¼ cup butter or margarine, melted
1 package dry yeast, dissolved in ¼ cup warm water

1. Combine the buckwheat flour, all-purpose flour, sugar, and salt in a large mixing bowl. Whisk to blend thoroughly.

2. In a separate bowl, whisk together the milk, eggs, and melted butter. Stir in the dissolved yeast. Make a well in the dry ingredients and pour in the egg mixture. Stir with a wooden spoon until well moistened. The batter will contain some lumps. Cover the bowl with plastic wrap and secure with an elastic band. Set aside to stand for 2 hours or refrigerate overnight.

3. Place a griddle over medium-high heat. Brush the surface with vegetable oil or rub with a strip of uncooked bacon as the griddle warms. When the griddle is hot, stir the batter, adding more milk if necessary to create a consistency like thick heavy cream. Take up the batter by scant ¼ cups and pour onto the hot griddle. Cook until the bubbles that have formed around the

outside edge are broken. Turn the pancakes over and cook the other side. Repeat with the remaining batter. Stir in additional milk as needed to maintain a pourable consistency. ❖

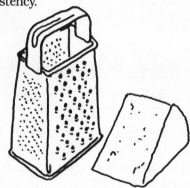

Cheddar Cheese Pancakes

MAKES 12

These savory hotcakes are excellent partners for thick slices of sizzled ham.

1¾ cups all-purpose flour, scoop measured
1 tablespoon sugar
3 teaspoons baking powder
¾ teaspoon salt
1½ cups milk
2 large eggs
¼ cup butter or margarine, melted
¾ cup shredded Cheddar cheese

1. Combine the flour, sugar, baking powder, and salt in a large mixing bowl. Whisk to blend thoroughly.

2. In a separate bowl, whisk together the milk, eggs, and melted butter. Stir in the cheese. Make a well in the dry ingredients and pour in the egg mixture. Stir with a wooden spoon until well moistened. The batter will contain some lumps. Set the batter aside.

3. Place a griddle over medium-high heat. Brush the surface with vegetable oil or rub with a strip of uncooked bacon as the griddle warms. When the griddle is hot, stir the batter, adding more milk if necessary to create a consistency like thick heavy cream. Take up the batter by scant ¼ cups and pour onto the hot griddle. Cook until

the bubbles that have formed around the outside edge are broken. Turn the pancakes over and cook the other side. Repeat with the remaining batter. Stir in additional milk as needed to maintain a pourable consistency.   ❖

Cornmeal Buttermilk Pancakes

MAKES 12

Yellow cornmeal adds a light crunch to these buttermilk pancakes.

1 cup all-purpose flour, scoop measured
1 cup yellow cornmeal
2 tablespoons sugar
2 teaspoons baking powder
½ teaspoon baking soda
¾ teaspoon salt
2 cups buttermilk
1 large egg
2 tablespoons butter or margarine, melted

1. Combine the flour, cornmeal, sugar, baking powder, baking soda, and salt in a large mixing bowl. Whisk to blend the dry ingredients thoroughly.

2. In a separate bowl, whisk together the buttermilk, egg, and melted butter. Make a well in the dry ingredients and pour in the egg mixture. Stir with a wooden spoon until well moistened. The batter will contain some lumps. Set the batter aside.

3. Place a griddle over medium-high heat. Brush the surface with vegetable oil or rub with a strip of uncooked bacon as the griddle warms. When the griddle is hot, stir the batter, adding more buttermilk if necessary to create a consistency like thick heavy cream. Take up the batter by scant ¼ cups and pour onto the hot griddle. Cook until the bubbles that have formed around the outside edge are broken. Turn the pancakes over and cook the other side. Repeat with the remaining batter. Stir in additional buttermilk as needed to maintain a pourable consistency.   ❖

Cornmeal Cranberry Pancakes

MAKES 12 LARGE PANCAKES

Sprightly chunks of tart red berries dot these cornmeal cakes. For a festive offering, cook up into tiny rounds and arrange beside sliced roast turkey.

1 cup all-purpose flour, scoop measured
1 cup yellow cornmeal
2 tablespoons sugar
2 teaspoons baking powder
½ teaspoon baking soda
¾ teaspoon salt
2 cups buttermilk
1 large egg
3 tablespoons vegetable oil
1 cup fresh cranberries, coarsely chopped

1. Combine the flour, cornmeal, sugar, baking powder, baking soda, and salt in a large mixing bowl. Whisk to blend the dry ingredients thoroughly.

2. In a separate bowl, whisk together the buttermilk, egg, and oil. Make a well in the dry ingredients and pour in the egg mixture. Stir with a wooden spoon until well moistened. The batter will contain some lumps. Stir in the cranberries and set the batter aside.

3. Place a griddle over medium-high heat. Brush the surface with vegetable oil as the griddle warms. When the griddle is hot, stir the batter, adding more buttermilk if necessary to create a consistency like thick heavy cream. Take up the batter by scant ¼ cups and pour onto the hot griddle. Cook until the bubbles that have formed around the outside edge are broken. Turn the pancakes over and cook the other side. Repeat with the remaining batter. Stir in additional buttermilk as needed to maintain a pourable consistency.   ❖

Lacy Corncakes

MAKES 48

These thin cornmeal pancakes develop delicate lacelike edges as they cook. Serve piping hot with roast pheasant or fresh pork.

1 cup yellow cornmeal
1 teaspoon baking soda
1 teaspoon salt
2 cups buttermilk
1 large egg

1. Combine the cornmeal, baking soda, and salt in a large mixing bowl. Whisk to blend thoroughly.

2. In a separate bowl, whisk together the buttermilk and egg. Make a well in the dry ingredients and pour in the egg mixture. Stir with a wooden spoon until smooth.

3. Place a griddle over medium-high heat. Brush the surface with vegetable oil as the griddle warms. When the griddle is hot, spoon the batter onto the griddle by scant tablespoonfuls. Cook until the edges are lacy. Turn the pancakes over and cook the other side. Repeat with the remaining batter and serve piping hot. ❖

Cranberry Pancakes

MAKES 12

Perfumed with almond, these pancakes are best when served with a heaping bowl of whipped unsalted butter.

2 cups all-purpose flour, scoop measured
¼ cup sugar
3 teaspoons baking powder
½ teaspoon salt
2 cups milk
2 large eggs, separated
1 teaspoon almond extract
2 tablespoons butter or margarine, melted
1 cup fresh cranberries, coarsely chopped

1. Combine the flour, sugar, baking powder, and salt in a large mixing bowl. Whisk to blend thoroughly.

2. In a separate bowl, whisk together the milk, egg yolks, almond extract, and melted butter. Make a well in the dry ingredients and pour in the egg yolk mixture. Stir with a wooden spoon until well moistened. The batter will contain some lumps. Stir in the cranberries. Whip the egg whites until soft peaks form, then fold into the batter. Set the batter aside.

3. Place a griddle over medium-high heat. Brush the surface with vegetable oil as the griddle warms. When the griddle is hot, stir the batter, adding more milk if necessary to create a consistency like thick heavy cream. Take up the batter by scant ¼ cups and pour onto the hot griddle. Cook until the bubbles that have formed around the outside edge are broken. Turn the pancakes over and cook the other side. Repeat with the remaining batter. Stir in additional milk as needed to maintain a pourable consistency. ❖

Four-Grain Pancakes

MAKES 12

These are no-nonsense, stick-to-your-ribs pancakes — hearty fare for wholesome eating.

⅔ cup quick-cooking rolled oats
⅓ cup quick-cooking barley
⅔ cup whole wheat flour, scoop measured
⅓ cup yellow cornmeal
2 teaspoons baking powder
½ teaspoon baking soda
½ teaspoon salt
2 cups buttermilk
⅓ cup honey
2 large eggs
4 tablespoons vegetable oil

1. Place the oats and barley in the container of a blender or processor and whirl until a coarse powdery consistency is attained. Transfer to a large mixing bowl. Add the whole wheat flour, cornmeal, baking powder, baking soda, and salt. Whisk to blend thoroughly.

2. In a separate bowl, whisk together the buttermilk, honey, eggs, and oil. Make a well in the dry ingredients and pour in the egg mixture. Stir with a wooden spoon until well moistened. The batter will contain some lumps. Set the batter aside.

3. Place a griddle over medium-high heat. Brush the surface with vegetable oil or rub with a strip of uncooked bacon as the griddle warms. When the griddle is hot, stir the batter, adding more buttermilk if necessary to create a consistency like thick heavy cream. Take up the batter by scant ¼ cups and pour onto the hot griddle. Cook until the bubbles that have formed around the outside edge are broken. Turn the pancakes over and cook the other side. Repeat with the remaining batter. Stir in additional buttermilk as needed to maintain a pourable consistency. ❖

Granola Pancakes

MAKES 12

Kids love these coarsely textured griddle cakes. Make up a batch and wrap singly to keep in the freezer. Then heat in the toaster or microwave on busy mornings.

¾ cup whole wheat flour, scoop measured
½ cup all-purpose flour, scoop measured
2 teaspoons baking powder
¾ teaspoon salt
1 cup granola cereal, crushed
2 cups milk
2 tablespoons honey
2 large eggs
2 tablespoons butter or margarine, melted

1. Combine the whole wheat flour, all-purpose flour, baking powder, and salt in a large mixing bowl. Whisk to blend thoroughly, then stir in the granola.

2. In a separate bowl, whisk together the milk, honey, eggs, and melted butter. Make a well in the dry ingredients and pour in the egg mixture. Stir with a wooden spoon until well moistened. The batter will contain some lumps. Set the batter aside.

3. Place a griddle over medium-high heat. Brush the surface with vegetable oil or rub with a strip of uncooked bacon as the griddle warms. When the griddle is hot, stir the batter, adding more milk if necessary to create a consistency like thick heavy cream. Take up the batter by scant ¼ cups and pour onto the hot griddle. Cook until the bubbles that have formed around the outside edge are broken. Turn the pancakes over and cook the other side. Repeat with the remaining batter. Stir in additional milk as needed to maintain a pourable consistency. ❖

Lemon Pancakes

MAKES 24

Serve these delicate cakes with a pitcher of warmed honey and thin slices of baked ham.

2 cups all-purpose flour, scoop measured
3 tablespoons sugar
2 teaspoons baking powder
½ teaspoon baking soda
½ teaspoon salt
2 cups milk
2 large eggs, separated
6 tablespoons butter or margarine, melted
2 tablespoons freshly squeezed lemon juice
1 tablespoon finely grated lemon zest

1. Combine the flour, sugar, baking powder, baking soda, and salt in a large mixing bowl. Whisk to blend thoroughly.

2. In a separate bowl, whisk together the milk, egg yolks, and melted butter. Stir in the lemon juice and lemon zest. Make a well in the dry ingredients and pour in the egg yolk mixture. Stir with a wooden spoon until well moistened. The batter will contain some lumps. Whip the egg whites until soft peaks form, then fold into the batter. Set the batter aside.

3. Place a griddle over medium-high heat. Brush the surface with vegetable oil as the griddle warms. When the griddle is hot, stir the batter, adding more milk if necessary to

create a consistency like thick heavy cream. Take up the batter by serving spoonfuls and pour onto the hot griddle. Cook until the bubbles that have formed around the outside edge are broken. Turn the pancakes over and cook the other side. Repeat with the remaining batter. Stir in additional milk as needed to maintain a pourable consistency.   ❖

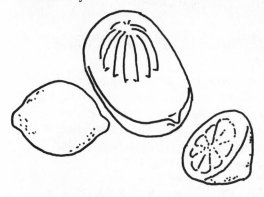

Light-as-Air Pancakes

MAKES 12

Carbonated bubbles of club soda make these pancakes incredibly light and tender.

2 cups all-purpose flour, scoop measured
2 tablespoons sugar
3 teaspoons baking powder
¾ teaspoon salt
2 cups club soda
2 large eggs, separated
3 tablespoons butter or margarine, melted

1. Combine the flour, sugar, baking powder, and salt in a large mixing bowl. Whisk to blend thoroughly.

2. In a separate bowl, whisk together 1 cup of the club soda, the egg yolks, and the melted butter. Whip the egg whites until soft peaks form and set aside. Make a well in the dry ingredients. Pour in the egg yolk mixture and the remaining cup of club soda. Stir with a wooden spoon until well moistened. The batter will contain some lumps. Fold in the whipped egg whites. Set the batter aside.

3. Place a griddle over medium-high heat. Brush the surface with vegetable oil as the griddle warms. When the griddle is hot, stir the batter, adding more club soda if necessary to create a consistency like thick heavy cream. Take up the batter by scant ¼ cups and pour onto the hot griddle. Cook until the bubbles that have formed around the outside edge are broken. Turn the pancakes over and cook the other side. Repeat with the remaining batter. Stir in additional club soda as needed to maintain a pourable consistency.   ❖

Oat Bran Pancakes

MAKES 12

The earthy flavor of oat bran is most welcome on those cold, damp mornings when the maple sap has just started to run.

1 cup all-purpose flour, scoop measured
¼ cup light brown sugar
2 teaspoons baking powder
½ teaspoon baking soda
½ teaspoon salt
1 cup oat bran
2¼ cups buttermilk
1 large egg
2 tablespoons butter or margarine, melted

1. Sift the flour and sugar into a large mixing bowl. Add the baking powder, baking soda, and salt, and whisk to blend thoroughly. Stir in the oat bran.

2. In a separate bowl, whisk together the buttermilk, egg, and melted butter. Make a well in the dry ingredients and pour in the egg mixture. Stir with a wooden spoon until well moistened. The batter will contain some lumps. Set the batter aside.

3. Place a griddle over medium-high heat. Brush the surface with vegetable oil or rub with a strip of uncooked bacon as the griddle warms. When the griddle is hot, stir the batter, adding more buttermilk if necessary to create a consistency like thick heavy cream. Take up the batter by scant ¼ cups

and pour onto the hot griddle. Cook until the bubbles that have formed around the outside edge are broken. Turn the pancakes over and cook the other side. Repeat with the remaining batter. Stir in additional buttermilk as needed to maintain a pourable consistency. ❖

Old-Fashioned Oatmeal Pancakes

MAKES 12

Coarsely ground oats contribute hearty flavor to these old-fashioned pancakes.

2 cups milk
½ cup steel-cut coarse oats
2 large eggs
¼ cup light brown sugar
3 teaspoons baking powder
¾ teaspoon salt
½ teaspoon cinnamon
¼ teaspoon nutmeg
¼ cup butter or margarine, melted
1 cup all-purpose flour, scoop measured

1. Heat the milk in a wide saucepan until bubbles begin to break the surface. Remove from the heat and stir in the oatmeal. Cover the pan and set aside for 20 minutes.

2. In a large mixing bowl, whisk together the eggs and sugar. Add the baking powder, salt, cinnamon, nutmeg, and melted butter. Blend well. Stir in the oatmeal and the flour. Set the batter aside.

3. Place a griddle over medium-high heat. Brush the surface with vegetable oil as the griddle warms. When the griddle is hot, stir the batter, adding more milk if necessary to create a consistency like thick heavy cream. Take up the batter by scant ¼ cups and pour onto the hot griddle. Cook until the bubbles that have formed around the outside edge are broken. Turn the pancakes over and cook the other side. Repeat with the remaining batter. Stir in additional milk as needed to maintain a pourable consistency. ❖

Herman Starter Pancakes

MAKES 12

The popular milk-based sourdough called "Herman" forms the basis of these robust pancakes. They are wonderful served with lightly stewed blueberries.

1 cup Herman sourdough starter (p. 49)
1 cup unflavored yogurt
½ cup warm water
1½ cups all-purpose flour, scoop measured
2 large eggs
2 tablespoons sugar
1 teaspoon baking soda
½ teaspoon salt
2 tablespoons vegetable oil

1. In a large mixing bowl, combine the sourdough starter, yogurt, and water. Add ½ cup of the flour and stir to blend. Cover the bowl with plastic wrap and secure with an elastic band. Let stand at room temperature overnight.

2. In a separate bowl, whisk together the eggs and sugar. Add the baking soda, salt, and oil, and blend well. Stir into the sourdough mixture. Add the remaining cup of flour and stir with a wooden spoon until well moistened. The batter will contain some lumps. Set the batter aside.

3. Place a griddle over medium-high heat. Brush the surface with vegetable oil or rub with a strip of uncooked bacon as the griddle warms. When the griddle is hot, stir the batter, adding some milk if necessary to create a consistency like thick heavy cream. Take up the batter by scant ¼ cups and pour onto the hot griddle. Cook until

the bubbles that have formed around the outside edge are broken. Turn the pancakes over and cook the other side. Repeat with the remaining batter. Stir in additional milk as needed to maintain a pourable consistency. ❖

Pumpkin Pancakes

MAKES 12

Scented with traditional spices, these pancakes beckon your family to a special holiday breakfast.

1½ cups all-purpose flour, scoop measured
½ cup light brown sugar
2 teaspoons baking powder
½ teaspoon baking soda
½ teaspoon salt
½ teaspoon cinnamon
¼ teaspoon ground cloves
¼ teaspoon allspice
1 cup buttermilk
2 large eggs
¼ cup butter or margarine, melted
1 cup pumpkin purée

1. Sift the flour and sugar into a large mixing bowl. Add the baking powder, baking soda, salt, cinnamon, cloves, and allspice, and whisk to blend thoroughly.

2. In a separate bowl, whisk together the buttermilk, eggs, and melted butter. Stir in the pumpkin purée. Make a well in the dry ingredients and pour in the egg mixture. Stir with a wooden spoon until well moistened. The batter will contain some lumps. Set the batter aside.

3. Place a griddle over medium-high heat. Brush the surface with vegetable oil as the griddle warms. When the griddle is hot, stir the batter, adding more buttermilk if necessary to create a consistency like thick heavy cream. Take up the batter by scant ¼ cups and pour onto the hot griddle. Cook until the bubbles that have formed around the outside edge are broken. Turn the pancakes over and cook the other side. Repeat with the remaining batter. Stir in additional buttermilk as needed to maintain a pourable consistency. ❖

Quick Oven Pancakes

MAKES 10

Baked in a large shallow pan, then cut into rectangles, these "pancakes" are just the thing for serving a crowd.

1 cup whole wheat flour, scoop measured
1 cup all-purpose flour, scoop measured
2 tablespoons sugar
1½ teaspoons baking powder
½ teaspoon baking soda
½ teaspoon salt
1½ cups buttermilk
2 large eggs
¼ cup butter or margarine, melted

1. Preheat the oven to 425°F. Combine the whole wheat flour and all-purpose flour in a large mixing bowl. Add the sugar, baking powder, baking soda, and salt, and whisk to blend thoroughly.

2. In a separate bowl, whisk together the buttermilk, eggs, and melted butter. Make a well in the dry ingredients and pour in the egg mixture. Stir with a wooden spoon until well moistened. The batter will contain some lumps.

3. Generously grease a 10x15-inch shallow baking pan. Pour in the batter and spread evenly across the surface. Place in the preheated oven and bake for 12 to 15 minutes, or until lightly browned. Remove from the oven and divide in half lengthwise. Then cut into ten 3x5-inch rectangles. ❖

Sour Milk Pancakes

MAKES 12

Sour milk produces pancakes with a tender, delicate crumb and a captivating taste.

2 cups milk
1 tablespoon freshly squeezed lemon juice

2 cups all-purpose flour, scoop measured
3 tablespoons sugar
2 teaspoons baking powder
½ teaspoon baking soda
¾ teaspoon salt
2 large eggs, separated
2 tablespoons butter or margarine, melted

1. Pour the milk into a glass measuring cup. Add the lemon juice and stir. Set aside for 10 minutes to thicken slightly and become sour.

2. Combine the flour, sugar, baking powder, baking soda, and salt in a large mixing bowl. Whisk to blend thoroughly.

3. In a separate bowl, whisk together the egg yolks and melted butter. Make a well in the dry ingredients. Pour in the sour milk, then add the egg yolk mixture. Stir with a wooden spoon until well moistened. The batter will contain some lumps. Whip the egg whites until soft peaks form and fold into the batter. Set the batter aside.

4. Place a griddle over medium-high heat. Brush the surface with vegetable oil or rub with a strip of uncooked bacon as the griddle warms. When the griddle is hot, stir the batter, adding some sweet milk if necessary to create a consistency like thick heavy cream. Take up the batter by scant ¼ cups and pour onto the hot griddle. Cook until the bubbles that have formed around the outside edge are broken. Turn the pancakes over and cook the other side. Repeat with the remaining batter. Stir in additional sweet milk as needed to maintain a pourable consistency.   ❖

Winter Squash Pancakes

MAKES 12

Here is a great way to use up leftover acorn or butternut squash. Serve these flavorful pancakes with bacon or sizzled ham.

1½ cups all-purpose flour, scoop measured
3 tablespoons light brown sugar

3 teaspoons baking powder
¾ teaspoon salt
½ teaspoon nutmeg
1 cup milk
1 large egg
3 tablespoons butter or margarine, melted
1 cup mashed acorn or butternut squash

1. Sift the flour and sugar into a large mixing bowl. Add the baking powder, salt, and nutmeg, and whisk to blend the dry ingredients thoroughly.

2. In a separate bowl, whisk together the milk, egg, and melted butter. Stir in the squash. Make a well in the dry ingredients and pour in the egg mixture. Stir with a wooden spoon until well moistened. The batter will contain some lumps. Set the batter aside.

3. Place a griddle over medium-high heat. Brush the surface with vegetable oil as the griddle warms. When the griddle is hot, stir the batter, adding more milk if necessary to create a consistency like thick heavy cream. Take up the batter by scant ¼ cups and pour onto the hot griddle. Cook until the bubbles that have formed around the outside edge are broken. Turn the pancakes over and cook the other side. Repeat with the remaining batter. Stir in additional milk as needed to maintain a pourable consistency.   ❖

Swedish Pancakes

MAKES 18

Whipped cream gives these small griddle cakes an exceptionally light texture. Serve for breakfast or as an accompaniment to roast pork.

1 cup all-purpose flour, scoop measured
½ cup whole wheat flour, scoop measured
2 tablespoons sugar
1½ teaspoons baking powder
½ teaspoon salt
¾ cup cold water
2 large eggs

2 tablespoons butter or margarine, melted
1 cup heavy cream

1. Combine the all-purpose flour, whole wheat flour, and sugar in a mixing bowl. Add the baking powder and salt, and whisk to blend thoroughly.

2. In a separate bowl, whisk together the water, eggs, and melted butter. Make a well in the dry ingredients and pour in the egg mixture. Stir with a wooden spoon until well moistened. The batter will contain some lumps. Whip the cream until stiff peaks form, then fold into the batter. Set the batter aside.

3. Place a griddle over medium-high heat. Brush the surface with vegetable oil as the griddle warms. When the griddle is hot, stir the batter, adding some milk if necessary to create a consistency like thick heavy cream. Take up the batter by generous serving spoonfuls and pour onto the hot griddle. Cook until the bubbles that have formed around the outside edge are broken. Turn the pancakes over and cook the other side. Repeat with the remaining batter. Stir in additional milk as needed to maintain a pourable consistency.   ❖

Sweet 'n' Light Pancakes

MAKES 12

Confectioners' sugar is the secret ingredient in these tender griddle cakes. Serve with sliced strawberries and sweetened whipped cream.

1½ cups all-purpose flour, scoop measured
¾ cup sifted confectioners' sugar
3 teaspoons baking powder
½ teaspoon salt
1¼ cups milk
2 large eggs
6 tablespoons butter or margarine, melted

1. Combine the flour, sugar, baking powder, and salt in a large mixing bowl. Whisk to blend thoroughly.

2. In a separate bowl, whisk together the milk, eggs, and melted butter. Make a well in the dry ingredients and pour in the egg mixture. Stir with a wooden spoon until well moistened. The batter will contain some lumps. Set the batter aside.

3. Place a griddle over medium-high heat. Brush the surface with vegetable oil as the griddle warms. When the griddle is hot, stir the batter, adding more milk if necessary to create a consistency like thick heavy cream. Take up the batter by scant ¼ cups and pour onto the hot griddle. Cook until the bubbles that have formed around the outside edge are broken. Turn the pancakes over and cook the other side. Repeat with the remaining batter. Stir in additional milk as needed to maintain a pourable consistency.   ❖

Wheat Germ Pancakes

MAKES 12

Delightfully nutritious. These pancakes will tempt your kids to eat the breakfast they should.

1 cup all-purpose flour, scoop measured
2 tablespoons light brown sugar
½ cup whole wheat flour, scoop measured
¾ cup wheat germ
1½ teaspoons baking powder
½ teaspoon baking soda
½ teaspoon salt
1¼ cups buttermilk
1 large egg
2 tablespoons vegetable oil

1. Sift the all-purpose flour and sugar into a large mixing bowl. Add the whole wheat flour, wheat germ, baking powder, baking soda, and salt, and whisk to blend thoroughly.

2. In a separate bowl, whisk together the buttermilk, egg, and oil. Make a well in the dry ingredients and pour in the egg mixture. Stir with a wooden spoon until well

moistened. The batter will contain some lumps. Set the batter aside.

3. Place a griddle over medium-high heat. Brush the surface with vegetable oil or rub with a strip of uncooked bacon as the griddle warms. When the griddle is hot, stir the batter, adding more buttermilk if necessary to create a consistency like thick heavy cream. Take up the batter by scant ¼ cups and pour onto the hot griddle. Cook until the bubbles that have formed around the outside edge are broken. Turn the pancakes over and cook the other side. Repeat with the remaining batter. Stir in additional buttermilk as needed to maintain a pourable consistency.   ❖

Maple Whole Wheat Pancakes

MAKES 12

The flavor of pure maple syrup is baked right into these luscious griddle cakes. Offer with sausage patties mounded on a paper napkin–lined plate.

1½ cups whole wheat flour, scoop measured
½ cup all-purpose flour, scoop measured
3 teaspoons baking powder
¾ teaspoon salt
1¾ cups milk
⅓ cup pure maple syrup
1 large egg
¼ cup butter or margarine, melted

1. Combine the whole wheat flour, all-purpose flour, baking powder, and salt in a large mixing bowl. Whisk to blend the dry ingredients thoroughly.

2. In a separate bowl, whisk together the milk, maple syrup, egg, and melted butter. Make a well in the dry ingredients and pour in the egg mixture. Stir with a wooden spoon until well moistened. The batter will contain some lumps. Set the batter aside.

3. Place a griddle over medium-high heat. Brush the surface with vegetable oil or rub with a strip of uncooked bacon as the grid-

dle warms. When the griddle is hot, stir the batter, adding more milk if necessary to create a consistency like thick heavy cream. Take up the batter by scant ¼ cups and pour onto the hot griddle. Cook until the bubbles that have formed around the outside edge are broken. Turn the pancakes over and cook the other side. Repeat with the remaining batter. Stir in additional milk as needed to maintain a pourable consistency.   ❖

Whole Wheat Yogurt Pancakes

MAKES 12

Unflavored yogurt lends a slightly sour tang to healthful whole wheat pancakes.

2 cups whole wheat flour, scoop measured
2 tablespoons sugar
2 teaspoons baking powder
½ teaspoon baking soda
¾ teaspoon salt
2 cups unflavored yogurt
2 large eggs
3 tablespoons vegetable oil

1. Combine the flour, sugar, baking powder, baking soda, and salt in a large mixing bowl. Whisk to blend thoroughly.

2. In a separate bowl, whisk together the yogurt, eggs, and oil. Make a well in the dry ingredients and pour in the egg mixture. Stir with a wooden spoon until well moistened. The batter will contain some lumps. Set the batter aside.

3. Place a griddle over medium-high heat. Brush the surface with vegetable oil or rub with a strip of uncooked bacon as the griddle warms. When the griddle is hot, stir the batter, adding some milk if necessary to create a consistency like thick heavy cream. Take up the batter by scant ¼ cups and pour onto the hot griddle. Cook until the bubbles that have formed around the outside edge are broken. Turn the pancakes over and cook the other side. Repeat with the remaining batter. Stir in additional milk as needed to maintain a pourable consistency.   ❖

Whole Wheat Apple Waffles

MAKES FOUR 7-INCH SQUARES

Hearty whole wheat waffles dotted with bits of tart, fresh apple.

1¾ cups all-purpose flour, scoop measured
2 tablespoons light brown sugar
1 cup whole wheat flour, scoop measured
¼ cup wheat germ
3 teaspoons baking powder
½ teaspoon salt
1 teaspoon cinnamon
3 large eggs, separated
2 cups milk
6 tablespoons vegetable oil
2 tart, fresh apples, peeled, cored, and
    chopped fine

1. Sift the all-purpose flour and sugar into a large mixing bowl. Add the whole wheat flour, wheat germ, baking powder, salt, and cinnamon, and whisk to blend thoroughly.

2. In a separate bowl, whisk together the egg yolks, milk, and oil. Make a well in the dry ingredients and pour in the egg yolk mixture. Stir with a wooden spoon until well moistened. The batter will contain some lumps. Set the batter aside. Divide the chopped apple into 4 equal portions and set aside.

3. Preheat a waffle iron. Meanwhile, whip the egg whites until soft peaks form, then fold into the batter. The consistency should be quite thick.

4. When the indicator signals that the waffle iron is hot, brush or spray the grids lightly with vegetable oil. Pour the batter into the center of the oiled waffle iron. As you pour, gently spread the batter over the grid with a kitchen knife. Scatter 1 portion of the apple over the batter and close the waffle iron. Cook for 3 to 4 minutes, or until the steam escaping from the sides is greatly reduced. Cautiously open the waffle iron. If it resists and seems to be sticking, the waffle is not yet done, so continue cooking for another minute. Remove the waffle with the tines of a fork and serve immediately. Brush or spray the grids of the waffle iron and repeat with the remaining batter and portions of apple.   ❖

Applesauce Waffles

MAKES THREE 9-INCH SQUARES

Homemade applesauce has been a favorite ingredient in New England baked goods for many years. If you don't make your own, canned applesauce is an acceptable stand-in.

1½ cups all-purpose flour, scoop measured
2 tablespoons sugar
2 teaspoons baking powder
½ teaspoon salt
½ teaspoon cinnamon
¼ teaspoon nutmeg
2 large eggs, separated
1 cup milk
⅓ cup vegetable oil
¾ cup applesauce

1. Combine the flour, sugar, baking powder, and salt in a large mixing bowl. Add the cinnamon and nutmeg, and whisk to blend thoroughly.

2. In a separate bowl, whisk together the egg yolks, milk, and oil. Stir in the applesauce. Make a well in the dry ingredients and pour in the egg yolk mixture. Stir with

a wooden spoon until well moistened. The batter will contain some lumps. Set the batter aside.

3. Preheat a waffle iron. Meanwhile, whip the egg whites until soft peaks form, then fold into the batter. The consistency should be quite thick.

4. When the indicator signals that the waffle iron is hot, brush or spray the grids lightly with vegetable oil. Pour the batter into the center of the oiled waffle iron. As you pour, gently spread the batter over the grid with a kitchen knife. Close the waffle iron and cook for 3 to 4 minutes, or until the steam escaping from the sides is greatly reduced. Cautiously open the waffle iron. If it resists and seems to be sticking, the waffle is not yet done, so continue cooking for another minute. Remove the waffle with the tines of a fork and serve immediately. Brush or spray the grids of the waffle iron and repeat with the remaining batter.   ❖

Banana Walnut Waffles

MAKES THREE 9-INCH SQUARES

Mashed banana contributes a homey flavor to these lovely waffles. Serve piping hot with butter and maple syrup.

1½ cups all-purpose flour, scoop measured
3 tablespoons sugar
3 teaspoons baking powder
½ teaspoon salt
2 large eggs, separated
1 cup milk
⅓ cup vegetable oil
¾ cup mashed banana (about 2 small bananas)
½ cup finely chopped walnuts

1. Combine the flour, sugar, baking powder, and salt in a large mixing bowl. Whisk to blend thoroughly.

2. In a separate bowl, whisk together the egg yolks, milk, and oil. Stir in the banana. Make a well in the dry ingredients and pour in the egg yolk mixture. Stir with a wooden spoon until well moistened. The batter will

contain some lumps. Set the batter aside. Divide the chopped walnuts into 3 equal portions and set aside.

3. Preheat a waffle iron. Meanwhile, whip the egg whites until soft peaks form, then fold into the batter. The consistency should be quite thick.

4. When the indicator signals that the waffle iron is hot, brush or spray the grids lightly with vegetable oil. Pour the batter into the center of the oiled waffle iron. As you pour, gently spread the batter over the grid with a kitchen knife. Scatter 1 portion of the walnuts over the batter and close the waffle iron. Cook for 3 to 4 minutes, or until the steam escaping from the sides is greatly reduced. Cautiously open the waffle iron. If it resists and seems to be sticking, the waffle is not yet done, so continue cooking for another minute. Remove the waffle with the tines of a fork and serve immediately. Brush or spray the grids of the waffle iron and repeat with the remaining batter and portions of walnuts.   ❖

Beer Waffles

MAKES THREE 9-INCH SQUARES

Dust these gorgeous waffles with confectioners' sugar and serve with hot apple slices that have been sautéed in butter.

1¾ cups all-purpose flour, scoop measured
2 tablespoons sugar
2 teaspoons baking powder
½ teaspoon salt
2 large eggs, separated
1 teaspoon vanilla extract
6 tablespoons butter or margarine, melted
1½ cups beer (one 12-ounce bottle)

1. Combine the flour, sugar, baking powder, and salt in a large mixing bowl. Whisk to blend thoroughly.

2. In a separate bowl, whisk together the egg yolks, vanilla, and melted butter. Stir in the beer. Make a well in the dry ingredients and pour in the egg yolk mixture. Stir with a wooden spoon until well moistened. The

batter will contain some lumps. Set the batter aside.

3. Preheat a waffle iron. Meanwhile, whip the egg whites until soft peaks form, then fold into the batter. The consistency should be quite thick.

4. When the indicator signals that the waffle iron is hot, brush or spray the grids lightly with vegetable oil. Pour the batter into the center of the oiled waffle iron. As you pour, gently spread the batter over the grid with a kitchen knife. Close the waffle iron and cook for 3 to 4 minutes, or until the steam escaping from the sides is greatly reduced. Cautiously open the waffle iron. If it resists and seems to be sticking, the waffle is not yet done, so continue cooking for another minute. Remove the waffle with the tines of a fork and serve immediately. Brush or spray the grids of the waffle iron and repeat with the remaining batter.   ❖

Blueberry Waffles

MAKES FOUR 7-INCH SQUARES

Yogurt is the ingredient that gives these blueberry waffles their slightly sour tang.

1¾ cups all-purpose flour, scoop measured
½ cup sugar
1½ teaspoons baking powder
½ teaspoon baking soda
½ teaspoon salt
½ teaspoon cinnamon
3 large eggs, separated
1 cup milk
1 teaspoon vanilla extract
¼ cup butter or margarine, melted
2 tablespoons vegetable oil
1 cup unflavored yogurt
1 cup small fresh blueberries, rinsed and
     gently patted dry

1. Combine the flour, sugar, baking powder, baking soda, salt, and cinnamon in a large mixing bowl. Whisk to blend the dry ingredients thoroughly.

2. In a separate bowl, whisk together the egg yolks, milk, vanilla, melted butter, and

oil. Stir in the yogurt. Make a well in the dry ingredients and pour in the egg yolk mixture. Stir with a wooden spoon until well moistened. The batter will contain some lumps. Set the batter aside.

3. Preheat a waffle iron. Meanwhile, whip the egg whites until soft peaks form, then fold into the batter. The consistency should be quite thick.

4. When the indicator signals that the waffle iron is hot, brush or spray the grids lightly with vegetable oil. Pour the batter into the center of the oiled waffle iron. As you pour, gently spread the batter over the grid with a kitchen knife. Scatter ¼ cup of the blueberries over the batter and close the waffle iron. Cook for 3 to 4 minutes, or until the steam escaping from the sides is greatly reduced. Cautiously open the waffle iron. If it resists and seems to be sticking, the waffle is not yet done, so continue cooking for another minute. Remove the waffle with the tines of a fork and serve immediately. Brush or spray the grids of the waffle iron and repeat with the remaining batter and blueberries.   ❖

Buttermilk Waffles

MAKES FOUR 7-INCH SQUARES

A combination of whole wheat flour, rolled oats, and cornmeal gives these waffles a hearty texture and a deep, robust flavor.

1 cup whole wheat flour, scoop measured
½ cup quick-cooking rolled oats
½ cup yellow cornmeal
2 tablespoons sugar
1½ teaspoons baking powder
½ teaspoon baking soda
¾ teaspoon salt
2 large eggs, separated
2 cups buttermilk
6 tablespoons butter or margarine, melted

1. Combine the flour, oats, and cornmeal in a large mixing bowl. Add the sugar, baking powder, baking soda, and salt, and whisk to blend thoroughly.

2. In a separate bowl, whisk together the egg yolks, buttermilk, and melted butter. Make a well in the dry ingredients and pour in the egg yolk mixture. Stir with a wooden spoon until well moistened. The batter will contain some lumps. Set the batter aside.

3. Preheat a waffle iron. Meanwhile, whip the egg whites until soft peaks form, then fold into the batter. The consistency should be quite thick.

4. When the indicator signals that the waffle iron is hot, brush or spray the grids lightly with vegetable oil. Pour the batter into the center of the oiled waffle iron. As you pour, gently spread the batter over the grid with a kitchen knife. Close the waffle iron and cook for 3 to 4 minutes, or until the steam escaping from the sides is greatly reduced. Cautiously open the waffle iron. If it resists and seems to be sticking, the waffle is not yet done, so continue cooking for another minute. Remove the waffle with the tines of a fork and serve immediately. Brush or spray the grids of the waffle iron and repeat with the remaining batter.   ❖

Chocolate Waffles

MAKES FOUR 7-INCH SQUARES

Kids love these chocolate waffles. For an "outta-sight" breakfast, serve them hot with a scoop of soft vanilla ice cream.

2 cups all-purpose flour, scoop measured
¼ cup sugar
1½ teaspoons baking powder
½ teaspoon baking soda
¼ teaspoon salt
2 large eggs, separated
1 cup milk
¼ cup butter or margarine, melted
½ cup chocolate-flavored syrup
½ cup sour cream

1. Combine the flour, sugar, baking powder, baking soda, and salt in a large mixing bowl. Whisk to blend thoroughly.

2. In a separate bowl, whisk together the egg yolks, milk, and melted butter. Stir in the chocolate-flavored syrup and sour cream. Make a well in the dry ingredients and pour in the egg yolk mixture. Stir with a wooden spoon until well moistened. The batter will contain some lumps. Set the batter aside.

3. Preheat a waffle iron. Meanwhile, whip the egg whites until soft peaks form, then fold into the batter. The consistency should be quite thick.

4. When the indicator signals that the waffle iron is hot, brush or spray the grids lightly with vegetable oil. Pour the batter into the center of the oiled waffle iron. As you pour, gently spread the batter over the grid with a kitchen knife. Close the waffle iron and cook for 3 to 4 minutes, or until the steam escaping from the sides is greatly reduced. Cautiously open the waffle iron. If it resists and seems to be sticking, the waffle is not yet done, so continue cooking for another minute. Remove the waffle with the tines of a fork and serve immediately. Brush or spray the grids of the waffle iron and repeat with the remaining batter.   ❖

Cinnamon Honey Waffles

MAKES FOUR 7-INCH SQUARES

There's something about the aroma of hot cinnamon and honey that evokes memories of my Connecticut childhood. These wonderful waffles taste every bit as good as they smell.

1 cup all-purpose flour, scoop measured
1 cup whole wheat flour, scoop measured
1 tablespoon sugar
3 teaspoons baking powder
½ teaspoon salt
1 teaspoon cinnamon
3 large eggs, separated
1⅔ cups milk
⅓ cup honey
½ cup vegetable oil

1. Combine the all-purpose flour and whole wheat flour in a large mixing bowl.

Add the sugar, baking powder, salt, and cinnamon, and whisk to blend thoroughly.

2. In a separate bowl, whisk together the egg yolks, milk, honey, and oil. Make a well in the dry ingredients and pour in the egg yolk mixture. Stir with a wooden spoon until well moistened. The batter will contain some lumps. Set the batter aside.

3. Preheat a waffle iron. Meanwhile, whip the egg whites until soft peaks form, then fold into the batter. The consistency should be quite thick.

4. When the indicator signals that the waffle iron is hot, brush or spray the grids lightly with vegetable oil. Pour the batter into the center of the oiled waffle iron. As you pour, gently spread the batter over the grid with a kitchen knife. Close the waffle iron and cook for 3 to 4 minutes, or until the steam escaping from the sides is greatly reduced. Cautiously open the waffle iron. If it resists and seems to be sticking, the waffle is not yet done, so continue cooking for another minute. Remove the waffle with the tines of a fork and serve immediately. Brush or spray the grids of the waffle iron and repeat with the remaining batter.   ❖

Fresh Corn Waffles

MAKES THREE 9-INCH SQUARES

Kernels of fresh corn are baked into these tender waffles. Serve for breakfast or as a late-night snack.

1¾ cups all-purpose flour, scoop measured
2 tablespoons sugar
3 teaspoons baking powder
½ teaspoon salt
2 large eggs, separated
1¾ cups milk
½ cup vegetable oil
1 cup fresh corn kernels

1. Combine the flour, sugar, baking powder, and salt in a large mixing bowl. Whisk to blend thoroughly.

2. In a separate bowl, whisk together the egg yolks, milk, and oil. Make a well in the

dry ingredients and pour in the egg yolk mixture. Stir with a wooden spoon until well moistened. The batter will contain some lumps. Set the batter aside.

3. Preheat a waffle iron. Meanwhile, whip the egg whites until soft peaks form, then fold into the batter. The consistency should be quite thick.

4. When the indicator signals that the waffle iron is hot, brush or spray the grids lightly with vegetable oil. Pour the batter into the center of the oiled waffle iron. As you pour, gently spread the batter over the grid with a kitchen knife. Scatter ⅓ cup of the corn over the batter and close the waffle iron. Cook for 3 to 4 minutes, or until the steam escaping from the sides is greatly reduced. Cautiously open the waffle iron. If it resists and seems to be sticking, the waffle is not yet done, so continue cooking for another minute. Remove the waffle with the tines of a fork and serve immediately. Brush or spray the grids of the waffle iron and repeat with the remaining batter and corn.   ❖

Cornmeal Waffles

MAKES FOUR 7-INCH SQUARES

Sausage links are just the thing to offer with these crunchy waffles.

1 cup yellow cornmeal
1 cup all-purpose flour, scoop measured
2 tablespoons sugar
3 teaspoons baking powder
½ teaspoon salt
3 large eggs, separated
2 cups milk
½ cup vegetable oil

1. Combine the cornmeal, flour, sugar, baking powder, and salt in a large mixing bowl. Whisk to blend thoroughly.

2. In a separate bowl, whisk together the egg yolks, milk, and oil. Make a well in the dry ingredients and pour in the egg yolk mixture. Stir with a wooden spoon until

well moistened. The batter will contain some lumps. Set the batter aside.

3. Preheat a waffle iron. Meanwhile, whip the egg whites until soft peaks form, then fold into the batter. The consistency should be quite thick.

4. When the indicator signals that the waffle iron is hot, brush or spray the grids lightly with vegetable oil. Pour the batter into the center of the oiled waffle iron. As you pour, gently spread the batter over the grid with a kitchen knife. Close the waffle iron and cook for 3 to 4 minutes, or until the steam escaping from the sides is greatly reduced. Cautiously open the waffle iron. If it resists and seems to be sticking, the waffle is not yet done, so continue cooking for another minute. Remove the waffle with the tines of a fork and serve immediately. Brush or spray the grids of the waffle iron and repeat with the remaining batter.   ❖

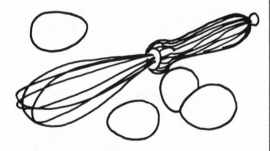

Eggnog Waffles

MAKES FOUR 7-INCH SQUARES

These rich waffles may be served hot with a scoop of vanilla ice cream for dessert, but I prefer them for breakfast, in the standard tradition, with butter and maple syrup.

2 cups all-purpose flour, scoop measured
2 tablespoons sugar
3 teaspoons baking powder
½ teaspoon salt
Generous amount of freshly grated nutmeg
2 large eggs, separated
2 cups commercially prepared eggnog
6 tablespoons butter or margarine, melted

1. Combine the flour, sugar, baking powder, salt, and nutmeg in a large mixing bowl. Whisk to blend thoroughly.

2. In a separate bowl, whisk together the egg yolks, eggnog, and melted butter. Make a well in the dry ingredients and pour in the egg yolk mixture. Stir with a wooden spoon until well moistened. The batter will contain some lumps. Set the batter aside.

3. Preheat a waffle iron. Meanwhile, whip the egg whites until soft peaks form, then fold into the batter. The consistency should be quite thick.

4. When the indicator signals that the waffle iron is hot, brush or spray the grids lightly with vegetable oil. Pour the batter into the center of the oiled waffle iron. As you pour, gently spread the batter over the grid with a kitchen knife. Close the waffle iron and cook for 3 to 4 minutes, or until the steam escaping from the sides is greatly reduced. Cautiously open the waffle iron. If it resists and seems to be sticking, the waffle is not yet done, so continue cooking for another minute. Remove the waffle with the tines of a fork and serve immediately. Brush or spray the grids of the waffle iron and repeat with the remaining batter.   ❖

Gingerbread Waffles

MAKES FOUR 7-INCH SQUARES

For a special occasion, serve these waffles with dollops of sweetened, lightly whipped cream. Dust the whipped cream with freshly grated nutmeg and garnish with slivers of lemon zest.

2 cups all-purpose flour, scoop measured
⅓ cup sugar
1½ teaspoons baking powder
½ teaspoon baking soda
½ teaspoon salt
½ teaspoon ground ginger
2 large eggs, separated
1½ cups buttermilk
½ cup molasses
½ cup vegetable oil

1. Combine the flour, sugar, baking powder, baking soda, salt, and ginger in a large mixing bowl. Whisk to blend thoroughly.

2. In a separate bowl, whisk together the egg yolks, buttermilk, molasses, and oil. Make a well in the dry ingredients and pour in the egg yolk mixture. Stir with a wooden spoon until well moistened. The batter will contain some lumps. Set the batter aside.

3. Preheat a waffle iron. Meanwhile, whip the egg whites until soft peaks form, then fold into the batter. The consistency should be quite thick.

4. When the indicator signals that the waffle iron is hot, brush or spray the grids lightly with vegetable oil. Pour the batter into the center of the oiled waffle iron. As you pour, gently spread the batter over the grid with a kitchen knife. Close the waffle iron and cook for 3 to 4 minutes, or until the steam escaping from the sides is greatly reduced. Cautiously open the waffle iron. If it resists and seems to be sticking, the waffle is not yet done, so continue cooking for another minute. Remove the waffle with the tines of a fork and serve immediately. Brush or spray the grids of the waffle iron and repeat with the remaining batter.   ❖

Honey Cream Waffles

MAKES FOUR 7-INCH SQUARES

Extravagant waffles to serve for brunch. Pass a generous bowl of unsalted butter that has been whipped with a small amount of honey and a dash of allspice.

2 cups all-purpose flour, scoop measured
1 tablespoon sugar
3 teaspoons baking powder
¾ teaspoon salt
2 large eggs, separated
1 cup medium or whipping cream
6 tablespoons butter or margarine, melted
⅔ cup milk
⅓ cup honey

1. Combine the flour, sugar, baking powder, and salt in a large mixing bowl. Whisk to blend thoroughly.

2. In a separate bowl, whisk together the egg yolks, cream, and melted butter. Stir in the milk and honey. Make a well in the dry ingredients and pour in the egg yolk mixture. Stir with a wooden spoon until well moistened. The batter will contain some lumps. Set the batter aside.

3. Preheat a waffle iron. Meanwhile, whip the egg whites until soft peaks form, then fold into the batter. The consistency should be quite thick.

4. When the indicator signals that the waffle iron is hot, brush or spray the grids lightly with vegetable oil. Pour the batter into the center of the oiled waffle iron. As you pour, gently spread the batter over the grid with a kitchen knife. Close the waffle iron and cook for 3 to 4 minutes, or until the steam escaping from the sides is greatly reduced. Cautiously open the waffle iron. If it resists and seems to be sticking, the waffle is not yet done, so continue cooking for another minute. Remove the waffle with the tines of a fork and serve immediately. Brush or spray the grids of the waffle iron and repeat with the remaining batter.   ❖

Honey Whole Wheat Waffles

MAKES FOUR 7-INCH SQUARES

The yeasted batter for these waffles ferments overnight to create a pleasant sourdough flavor.

1¾ cups milk
⅓ cup honey
6 tablespoons butter or margarine
½ teaspoon salt
1 package dry yeast, dissolved in ¼ cup warm water
2 large eggs, beaten
2 cups whole wheat flour, scoop measured

1. In a wide saucepan, combine the milk, honey, butter, and salt. Place over medium

heat and stir until the butter is melted. Transfer to a large mixing bowl to cool.

2. When the mixture is barely warm to the touch, stir in the dissolved yeast and beaten egg. Blend in the flour. Cover the bowl with plastic wrap and secure with an elastic band. Refrigerate overnight.

3. Take the batter from the refrigerator and let stand for 30 minutes to warm. Meanwhile, preheat a waffle iron. When the indicator signals that the waffle iron is hot, brush or spray the grids lightly with vegetable oil. Stir the batter down, then pour into the center of the oiled waffle iron. As you pour, gently spread the batter over the grid with a kitchen knife. Close the waffle iron and cook for 3 to 4 minutes, or until the steam escaping from the sides is greatly reduced. Cautiously open the waffle iron. If it resists and seems to be sticking, the waffle is not yet done, so continue cooking for another minute. Remove the waffle with the tines of a fork and serve immediately. Brush or spray the grids of the waffle iron and repeat with the remaining batter.   ❖

and pour in the egg yolk mixture. Stir with a wooden spoon until well moistened. The batter will contain some lumps. Set the batter aside. Divide the chopped pecans into 3 equal portions and set aside.

3. Preheat a waffle iron. Meanwhile, whip the egg whites until soft peaks form, then fold into the batter. The consistency should be quite thick.

4. When the indicator signals that the waffle iron is hot, brush or spray the grids lightly with vegetable oil. Pour the batter into the center of the oiled waffle iron. As you pour, gently spread the batter over the grid with a kitchen knife. Scatter 1 portion of the pecans over the batter and close the waffle iron. Cook for 3 to 4 minutes, or until the steam escaping from the sides is greatly reduced. Cautiously open the waffle iron. If it resists and seems to be sticking, the waffle is not yet done, so continue cooking for another minute. Remove the waffle with the tines of a fork and serve immediately. Brush or spray the grids of the waffle iron and repeat with the remaining batter and portions of pecans.   ❖

Maple Pecan Waffles

MAKES THREE 9-INCH SQUARES

Slices of sizzled ham are the perfect partner for these maple-flavored waffles.

2 cups all-purpose flour, scoop measured
¼ cup light brown sugar
3 teaspoons baking powder
½ teaspoon salt
2 large eggs, separated
1⅔ cups milk
6 tablespoons butter or margarine, melted
⅓ cup pure maple syrup
⅔ cup finely chopped pecans

1. Sift the flour and sugar into a large mixing bowl. Add the baking powder and salt, and whisk to blend thoroughly.

2. In a separate bowl, whisk together the egg yolks, milk, melted butter, and maple syrup. Make a well in the dry ingredients

Pineapple Waffles

MAKES FOUR 7-INCH SQUARES

Bits of succulent pineapple are a cheerful addition to tender waffles. Serve with dollops of sweetened whipped cream.

2 cups all-purpose flour, scoop measured
2 tablespoons sugar
3 teaspoons baking powder
¾ teaspoon salt
2 large eggs, separated
2 cups milk
½ cup vegetable oil
1 cup drained, crushed canned pineapple

1. Combine the flour, sugar, baking powder, and salt in a large mixing bowl. Whisk to blend thoroughly.

2. In a separate bowl, whisk together the egg yolks, milk, and oil. Stir in the pineapple. Make a well in the dry ingredients and

pour in the egg yolk mixture. Stir with a wooden spoon until well moistened. The batter will contain some lumps. Set the batter aside.

3. Preheat a waffle iron. Meanwhile, whip the egg whites until soft peaks form, then fold into the batter. The consistency should be quite thick.

4. When the indicator signals that the waffle iron is hot, brush or spray the grids lightly with vegetable oil. Pour the batter into the center of the oiled waffle iron. As you pour, gently spread the batter over the grid with a kitchen knife. Close the waffle iron and cook for 3 to 4 minutes, or until the steam escaping from the sides is greatly reduced. Cautiously open the waffle iron. If it resists and seems to be sticking, the waffle is not yet done, so continue cooking for another minute. Remove the waffle with the tines of a fork and serve immediately. Brush or spray the grids of the waffle iron and repeat with the remaining batter. ❖

Raised Waffles

MAKES FOUR 7-INCH SQUARES

Heady with the fragrance of yeast, these waffles are excellent as a savory base for an entrée. Spoon on creamed chicken, lobster Newburg, or creamed chipped beef.

1¾ cups milk
6 tablespoons butter or margarine
1 teaspoon sugar
¾ teaspoon salt
1 package dry yeast, dissolved in ¼ cup warm
    water
2 large eggs, beaten
2 cups all-purpose flour, scoop measured

1. In a wide saucepan, combine the milk, butter, sugar, and salt. Place over medium heat and stir until the butter is melted. Transfer to a large mixing bowl to cool.

2. When the mixture is barely warm to the touch, stir in the dissolved yeast and beaten egg. Blend in the flour, cover with a

clean kitchen towel and set aside to stand for 30 minutes.

3. Meanwhile, preheat a waffle iron. When the indicator signals that the waffle iron is hot, brush or spray the grids lightly with vegetable oil. Stir the batter down, then pour into the center of the oiled waffle iron. As you pour, gently spread the batter over the grid with a kitchen knife. Close the waffle iron and cook for 3 to 4 minutes, or until the steam escaping from the sides is greatly reduced. Cautiously open the waffle iron. If it resists and seems to be sticking, the waffle is not yet done, so continue cooking for another minute. Remove the waffle with the tines of a fork and serve immediately. Brush or spray the grids of the waffle iron and repeat with the remaining batter. ❖

Pumpkin Waffles

MAKES THREE 9-INCH SQUARES

One sniff of these spicy waffles will banish your winter-morning blues. Serve with butter that has been whipped with a small amount of orange marmalade and a pinch of ground ginger.

1¾ cups all-purpose flour, scoop measured
¼ cup light brown sugar
2 teaspoons baking powder
½ teaspoon salt
1 teaspoon cinnamon
½ teaspoon nutmeg
½ teaspoon ground ginger
2 large eggs, separated
1 cup milk
6 tablespoons butter or margarine, melted
¾ cup pumpkin purée

1. Sift the flour and sugar into a large bowl. Add the baking powder, salt, cinnamon, nutmeg, and ginger, and whisk to blend thoroughly.

2. In a separate bowl, whisk together the egg yolks, milk, and melted butter. Stir in the pumpkin purée. Make a well in the dry ingredients and pour in the egg yolk mix-

ture. Stir with a wooden spoon until well moistened. The batter will contain some lumps. Set the batter aside.

3. Preheat a waffle iron. Meanwhile, whip the egg whites until soft peaks form, then fold into the batter. The consistency should be quite thick.

4. When the indicator signals that the waffle iron is hot, brush or spray the grids lightly with vegetable oil. Pour the batter into the center of the oiled waffle iron. As you pour, gently spread the batter over the grid with a kitchen knife. Close the waffle iron and cook for 3 to 4 minutes, or until the steam escaping from the sides is greatly reduced. Cautiously open the waffle iron. If it resists and seems to be sticking, the waffle is not yet done, so continue cooking for another minute. Remove the waffle with the tines of a fork and serve immediately. Brush or spray the grids of the waffle iron and repeat with the remaining batter.   ❖

Club Soda Waffles

MAKES THREE 9-INCH SQUARES

The carbon dioxide bubbles in club soda make these waffles exceptionally light. Heat some strawberry jelly until it liquefies, then drizzle on top before serving.

1½ cups all-purpose flour, scoop measured
2 tablespoons sugar
2 teaspoons baking powder
¾ teaspoon salt
2 large eggs, separated
½ cup light cream
6 tablespoons butter or margarine, melted
1 cup club soda

1. Combine the flour, sugar, baking powder, and salt in a large mixing bowl. Whisk to blend thoroughly.

2. In a separate bowl, whisk together the egg yolks, cream, and melted butter. Stir in the club soda. Make a well in the dry ingredients and pour in the egg yolk mixture. Stir with a wooden spoon until well moist-

ened. The batter will contain some lumps. Set the batter aside.

3. Preheat a waffle iron. Meanwhile, whip the egg whites until soft peaks form, then fold into the batter. The consistency should be quite thick.

4. When the indicator signals that the waffle iron is hot, brush or spray the grids lightly with vegetable oil. Pour the batter into the center of the oiled waffle iron. As you pour, gently spread the batter over the grid with a kitchen knife. Close the waffle iron and cook for 3 to 4 minutes, or until the steam escaping from the sides is greatly reduced. Cautiously open the waffle iron. If it resists and seems to be sticking, the waffle is not yet done, so continue cooking for another minute. Remove the waffle with the tines of a fork and serve immediately. Brush or spray the grids of the waffle iron and repeat with the remaining batter.   ❖

Sour Cream Waffles

MAKES FOUR 7-INCH SQUARES

Serve these golden brown waffles with plenty of butter and a pitcher of blackberry syrup.

1¾ cups all-purpose flour, scoop measured
2 tablespoons sugar
1½ teaspoons baking powder
½ teaspoon baking soda
½ teaspoon salt
3 large eggs, separated
1⅓ cups milk
¼ cup butter or margarine, melted
2 tablespoons vegetable oil
1 cup sour cream

1. Combine the flour, sugar, baking powder, baking soda, and salt in a large mixing bowl. Whisk to blend thoroughly.

2. In a separate bowl, whisk together the egg yolks, milk, melted butter, and oil. Stir in the sour cream. Make a well in the dry ingredients and pour in the egg yolk mixture. Stir with a wooden spoon until well

moistened. The batter will contain some lumps. Set the batter aside.

3. Preheat a waffle iron. Meanwhile, whip the egg whites until soft peaks form, then fold into the batter. The consistency should be quite thick.

4. When the indicator signals that the waffle iron is hot, brush or spray the grids lightly with vegetable oil. Pour the batter into the center of the oiled waffle iron. As you pour, gently spread the batter over the grid with a kitchen knife. Close the waffle iron and cook for 3 to 4 minutes, or until the steam escaping from the sides is greatly reduced. Cautiously open the waffle iron. If it resists and seems to be sticking, the waffle is not yet done, so continue cooking for another minute. Remove the waffle with the tines of a fork and serve immediately. Brush or spray the grids of the waffle iron and repeat with the remaining batter. ❖

Sweet Potato Waffles

MAKES FOUR 7-INCH SQUARES

These waffles look beautiful. Serve with whipped butter, to which a small amount of thawed orange-juice concentrate has been added.

2 cups all-purpose flour, scoop measured
¼ cup light brown sugar
3 teaspoons baking powder
¾ teaspoon salt
3 large eggs, separated
1½ cups milk
½ cup butter or margarine, melted
2 tablespoons honey
1 tablespoon finely grated orange zest
1 cup mashed baked sweet potato

1. Sift the flour and sugar into a large mixing bowl. Add the baking powder and salt, and whisk to blend thoroughly.

2. In a separate bowl, whisk together the egg yolks, milk, melted butter, and honey. Stir in the orange zest and sweet potato. Make a well in the dry ingredients and pour in the egg yolk mixture. Stir with a wooden

spoon until well moistened. The batter will contain some lumps. Set the batter aside.

3. Preheat a waffle iron. Meanwhile, whip the egg whites until soft peaks form, then fold into the batter. The consistency should be quite thick.

4. When the indicator signals that the waffle iron is hot, brush or spray the grids lightly with vegetable oil. Pour the batter into the center of the oiled waffle iron. As you pour, gently spread the batter over the grid with a kitchen knife. Close the waffle iron and cook for 3 to 4 minutes, or until the steam escaping from the sides is greatly reduced. Cautiously open the waffle iron. If it resists and seems to be sticking, the waffle is not yet done, so continue cooking for another minute. Remove the waffle with the tines of a fork and serve immediately. Brush or spray the grids of the waffle iron and repeat with the remaining batter. ❖

Walnut Spice Waffles

MAKES THREE 9-INCH SQUARES

Make these yummy waffles for the favorite kids in your life. Pass bowls of sour cream and warm applesauce to spoon on top.

2 cups all-purpose flour, scoop measured
3 tablespoons sugar
3 teaspoons baking powder
½ teaspoon salt
1 teaspoon cinnamon
½ teaspoon nutmeg
2 large eggs, separated
2 cups milk
6 tablespoons butter or margarine, melted
½ cup finely chopped walnuts

1. Combine the flour, sugar, baking powder, and salt in a large mixing bowl. Add the

cinnamon and nutmeg and whisk to blend thoroughly.

2. In a separate bowl, whisk together the egg yolks, milk, and melted butter. Make a well in the dry ingredients and pour in the egg yolk mixture. Stir with a wooden spoon until well moistened. The batter will contain some lumps. Set the batter aside. Divide the walnuts into 3 equal portions and set aside.

3. Preheat a waffle iron. Meanwhile, whip the egg whites until soft peaks form, then fold into the batter. The consistency should be quite thick.

4. When the indicator signals that the waffle iron is hot, brush or spray the grids lightly with vegetable oil. Pour the batter into the center of the oiled waffle iron. As you pour, gently spread the batter over the grid with a kitchen knife. Scatter 1 portion of the walnuts over the batter and close the waffle iron. Cook for 3 to 4 minutes, or until the steam escaping from the sides is greatly reduced. Cautiously open the waffle iron. If it resists and seems to be sticking, the waffle is not yet done, so continue cooking for another minute. Remove the waffle with the tines of a fork and serve immediately. Brush or spray the grids of the waffle iron and repeat with the remaining batter and portions of walnuts. ❖

Wheat Bran Waffles

MAKES THREE 9-INCH SQUARES

The goodness of wheat bran comes alive in these full-bodied waffles. Serve with peach slices that have been heated in a saucepan with some sugar and a touch of cinnamon.

1 cup 100% bran cereal (not flakes)
2 cups milk
2 large eggs, separated
½ cup vegetable oil
3 tablespoons sugar
3 teaspoons baking powder
¾ teaspoon salt
1 cup all-purpose flour, scoop measured

1. In a large mixing bowl, combine the bran and 1 cup of the milk. Set aside for 10 minutes to soften.

2. In a separate bowl, whisk together the egg yolks, the remaining cup of milk, and the oil. Blend into the softened bran. Add the sugar, baking powder, and salt, and beat with a wooden spoon. Blend in the flour until well moistened. The batter will contain some lumps. Set the batter aside.

3. Preheat a waffle iron. Meanwhile, whip the egg whites until soft peaks form, then fold into the batter. The consistency should be quite thick.

4. When the indicator signals that the waffle iron is hot, brush or spray the grids lightly with vegetable oil. Pour the batter into the center of the oiled waffle iron. As you pour, gently spread the batter over the grid with a kitchen knife. Close the waffle iron and cook for 3 to 4 minutes, or until the steam escaping from the sides is greatly reduced. Cautiously open the waffle iron. If it resists and seems to be sticking, the waffle is not yet done, so continue cooking for another minute. Remove the waffle with the tines of a fork and serve immediately. Brush or spray the grids of the waffle iron and repeat with the remaining batter. ❖

❖ Doughnuts and Fried Breads ❖

WHEN I WAS a child growing up in the country, we had a neighbor who made her own doughnuts. The whole idea so fascinated me that I would have given my eyeteeth to stand and watch her. My mother wouldn't allow it, of course, and I considered that one of the great deprivations of my youth.

Today the process of making doughnuts still intrigues me: the amazing manner in which the pieces of dough puff and swell, then turn golden brown; the irresistible aroma as they sputter in the hot fat. And the flavor. Ah yes, the flavor. Once you've tasted homemade doughnuts, still warm from the fat, store-bought never seem the same again.

Doughnuts have long-established ties with New England cookery. Colonial women learned to make dropped doughnuts from the Dutch settlers of New Amsterdam, and the familiar ring-shaped doughnut has a past that has become a Yankee legend. Captain Hanson Gregory, a Maine settler, is credited with inventing the hole in a doughnut. The story goes that he was unhappy with his mother's undercooked doughnuts, so he suggested that she cut a hole in the middle before frying the dough to eliminate the soggy center.

Fried breads, like doughnuts, have deep New England roots. According to some sources, Northeast Indians cooked pieces of unleavened dough in rendered bear fat.

213

This practice probably evolved into the making of fried breads, wherein pieces of dough leavened with baking powder or yeast are cooked in deep fat. New England cooks were the first to add chopped clams to baking powder dough and fry small spheres into clam fritters.

Success in making doughnuts and fried breads can be tricky. The crucial factor is temperature — the temperature of the batter or dough, and the temperature of the fat it is cooked in.

When fat is too hot, the exterior crust browns before the inside is cooked. On the other hand, when fat is too cool, the exterior crust forms slowly and excessive grease is absorbed by the dough. The recommended temperature for fat is between 365°F. and 375°F. The recommended temperature for batter and dough is between 70°F. and 80°F. If the dough is cold, it lowers the temperature of the fat to the point where it is too cool to create a crust rapidly. In view of that, I have avoided any suggestions that doughnuts be shaped and then refrigerated.

Doughnuts are at their best when eaten slightly warm. Fried breads and fritters should be served piping hot. If necessary, it is possible to store cooled doughnuts in an airtight metal tin or cookie jar. You also may freeze them in a plastic bag secured with a wire twist. Fried breads may be kept at room temperature, wrapped in aluminum foil. Unwrap them and warm directly on the oven rack of a preheated 400°F. oven until they become crisp. Fritters may be covered and refrigerated for 24 hours. To reheat, arrange them in a single layer on a baking sheet and place in a preheated 375°F. oven for 5 to 8 minutes. Do not attempt to heat doughnuts, fried breads, or fritters in a microwave oven.

Applesauce Doughnuts

MAKES 24

Apple juice and applesauce combine to give these doughnuts a harvest flavor.

3½ to 4 cups all-purpose flour, scoop measured
2 teaspoons baking powder
1 teaspoon baking soda
¾ teaspoon salt
1 teaspoon cinnamon
½ teaspoon nutmeg
2 large eggs
¾ cup sugar
¼ cup butter or margarine, melted
1 cup applesauce
¼ cup apple juice
Vegetable oil for deep-frying

1. In a large mixing bowl, combine 3½ cups of the flour with the baking powder, baking soda, and salt. Add the cinnamon and nutmeg. Whisk to blend thoroughly.

2. Combine the eggs and sugar in the bowl of an electric mixer. Beat at high speed until pale yellow and slightly thickened. Gradually beat in the melted butter. Add the applesauce and apple juice, and blend well. With the mixer on low speed, sprinkle in the dry ingredients. Beat until a moist, stiff dough is formed.

3. Turn out onto a lightly floured surface. Knead gently, working in additional flour if necessary to create a soft, smooth dough. Cover the dough with a clean kitchen towel and let rest for 30 minutes. Roll the dough to a ½-inch thickness and cut out with a 2½-inch doughnut cutter.

4. Heat the oil to 370°F. Using a perforated metal spatula, transfer the doughnuts to the hot oil. Do not overcrowd the pan; cook only a few doughnuts at one time. Fry for 3 to 4 minutes, or until golden brown on both sides. Transfer to absorbent paper to drain. Repeat with the remaining doughnuts. When cool, dust with cinnamon sugar if you wish. ❖

Baked Spice Doughnuts

MAKES 36

These wonderful doughnuts are not fried in deep fat. Instead, they are brushed with melted butter and baked on a cookie sheet.

1½ cups milk
⅓ cup solid vegetable shortening
½ cup sugar
1 teaspoon salt
½ teaspoon nutmeg
½ teaspoon cinnamon
1 package dry yeast, dissolved in ¼ cup warm water
2 large eggs, beaten
4 to 4½ cups all-purpose flour, scoop measured
½ cup butter or margarine, melted
2 teaspoons cinnamon, mixed with ½ cup sugar

1. In a wide saucepan, combine the milk, shortening, sugar, and salt. Place over medium heat and stir until the shortening is melted. Remove from the heat and whisk in the nutmeg and cinnamon. Transfer to a large mixing bowl to cool.

2. When the mixture is barely warm to the touch, stir in the dissolved yeast and beaten egg. Add 2 cups of the flour and beat with a wooden spoon until smooth. Stir in enough of the remaining flour to create a moist, stiff dough.

3. Turn out onto a lightly floured surface. Knead gently, working in additional flour if necessary. The dough should be soft but not sticky. Cover the dough with a clean kitchen towel and let rest for 30 minutes.

4. Generously grease 2 baking sheets. Roll the dough to a ½-inch thickness and cut out with a 2½-inch doughnut cutter. Transfer to the prepared baking sheets. Brush with ¼ cup of the butter. Cover loosely with plastic wrap and let rise. When double in bulk, brush the doughnuts with the remaining ¼ cup melted butter. Place in a preheated 425°F. oven and bake for 12 to 15 minutes, or until lightly browned. Cool on a rack for 5 minutes, then sprinkle the cinnamon sugar on top of the warm doughnuts.   ❖

Banana Ginger Doughnuts

MAKES 24

The flavor of banana is spiked with ginger in these aromatic doughnuts. Serve warm with apple cider.

3½ to 4 cups all-purpose flour, scoop measured
2 teaspoons baking powder
½ teaspoon baking soda
¾ teaspoon salt
½ teaspoon ground ginger
2 large eggs
¾ cup sugar
¼ cup butter or margarine, melted
1 cup mashed very ripe banana (about 2 large bananas)
¼ cup milk
Vegetable oil for deep-frying

1. In a large mixing bowl, combine 3½ cups of the flour with the baking powder, baking soda, salt, and ginger. Whisk to blend thoroughly.

2. Combine the eggs and sugar in the bowl of an electric mixer. Beat at high speed until pale yellow and slightly thickened. Gradually beat in the melted butter. Add the banana and milk, and blend well. With the mixer on low speed, sprinkle in the dry ingredients. Beat until a moist, stiff dough is formed.

3. Turn out onto a lightly floured surface. Knead gently, working in additional flour if necessary to create a soft, smooth dough. Cover the dough with a clean kitchen towel and let rest for 30 minutes. Roll the dough to a ½-inch thickness and cut out with a 2½-inch doughnut cutter.

4. Heat the oil to 370°F. Using a perforated metal spatula, transfer the doughnuts to the hot oil. Do not overcrowd the pan; cook only a few doughnuts at one time. Fry for 3

to 4 minutes, or until golden brown on both sides. Transfer to absorbent paper to drain. Repeat with the remaining doughnuts. When cool, dust with confectioners' sugar if you wish.   ❖

Doughnut Bows

MAKES 40

In the fall, the New England countryside is alive with ethnic fairs and festivals. These citrus-flavored doughnuts are a favorite at Polish church fairs.

3½ to 4 cups all-purpose flour, scoop
   measured
3 teaspoons baking powder
1 teaspoon salt
2 large eggs
½ cup sugar
1 tablespoon finely grated lemon zest
2 tablespoons finely grated orange zest
1½ cups heavy cream
Vegetable oil for deep-frying

1. In a large mixing bowl, combine 3½ cups of the flour with the baking powder and salt. Whisk to blend thoroughly.

2. Combine the eggs and sugar in the bowl of an electric mixer. Beat at high speed until pale yellow and slightly thickened. Blend in the lemon zest and orange zest. Gradually beat in the cream. With the mixer on low speed, sprinkle in the dry ingredients. Beat until a moist, stiff dough is formed.

3. Turn out onto a lightly floured surface. Knead gently, working in additional flour if necessary to create a soft, smooth dough. Divide the dough in half and cover with a clean kitchen towel. Set the dough aside and let it rest for 30 minutes.

4. Roll one portion of dough into a 10x12-inch rectangle. Trim the edges to square off the rectangle. Lift the dough to loosen it from the work surface. Cut the rectangle into five 2x12-inch strips. Then cut the strips crosswise into four 2x3-inch pieces. Make a small lengthwise slit in each piece. Tuck one end of each piece through the slit

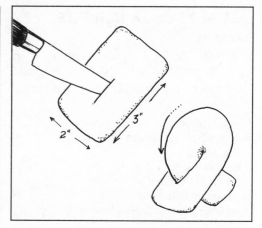

To make Doughnut Bows, make a small length-wise slit in each 2x3-inch piece of dough. Tuck one end of each piece through the slit and pull it through to the other side.

and pull it through to the other side. (See illustration.) Repeat this process with the remaining portion of the dough.

5. Heat the oil to 370°F. Using a perforated metal spatula, transfer the doughnuts to the hot oil. Do not overcrowd the pan; cook only a few doughnuts at one time. Fry for 3 to 4 minutes, or until golden brown on both sides. Transfer to absorbent paper to drain. Repeat with the remaining doughnuts. When cool, dust with sifted confectioners' sugar if you wish.   ❖

Brown Sugar Doughnuts

MAKES 24

A touch of dark rum lends an inimitable flavor to these old-time favorites.

3½ to 4 cups all-purpose flour, scoop
   measured
2 teaspoons baking powder
½ teaspoon baking soda
¾ teaspoon salt
½ teaspoon cinnamon
2 large eggs
1 cup light brown sugar
¼ cup butter or margarine, melted
2 tablespoons dark rum

1 cup milk
Vegetable oil for deep-frying
½ cup granulated sugar, mixed with ½ cup
  light brown sugar

1. In a large mixing bowl, combine 3½ cups of the flour with the baking powder, baking soda, salt, and cinnamon. Whisk to blend thoroughly.

2. Combine the eggs and sugar in the bowl of an electric mixer. Beat at high speed until light in color and slightly thickened. Gradually beat in the melted butter. Add the rum and milk, and blend well. With the mixer on low speed, sprinkle in the dry ingredients. Beat until a moist, stiff dough is formed.

3. Turn out onto a lightly floured surface. Knead gently, working in additional flour if necessary to create a soft, smooth dough. Cover the dough with a clean kitchen towel and let rest for 30 minutes. Roll the dough to a ½-inch thickness and cut out with a 2½-inch doughnut cutter.

4. Heat the oil to 370°F. Using a perforated metal spatula, transfer the doughnuts to the hot oil. Do not overcrowd the pan; cook only a few doughnuts at one time. Fry for 3 to 4 minutes, or until golden brown on both sides. Transfer to absorbent paper to drain. Repeat with the remaining doughnuts. When cool, dust with the mixture of granulated and brown sugar. ❖

Chocolate Doughnuts

MAKES 24

The ultimate in doughnut decadence. You may dust these chocolate treats with sifted confectioners' sugar or lightly spread on a chocolate glaze made by heating together 3 squares of semisweet chocolate and 2 tablespoons of white corn syrup.

3½ to 4 cups all-purpose flour, scoop
  measured
2 teaspoons baking powder
½ teaspoon baking soda
¾ teaspoon salt

¼ teaspoon cinnamon
2 large eggs
1 cup sugar
¼ cup butter or margarine, melted
2 ounces semisweet chocolate, melted
1 cup buttermilk
Vegetable oil for deep-frying

1. In a large mixing bowl, combine 3½ cups of the flour with the baking powder, baking soda, salt, and cinnamon. Whisk to blend thoroughly.

2. Combine the eggs and sugar in the bowl of an electric mixer. Beat at high speed until pale yellow and slightly thickened. Gradually beat in the melted butter. Blend in the chocolate. Add the buttermilk and blend well. With the mixer on low speed, sprinkle in the dry ingredients. Beat until a moist, stiff dough is formed.

3. Turn out onto a lightly floured surface. Knead gently, working in additional flour if necessary to create a soft, smooth dough. Cover the dough with a clean kitchen towel and let rest for 30 minutes. Roll the dough to a ½-inch thickness and cut out with a 2½-inch doughnut cutter.

4. Heat the oil to 370°F. Using a perforated metal spatula, transfer the doughnuts to the hot oil. Do not overcrowd the pan; cook only a few doughnuts at one time. Fry for 3 to 4 minutes, or until cooked through. Transfer to absorbent paper to drain. Repeat with the remaining doughnuts. ❖

Crullers

MAKES 24

These are the classic doughnut twists served every morning throughout New England at tiny corner coffee shops.

3½ to 4 cups all-purpose flour, scoop
  measured
3 teaspoons baking powder
¾ teaspoon salt
½ teaspoon mace
2 large eggs
⅔ cup sugar

¼ cup solid vegetable shortening, melted
1 tablespoon finely grated lemon zest
1 cup milk
Vegetable oil for deep-frying

1. In a large mixing bowl, combine 3½ cups of the flour with the baking powder, salt, and mace. Whisk to blend thoroughly.

2. Combine the eggs and sugar in the bowl of an electric mixer. Beat at high speed until pale yellow and slightly thickened. Gradually beat in the melted shortening. Add the lemon zest and milk, and blend well. With the mixer on low speed, sprinkle in the dry ingredients. Beat until a moist, stiff dough is formed.

3. Turn out onto a lightly floured surface. Knead gently, working in additional flour if necessary to create a soft, smooth dough. Cover the dough with a clean kitchen towel and let rest for 30 minutes.

4. Divide the dough in half. Roll one portion into an 8x12-inch rectangle. Trim the edges to square off the rectangle. Lift the dough to loosen it from the work surface. Cut into twelve 8-inch-long strips. Fold the

---

To make Crullers, fold the strips of dough in half and pinch the ends together. Stretch and twist the double strip to create a cruller 6 inches long.

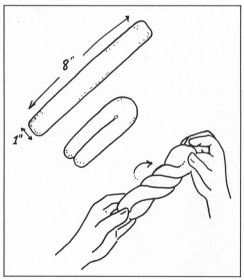

strips in half and bring the ends together. Moisten the ends with water and pinch them together. Stretch and twist the double strip to create a cruller 6 inches long. (See illustration.) Repeat this process with the remaining portion of dough.

5. Heat the oil to 370°F. Using a perforated metal spatula, transfer the crullers to the hot oil. Do not overcrowd the pan; cook only a few crullers at one time. Fry for 3 to 4 minutes, or until golden brown on both sides. Transfer to absorbent paper to drain. Repeat with the remaining crullers.   ❖

Drop Doughnuts

MAKES 36

These doughnuts are so easy to make you can surprise your family with them on a Sunday morning. Serve plain or with warm maple syrup.

2½ cups all-purpose flour, scoop measured
¼ cup sugar
3 teaspoons baking powder
½ teaspoon salt
1 teaspoon mace
Generous amount of freshly grated nutmeg
¾ cup milk
1 large egg
¼ cup vegetable oil
½ teaspoon almond extract
Vegetable oil for deep-frying

1. Combine the flour, sugar, baking powder, and salt in a large mixing bowl. Add the mace and nutmeg. Whisk to blend the dry ingredients thoroughly.

2. In a separate bowl, whisk together the milk, egg, oil, and almond extract. Make a well in the dry ingredients and pour in the egg mixture. Blend with a wooden spoon until well moistened.

3. Heat the oil to 370°F. Coat 2 teaspoons with oil by dipping them in the hot fat. Scoop up the batter by rounded teaspoonfuls and drop into the oil, using one spoon to push the dough off the other. Do not overcrowd the pan; cook only a few doughnuts at

one time. Fry for 3 to 4 minutes, turning the doughnuts as they puff to encourage even browning. Transfer to absorbent paper with a slotted spoon. Repeat with the remaining batter.   ❖

Egg Doughnuts

MAKES 30

Egg doughnuts are like discs of fried dough, except that they are unusually rich. Serve plain or dust with confectioners' sugar.

3 to 3½ cups all-purpose flour, scoop
   measured
3 teaspoons baking powder
¾ teaspoon salt
3 large eggs
½ cup sugar
½ cup butter or margarine, melted
⅓ cup milk
Vegetable oil for deep-frying

1. In a large mixing bowl, combine 3 cups of the flour with the baking powder and salt. Whisk to blend thoroughly.

2. Combine the eggs and sugar in the bowl of an electric mixer. Beat at high speed until pale yellow and slightly thickened. Gradually beat in the melted butter. Add the milk and blend well. With the mixer on low speed, sprinkle in the dry ingredients. Beat until a moist, stiff dough is formed.

3. Turn out onto a lightly floured surface. Knead gently, working in additional flour if necessary to create a soft, smooth dough. Cover the dough with a clean kitchen towel and let rest for 30 minutes. Roll the dough to a ¼-inch thickness and cut out with a 2-inch biscuit cutter.

4. Heat the oil to 370°F. Using a perforated metal spatula, transfer the doughnuts to the hot oil. Do not overcrowd the pan; cook only a few doughnuts at one time. Fry for 3 to 4 minutes, or until golden brown on both sides. Transfer to absorbent paper to drain. Repeat with the remaining doughnuts.   ❖

Herman Starter Doughnuts

MAKES 24

Tangy sourdough starter creates doughnuts with superb flavor and texture. Serve warm to fully appreciate their unique character.

3 to 3½ cups all-purpose flour
2 teaspoons baking powder
½ teaspoon baking soda
¾ teaspoon salt
1 teaspoon cinnamon
½ teaspoon nutmeg
2 large eggs
½ cup sugar
¼ cup butter or margarine, melted
1 teaspoon vanilla extract
1 cup Herman sourdough starter (p. 49), at
   room temperature
⅔ cup buttermilk
Vegetable oil for deep-frying

1. In a large mixing bowl, combine 3 cups of the flour with the baking powder, baking soda, and salt. Add the cinnamon and nutmeg, and whisk to blend thoroughly.

2. Combine the eggs and sugar in the bowl of an electric mixer. Beat at high speed until pale yellow and slightly thickened. Gradually beat in the melted butter. Add the vanilla, sourdough starter, and buttermilk, and blend well. With the mixer on low speed, sprinkle in the dry ingredients. Beat until a moist, stiff dough is formed.

3. Turn out onto a lightly floured surface. Knead gently, working in additional flour if necessary. The dough should be soft but not sticky. Cover the dough with a clean kitchen towel and let rest for 30 minutes.

4. Dust 2 baking sheets with flour. Roll the dough to a ½-inch thickness and cut out with a 2½-inch doughnut cutter. Transfer to the floured baking sheets. Cover loosely with plastic wrap and let rise. When double in bulk, begin heating the vegetable oil to 370°F. Using a perforated metal spatula, transfer the doughnuts to the hot oil. Do not overcrowd the pan; cook only a few doughnuts at one time. Fry for 3 to 4 minutes, or

until golden brown on both sides. Transfer to absorbent paper to drain. Repeat with the remaining doughnuts.   ❖

Honey Doughnut Puffs

MAKES 36

A yeast-leavened batter, flavored with honey, is dropped by generous teaspoonfuls to create luscious doughnut spheres. Serve plain or dip into a combination of 3 tablespoons honey and 3 tablespoons butter that has been heated until it has liquefied.

⅓ cup honey
2 tablespoons butter, cut into small pieces
1 cup boiling water
1 package dry yeast
½ teaspoon salt
2½ cups all-purpose flour, scoop measured
Generous amount of freshly grated nutmeg
Vegetable oil for deep-frying

1. Combine the honey and butter in a large mixing bowl. Pour in the boiling water and stir until the butter is melted. Set aside to cool.

2. When the mixture is barely warm to the touch, sprinkle on the yeast and stir to dissolve. Blend in the salt. Add the flour and beat with a wooden spoon until well moistened. Stir in the nutmeg. Cover the bowl with a clean kitchen towel and set aside to rise.

3. When double in bulk, stir the dough down. Heat the oil to 370°F. Coat 2 teaspoons with oil by dipping them in the hot fat. Scoop up the batter by rounded teaspoonfuls and drop into the oil. Do not overcrowd the pan; cook only a few doughnuts at a time. Fry for 3 to 4 minutes, turning the doughnuts as they puff to encourage even browning. Transfer to absorbent paper with a slotted spoon. Repeat with the remaining batter.   ❖

Honey Raised Doughnuts

MAKES 24

Light, puffy whole wheat doughnuts, scented with honey. These are a welcome contribution to the bakery booth at a church bazaar.

¾ cup milk
¼ cup butter or margarine
¼ cup honey
¼ cup sugar
¾ teaspoon salt
½ teaspoon cinnamon
¼ teaspoon nutmeg
1 package dry yeast, dissolved in ¼ cup warm water
2 large eggs, beaten
2 cups whole wheat flour, scoop measured
1½ to 2 cups all-purpose flour, scoop measured
Vegetable oil for deep-frying

1. In a wide saucepan, combine the milk, butter, honey, sugar, and salt. Place over medium heat and stir until the butter is melted. Remove from the heat and whisk in the cinnamon and nutmeg. Transfer to a large mixing bowl to cool.

2. When the mixture is barely warm to the touch, stir in the dissolved yeast and beaten egg. Add the whole wheat flour and beat with a wooden spoon until smooth. Stir in enough of the all-purpose flour to create a moist, stiff dough.

3. Turn out onto a lightly floured surface. Knead gently, working in additional all-

purpose flour if necessary. The dough should be soft but not sticky. Transfer to a greased bowl and cover with a clean kitchen towel. Set aside to rise until double in bulk.

4. Punch the dough down, then turn it out onto a floured surface. Roll to a ½-inch thickness and cut out with a 2½-inch doughnut cutter. Transfer to a floured baking sheet. Cover with a clean kitchen towel and set aside to rise for 20 minutes.

5. Heat the oil to 370°F. Using a perforated metal spatula, transfer the doughnuts to the hot oil. Do not overcrowd the pan; cook only a few doughnuts at one time. Fry for 3 to 4 minutes, or until golden brown on both sides. Transfer to absorbent paper to drain. Repeat with the remaining doughnuts. ❖

Jelly Doughnuts

MAKES 24

These technically should be called "jam doughnuts," since they are filled with jam. When frying doughnuts that are already filled, it's a good idea to use jam because it's thicker and doesn't liquefy as fast as jelly upon contact with hot fat.

¾ cup milk
¼ cup butter or margarine
¼ cup sugar
½ teaspoon salt
½ teaspoon vanilla extract
1 teaspoon finely grated lemon zest
1 package dry yeast, dissolved in ¼ cup warm
   water
2 large eggs
3½ to 4 cups all-purpose flour, scoop
   measured
⅔ cup grape, blueberry, or raspberry jam
Vegetable oil for deep-frying

1. In a wide saucepan, combine the milk, butter, sugar, and salt. Place over medium heat and stir until the butter is melted. Transfer to a large mixing bowl and blend in the vanilla and lemon zest. Set aside to cool.

2. When the mixture is barely warm to the touch, stir in the dissolved yeast. Separate 1 of the eggs, reserving the white. Beat the yolk and the other whole egg together, and add to the milk mixture. Add 3 cups of the flour and beat with a wooden spoon until a moist, stiff dough is formed.

3. Turn out onto a lightly floured surface. Knead in enough of the remaining flour to create a dough that is soft but not sticky. Transfer to a greased bowl and cover with a clean kitchen towel. Set aside to rise until double in bulk.

4. Punch the dough down, then turn it out onto a floured surface. Roll to a ¼-inch thickness and cut out with a 3-inch biscuit cutter. Spoon a generous dollop of jam onto the center of half the rounds. Whisk the egg white until foamy, then lightly brush the dough surrounding the jam. Top with the remaining dough rounds and press to seal. Transfer to a baking sheet. Loosely cover the doughnuts with a kitchen towel and let them rest for 10 minutes.

5. Heat the oil to 370°F. Using a perforated metal spatula, transfer the doughnuts to the hot oil. Do not overcrowd the pan; cook only a few doughnuts at one time. Fry for 3 to 4 minutes, or until golden brown on both sides. Transfer to absorbent paper to drain. Repeat with the remaining doughnuts. ❖

Filled Molasses Doughnuts

MAKES 24

Ginger marmalade is the exotic filling for these delicious doughnuts. Dust with sifted confectioners' sugar and serve warm to eat with a fork.

3½ to 4 cups all-purpose flour, scoop
   measured
2 teaspoons baking powder
1 teaspoon baking soda
½ teaspoon salt
1½ teaspoons ground ginger
¼ teaspoon cinnamon

¼ teaspoon nutmeg
3 large eggs
1 cup sugar
½ cup molasses
2 tablespoons solid vegetable shortening, melted
1 tablespoon finely grated lemon zest
1 cup sour cream
⅔ cup ginger marmalade
Vegetable oil for deep-frying

1. In a large mixing bowl, combine 3½ cups of the flour with the baking powder, baking soda, and salt. Add the ginger, cinnamon, and nutmeg. Whisk to blend the dry ingredients thoroughly.

2. Combine the eggs and sugar in the bowl of an electric mixer. Beat at high speed until pale yellow and slightly thickened. Gradually beat in the molasses and melted shortening. Add the lemon zest and sour cream, and blend well. With the mixer on low speed, sprinkle in the dry ingredients. Beat until a moist, stiff dough is formed.

3. Turn out onto a lightly floured surface. Knead gently, working in additional flour if necessary to create a soft, smooth dough. Cover the dough with a clean kitchen towel and let rest for 30 minutes. Roll the dough to a ¼-inch thickness and cut out with a 3-inch biscuit cutter. Spoon a generous dollop of ginger marmalade onto the center of half the rounds. Moisten the surrounding dough with warm water. Top with the remaining dough rounds and press to seal.

4. Heat the oil to 370°F. Using a perforated metal spatula, transfer the doughnuts to the hot oil. Do not overcrowd the pan; cook only a few doughnuts at one time. Fry for 3 to 4 minutes, or until nicely browned on both sides. Transfer to absorbent paper to drain, then repeat with the remaining doughnuts.   ❖

Molasses Spice Doughnuts

MAKES 24

Old-fashioned spice doughnuts, flavored with molasses, make a special Halloween treat.

3½ to 4 cups all-purpose flour, scoop measured
1 teaspoon baking powder
1 teaspoon baking soda
½ teaspoon salt
½ teaspoon cinnamon
½ teaspoon allspice
½ teaspoon ground cloves
2 large eggs
¾ cup sugar
5 tablespoons butter or margarine, melted
½ cup molasses
1 cup buttermilk
Vegetable oil for deep-frying.

1. In a large mixing bowl, combine 3½ cups of the flour with the baking powder, baking soda, and salt. Add the cinnamon, allspice, and cloves. Whisk to blend the dry ingredients thoroughly.

2. Combine the eggs and sugar in the bowl of an electric mixer. Beat at high speed until pale yellow and slightly thickened. Gradually beat in the melted butter. Add the molasses and buttermilk, and blend well. With the mixer on low speed, sprinkle in the dry ingredients. Beat until a moist, stiff dough is formed.

3. Turn out onto a lightly floured surface. Knead gently, working in additional flour if necessary to create a soft, smooth dough. Cover the dough with a clean kitchen towel and let rest for 30 minutes. Roll the dough

to a ½-inch thickness and cut out with a 2½-inch doughnut cutter.

4. Heat the oil to 370°F. Using a perforated metal spatula, transfer the doughnuts to the hot oil. Do not overcrowd the pan; cook only a few doughnuts at one time. Fry for 3 to 4 minutes, or until golden brown on both sides. Transfer to absorbent paper to drain. Repeat with the remaining doughnuts. When cool, dust with sifted confectioners' sugar if you wish.   ❖

Old-Fashioned Doughnuts

MAKES 24

These are doughnuts like Grandma used to make. Once you taste one, freshly made, you'll wonder why you ever ate store-bought.

3½ to 4 cups all-purpose flour, scoop measured
3 teaspoons baking powder
1 teaspoon salt
½ teaspoon cinnamon
¼ teaspoon nutmeg
⅛ teaspoon ground cloves
2 large eggs
⅔ cup sugar
5 tablespoons butter or margarine, melted
1 cup milk
1 teaspoon vanilla extract
Vegetable oil for deep-frying.

1. In a large mixing bowl, combine 3½ cups of the flour with the baking powder and salt. Add the cinnamon, nutmeg, and cloves. Whisk to blend thoroughly.

2. Combine the eggs and sugar in the bowl of an electric mixer. Beat at high speed until pale yellow and slightly thickened. Gradually beat in the melted butter. Add the milk and vanilla, and blend well. With the mixer on low speed, sprinkle in the dry ingredients. Beat until a moist, stiff dough is formed.

3. Turn out onto a lightly floured surface. Knead gently, working in additional flour if

necessary to create a soft, smooth dough. Cover the dough with a clean kitchen towel and let rest for 30 minutes. Roll the dough to a ½-inch thickness and cut out with a 2½-inch doughnut cutter.

4. Heat the oil to 370°F. Using a perforated metal spatula, transfer the doughnuts to the hot oil. Do not overcrowd the pan; cook only a few doughnuts at one time. Fry for 3 to 4 minutes, or until golden brown on both sides. Transfer to absorbent paper to drain. Repeat with the remaining doughnuts.   ❖

Orange Drop Doughnuts

MAKES 36

Bright sunny doughnuts to serve at a springtime brunch with sliced fresh strawberries and softly whipped cream.

1 cup all-purpose flour, scoop measured
1 cup whole wheat flour, scoop measured
¼ cup sugar
2 teaspoons baking powder
½ teaspoon baking soda
½ teaspoon salt
½ cup freshly squeezed orange juice
2 large eggs
3 tablespoons butter or margarine, melted
1 tablespoon finely grated orange zest
Vegetable oil for deep-frying

1. Combine the all-purpose flour, whole wheat flour, sugar, baking powder, baking soda, and salt in a large mixing bowl. Whisk to blend thoroughly.

2. In a separate bowl, whisk together the orange juice, eggs, and melted butter. Stir in the orange zest. Make a well in the dry ingredients and pour in the egg mixture. Blend with a wooden spoon until thoroughly moistened.

3. Heat the oil to 370°F. Coat 2 teaspoons with oil by dipping them in the hot fat. Scoop up the batter by rounded teaspoonfuls and drop into the oil, using one spoon to push the dough off the other. Do not overcrowd the pan; cook only a few doughnuts at

one time. Fry for 3 to 4 minutes, turning the doughnuts as they puff to encourage even browning. Transfer to absorbent paper with a slotted spoon. Repeat with the remaining batter.　❖

Potato Doughnuts

MAKES 24

New England cooks have traditionally used mashed potato as an ingredient in baked goods. Here it helps create light, exceptionally tender doughnuts. Don't forget to fry up the "holes" for finger snacks.

1 cup milk
¼ cup butter or margarine
¾ cup sugar
¾ teaspoon salt
½ teaspoon cinnamon
1 package dry yeast, dissolved in ¼ cup warm water
2 large eggs, beaten
1 cup warm mashed potato
3½ to 4 cups all-purpose flour, scoop measured
Vegetable oil for deep-frying

1. In a wide saucepan, combine the milk, butter, sugar, and salt. Place over medium heat and stir until the butter is melted. Remove from the heat and whisk in the cinnamon. Transfer to a large mixing bowl to cool.

2. When the mixture is barely warm to the touch, stir in the dissolved yeast and beaten egg. Blend in the mashed potato. Add 3½ cups of the flour and beat with a wooden spoon until a moist, stiff dough is formed.

3. Turn out onto a lightly floured surface. Knead gently, working in additional flour if necessary. The dough should be soft but not sticky. Cover the dough with a clean kitchen towel and let rest for 30 minutes.

4. Dust 2 baking sheets with flour. Roll the dough to a ½-inch thickness and cut out with a 2½-inch doughnut cutter. Transfer

to the floured baking sheets. Cover loosely with plastic wrap and let rise. When double in bulk, begin heating the vegetable oil to 370°F. Using a perforated metal spatula, transfer the doughnuts to the hot oil. Do not overcrowd the pan; cook only a few doughnuts at one time. Fry for 3 to 4 minutes, or until golden brown on both sides. Transfer to absorbent paper to drain. Repeat with the remaining doughnuts.　❖

Pumpkin Doughnuts

MAKES 24

Reassuring doughnuts to offer your after-school snackers on a cold winter day, accompanied by a glass of milk.

3½ to 4 cups all-purpose flour, scoop measured
2 teaspoons baking powder
½ teaspoon baking soda
¾ teaspoon salt
1 teaspoon cinnamon
½ teaspoon allspice
¼ teaspoon ground cloves
2 large eggs
½ cup light brown sugar
¼ cup granulated sugar
¼ cup butter or margarine, melted
1 cup pumpkin purée
½ cup milk
1 teaspoon vanilla extract
Vegetable oil for deep-frying

1. In a large mixing bowl, combine 3½ cups of the flour with the baking powder, baking soda, and salt. Add the cinnamon, allspice, and cloves. Whisk to blend the dry ingredients thoroughly.

2. Combine the eggs and brown sugar in the bowl of an electric mixer. Add the granulated sugar and beat at high speed until light in color and slightly thickened. Gradually beat in the melted butter. Add the pumpkin purée and blend in. Stir in the milk and vanilla. With the mixer on low speed, sprinkle in the dry ingredients. Beat until a moist, stiff dough is formed.

3. Turn out onto a lightly floured surface. Knead gently, working in additional flour if necessary to create a soft, smooth dough. Cover the dough with a clean kitchen towel and let rest for 30 minutes. Roll the dough to a ½-inch thickness and cut out with a 2½-inch doughnut cutter.

4. Heat the oil to 370°F. Using a perforated metal spatula, transfer the doughnuts to the hot oil. Do not overcrowd the pan; cook only a few doughnuts at one time. Fry for 3 to 4 minutes, or until golden brown on both sides. Transfer to absorbent paper to drain. Repeat with the remaining doughnuts.   ❖

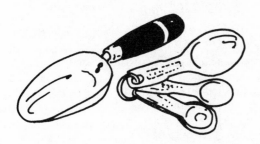

Raisin Drop Doughnuts

MAKES 36

Raisins dot these puffy doughnut balls. Eat out of hand or drizzle with fruit syrup and eat with a fork.

2⅔ cups all-purpose flour, scoop measured
⅓ cup sugar
3 teaspoons baking powder
¾ teaspoon salt
¾ cup milk
2 large eggs
2 tablespoons butter or margarine, melted
1 cup raisins
Vegetable oil for deep-frying

1. Combine the flour, sugar, baking powder, and salt in a large mixing bowl. Whisk to blend thoroughly.

2. In a separate bowl, whisk together the milk, eggs, and melted butter. Make a well in the dry ingredients and pour in the egg mixture. Blend with a wooden spoon until well moistened. Stir in the raisins.

3. Heat the oil to 370°F. Coat 2 teaspoons with oil by dipping them in the hot fat. Scoop up the batter by rounded teaspoonfuls and drop into the oil, using one spoon to push the dough off the other. Do not overcrowd the pan; cook only a few doughnuts at one time. Fry for 3 to 4 minutes, turning the doughnuts as they puff to encourage even browning. Transfer to absorbent paper with a slotted spoon. Repeat with the remaining batter.   ❖

Quick Rolled Doughnuts

MAKES 18

Mixed like muffin batter, these doughnuts are quick and easy to prepare. Dust with sifted confectioners' sugar if you like.

2 cups all-purpose flour, scoop measured
¼ cup sugar
2 teaspoons baking powder
½ teaspoon baking soda
½ teaspoon salt
½ teaspoon cinnamon
¼ teaspoon nutmeg
½ cup buttermilk
2 large eggs
2 tablespoons vegetable oil
Vegetable oil for deep-frying

1. Combine the flour, sugar, baking powder, baking soda, and salt in a large mixing bowl. Add the cinnamon and nutmeg, and whisk to blend thoroughly.

2. In a separate bowl, whisk together the buttermilk, eggs, and oil. Make a well in the dry ingredients and pour in the egg mixture. Blend with a wooden spoon until well moistened.

3. Turn out onto a lightly floured surface. Knead gently, for 20 to 25 strokes, sprinkling on flour if necessary to prevent sticking. Roll the dough to a ½-inch thickness and cut out using a 2½-inch doughnut cutter.

4. Heat the oil to 370°F. Using a perforated metal spatula, transfer the doughnuts to the hot oil. Do not overcrowd the pan; cook

only a few doughnuts at one time. Fry for 3 to 4 minutes, or until golden brown on both sides. Transfer to absorbent paper to drain. Repeat with the remaining doughnuts. ❖

Sour Cream Doughnuts

MAKES 24

These rich, flavorful doughnuts are baked in the oven and then topped with a maple glaze.

3½ to 4 cups all-purpose flour, scoop
   measured
2 teaspoons baking powder
½ teaspoon baking soda
¾ teaspoon salt
½ teaspoon cinnamon
¼ teaspoon nutmeg
2 large eggs
½ cup granulated sugar
½ cup butter or margarine, melted
1 cup sour cream
1½ cups confectioners' sugar, sifted
1 tablespoon warm water
2 tablespoons pure maple syrup

1. In a large mixing bowl, combine 3½ cups of the flour with the baking powder, baking soda, and salt. Add the cinnamon and nutmeg, and whisk to blend the dry ingredients thoroughly.

2. Combine the eggs and granulated sugar in the bowl of an electric mixer. Beat at high speed until pale yellow and slightly thickened. Gradually beat in ¼ cup of the melted butter. Add the sour cream and blend well. With the mixer on low speed, sprinkle in the dry ingredients. Beat until a moist, stiff dough is formed.

3. Turn out onto a lightly floured surface. Knead gently, working in additional flour if necessary to create a soft, smooth dough. Cover the dough with a clean kitchen towel and let rest for 30 minutes.

4. Preheat the oven to 425°F. Generously grease 2 baking sheets. Roll the dough to a ½-inch thickness and cut out with a 2½-inch doughnut cutter. Transfer to the pre-

pared baking sheets. Brush with the remaining ¼ cup melted butter. Bake for 12 to 15 minutes, or until lightly browned. Transfer to a cooling rack.

5. When the doughnuts are completely cooled, combine the confectioners' sugar, water, and maple syrup in a small bowl. Blend until smooth, then spread over the surface of each doughnut. ❖

Sweet Potato Doughnuts

MAKES 24

Baked sweet potatoes that have been puréed form the basis for these sensational spiced doughnuts.

3½ to 4 cups all-purpose flour, scoop
   measured
3 teaspoons baking powder
¾ teaspoon salt
½ teaspoon cinnamon
¼ teaspoon nutmeg
⅛ teaspoon ground cloves
2 large eggs
1 cup sugar
¼ cup butter or margarine, melted
1 cup baked sweet potato purée
¼ cup milk
Vegetable oil for deep-frying

1. In a large mixing bowl, combine 3½ cups of the flour with the baking powder and salt. Add the cinnamon, nutmeg, and cloves. Whisk to blend thoroughly.

2. Combine the eggs and sugar in the bowl of an electric mixer. Beat at high speed until pale yellow and slightly thickened. Gradually beat in the melted butter. Add the sweet potato purée and milk, and blend well. With the mixer on low speed, sprinkle in the dry ingredients. Beat until a moist, stiff dough is formed.

3. Turn out onto a lightly floured surface. Knead gently, working in additional flour if necessary to create a soft, smooth dough. Cover the dough with a clean kitchen towel and let rest for 30 minutes. Roll the dough

to a ½-inch thickness and cut out with a 2½-inch doughnut cutter.

4. Heat the oil to 370°F. Using a perforated metal spatula, transfer the doughnuts to the hot oil. Do not overcrowd the pan; cook only a few doughnuts at one time. Fry for 3 to 4 minutes, or until golden brown on both sides. Transfer to absorbent paper to drain. Repeat with the remaining doughnuts. ❖

Fried Dough

MAKES 24

Fried dough has been a Yankee staple for years. The shape it takes varies with its creator — some cooks fashion strips of dough, others fry small rounds, and still others create discs. In this recipe, egg-sized pieces of dough are dropped into hot fat to produce fluffy orbs. Whatever the shape, fried dough is best when sprinkled with confectioners' sugar and served hot with maple syrup and bacon.

1 cup warm water
1 package dry yeast
1 teaspoon sugar
1 teaspoon salt
1 tablespoon olive oil
3 cups all-purpose flour, scoop measured
Vegetable oil for deep-frying

1. Measure the warm water into a large mixing bowl. Sprinkle in the yeast and stir to dissolve. Blend in the sugar and salt. Stir in the olive oil. Add 2 cups of the flour and beat with a wooden spoon until smooth. Stir in the remaining cup of flour. Cover the bowl with plastic wrap and secure with an elastic band. Set aside to rise.

2. When double in bulk, stir the dough down. Heat the vegetable oil to 370°F. Coat 2 tablespoons with oil by dipping them in the hot fat. Scoop up the dough by rounded tablespoonfuls and drop into the oil. Do not overcrowd the pan; cook only a few pieces at a time. Fry for 3 to 4 minutes, turning the dough balls as they puff to encourage even

browning. Transfer to absorbent paper with a slotted spoon. Repeat with the remaining batter. ❖

Fried Dough, Portuguese-Style

MAKES 8

In the Portuguese community of Province-town, Massachusetts, fried dough is made by cutting the dough into small pieces, then stretching them into flat rounds. The resulting puffy discs are called "flippers" by the locals. They may be served anytime, but the customary practice is to offer them at breakfast, either tossed in cinnamon sugar or with butter and maple syrup. This recipe, which is leavened with baking powder, is faster to prepare than the preceding yeast-leavened fried dough recipe.

2 to 2½ cups all-purpose flour, scoop measured
1½ teaspoons sugar
2 teaspoons baking powder
¾ teaspoon salt
⅔ cup warm water
1 tablespoon olive oil
Vegetable oil for deep-frying

1. In a large mixing bowl, combine 2 cups of the flour with the sugar, baking powder, and salt. Whisk to blend thoroughly.

2. Combine the water and olive oil in a glass measuring cup. Make a well in the dry ingredients. Pour in the liquid and toss with a fork until the dough holds together. Gather the dough into a ball and roll it around the inside of the bowl to pick up any stray particles. Transfer to a lightly floured surface and knead in enough of the remaining flour to create a soft dough that is moist but not sticky. Shape the dough into a 16-inch rope. Cut the rope into 8 equal portions, then flatten each portion into a thin disc.

3. Heat the vegetable oil to 370°F. Fry 1 disc at a time, turning it once to brown both

sides evenly. Using a perforated metal spatula, transfer the cooked dough to absorbent paper to drain. Repeat with the remaining discs.   ❖

Deep-Fried Biscuits

MAKES 18

Similar to fried dough, these yeast-leavened biscuits are cut into 2-inch rounds and fried in deep fat. Serve as you would baked biscuits or rolls.

2 cups milk
1 package dry yeast
2½ to 3 cups all-purpose flour, scoop measured
2 tablespoons sugar
1 teaspoon salt
¼ cup butter or margarine, melted
Vegetable oil for deep-frying

1. Measure the milk into a large mixing bowl. Sprinkle in the yeast and set aside for 10 minutes. Stir to dissolve the yeast and add 1 cup of the flour. Beat with a wooden spoon until smooth. Cover the bowl with plastic wrap and secure with an elastic band. Set aside to rise until light and foamy.

2. Sprinkle on the sugar and salt. Stir the dough down. Add the melted butter and 1½ cups of the remaining flour. Beat until smooth. Turn out onto a lightly floured surface and knead in enough of the remaining flour to create a soft dough that is moist but not sticky. Roll to a ½-inch thickness and cut out with a 2-inch biscuit cutter.

3. Heat the oil to 370°F. Using a perforated metal spatula, transfer the biscuits to the hot oil. Do not overcrowd the pan; cook only a few biscuits at one time. Fry for 3 to 4 minutes, or until golden brown on both sides. Transfer to absorbent paper to drain. Repeat with the remaining biscuits.   ❖

Apple Fritters

MAKES 18

Chunks of fresh apple are contained inside these puffy deep-fried spheres. Dust with confectioners' sugar and serve for dessert or as a special-occasion snack.

1¾ cups all-purpose flour, scoop measured
2 tablespoons sugar
2 teaspoons baking powder
½ teaspoon salt
½ teaspoon cinnamon
¼ teaspoon nutmeg
¾ cup milk
2 large eggs, separated
2 tablespoons butter or margarine, melted
1 cup peeled, cored, and coarsely chopped apple
Vegetable oil for deep-frying

1. Combine the flour, sugar, baking powder, and salt in a large mixing bowl. Add the cinnamon and nutmeg, and whisk to blend thoroughly.

2. In a separate bowl, whisk together the milk, egg yolks, and melted butter. In another bowl, whip the egg whites until soft peaks form. Make a well in the dry ingredients. Pour in the egg yolk mixture and beat until well moistened. Stir in the apple, then fold in the egg whites.

3. Heat the vegetable oil to 370°F. Coat 2 tablespoons with oil by dipping them in the hot fat. Scoop up the dough by rounded tablespoonfuls and drop into the oil. Do not overcrowd the pan; cook only a few fritters at one time. Fry for 3 to 4 minutes, turning the fritters as they puff to encourage even browning. Transfer to absorbent paper with a slotted spoon. Repeat with the remaining batter.   ❖

Clam Fritters

MAKES 18

A collection of New England fried breads would be incomplete without a recipe for clam fritters, that ubiquitous specialty of the Northeast shoreline. In this recipe, lemon juice provides a lively accent.

24 fresh cherrystone clams
Juice of 1 lemon
1½ cups all-purpose flour, scoop measured
2 teaspoons baking powder
1 teaspoon salt
Generous amount of freshly ground black
  pepper
¼ cup milk
2 large eggs, separated
Vegetable oil for deep-frying

1. Open the clams and remove them from their shells, reserving the liquid. Chop the clams finely. Strain the broth and measure out ½ cup. Combine the broth and chopped clams in a large mixing bowl. Sprinkle on the lemon juice and stir to blend.

2. In a separate bowl, combine the flour, baking powder, salt, and pepper. Whisk to blend thoroughly. Beat the milk and egg yolks together. Pour over the chopped clams and stir to combine.

3. Whip the egg whites until soft peaks form. Sprinkle the dry ingredients over the clam mixture and stir until well moistened. Fold in the egg whites.

4. Heat the oil to 370°F. Coat 2 tablespoons with oil by dipping them in the hot fat. Scoop up the dough by rounded tablespoonfuls and drop into the oil. Do not overcrowd the pan; cook only a few fritters at one time. Fry for 3 to 4 minutes, turning the fritters as they puff to encourage even browning. Transfer to absorbent paper with a slotted spoon. Repeat with the remaining batter.   ❖

Clam and Onion Fritters

MAKES 18

Adding club soda to the batter creates exceptionally light clam fritters. Serve hot with thick slices of peeled, fresh tomato and a scoop of coleslaw.

24 fresh cherrystone clams
1¾ cups all-purpose flour, scoop measured

2 teaspoons baking powder
1 teaspoon salt
Generous amount of freshly ground black
  pepper
1 large egg
1 medium onion, finely chopped
1 tablespoon finely chopped fresh parsley
1 teaspoon freshly squeezed lemon juice
1 cup club soda
Vegetable oil for deep-frying

1. Open the clams and remove them from their shells. Discard the liquid or save for another use. Chop the clams finely and set aside.

2. In a large mixing bowl, combine the flour, baking powder, salt, and pepper. Whisk to blend thoroughly. Beat the egg in a separate bowl. Stir in the onion, parsley, and lemon juice.

3. Make a well in the dry ingredients. Pour in the egg mixture. Add the club soda and immediately stir to combine. Beat until the foam subsides. Stir in the chopped clams.

4. Heat the oil to 370°F. Coat 2 tablespoons with oil by dipping them in the hot fat. Scoop up the dough by rounded tablespoonfuls and drop into the oil. Do not overcrowd the pan; cook only a few fritters at one time. Fry for 3 to 4 minutes, turning the fritters as they puff to encourage even browning. Transfer to absorbent paper with a slotted spoon. Repeat with the remaining batter.   ❖

Corn Fritters

MAKES 18

Corn fritters may be served in place of biscuits with baked ham or fried chicken, but they are also good for breakfast, with maple syrup and bacon.

1½ cups all-purpose flour, scoop measured
2 teaspoons baking powder
1 teaspoon salt
Generous amount of freshly ground black
  pepper
¾ cup milk

2 large eggs, separated
2 tablespoons butter or margarine, melted
1 cup fresh corn kernels
Vegetable oil for deep-frying

1. Combine the flour, baking powder, salt, and pepper in a large mixing bowl. Whisk to blend thoroughly.

2. In a separate bowl, whisk together the milk, egg yolks, and melted butter. In another bowl, whip the egg whites until soft peaks form. Make a well in the dry ingredients. Pour in the egg yolk mixture and beat until well moistened. Stir in the corn, then fold in the egg whites.

3. Heat the oil to 370°F. Coat 2 tablespoons with oil by dipping them in the hot fat. Scoop up the dough by rounded tablespoonfuls and drop into the oil. Do not overcrowd the pan; cook only a few fritters at one time. Fry for 3 to 4 minutes, turning the fritters as they puff to encourage even browning. Transfer to absorbent paper with a slotted spoon. Repeat with the remaining batter.   ❖

Pumpkin Fritters

MAKES 36

Tiny puffs of fried pumpkin bread are a delightful partner to roast turkey or pork.

Present them piled around the roast or arranged in a napkin-lined basket.

2 cups all-purpose flour, scoop measured
2 tablespoons light brown sugar
2 teaspoons baking powder
½ teaspoon salt
½ teaspoon allspice
2 tablespoons half-and-half or light cream
1 large egg
2 tablespoons butter or margarine, melted
¾ cup pumpkin purée
Vegetable oil for deep-frying

1. Sift the flour and sugar into a large mixing bowl. Add the baking powder, salt, and allspice. Whisk to blend thoroughly.

2. In a separate bowl, whisk together the half-and-half, egg, and melted butter. Stir in the pumpkin purée. Make a well in the dry ingredients. Pour in the egg mixture and beat with a wooden spoon until well moistened.

3. Heat the oil to 370°F. Coat 2 teaspoons with oil by dipping them in the hot fat. Scoop up the dough by rounded teaspoonfuls and drop into the oil. Do not overcrowd the pan; cook only a few fritters at one time. Fry for 3 to 4 minutes, turning the fritters as they puff to encourage even browning. Transfer to absorbent paper with a slotted spoon. Repeat with the remaining batter. ❖

❖ Griddle, Skillet, and Flat Breads ❖

FLAT BREAD, baked on hot stones, was a culinary staple of all early civilizations. In the Northeast, the Narragansett Indians made cakes from ground corn and water, and cooked them on the hot stones of their campfires, a practice they taught to the Pilgrims.

Ever since that time, cooking breads on a hot surface has remained a favorite Yankee technique. The corncakes of the Indians eventually became jonnycakes, which today are cooked on a griddle. A variety of other griddle breads, such as English muffins and oatcakes, are also part of the contemporary New England cuisine.

Skillet breads, such as large popovers and skillet pancakes, are an extension of the griddle-cooking method. The skillet is first heated on the stove top, then the batter is poured in and baked in the oven. Quite often skillet breads are sweet, and consequently they are served for breakfast, brunch, or dessert.

Flat breads, which may or may not be leavened, are cooked on a metal baking sheet or baking stone. A baking stone is preferred because it is made of ceramic ware that has been fired by intense heat. This results in a baking surface that will absorb and retain heat in much the same way as the floor of a brick oven. Flat breads baked on such a surface develop a remarkably crisp underside.

The quality and material of the cooking surface also are important in preparing griddle breads and skillet breads. A heavy griddle that absorbs heat quickly and evenly is the most desirable. A nonstick surface is a welcome feature, though a light film of oil or grease must still be applied.

Many New England cooks prefer a griddle made from soapstone. These attractive griddles consist of a slab of soapstone banded by a strip of copper. Soapstone, which is a natural material mined in Vermont, retains heat evenly and never needs greasing, so it creates exceptionally fine griddle breads.

Skillet breads may be made in any frying pan that has an ovenproof handle. There is available, however, a specially designed black steel pan that is wonderful for baking these unique breads. It is shaped like a skillet, except it has two small hooklike handles and the sides are curved and rounded. The black metal holds the heat and distributes it evenly, while the curved sides promote puffing to create a light, evenly cooked skillet bread.

Some griddle breads are best when eaten immediately; others, such as English muffins, may be stored in an airtight plastic bag. Crisp flat breads, such as cracker breads, should be kept in an airtight plastic container or metal tin. Other types may be stored in a plastic bag secured with a wire twist. Skillet breads are meant to be eaten straight from the oven. Griddle breads and flat breads may be successfully frozen. To defrost, allow them to come to room temperature inside the plastic bag.

Cornmeal Griddle Muffins

MAKES 12

These crunchy griddle breads may be drizzled with syrup and eaten with a fork. They also may be split and buttered and eaten out of hand.

1½ cups yellow cornmeal
1½ cups all-purpose flour, scoop measured
2 tablespoons sugar

4 teaspoons baking powder
¾ teaspoon salt
1 cup milk
2 large eggs
¼ cup vegetable oil

1. Combine the cornmeal, flour, sugar, baking powder, and salt in a large mixing bowl. Whisk to blend thoroughly.

2. In a separate bowl, whisk together the milk, eggs, and oil. Make a well in the dry ingredients and pour in the egg mixture. Blend with a wooden spoon until a moist, lumpy batter is formed. Set the batter aside.

3. Place a griddle over medium-high heat. Brush the surface with vegetable oil. When the griddle is hot, spoon the batter onto the surface, forming 3-inch rounds. Cook for 3 to 5 minutes, or until nicely browned. Turn and cook the other side. Repeat with the remaining batter.   ❖

Cheddar Cheese Griddle Muffins

MAKES 15

Shaped into squares, these unusual griddle cakes are similar to English muffins. Serve hot with butter and syrup, or allow to cool and then split and toast.

1 cup milk
2 tablespoons butter or margarine
1 tablespoon sugar
1 teaspoon salt
1 package dry yeast, dissolved in ¼ cup warm water
½ cup Herman sourdough starter (p. 49), at room temperature
1 cup shredded Cheddar cheese
4 to 4½ cups all-purpose flour, scoop measured

1. In a wide saucepan, combine the milk, butter, sugar, and salt. Place over medium heat and stir until the butter is melted. Transfer to a large mixing bowl.

2. When the mixture is barely warm to the touch, stir in the dissolved yeast. Blend in the sourdough starter and cheese. Add 2

cups of the flour and beat with a wooden spoon until smooth. Gradually blend in additional flour until the dough becomes too difficult to stir. Turn out onto a floured surface and knead in as much of the remaining flour as necessary to form a cohesive dough. Continue kneading in flour until the dough is soft and moist yet no longer sticks to the work surface. Transfer to a greased bowl and cover with plastic wrap. Secure with an elastic band and set aside to rise until double in bulk.

3. Generously dust a baking sheet with cornmeal. Punch the dough down, then turn it out onto a floured surface. Roll into a 9x15-inch rectangle. Trim the edges to square off the rectangle. Lift the dough to loosen it from the work surface. Cut the rectangle into five 3-inch-wide strips, then cut the strips into squares. Transfer the squares to the prepared baking sheet. Cover loosely with plastic wrap and let rise for 30 minutes.

4. Grease a griddle by spraying it with vegetable shortening. Place the griddle over medium-high heat. When the griddle is hot, arrange the squares over the surface. Cook for 3 to 5 minutes, or until nicely browned. Turn the squares over and cook the other side. ❖

Whole Wheat Griddle Muffins

MAKES 12

These tender griddle breads have a crumbly, biscuitlike texture. Split with the tines of a fork and toast to serve with honey or butter and jam.

1½ cups whole wheat flour, scoop measured
½ cup all-purpose flour, scoop measured
2 tablespoons sugar
1 teaspoon baking powder
1 teaspoon baking soda
½ teaspoon salt
¾ cup buttermilk
¼ cup butter or margarine, melted

1. Combine the whole wheat flour, all-purpose flour, sugar, baking powder, baking soda, and salt in a large mixing bowl. Whisk to blend thoroughly.

2. Make a well in the dry ingredients. Pour in the buttermilk and melted butter. Toss with a fork until the dough holds together. Gather the dough into a ball and roll it around the inside of the bowl to pick up any stray particles. Transfer to a lightly floured surface and knead 20 to 25 times, sifting on flour if necessary to prevent sticking. Roll to a ½-inch thickness and cut out with a 2-inch biscuit cutter.

3. Place a griddle over medium-high heat. Brush the surface with vegetable oil. When the griddle is hot, place the muffins on the surface and cook for 5 to 7 minutes, or until lightly browned on both sides. Serve hot or transfer to a cooling rack. ❖

Egg Cakes

MAKES 10

These puffy cakes are a cross between a pancake and an English muffin. Serve with hot apple slices or blueberries cooked with sugar and a small amount of water. Top with a dollop of sour cream.

½ cup all-purpose flour, scoop measured
¾ teaspoon salt
¾ teaspoon baking powder
¼ teaspoon baking soda
½ cup buttermilk
6 large eggs, separated
1 teaspoon vanilla extract
½ teaspoon cream of tartar
2 tablespoons sugar

1. Combine the flour, salt, baking powder, and baking soda in a large mixing bowl. Whisk to blend thoroughly.

2. In a separate bowl, whisk together the buttermilk, egg yolks, and vanilla. Set aside. Beat the egg whites until foamy. Add the cream of tartar and beat until soft peaks form. Gradually sprinkle in the sugar, beating until the egg whites are glossy.

3. Place a griddle over medium-high heat. Brush the surface with vegetable oil. While the griddle heats, make a well in the dry ingredients and pour in the egg yolk mixture. Stir with a wooden spoon until well moistened. Fold in the whipped egg whites. When the griddle is hot, take up the batter by ½ cups and pour onto the hot surface. Cook for 3 to 4 minutes, or until the bottoms are golden. Turn and cook the other side. Repeat with the remaining batter. ❖

English Muffins

MAKES 12

Light, open-textured English muffins with a tantalizing yeasty aroma. Once you try these, you'll never be happy with store-bought.

¾ cup warm water
1 package dry yeast
2 tablespoons sugar
1 teaspoon salt
1 large egg, beaten
3 tablespoons butter or margarine, melted
2½ to 3 cups bread flour, preferably bromated, scoop measured

1. Measure the water into a large mixing bowl. Sprinkle on the yeast and stir to dissolve. Stir in the sugar and salt. Blend in the beaten egg and melted butter. Add 2 cups of the flour and beat with a wooden spoon until smooth. Gradually blend in additional flour until the dough becomes too difficult to stir. Turn out onto a floured surface and knead in as much of the remaining flour as necessary to form a soft dough that is moist yet no longer sticks to the work surface. Transfer to a greased bowl and cover with plastic wrap. Secure with an elastic band and set aside to rise until double in bulk.

2. Punch the dough down and turn it out onto a floured surface. Knead until the dough is smooth and resilient. Cover loosely with plastic wrap and let rest for 20 minutes. Roll the dough to a ½-inch thickness.

Cut out with a 3-inch biscuit cutter and transfer to a baking sheet sprinkled with cornmeal. Sprinkle cornmeal over the tops of the muffins and cover with a clean kitchen towel. Set aside to rise for 45 minutes.

3. Grease a griddle by spraying it with vegetable shortening. Place the griddle over medium-high heat. When the griddle is hot, arrange some of the muffins on the surface. Cook for 5 to 8 minutes, or until both sides are nicely browned. Transfer to a rack to cool. Repeat with the remaining muffins. ❖

Sourdough English Muffins

MAKES 12

The tang of sourdough starter gives these English muffins an extra measure of flavor. Be sure to split them with the tines of a fork to appreciate their wonderful texture. Toast and spread with butter.

½ cup warm water
1 package dry yeast
1 teaspoon salt
1 cup Herman sourdough starter (p. 49), at room temperature
1 large egg, beaten
3 tablespoons butter or margarine, melted
2 to 2½ cups bread flour, preferably bromated, scoop measured

1. Measure the water into a large mixing bowl. Sprinkle on the yeast and stir to dissolve. Stir in the salt, then blend in the sourdough starter, beaten egg, and melted butter. Add 1 cup of the flour and beat with a wooden spoon until smooth. Gradually blend in additional flour until the dough becomes too difficult to stir. Turn out onto a floured surface and knead in as much of the remaining flour as necessary to form a soft dough that is moist yet no longer sticks to the work surface. Transfer to a greased bowl and cover with plastic wrap. Secure with an elastic band and set aside to rise until double in bulk.

2. Punch the dough down and turn it out onto a floured surface. Knead until the dough is smooth and resilient. Cover loosely with plastic wrap and let rest for 20 minutes. Roll the dough to a ½-inch thickness. Cut out with a 3-inch biscuit cutter and transfer to a baking sheet sprinkled with cornmeal. Sprinkle cornmeal over the tops of the muffins and cover with a clean kitchen towel. Set aside to rise for 45 minutes.

3. Grease a griddle by spraying it with vegetable shortening. Place the griddle over medium-high heat. When the griddle is hot, arrange some of the muffins on the surface. Cook for 5 to 8 minutes, or until both sides are nicely browned. Transfer to a rack to cool. Repeat with the remaining muffins. ❖

Whole Wheat English Muffins

MAKES 12

The fragrance of honey enlivens these satisfying English muffins. Split with the tines of a fork and toast, then spread with butter that has been whipped with a touch of allspice.

¾ cup warm water
1 package dry yeast
⅓ cup honey
1 teaspoon salt
1 large egg, beaten
3 tablespoons butter or margarine, melted
2 cups whole wheat flour, scoop measured
1 to 1½ cups bread flour, preferably
  bromated, scoop measured

1. Measure the water into a large mixing bowl. Sprinkle on the yeast and stir to dissolve. Stir in the honey and salt. Blend in the beaten egg and melted butter. Add the whole wheat flour and beat with a wooden spoon until smooth. Gradually blend in the bread flour until the dough becomes too difficult to stir. Turn out onto a floured surface and knead in as much of the remaining bread flour as necessary to form a soft dough that is moist yet no longer sticks to the work surface. Transfer to a greased bowl and cover with plastic wrap. Secure with an elastic band and set aside to rise until double in bulk.

2. Punch the dough down and turn it out onto a floured surface. Knead until the dough is smooth and resilient. Cover loosely with plastic wrap and let rest for 20 minutes. Roll the dough to a ½-inch thickness. Cut out with a 3-inch biscuit cutter and transfer to a baking sheet sprinkled with cornmeal. Sprinkle cornmeal over the tops of the muffins and cover with a clean kitchen towel. Set aside to rise for 45 minutes.

3. Grease a griddle by spraying it with vegetable shortening. Place the griddle over medium-high heat. When the griddle is hot, arrange some of the muffins on the surface. Cook for 5 to 8 minutes, or until both sides are nicely browned. Transfer to a rack to cool. Repeat with the remaining muffins. ❖

Jonnycakes

MAKES 12

Jonnycake, spelled without the h, is a cornmeal griddle cake that has been made in Rhode Island since the days of the Pilgrims. Much dispute exists over its authentic thickness, width, and various other characteristics. Everyone agrees, however, that white cornmeal is the essential ingredient.

1 cup white cornmeal
1 teaspoon sugar
½ teaspoon salt
1 cup boiling water
¼ cup milk

1. Combine the cornmeal, sugar, and salt in a large mixing bowl. Pour in the boiling water and beat until well moistened. Stir in the milk. Set the batter aside.

2. Place a griddle over medium-high heat. Brush the surface with vegetable oil or rub with a strip of uncooked bacon as the griddle warms. When the griddle is hot, spoon the batter onto the surface. The batter should be as thick as mashed potatoes. Form the batter into cakes about ½-inch thick and 2½ inches across. Cook until a crunchy, light brown crust forms on the underside. Turn the cakes over and cook the other side. Repeat with the remaining batter.   ❖

Thin Jonnycakes

MAKES 12

These thin corncakes are associated with Newport County, or that part of Rhode Island known as East-of-Bay. Serve jonnycakes with butter and maple syrup, just as you would pancakes.

1 cup white cornmeal
½ teaspoon salt
2 cups milk

1. Combine the cornmeal and salt in a large mixing bowl. Measure out 2 tablespoons of the milk and set it aside. Pour in the remaining milk. Beat until well moistened. Set the batter aside.

2. Place a griddle over medium-high heat. Brush the surface with vegetable oil or rub with a strip of uncooked bacon as the griddle warms. When the griddle is hot, spoon the batter onto the surface to form cakes ⅛ inch thick and 5 inches across. The batter should be very thin. As the cakes cook, they should develop open, lacy edges. If necessary, add the reserved milk to achieve the desired effect. Cook until a crunchy, light brown crust forms on the underside. Turn the cakes over and cook the other side. Repeat with the remaining batter.   ❖

Molasses Jonnycakes

MAKES 18

Jonnycakes sweetened with molasses and speckled with pecans are a contemporary variation on the colonial theme.

2 cups white cornmeal
1 teaspoon salt
4 tablespoons butter or margarine, cut into small pieces
1½ cups boiling water
¼ cup molasses
¼ cup half-and-half or light cream
½ cup coarsely chopped pecans

1. Combine the cornmeal and salt in a large mixing bowl. Add the butter. Pour on the boiling water, then immediately add the molasses. Beat until the butter is melted and the batter is moistened. Stir in the half-and-half. Set the batter aside.

2. Place a griddle over medium-high heat. Brush the surface with vegetable oil or rub with a strip of uncooked bacon as the griddle warms. When the griddle is hot, stir the pecans into the batter, then spoon the batter onto the griddle. The consistency should be very thick. Form the batter into cakes about ½ inch thick and 2½ inches across. Cook until a crunchy, light brown crust forms on the underside. Turn the cakes over and cook the other side. Repeat with the remaining batter.   ❖

Oatcakes

MAKES 12

Replete with hearty oats, these hotcakes make a tempting addition to a plate of scrambled eggs and ham.

1½ cups quick-cooking rolled oats
¾ cup all-purpose flour, scoop measured
2 teaspoons baking powder
½ teaspoon salt
1 cup milk
¼ cup butter or margarine

1. Combine the oats, flour, baking powder, and salt in a large mixing bowl. Whisk to blend thoroughly.

2. In a small saucepan, combine the milk and butter. Place over medium heat and stir until the butter is melted. Make a well in the dry ingredients. Pour in the warm milk and toss with a fork until the dough holds together. Gather the dough into a ball and roll it around the inside of the bowl to pick up any stray particles. Scatter additional oats on a work surface. Place the dough on the oats and press into a flat circle. Scatter more oats over the top. Roll to a ¼-inch thickness, scattering on additional oats if necessary to prevent the rolling pin from sticking. Cut out the dough with a 3-inch biscuit cutter.

3. Place a griddle over medium-high heat. Brush the surface with vegetable oil. When the griddle is hot, place the cakes on the surface and cook for 5 to 7 minutes, or until lightly browned on both sides. Serve hot or transfer to a cooling rack.   ❖

Welsh Cakes

MAKES 18

These delightful cakes resemble rich biscuits that have been cooked on a griddle. Serve warm, sprinkled with confectioners' sugar.

3 cups all-purpose flour, scoop measured
¾ cup sugar
3 teaspoons baking powder
½ teaspoon salt
½ teaspoon cinnamon
¼ teaspoon nutmeg
8 tablespoons butter or margarine, cut into small pieces
½ cup solid vegetable shortening
1 cup dried currants
¾ cup milk
2 large eggs

1. Combine the flour, sugar, baking powder, and salt in a large mixing bowl. Add the cinnamon and nutmeg, and whisk to blend thoroughly. Add the butter and shortening, and cut in with a knife until the mixture is crumbly. Add the currants and toss to mix.

2. In a separate bowl, whisk together the milk and eggs. Make a well in the dry ingredients. Pour in the egg mixture and toss with a fork until the dough holds together. Gather the dough into a ball and roll it around the inside of the bowl to pick up any stray particles. Transfer to a lightly floured surface and form into a flat round. The dough will have a firm, piecrust–type consistency. Roll to a ¼-inch thickness and cut out with a 3-inch biscuit cutter.

3. Place a griddle over medium-high heat. Brush the surface with vegetable oil. When the griddle is hot, place the cakes on the surface and cook for 5 to 7 minutes, or until lightly browned on both sides. Serve hot or transfer to a cooling rack.   ❖

Skillet Popover

MAKES ONE 10-INCH POPOVER

This well-loved skillet bread is also known as a Dutch baby or oven pancake. Serve with fresh strawberries, sliced bananas, or sliced fresh peaches.

½ cup milk
2 large eggs
¼ teaspoon salt
½ cup all-purpose flour, scoop measured
Generous amount of freshly grated nutmeg
¼ cup butter or margarine
1 tablespoon freshly squeezed lemon juice
2 tablespoons sifted confectioners' sugar

1. Preheat the oven to 425°F. Combine the milk and eggs in a large mixing bowl, and whisk to blend. Stir in the salt. Add the flour and nutmeg, and beat with a whisk until smooth.

2. Place the butter in a 10-inch skillet with an ovenproof handle. Put the skillet in the oven and heat until the butter is melted. Immediately pour the batter into the skillet and return to the oven. Bake for 15 to 20

minutes, or until puffed and lightly browned. Sprinkle on the lemon juice and dust with the confectioners' sugar. Return the popover to the oven for 2 minutes. Cut into wedges and serve hot. ❖

Spiced Apple Skillet Pancake

MAKES ONE 10-INCH PANCAKE

Cut into wedges and served hot, this apple skillet bread makes a glorious treat for brunch. It is especially good with slices of honey-baked ham.

1 cup milk
4 large eggs
6 tablespoons butter or margarine, melted
1 teaspoon vanilla extract
½ cup all-purpose flour, scoop measured
2 tablespoons sugar, plus ⅔ cup
1 teaspoon baking powder
¼ teaspoon salt
½ teaspoon nutmeg
½ teaspoon cinnamon
2 tart apples, peeled, cored, and sliced

1. Preheat the oven to 425°F. Combine the milk, eggs, 2 tablespoons of the melted butter, and the vanilla in a large mixing bowl. Whisk to blend.

2. In a separate bowl, combine the flour, 2 tablespoons of the sugar, the baking powder, the salt, and ¼ teaspoon of the nutmeg. Whisk to blend thoroughly. Add to the egg mixture and whisk until smooth.

3. Pour the remaining 4 tablespoons melted butter into a 10-inch skillet with an ovenproof handle. Tilt to coat the bottom and sides. Place over medium-high heat and warm until the butter begins to bubble. Immediately remove from the heat. In a small bowl, combine the remaining ⅔ cup sugar, the cinnamon, and the remaining ¼ teaspoon nutmeg. Whisk to blend thoroughly. Sprinkle half the mixture over the warm butter. Arrange the apple slices over the mixture in an overlapping layer. Sprinkle on the remaining sugar mixture. Return

to medium-high heat and warm until the butter bubbles. Pour on the batter and immediately transfer to the preheated oven. Bake for 15 minutes. Reduce the oven temperature to 375°F. and continue baking for 10 to 15 minutes, or until the surface is nicely browned. Slide out onto a warm platter and cut into wedges. Serve immediately with sweetened whipped cream or vanilla ice cream on the side. ❖

Peach Skillet Pancakes

MAKES TWO 10-INCH CAKES

Kissed with almond liqueur, these are definitely grown-up pancakes. Serve with roasted fresh ham or grilled pork sausage links.

8 tablespoons unsalted butter (Do not substitute margarine.)
3 large fresh peaches, peeled and sliced
¼ cup amaretto
¾ cup milk
3 large eggs, separated
½ teaspoon cinnamon
½ teaspoon salt
½ cup all-purpose flour, scoop measured
1 tablespoon granulated sugar
3 tablespoons light brown sugar

1. Melt 4 tablespoons of the butter in a wide saucepan. Add the peaches and amaretto, and toss to coat. Stir over medium heat until the peaches are crisp-tender and the liqueur has evaporated. Set aside.

2. Combine the milk and egg yolks in a large mixing bowl. Whisk to blend. Whisk in the cinnamon and salt. Add the flour and whisk until smooth. In a separate bowl, whisk the egg whites until soft peaks form. Gradually sprinkle in the granulated sugar and continue whisking until the egg whites are glossy. Fold into the egg yolk mixture.

3. Melt 2 tablespoons of the remaining butter in a 10-inch skillet with an ovenproof handle. Pour in half the batter. Place over medium heat and cook for about 3

minutes, or until set. Arrange half the peach slices over the batter. Sift half the brown sugar over the peaches. Slide under a broiler and cook for 2 to 3 minutes, or until the pancake is puffed and golden. Slide out onto a warm platter. Make another pancake with the remaining batter and peaches. Cut into generous wedges to serve.   ❖

Pita Bread

MAKES 12

These pocket breads have become increasingly popular, especially for sandwiches. They will puff considerably as they bake, then deflate. When cool, gently pry them apart to form a pocket.

1½ cups warm water
1 package dry yeast
1 teaspoon salt
1 tablespoon olive oil
3½ to 4 cups bread flour, preferably
  bromated, scoop measured

1. Measure the water into a large mixing bowl. Sprinkle on the yeast and stir to dissolve. Stir in the salt and olive oil.

2. Add 2 cups of the flour and beat with a wooden spoon until smooth. Gradually blend in additional flour until the dough becomes too difficult to stir. Turn out onto a floured surface and knead in as much of the remaining flour as necessary to form a cohesive dough. Continue kneading in flour until the dough is firm and resilient and no longer sticks to the work surface. Transfer to a greased bowl and cover with plastic wrap. Secure with an elastic band and set aside to rise until double in bulk.

3. Punch the dough down and turn it out onto a floured surface. Knead vigorously until the dough is firm and resilient. Return to the greased bowl. Cover and let rise until double in bulk.

4. Punch the dough down and turn it out onto a floured surface. Shape into an 18-inch rope by rolling it under the palms of your hands. Cut the rope into twelve 1½-inch lengths. Shape each portion into a ball. Cover the balls with a clean kitchen towel and let rest for 30 minutes.

5. Pat the dough balls into flat circles. Using a rolling pin, roll them into ¼-inch-thick rounds. Cover with a clean kitchen towel and let rest for 30 minutes.

6. Meanwhile, place a baking stone on the center rack of the oven and preheat to 500°F. for 20 minutes. Heavily dust both sides of each pita with flour. Transfer 3 floured rounds to a baking sheet without sides. When the baking stone is hot, tip the sheet and allow the pita rounds to slide onto the stone. Bake for 3 to 5 minutes, or until puffed and lightly browned. It is not necessary to turn them. Use a perforated metal spatula to transfer the breads to a cooling rack and repeat the baking process with 3 more pita rounds.   ❖

Wheat Germ Pita

MAKES 12

Wheat germ contributes a coarse, hearty texture to pita bread. These rounds are particularly good stuffed with cucumber slices and onion rings tossed with unflavored yogurt.

1½ cups warm water
1 package dry yeast
1 teaspoon sugar
1 teaspoon salt
1 tablespoon olive oil
1 cup wheat germ
3 to 3½ cups bread flour, preferably
  bromated, scoop measured

1. Measure the water into a large mixing bowl. Sprinkle on the yeast and stir to dissolve. Stir in the sugar, salt, and olive oil.

2. Add the wheat germ and 1 cup of the flour. Beat with a wooden spoon until smooth. Gradually blend in additional flour until the dough becomes too difficult to stir. Turn out onto a floured surface and knead in as much of the remaining flour as necessary to form a cohesive dough. Continue kneading in flour until the dough is firm and resilient and no longer sticks to the work surface. Transfer to a greased bowl and cover with plastic wrap. Secure with an elastic band and set aside to rise until double in bulk.

3. Punch the dough down and turn it out onto a floured surface. Knead vigorously until the dough is firm and resilient. Return to the greased bowl. Cover and let rise until double in bulk.

4. Punch the dough down and turn it out onto a floured surface. Shape into an 18-inch rope by rolling it under the palms of your hands. Cut the rope into twelve 1½-inch lengths. Shape each portion into a ball. Cover the balls with a clean kitchen towel and let rest for 30 minutes.

5. Pat the dough balls into flat circles. Using a rolling pin, roll them into ¼-inch-thick rounds. Cover with a clean kitchen towel and let rest for 30 minutes.

6. Meanwhile, place a baking stone on the center rack of the oven and preheat to 500°F. for 20 minutes. Heavily dust both sides of each pita with flour. Transfer 3 floured rounds to a baking sheet without

sides. When the baking stone is hot, tip the sheet and allow the pita rounds to slide onto the stone. Bake for 3 to 5 minutes, or until puffed and lightly browned. It is not necessary to turn them. Use a perforated metal spatula to transfer the breads to a cooling rack and repeat the baking process with 3 more pita rounds.   ❖

Whole Wheat Pita

MAKES 12

In addition to their role as sandwich shells, pita breads also may be separated, cut into wedges, and toasted until crisp. The resulting triangles are wonderful served with dips and spreads.

1½ cups warm water
1 package dry yeast
1 teaspoon salt
2 cups whole wheat flour, scoop measured
1½ to 2 cups bread flour, preferably
    bromated, scoop measured

1. Measure the water into a large mixing bowl. Sprinkle on the yeast and stir to dissolve. Stir in the salt.

2. Add the whole wheat flour and beat with a wooden spoon until smooth. Gradually blend in the bread flour until the dough becomes too difficult to stir. Turn out onto a floured surface and knead in as much of the remaining bread flour as necessary to form a cohesive dough. Continue kneading in bread flour until the dough is firm and resilient and no longer sticks to the work surface. Transfer to a greased bowl and cover with plastic wrap. Secure with an elastic band and set aside to rise until double in bulk.

3. Punch the dough down and turn it out onto a floured surface. Knead vigorously until the dough is firm and resilient. Return to the greased bowl. Cover and let rise until double in bulk.

4. Punch the dough down and turn it out onto a floured surface. Shape into an 18-

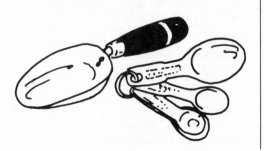

inch rope by rolling it under the palms of your hands. Cut the rope into twelve 1½-inch lengths. Shape each portion into a ball. Cover the balls with a clean kitchen towel and let rest for 30 minutes.

5. Pat the dough balls into flat circles. Using a rolling pin, roll them into ¼-inch-thick rounds. Cover with a clean kitchen towel and let rest for 30 minutes.

6. Meanwhile, place a baking stone on the center rack of the oven and preheat to 500°F. for 20 minutes. Heavily dust both sides of each pita with flour. Transfer 3 floured rounds to a baking sheet without sides. When the baking stone is hot, tip the sheet and allow the pita rounds to slide onto the stone. Bake for 3 to 5 minutes, or until puffed and lightly browned. It is not necessary to turn them. Use a perforated metal spatula to transfer the breads to a cooling rack and repeat the baking process with 3 more pita rounds.   ❖

Herbed Bread Rounds

MAKES 12

Chewy rounds of flat bread are brushed with olive oil and sprinkled with herbs. These are just the thing to take along on a picnic.

1½ cups warm water
1 package dry yeast
1½ teaspoons sugar
1 teaspoon salt
4 tablespoons olive oil
4½ to 5 cups bread flour, preferably
   bromated, scoop measured
2 teaspoons dried oregano
1 teaspoon dried basil
1 teaspoon dried rosemary, crushed with a
   mortar and pestle

1. Measure the water into a large mixing bowl. Sprinkle on the yeast and stir to dissolve. Stir in the sugar, salt, and 1 tablespoon of the olive oil.

2. Add 2 cups of the flour and beat with a wooden spoon until smooth. Gradually blend in additional flour until the dough becomes too difficult to stir. Turn out onto a floured surface and knead in as much of the remaining flour as necessary to form a cohesive dough. Continue kneading in flour until the dough is firm and resilient and no longer sticks to the work surface. Transfer to a greased bowl and cover with plastic wrap. Secure with an elastic band and set aside to rise until double in bulk.

3. Generously grease 2 baking sheets. Punch down the dough and turn it out onto a floured surface. Divide the dough into 12 equal portions. Roll each portion into a ball. Cover with a clean kitchen towel and let rest for 20 minutes. Using a rolling pin, roll a ball of dough into a 6-inch circle. Transfer to a prepared baking sheet. Repeat with the remaining balls of dough, placing two or three circles on each sheet. Brush the surface of the dough rounds with the remaining 3 tablespoons olive oil. In a small bowl, combine the oregano, basil, and rosemary. Toss with a fork to mix, then scatter over the flat breads. Set aside and let stand, uncovered, for 20 minutes. Preheat the oven to 400°F. Place 1 baking sheet in the oven and bake the bread rounds for 15 to 20 minutes, or until lightly browned around the edges. Serve immediately or transfer to a rack to cool. Bake the remaining sheet, allowing the first sheet to cool before transferring more uncooked rounds to the oven. Repeat the procedure with any remaining rounds.   ❖

Rye Flat Bread

MAKES 6

Crisp and substantial, this is a great bread to serve with homemade soup. The hearty rye flavor is accentuated by the caraway seeds.

2 cups warm water
1 package dry yeast
2 teaspoons sugar

1 teaspoon salt
2½ cups rye flour, scoop measured
1 tablespoon caraway seeds
2½ to 3 cups bread flour, scoop measured
1 large egg white, whisked with 1 tablespoon
cold water

1. Measure the water into a large mixing bowl. Sprinkle on the yeast and stir to dissolve. Stir in the sugar and salt.

2. Add the rye flour and caraway seeds, and beat with a wooden spoon until smooth. Gradually blend in the bread flour until the dough becomes too difficult to stir. Turn out onto a floured surface and knead in as much of the remaining bread flour as necessary to form a cohesive dough. Continue kneading in bread flour until the dough is firm and resilient and no longer sticks to the work surface. Transfer to a greased bowl and cover with plastic wrap. Secure with an elastic band and set aside to rise until double in bulk.

3. Preheat the oven to 375°F. Generously grease 2 baking sheets. Punch the dough down and turn it out onto a floured surface. Divide the dough into 6 equal portions. Roll each portion into a ball. Using a rolling pin, roll a ball of dough into an 8-inch circle. Transfer to a prepared baking sheet. Repeat with the remaining balls of dough. Cover with a clean kitchen towel and let rise for 45 minutes. Prick the surface of the flat breads with the tines of a fork. Brush with the egg white and water. Bake in the preheated oven for 30 to 35 minutes, or until crisp. Transfer to a cooling rack.   ❖

Puffy Onion Flat Bread

MAKES 6

Topped with a liberal sprinkling of green onion, these sensational flat breads are a perfect accompaniment to hearty stews and casseroles. Pass the breads whole, allowing each person to pull off an individual portion.

2 cups warm water
1 package dry yeast
2 tablespoons sugar
1 teaspoon salt
5 to 5½ cups bread flour, preferably
bromated, scoop measured
1 large egg yolk, whisked with 1 tablespoon
cold water
6 green onions, thinly sliced

1. Measure the water into a large mixing bowl. Sprinkle on the yeast and stir to dissolve. Stir in the sugar and salt.

2. Add 3 cups of the flour and beat with a wooden spoon until smooth. Gradually blend in additional flour until the dough becomes too difficult to stir. Turn out onto a floured surface and knead in as much of the remaining flour as necessary to form a cohesive dough. Continue kneading in flour until the dough is firm and resilient and no longer sticks to the work surface. Transfer to a greased bowl and cover with plastic wrap. Secure with an elastic band and set aside to rise until double in bulk.

3. Generously grease 3 baking sheets. Punch the dough down and turn it out onto a floured surface. Divide the dough into 6 equal portions. Cover with a clean kitchen towel and let rest for 20 minutes. Roll a portion of dough into a 7x11-inch rectangle. Transfer to a prepared baking sheet. Repeat with the remaining portions of dough, arranging them 2 to a baking sheet. Brush the surface of the rectangles with the egg yolk and scatter on the onion. Set aside and let stand, uncovered, for 30 minutes. Preheat the oven to 425°F. Bake the breads for 15 to 20 minutes, or until golden brown. Serve immediately or transfer to a rack to cool.   ❖

Cinnamon Flat Bread

MAKES 1 ROUND LOAF

Warm wedges of this raisin-dotted loaf are a welcome treat on a cool spring afternoon. Serve with tea or hot chocolate.

1¼ cups all-purpose flour, scoop measured
¾ cup whole wheat flour, scoop measured
4 tablespoons sugar
2 teaspoons baking powder
½ teaspoon baking soda
½ teaspoon salt
3 tablespoons butter or margarine, cut into
    small pieces, plus 2 tablespoons
½ cup raisins
1 cup unflavored yogurt
1 teaspoon cinnamon

1. Preheat the oven to 425°F. Lightly grease a baking sheet without sides. Combine the all-purpose flour, whole wheat flour, 2 tablespoons of the sugar, the baking powder, the baking soda, and the salt in a large mixing bowl. Whisk to blend thoroughly. Add 3 tablespoons of the butter and cut in with a knife until the mixture is crumbly. Add the raisins and toss to mix.

2. Make a well in the dry ingredients. Pour in the yogurt and toss with a fork until the dough holds together. Gather the dough into a ball and roll it around the inside of the bowl to pick up any stray particles. Transfer to a lightly floured surface and shape into a small, flat round. Transfer to the prepared baking sheet. Press the dough into a 10-inch circle. Smooth the top with a rolling pin. Place in the preheated oven and bake for 10 minutes. Meanwhile, heat the remaining 2 tablespoons butter and 2 tablespoons sugar along with the cinnamon in a small saucepan. Remove the bread from the oven and brush the butter mixture over the top. Return to the oven and bake for 8 to 10 minutes more, or until lightly browned around the edges. Cut into wedges to serve.   ❖

Quick Flat Bread

MAKES ONE 9x13-INCH LOAF

This savory bread can be put together in minutes. Flavored with Parmesan cheese and chives, it makes a tasty accompaniment to grilled chicken.

3 cups all-purpose flour, scoop measured
1 tablespoon sugar
3 teaspoons baking powder
½ teaspoon salt
¾ cup freshly grated Parmesan cheese
2 tablespoons chopped fresh chives
1½ cups milk
⅓ cup butter or margarine

1. Preheat the oven to 400°F. Generously grease a 9x13-inch baking dish. Combine the flour, sugar, baking powder, and salt in a large mixing bowl. Whisk to blend thoroughly. Stir in ½ cup of the Parmesan cheese and the chives.

2. In a small saucepan, combine the milk and butter. Place over medium heat and stir until the butter is melted. Make a well in the dry ingredients. Pour in the warm milk and beat with a wooden spoon until well moistened. Pour into the prepared baking dish. Sprinkle the surface with the remaining ¼ cup cheese and bake for 20 to 25 minutes, or until the top is nicely browned. Cut into squares and serve while still hot.   ❖

Poppy Seed Cracker Bread

MAKES 8

Rolling the dough directly on a greased baking sheet enables you to create exceptionally thin cracker bread. Present the irregularly shaped rounds whole or break them into large pieces.

¾ cup warm water
1 package dry yeast
1 teaspoon sugar
1 teaspoon salt
1 egg, beaten
3 to 3½ cups bread flour, scoop measured
Cold water
2 tablespoons poppy seeds

1. Measure the water into a large mixing bowl. Sprinkle on the yeast and stir to dissolve. Stir in the sugar and salt. Blend in the beaten egg.

2. Add 1 cup of the flour and beat with a wooden spoon until smooth. Gradually

blend in additional flour until the dough becomes too difficult to stir. Turn out onto a floured surface and knead in as much of the remaining flour as necessary to form a cohesive dough. Continue kneading in flour until the dough is firm and resilient and no longer sticks to the work surface. Transfer to a greased bowl and cover with plastic wrap. Secure with an elastic band and set aside to rise until double in bulk.

3. Preheat the oven to 425°F. Generously grease 3 baking sheets without sides. Punch the dough down and turn it out onto a floured surface. Divide the dough into 8 equal portions. Place 1 portion on a greased baking sheet. Using a rolling pin, roll the dough as thinly as possible, forming an irregular circle. Brush the surface with cold water, then scatter on some poppy seeds. Gently press the seeds into the dough with your fingertips. Bake in the preheated oven for 5 to 7 minutes.

4. Repeat the procedure with another portion of dough. When the first bread is lightly browned around the edges, remove it from the oven and transfer to a cooling rack. Bake the second portion of dough while you roll out a third portion on another baking sheet. Be sure to let the first baking sheet cool completely before rolling another portion of dough on it. Alternate baking sheets until all 8 portions of dough are cooked.   ❖

Sesame Cracker Bread

MAKES 30

Paper-thin rounds of sesame-flavored bread. Pile them in a napkin-lined basket and offer with chilled lobster salad.

1¾ cups all-purpose flour, scoop measured
½ cup yellow cornmeal
2 tablespoons sugar
½ teaspoon salt
½ teaspoon baking soda
⅓ cup butter or margarine, cut into small pieces
½ cup cold water
2 tablespoons white vinegar
¼ cup sesame seeds

1. Combine the flour, cornmeal, sugar, salt, and baking soda in a large mixing bowl. Whisk to blend thoroughly. Add the butter and cut in with a knife until the mixture is crumbly.

2. Combine the water and vinegar in a glass measuring cup. Make a well in the dry ingredients. Pour in the water and vinegar, and toss with a fork until the dough holds together. Gather the dough into a ball and roll it around the inside of the bowl to pick up any stray particles. Transfer to a lightly floured surface and knead 20 to 25 times, sifting on flour if necessary to prevent sticking. Cover with a clean kitchen towel and let rest for 30 minutes.

3. Preheat the oven to 375°F. Lightly grease 3 baking sheets. Divide the dough into 30 equal portions and roll each portion into a ball. Scatter some sesame seeds over the work surface. Place a ball of dough on top of the seeds and roll out into an irregular round. Roll the dough as thinly as possible. Scatter additional sesame seeds over the surface of the round and roll to press in. Transfer the round to a prepared baking sheet. Repeat with the remaining balls of dough. Place 1 baking sheet in the preheated oven and bake for 8 to 10 minutes, or until lightly browned around the edges. Transfer to a cooling rack. Bake the remaining sheets, one at a time.   ❖

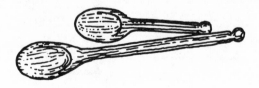

❖ Pizza, Calzone, and Bread Sticks ❖

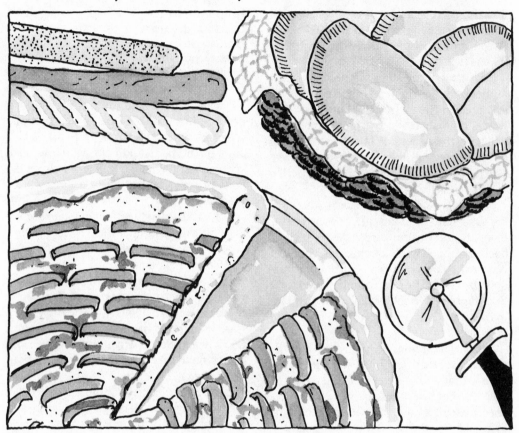

ONE MIGHT justifiably wonder how it is that austere, taciturn New Englanders adopted pizza as one of their own. Pizza, that brazen, lusty concoction, embraced by the Land of Steady Habits.

It is futile to try and find logical reasons for infatuation. Pizza was introduced to the East Coast by Italian immigrants in the early twentieth century, and the love affair began. Its popularity was bolstered by American soldiers, who returned from World War II with a desire to taste once again a dish they had grown fond of abroad. But nothing can explain the unabashed enthusiasm with which reticent Yankees accepted this cheese and tomato pie.

Opinions on what constitutes an excellent pizza are diverse. Most people agree

that the crust should be crisp, but beyond that there is little consensus. Thick crust, thin crust, and very thin crust all have ardent admirers. Favorite traditional toppings run the gamut from peppers to onions to anchovies. Whether pizza is best when cooked in a pan or directly on the floor of a brick oven is a matter of debate. All in all, the standards by which a pizza is judged are personal and subjective.

Due to the fact that it is impossible to heat a home oven to the high temperatures attained by commercial pizza ovens, it can be difficult to duplicate pizzeria-type pizza. I've found, however, that by using a baking stone you can create an exceptionally fine pizza at home. Many specialty cookware stores and gourmet shops offer these stones

245

for sale at a reasonable price. If you cannot obtain one locally, write to the Old Stone Oven Corporation, P.O. Box 141, Elmhurst, Illinois 60126.

Place the baking stone on the center rack of the oven. Set the temperature to 500°F. and preheat the stone for 20 minutes. The heat that is absorbed by the baking stone will cook the underside of a pizza in much the same way the floor of a brick oven does. The result is a crust that is uniformly crisp across its entire surface.

Pizza can be made with classic toppings such as tomato sauce and pepperoni or more up-to-the minute ingredients such as duck sausage, wild mushrooms, or goat cheese. In size, pizzas range from 2½-inch appetizers to a 6-inch round, served as a first course or luncheon. A 10-inch pizza makes an adequate entrée, and a 14-inch pizza feeds two.

Calzone is similar to pizza in that the same basic bread dough is used. The difference is that a calzone is folded like a turnover so that the topping ingredients are used instead as a filling. Calzone may be baked or deep-fried. Baking is a lighter, healthier alternative, however, so it is the recommended method.

Bread sticks are a delightful offshoot of the Italian-bread theme. They, too, have become popular in New England and are often seen on restaurant tables standing on end in a long, narrow glass. Bread sticks should be dry and crisp and break with a sharp snap. They are customarily eaten plain; it is considered poor form to spread them with butter.

Puffy Pizza Crust

MAKES ONE 14-INCH CRUST

Bromated bread flour is essential in creating this exceptionally airy crust because the proportion of water to flour is unusually high. For best results, bake on a preheated baking stone.

1 cup warm water
1 package dry yeast
½ teaspoon sugar
½ teaspoon salt
2 to 2½ cups bromated bread flour, scoop measured

1. Measure the water into a large mixing bowl. Sprinkle on the yeast and stir to dissolve. Blend in the sugar and salt. Add 2 cups of the flour and beat with a wooden spoon until the dough pulls away from the bowl in ropy strands. The mixture will be very wet.

2. Turn the dough out onto a floured surface and dust lightly with flour. Using a pastry scraper, lift and fold the dough over on itself. Press down to work the flour in. Repeat the process of folding and pressing with the pastry scraper until the dough holds together in a flabby mass. Dust lightly with flour and transfer to a greased bowl. Cover with plastic wrap. Secure with an elastic band and set aside to rise until double in bulk.

3. Turn the dough out onto a floured surface. Pat down into a flat circle, dusting any moist spots with flour. Press the circle as flat as you can, working out any air bubbles you see. Fold the dough in half, dust with flour, and press into a flat semicircle. Fold into quarters, dust with flour, and press flat. Tucking the corners underneath, form the dough into a ball. Dust with flour and return to the bowl. Cover with plastic wrap. Secure with an elastic band and set aside to rise until double in bulk.

4. Use this dough in preparing any of the pizza recipes in this chapter, especially Fresh Tomato Pizza (p. 250) and Zucchini and Bel Paese Pizza (p. 251).   ❖

Thin and Crispy Pizza Crust

MAKES ONE 14-INCH CRUST

The addition of oil to pizza dough helps produce a thin, densely textured crust.

For best results, add the toppings and bake as quickly as possible. Do not allow the shaped crust to stand at room temperature any longer than necessary.

¾ cup warm water
1 package dry yeast
¾ teaspoon salt
2 tablespoons olive oil
2 to 2½ cups all-purpose flour, scoop
   measured

1. Measure the water into a large mixing bowl. Sprinkle on the yeast and stir to dissolve. Blend in the salt and oil. Add 2 cups of the flour and beat with a wooden spoon until a smooth, stiff dough is formed.

2. Turn out onto a floured surface and knead, working in as much additional flour as necessary to form a resilient, nonsticky dough. Transfer to a greased bowl and cover with plastic wrap. Secure with an elastic band and set aside to rise until double in bulk.

3. Use this dough in preparing any of the pizza recipes in this chapter.   ❖

Deep-Pan Pizza Crust

MAKES ONE 14-INCH CRUST

The best utensil for cooking this type of crust is a black steel pan with a removable bottom. The black metal conducts heat exceptionally well, producing a crispy, thick crust with a light texture. The removable bottom facilitates slicing and serving.

1 cup warm water
1 package dry yeast
½ teaspoon sugar
¾ teaspoon salt
¼ cup whole wheat flour, scoop measured
2 to 2½ cups bread flour, preferably
   bromated, scoop measured

1. Measure the water into a large mixing bowl. Sprinkle on the yeast and stir to dissolve. Blend in the sugar and salt. Add the whole wheat flour and 2 cups of the bread flour, and beat with a wooden spoon until a smooth, stiff dough is formed.

2. Turn out onto a floured surface and knead, working in as much additional bread flour as necessary to form a resilient, nonsticky dough. Transfer to a greased bowl and cover with plastic wrap. Secure with an elastic band and set aside to rise until double in bulk.

3. Use this dough in preparing any of the pizza recipes in this chapter.   ❖

Whole Wheat Pizza Crust

MAKES ONE 14-INCH CRUST

A combination of whole wheat and bromated bread flours produces a pizza crust with distinctive flavor and a slightly chewy consistency. You may use this crust with any of the following pizza recipes, but it is especially good topped with red onions and Gorgonzola cheese (pp. 252-253).

¾ cup warm water
1 package dry yeast
½ teaspoon sugar
½ teaspoon salt
1 cup whole wheat flour, scoop measured
1 to 1½ cups bread flour, preferably
   bromated, scoop measured

1. Measure the water into a large mixing bowl. Sprinkle on the yeast and stir to dissolve. Blend in the sugar and salt. Add the whole wheat flour and 1 cup of the bread flour, and beat with a wooden spoon until a smooth, stiff dough is formed.

2. Turn out onto a floured surface and knead, working in as much additional bread flour as necessary to form a resilient, nonsticky dough. Transfer to a greased bowl and cover with plastic wrap. Secure with an elastic band and set aside to rise until double in bulk.

3. Use this dough in preparing any of the pizza recipes in this chapter.   ❖

Processor Pizza Crust

MAKES ONE 14-INCH CRUST

It is easy and quick to produce pizza dough in the food processor because the kneading step is eliminated.

⅔ cup warm water
1 package dry yeast
2 cups bread flour, scoop measured
½ teaspoon sugar
½ teaspoon salt
1 tablespoon olive oil

1. Measure the water into a large mixing bowl. Sprinkle on the yeast and stir to dissolve. Set aside.

2. Combine the flour, sugar, and salt in the bowl of a food processor. Pulse briefly to blend. Add the olive oil to the dissolved yeast. With the processor running, slowly pour the liquid mixture into the dry ingredients. Process until a ball of dough forms on top of the blades. Add more flour if necessary to create a resilient, nonsticky dough. Turn the dough out onto a floured surface and dust with flour. Transfer to a greased bowl and cover with plastic wrap. Secure with an elastic band and set aside to rise until double in bulk.

3. Use this dough in preparing any of the pizza recipes in this chapter.   ❖

No-Yeast Pizza Crust

MAKES ONE 14-INCH CRUST

A crumbly, biscuitlike crust. This dough may be used with any of the following recipes. It must, however, be baked in a pan rather than on a baking stone.

2 cups all-purpose flour, scoop measured
2 teaspoons baking powder
½ teaspoon sugar
½ teaspoon salt
¼ cup solid vegetable shortening
¾ cup cold water

1. Preheat the oven to 425°F. Generously grease a 14-inch pizza pan. Combine the flour, baking powder, sugar, and salt in a large mixing bowl. Whisk to blend thoroughly. Add the shortening and cut in with a knife until the mixture is crumbly.

2. Make a well in the dry ingredients. Pour in the water and toss with a fork until the dough holds together. Gather the dough into a ball and roll it around the inside of the bowl to pick up any stray particles. Transfer to a floured surface and knead 20 to 25 times. Pat into a flat circle and transfer to the prepared pan. Pat the dough to fit the pan and form a rim around the outside edge. Brush with olive oil and top with pizza ingredients. Bake in the preheated oven for 20 to 25 minutes, or until the rim of the crust is nicely browned.   ❖

Honey Whole Wheat Pizza Crust

MAKES ONE 14-INCH CRUST

A soft crust made solely from whole wheat flour. The final texture is somewhat dense, yet the crust is light. Its honey-flavored character is especially good when paired with vegetable toppings.

¾ cup warm water
1 package dry yeast
2 tablespoons honey
½ teaspoon salt
2 to 2½ cups whole wheat flour, scoop measured

1. Measure the water into a large mixing bowl. Sprinkle on the yeast and stir to dissolve. Blend in the honey and salt. Add 2 cups of the flour and beat with a wooden spoon until a smooth, stiff dough is formed.

2. Turn out onto a floured surface and knead, working in as much additional flour as necessary to form a soft, moist dough. Dust with flour and transfer to a greased bowl. Cover with plastic wrap. Secure with an elastic band and set aside to rise until double in bulk.

3. Use this dough in preparing any of the pizza recipes in this chapter.   ❖

Pizza Sauce

MAKES ENOUGH FOR ONE 14-INCH PIZZA

This is a slightly chunky tomato sauce to use atop any pizza crust. This recipe may be doubled or tripled and then frozen for later use.

1 can (35 ounces) Italian plum tomatoes, undrained
1 teaspoon dried basil
½ teaspoon dried oregano
½ teaspoon dried rosemary, crushed with a mortar and pestle
½ teaspoon sugar
1 bay leaf, broken in half
1 clove garlic, peeled and cut in half
Salt and freshly ground black pepper

1. In a wide saucepan, combine the tomatoes, basil, oregano, and rosemary. Stir in the sugar. Add the bay leaf and garlic. Place over medium heat and cook, uncovered, until the mixture bubbles vigorously. Reduce the heat and simmer uncovered for 2 hours, or until the excess moisture has evaporated and the sauce has thickened. Stir occasionally to break up the tomatoes.

2. Test for doneness by spooning a dollop of sauce onto a plate. The sauce has thickened sufficiently when only a negligible amount of liquid seeps out around the edge of the dollop. Remove the bay leaf and garlic, and season with salt and pepper. Use immediately or refrigerate for later use.   ❖

Sausage Pizza

MAKES ONE 14-INCH PIZZA

This is the classic tomato-sauce pizza associated with corner pizza shops throughout New England. Using the basic recipe, you may substitute topping ingredients in any combination. Cooked hamburger or sliced pepperoni stands in for the sausage; add sliced mushrooms, roasted peppers, anchovies, onions, or whatever strikes your fancy.

One 14-inch pizza crust (pp. 246-248)
2 links hot Italian sausage, casings removed
Pizza Sauce (see recipe above)
1 green bell pepper, cut into thin strips
½ cup freshly grated Parmesan cheese
6 ounces mozzarella cheese, shredded

1. Prepare pizza dough from one of the preceding recipes. Generously grease a 14-inch pizza pan or place a baking stone on the center rack of the oven and preheat to 500°F. for 20 minutes. Crumble the sausage into a small nonstick skillet and cook until it is no longer pink. Drain off the fat and set the sausage aside.

2. If using a baking stone, place a sheet of 18-inch extra-heavy aluminum foil on a large pastry board. Grease the foil generously with solid vegetable shortening. Turn the dough out onto a lightly floured surface and flatten into a large circle by pressing down with your hands. Fold in half and transfer to the greased foil or pizza pan. Unfold the dough and shape into a 14-inch circle, forming a rim around the outside edge.

4. Spoon the pizza sauce over the dough. Scatter on the cooked sausage, then arrange the green pepper on top. Place the pan in the oven or carefully slide the pizza and underlying foil from the pastry board to the preheated baking stone. Bake at 500°F. for 5 minutes. Then reduce the heat to 425°F. If using a baking stone, lift the pizza with a long spatula and pull the foil out from underneath. Continue baking the pizza for 10 to 15 minutes, or until the crust is lightly browned. During the last 5 minutes of cooking time, sprinkle on the Parmesan cheese and then scatter on the mozzarella. Bake until the mozzarella is melted. Transfer to a cutting board and slice into wedges. (After removing the pizza, allow the baking stone to cool completely inside the oven.) ❖

Fresh Tomato Pizza

MAKES ONE 14-INCH PIZZA

*Slices of fresh tomato take the place of to-
mato sauce in this contemporary pizza. To
appreciate the character of this pizza fully, use a high-quality olive oil, preferably
a pale green first pressing.*

1 Puffy Pizza Crust (p. 246)
Olive oil
4 medium tomatoes, peeled and sliced
Salt and freshly ground black pepper
6 slices smoked ham, cut into ½-inch squares
1 green bell pepper, cut into thin strips
2 ounces herbed Boursin cheese
2 ounces feta cheese, crumbled
1 tablespoon chopped fresh thyme

1. Prepare the pizza dough.
2. Place a baking stone on the center rack
of the oven and preheat to 500°F. for 20
minutes. Meanwhile, place a sheet of 18-
inch extra-heavy aluminum foil on a large
pastry board. Grease the foil generously
with solid vegetable shortening. Turn the
dough out onto a lightly floured surface and
flatten into a large circle by pressing down
with your hands. Fold the dough in half and
transfer to the greased foil. Unfold the
dough and shape into a 14-inch circle,
forming a rim around the outside edge.
3. Generously spread the oil over the surface of the dough with your fingertips. Arrange the tomato slices over the dough in
concentric circles, but do not overlap them.
Sprinkle with salt and pepper. Scatter the
ham over the tomatoes and lay on the strips
of green pepper in an attractive pattern.
4. Drop small dollops of the Boursin
cheese over the pepper strips and sprinkle
on the feta cheese. Scatter the thyme over
the top. Carefully slide the pizza and underlying foil from the pastry board to the preheated baking stone. Bake at 500°F. for 5
minutes. Then lift the pizza with a long
spatula and pull the foil out from underneath. Reduce the heat to 425°F. and continue baking the pizza directly on the stone
for 10 to 15 minutes, or until the crust is
lightly browned. Transfer to a cutting board
and slice into wedges. (After removing the
pizza, allow the baking stone to cool completely inside the oven.)   ❖

White Clam Pizza

MAKES ONE 14-INCH PIZZA

*This popular New England pizza is
thought to have originated, at least in this
country, in New Haven, Connecticut. If
you partially bake the oil-brushed crust
before adding the clams, you will produce
a crispy pizza without toughening the
clams by overcooking them.*

One 14-inch pizza crust (pp. 246-248)
24 littleneck clams
¼ cup olive oil
2 cloves garlic, pressed
1 teaspoon dried oregano
Salt and freshly ground black pepper

1. Prepare pizza dough from one of the
preceding recipes. Generously grease a 14-
inch pizza pan or place a baking stone on
the center rack of the oven and preheat to
500°F. for 20 minutes. Open the clams, reserving the broth for another use. Chop the
clams and refrigerate.
2. Heat the oil in a small saucepan. Remove from the heat and add the garlic by
forcing it through a press. It should sizzle
slightly as it hits the oil, but it shouldn't
turn brown. Stir in the oregano and set
aside.
3. If using a baking stone, place a sheet of
18-inch extra-heavy aluminum foil on a
large pastry board. Grease the foil generously with solid vegetable shortening. Turn
the dough out onto a lightly floured surface
and flatten into a large circle by pressing
down with your hands. Fold in half and
transfer to the greased foil or pizza pan.
Unfold the dough and shape into a 14-inch
circle, forming a rim around the outside
edge.
4. Brush the oil and garlic over the surface of the dough. Sprinkle with salt and

pepper. Place the pan in the oven or carefully slide the pizza and underlying foil from the pastry board to the preheated baking stone. Bake at 500°F. for 8 minutes. Then lift the pizza with a long spatula and pull the foil out from underneath. Scatter the chopped clams over the pizza. Reduce the heat to 425°F. and continue baking the pizza directly on the stone for 10 to 15 minutes, or until the crust is lightly browned. Transfer to a cutting board and slice into wedges. (After removing the pizza, allow the baking stone to cool completely inside the oven.)   ❖

Zucchini and Bel Paese Pizza

MAKES ONE 14-INCH PIZZA

Instead of a sauce, shredded Bel Paese cheese is distributed over the crust, where it melts to form a base for rounds of fresh sliced zucchini.

1 Puffy Pizza Crust (p. 246)
Olive oil
8 ounces Bel Paese cheese, shredded
4 slim zucchini squash, thinly sliced
Salt and freshly ground black pepper
2 tablespoons whole fresh oregano leaves
½ cup freshly grated Parmesan cheese

1. Prepare the pizza dough.
2. Place a baking stone on the center rack of the oven and preheat to 500°F. for 20 minutes. Meanwhile, place a sheet of 18-inch extra-heavy aluminum foil on a large pastry board. Grease the foil generously with solid vegetable shortening. Turn the dough out onto a lightly floured surface and flatten into a large circle by pressing down with your hands. Fold the dough in half and transfer to the greased foil. Unfold the dough and shape into a 14-inch circle, forming a rim around the outside edge.
3. Generously spread the olive oil over the surface of the dough with your fingertips. Scatter the Bel Paese cheese over the dough. Arrange the zucchini slices over the dough in concentric circles, overlapping the slices.

Sprinkle with salt and pepper. Scatter the oregano over the top. Carefully slide the pizza and underlying foil from the pastry board to the preheated baking stone. Bake at 500°F. for 5 minutes. Then lift the pizza with a long spatula and pull the foil out from underneath. Reduce the heat to 425°F. and continue baking the pizza directly on the stone for 10 to 15 minutes, or until the crust is lightly browned. During the last 5 minutes of baking, sprinkle on the Parmesan cheese. Transfer the pizza to a cutting board and slice into wedges. (After removing the pizza, allow the baking stone to cool completely inside the oven.)   ❖

Three-Pepper Pizza

MAKES ONE 14-INCH PIZZA

Thin strips of green, red, and yellow peppers intermingle to create a visually stunning pizza. Use with any of the preceding crust recipes.

One 14-inch pizza crust (pp. 246-248)
Olive oil
1 large green bell pepper, cut into thin strips
1 large red bell pepper, cut into thin strips
1 large yellow bell pepper, cut into thin strips
Salt and freshly ground black pepper
6 ounces Montrachet cheese, crumbled
1 tablespoon chopped fresh thyme

1. Prepare pizza dough from one of the preceding recipes. Generously grease a 14-inch pizza pan or place a baking stone on the center rack of the oven and preheat to 500°F. for 20 minutes.
2. If using a baking stone, place a sheet of 18-inch extra-heavy aluminum foil on a large pastry board. Grease the foil generously with solid vegetable shortening. Turn the dough out onto a lightly floured surface and flatten into a large circle by pressing down with your hands. Fold the dough in half and transfer to the greased foil or pizza pan. Unfold the dough and shape into a 14-inch circle, forming a rim around the outside edge.

3. Generously spread the oil over the surface of the dough with your fingertips. Arrange the strips of pepper over the dough in concentric circles, alternating the colors of strips to create an attractive design. Sprinkle with salt and pepper. Sprinkle on the Montrachet cheese, then scatter the thyme over the top. Place the pan in the oven or carefully slide the pizza and underlying foil from the pastry board to the preheated baking stone. Bake at 500°F. for 5 minutes. Then lift the pizza with a long spatula and pull the foil out from underneath. Reduce the heat to 425°F. and continue baking the pizza directly on the stone for 10 to 15 minutes, or until the crust is lightly browned. Transfer the pizza to a cutting board and slice into wedges. (After removing the pizza, allow the baking stone to cool completely inside the oven.)   ❖

Pesto Pizza

MAKES ONE 14-INCH PIZZA

The puréed blend of fresh basil and Parmesan cheese referred to as "pesto" is here spread over pizza dough and baked with sun-dried tomatoes.

One 14-inch pizza crust (pp. 246-248)
2 tablespoons butter or margarine'
2 tablespoons olive oil
1 clove garlic
¼ teaspoon salt
6 tablespoons freshly grated Parmesan cheese
18 large fresh basil leaves
5 tablespoons pine nuts
⅓ cup coarsely chopped sun-dried tomatoes

1. Prepare pizza dough from one of the preceding recipes. Generously grease a 14-inch pizza pan or place a baking stone on the center rack of the oven and preheat to 500°F. for 20 minutes. Combine the butter, oil, and garlic in a blender. Whirl until smooth. Add the salt, 3 tablespoons of the cheese, and the basil. Whirl to purée the basil leaves. Add 2 tablespoons of the pine

nuts and whirl briefly to achieve a spreadable but coarse texture.

2. If using a baking stone, place a sheet of 18-inch extra-heavy aluminum foil on a large pastry board. Grease the foil generously with solid vegetable shortening. Turn the dough out onto a lightly floured surface and flatten into a large circle by pressing down with your hands. Fold the dough in half and transfer to the greased foil or pizza pan. Unfold the dough and shape into a 14-inch circle, forming a rim around the outside edge.

3. Spread the pesto over the surface of the dough. Distribute the tomatoes over the pesto, then scatter on the remaining 3 tablespoons pine nuts. Place the pan in the oven or carefully slide the pizza and underlying foil from the pastry board to the preheated baking stone. Bake at 500°F. for 5 minutes. Then lift the pizza with a long spatula and pull the foil out from underneath. Reduce the heat to 425°F. and continue baking the pizza directly on the stone for 10 to 15 minutes, or until the crust is lightly browned. During the last 5 minutes of baking, sprinkle on the remaining 3 tablespoons cheese. Transfer the pizza to a cutting board and slice into wedges. (After removing the pizza, allow the baking stone to cool completely inside the oven.)   ❖

Red Onion and Gorgonzola Pizza

MAKES ONE 14-INCH PIZZA

This delicious and sophisticated pizza makes a memorable appetizer when sliced into thin wedges. Serve with a knife and fork or eat out of hand.

One 14-inch pizza crust (pp. 246-248)
Olive oil
Salt and freshly ground black pepper
4 ounces prosciutto, finely chopped
2 medium red onions, thinly sliced and
     separated into rings
1 cup crumbled Gorgonzola cheese

1. Prepare pizza dough from one of the preceding recipes. Generously grease a 14-inch pizza pan or place a baking stone on the center rack of the oven and preheat to 500°F. for 20 minutes.

2. If using a baking stone, place a sheet of 18-inch extra-heavy aluminum foil on a large pastry board. Grease the foil generously with solid vegetable shortening. Turn the dough out onto a lightly floured surface and flatten into a large circle by pressing down with your hands. Fold the dough in half and transfer to the greased foil. Unfold the dough and shape into a 14-inch circle, forming a rim around the outside edge.

3. Generously spread the oil over the surface of the dough with your fingertips. Sprinkle with salt and pepper. Scatter the prosciutto over the surface. Arrange the onion rings over the prosciutto in an overlapping manner. Sprinkle on the Gorgonzola. Place the pan in the oven or carefully slide the pizza and underlying foil from the pastry board to the preheated baking stone. Bake at 500°F. for 5 minutes. Then lift the pizza with a long spatula and pull the foil out from underneath. Reduce the heat to 425°F. and continue baking the pizza directly on the stone for 10 to 15 minutes, or until the crust is lightly browned. Transfer the pizza to a cutting board and slice into wedges. (After removing the pizza, allow the baking stone to cool completely inside the oven.) ❖

Spinach and Ricotta Pizza

MAKES ONE 14-INCH PIZZA

The combination of spinach and ricotta cheese is a familiar one. Here the treatment is slightly different, though. The ricotta cheese is spread over pizza dough, then topped with coarsely chopped raw spinach. A creamy saucelike texture is the result.

One 14-inch pizza crust (pp. 246-248)
1 pound fresh spinach, tough stems removed
Olive oil
1 pound ricotta cheese
Salt and freshly ground black pepper
½ cup freshly grated Parmesan cheese
3 green onions, sliced
½ cup freshly grated Gruyère cheese

1. Prepare pizza dough from one of the preceding recipes. Generously grease a 14-inch pizza pan or place a baking stone on the center rack of the oven and preheat to 500°F. for 20 minutes. Coarsely chop the spinach and set aside.

2. If using a baking stone, place a sheet of 18-inch extra-heavy aluminum foil on a large pastry board. Grease the foil generously with solid vegetable shortening. Turn the dough out onto a lightly floured surface and flatten into a large circle by pressing down with your hands. Fold the dough in half and transfer to the greased foil. Unfold the dough and shape into a 14-inch circle, forming a rim around the outside edge.

3. Generously spread the oil over the surface of the dough with your fingertips. Spoon the ricotta cheese onto the dough and spread it evenly over the surface. Sprinkle with salt and pepper. Scatter the Parmesan cheese over the ricotta. Distribute the spinach over the top. Scatter on the onions. Place the pan in the oven or carefully slide the pizza and underlying foil from the pastry board to the preheated baking stone. Bake at 500°F. for 5 minutes. Then lift the pizza with a long spatula and pull the foil out from underneath. Reduce the

heat to 425°F. and continue baking the pizza directly on the stone for 10 to 15 minutes, or until the crust is lightly browned.
During the last 5 minutes of cooking time,
sprinkle on the Gruyère cheese and bake
until melted. Transfer the pizza to a cutting
board and slice into wedges. (After removing the pizza, allow the baking stone to cool
completely inside the oven.)   ❖

Cheese Calzone

MAKES 4

*These individual dough pockets may be
baked or fried. If baked, they are served
plain; if fried, they are usually served
with a tomato sauce. Baked calzone tend
to be lighter. They may be eaten with a
knife and fork or out of hand.*

1 cup warm water
1 package dry yeast
1 teaspoon salt
1 tablespoon olive oil
2½ to 3 cups bread flour, preferably
   bromated, scoop measured
1 large egg
1 pound ricotta cheese
½ cup shredded mozzarella cheese
½ cup freshly grated Parmesan cheese
1 tablespoon freeze-dried chives
Salt and freshly ground black pepper to taste

   1. Measure the water into a large mixing
bowl. Sprinkle on the yeast and stir to dissolve. Blend in the salt and olive oil. Add 2
cups of the flour and beat with a wooden
spoon until a smooth, stiff dough is formed.
Turn out onto a floured surface and knead,
working in as much additional flour as necessary to form a smooth, resilient dough.
Transfer to a greased bowl and cover with
plastic wrap. Secure with an elastic band
and set aside to rise until double in bulk.
   2. Punch the dough down and turn out
onto a floured surface. Divide into 4 equal
portions. Shape each portion into a ball
and set aside. Cover loosely with plastic
wrap and let rest for 30 minutes.

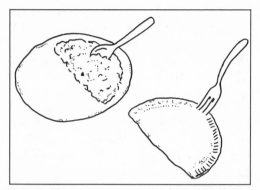

*To make calzone, spoon filling onto one half of
each rolled-out portion of dough. Spread evenly, leaving a 1-inch margin for sealing. Fold the
dough over the filling and moisten with water if
necessary to seal the edges. Press the dough
together with the tines of a fork.*

---

   3. Meanwhile, beat the egg in a large mixing bowl. Add the ricotta cheese and blend
well. Stir in the mozzarella cheese, Parmesan cheese, chives, and salt and pepper.
   4. Preheat the oven to 425°F. Generously
grease a baking sheet. Roll each ball of
dough into an 8-inch round. Spoon equal
amounts of the cheese mixture onto one
half of each portion of dough. Spread evenly,
leaving a 1-inch margin for sealing. Fold
the dough over the filling and moisten with
water if necessary to seal the edges. Press
the dough together with the tines of a fork.
(See illustration.) Transfer to the prepared
sheet and bake for 20 to 30 minutes, or
until nicely browned. Serve immediately.
   NOTE: To fry calzone, submerge the
sealed packets in vegetable oil that has
been heated to 375°F. Cook until browned,
then drain on absorbent paper. Serve with
Pizza Sauce (p. 249).   ❖

Sausage Calzone

MAKES 1

*This large baked calzone may be cut in
half and served as two dinner portions. It
also may be sliced into slender strips and*

offered as an appetizer to be eaten with the fingers.

1 cup warm water
1 package dry yeast
1 teaspoon salt
1 tablespoon olive oil
2½ to 3 cups bread flour, preferably
   bromated, scoop measured
4 links hot Italian sausage, casings removed
1 large egg
1 pound ricotta cheese
1 cup shredded fontina cheese
1 teaspoon dried basil
½ teaspoon dried oregano
Salt and freshly ground black pepper to taste

1. Measure the water into a large mixing bowl. Sprinkle on the yeast and stir to dissolve. Blend in the salt and olive oil. Add 2 cups of the flour and beat with a wooden spoon until a smooth, stiff dough is formed. Turn out onto a floured surface and knead, working in as much additional flour as necessary to form a smooth, resilient dough. Transfer to a greased bowl and cover with plastic wrap. Secure with an elastic band and set aside to rise until double in bulk.

2. Punch the dough down and turn out onto a floured surface. Roll into a 14-inch round. Cover loosely with plastic wrap and let rest for 30 minutes.

3. Meanwhile, crumble the sausage into a small nonstick skillet and cook until no longer pink. Drain off the fat and set the sausage aside. Beat the egg in a large mixing bowl. Add the ricotta cheese and blend well. Stir in the fontina cheese, basil, oregano, and salt and pepper. Blend in the cooked sausage.

4. Preheat the oven to 425°F. Generously grease a baking sheet. Spoon the sausage mixture over one half of the dough. Spread evenly, leaving a 1-inch margin for sealing. Fold the dough over the filling and moisten with water if necessary to seal the edges. Press the dough together with the tines of a fork. (See illustration.) Transfer to the prepared sheet and bake for 35 to 45 minutes, or until nicely browned. Serve immediately. ❖

Mushroom Prosciutto Calzone

MAKES 4

The Italian cuisine has long been popular in New England, and stuffed pizza dough, like this calzone, still lures customers into small ethnic restaurants.

1 cup warm water
1 package dry yeast
1 teaspoon salt
1 tablespoon olive oil
2½ to 3 cups bread flour, preferably
   bromated, scoop measured
2 tablespoons butter or margarine
8 ounces fresh mushrooms, coarsely chopped
1 teaspoon dried thyme
1 large egg
1 pound ricotta cheese
1 cup crumbled feta cheese
4 ounces prosciutto, coarsely chopped
Salt and freshly ground black pepper to taste

1. Measure the water into a large mixing bowl. Sprinkle on the yeast and stir to dissolve. Blend in the salt and olive oil. Add 2 cups of the flour and beat with a wooden spoon until a smooth, stiff dough is formed. Turn out onto a floured surface and knead, working in as much additional flour as necessary to form a smooth, resilient dough. Transfer to a greased bowl and cover with plastic wrap. Secure with an elastic band and set aside to rise until double in bulk.

2. Punch the dough down and turn out onto a floured surface. Divide into 4 equal portions. Shape each portion into a ball and set aside. Cover loosely with plastic wrap and let rest for 30 minutes.

3. Meanwhile, melt the butter in a skillet and add the mushrooms, tossing to coat. Cook until the mushrooms are tender and all the moisture in the pan has evaporated. Stir in the thyme and remove from the heat. Beat the egg in a large mixing bowl. Add the ricotta cheese and blend well. Stir in the feta cheese, prosciutto, and salt and pepper. Blend in the cooked mushrooms.

4. Preheat the oven to 425°F. Generously grease a baking sheet. Roll each ball of dough into an 8-inch round. Spoon equal amounts of the cheese mixture onto one half of each portion of dough. Spread evenly, leaving a 1-inch margin for sealing. Fold the dough over the filling and moisten with water if necessary to seal the edges. Press the dough together with the tines of a fork. (See illustration on page 254.) Transfer to the prepared sheet and bake for 20 to 30 minutes, or until nicely browned. Serve immediately.   ❖

Salami Calzone

MAKES 4

The aroma of salami always brings back memories of the first time I walked into an Italian deli. That wonderful, overwhelming smell — and all those sausages and pungent cheeses. For me, part of the fun of cooking Italian food is shopping for the ingredients.

1 cup warm water
1 package dry yeast
1 teaspoon salt
1 tablespoon olive oil
2½ to 3 cups bread flour, preferably
    bromated, scoop measured
1 large egg
1 pound ricotta cheese
1 cup shredded provolone cheese
4 ounces Italian salami, coarsely chopped
1 teaspoon dried oregano
½ teaspoon dried basil
2 green onions, thinly sliced
Salt and freshly ground black pepper to taste

1. Measure the water into a large mixing bowl. Sprinkle on the yeast and stir to dissolve. Blend in the salt and olive oil. Add 2 cups of the flour and beat with a wooden spoon until a smooth, stiff dough is formed. Turn out onto a floured surface and knead, working in as much additional flour as necessary to form a smooth, resilient dough. Transfer to a greased bowl and cover with

plastic wrap. Secure with an elastic band and set aside to rise until double in bulk.

2. Punch the dough down and turn out onto a floured surface. Divide into 4 equal portions. Shape each portion into a ball and set aside. Cover loosely with plastic wrap and let rest for 30 minutes.

3. Meanwhile, beat the egg in a large mixing bowl. Add the ricotta cheese and blend well. Stir in the provolone cheese and salami. Blend in the oregano, basil, onions, and salt and pepper.

4. Preheat the oven to 425°F. Generously grease a baking sheet. Roll each ball of dough into an 8-inch round. Spoon equal amounts of the cheese mixture onto one half of each portion of dough. Spread evenly, leaving a 1-inch margin for sealing. Fold the dough over the filling and moisten with water if necessary to seal the edges. Press the dough together with the tines of a fork. (See illustration on page 254.) Transfer to the prepared sheet and bake for 20 to 30 minutes, or until nicely browned. Serve immediately.   ❖

Spinach and Ricotta Calzone

MAKES 4

Eat these individual turnovers warm or at room temperature. They make especially good picnic fare.

1 cup warm water
1 package dry yeast
1 teaspoon salt
1 tablespoon olive oil
2½ to 3 cups bread flour, preferably
    bromated, scoop measured
1 large egg
1 pound ricotta cheese
1 pound spinach, stemmed, cooked, and
    chopped
½ cup shredded mozzarella cheese
½ cup freshly grated Parmesan cheese
Generous amount of freshly grated nutmeg
Salt and freshly ground black pepper to taste

1. Measure the water into a large mixing bowl. Sprinkle on the yeast and stir to dis-

solve. Blend in the salt and olive oil. Add 2 cups of the flour and beat with a wooden spoon until a smooth, stiff dough is formed. Turn out onto a floured surface and knead, working in as much additional flour as necessary to form a smooth, resilient dough. Transfer to a greased bowl and cover with plastic wrap. Secure with an elastic band and set aside to rise until double in bulk.

2. Punch the dough down and turn out onto a floured surface. Divide into 4 equal portions. Shape each portion into a ball and set aside. Cover loosely with plastic wrap and let rest for 30 minutes.

3. Meanwhile, beat the egg in a large mixing bowl. Add the ricotta cheese and blend well. Stir in the spinach. Blend in the mozzarella cheese, Parmesan cheese, nutmeg, and salt and pepper.

4. Preheat the oven to 425°F. Generously grease a baking sheet. Roll each ball of dough into an 8-inch round. Spoon equal amounts of the cheese mixture onto one half of each portion of dough. Spread evenly, leaving a 1-inch margin for sealing. Fold the dough over the filling and moisten with water if necessary to seal the edges. Press the dough together with the tines of a fork. (See illustration page on 254.) Transfer to the prepared sheet and bake for 20 to 30 minutes, or until nicely browned. Serve immediately or cool on a rack. ❖

Vegetable Calzone

MAKES 4

The colorful, abundant filling of this calzone oozes out when you cut into it, so plan to eat it with a knife and fork.

1 cup warm water
1 package dry yeast
1 teaspoon salt
1 tablespoon olive oil
2½ to 3 cups bread flour, preferably bromated, scoop measured
1 tablespoon vegetable oil
1 tablespoon butter or margarine
1 small onion, sliced

1 clove garlic, minced or pressed
8 medium mushrooms, sliced
1 medium green bell pepper, cut into thin strips
1 medium red bell pepper, cut into thin strips
1 tablespoon flour
Salt and freshly ground black pepper to taste
1 cup heavy cream
½ cup shredded mozzarella cheese
½ cup freshly grated Parmesan cheese
1 large egg, beaten

1. Measure the water into a large mixing bowl. Sprinkle on the yeast and stir to dissolve. Blend in the salt and olive oil. Add 2 cups of the flour and beat with a wooden spoon until a smooth, stiff dough is formed. Turn out onto a floured surface and knead, working in as much additional flour as necessary to form a smooth, resilient dough. Transfer to a greased bowl and cover with plastic wrap. Secure with an elastic band and set aside to rise until double in bulk.

2. Punch the dough down and turn out onto a floured surface. Divide into 4 equal portions. Shape each portion into a ball and set aside. Cover loosely with plastic wrap and let rest for 30 minutes.

3. Meanwhile, heat the vegetable oil and butter in a skillet until the butter is melted. Add the onion and garlic, tossing to coat. Scatter on the mushrooms, green pepper, and red pepper. Cover the pan and reduce the heat. Cook slowly until the vegetables are tender. Sprinkle on the flour and salt and pepper. Increase the heat and cook, stirring, until the moisture in the pan evaporates. Pour on the cream and add the mozzarella cheese. Stir over medium heat until very thick. Transfer to a bowl and allow to cool. Blend in the Parmesan cheese and beaten egg.

4. Preheat the oven to 425°F. Generously grease a baking sheet. Roll each ball of dough into an 8-inch round. Spoon equal amounts of the vegetable mixture onto one half of each portion of dough. Spread evenly, leaving a 1-inch margin for sealing. Fold the dough over

the filling and moisten with water if necessary to seal the edges. Press the dough together with the tines of a fork. (See illustration on page 254.) Transfer to the prepared sheet and bake for 20 to 30 minutes, or until nicely browned. Serve immediately. ❖

Cheddar Cheese Bread Sticks

MAKES 36

Sharp Cheddar cheese is baked right into these bread sticks to give them a distinctively New England flavor.

⅔ cup milk
2 tablespoons butter or margarine
¾ teaspoon sugar
¾ teaspoon salt
1 package dry yeast, dissolved in ¼ cup warm
    water
¾ cup shredded sharp Cheddar cheese
2½ to 3 cups bread flour, scoop measured

1. In a wide saucepan, combine the milk, butter, sugar, and salt. Place over medium heat and stir until the butter is melted. Transfer to a mixing bowl to cool.

To make bread sticks, roll each strip of dough under the palms of your hands to form an 8-inch length. To make bread twists, roll each strip into an 8-inch twisted length by holding one end of the dough stationary and rolling with the palm of the other hand.

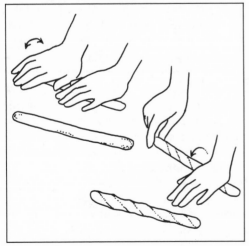

2. When the mixture is barely warm to the touch, stir in the dissolved yeast. Blend in the cheese. Add 2 cups of the flour and beat with a wooden spoon until a smooth, stiff dough is formed. Turn out onto a floured surface and knead, working in as much additional flour as necessary to form a smooth, resilient dough. Transfer to a greased bowl and cover with plastic wrap. Secure with an elastic band and set aside to rise until double in bulk.

3. Generously grease 2 baking sheets. Punch the dough down and turn out onto a floured surface. Roll to a 9x12-inch rectangle. Trim the edges to square off the rectangle. Lift the dough to loosen it from the work surface. Using a pastry wheel, cut the dough lengthwise into eighteen ½-inch strips. Cut the strips in half crosswise. Roll each strip under the palms of your hands to form an 8-inch length. (See illustration.) Transfer the strips to the prepared sheets, placing them well apart. Cover with a clean kitchen towel and let stand for 20 minutes. Bake in a preheated 375°F. oven for 20 to 25 minutes, or until lightly browned. Turn the oven off and leave the door ajar, allowing the bread sticks to cool inside the oven to become crisp. ❖

Garlic Parmesan Twists

MAKES 36

Redolent of garlic, these crispy bread sticks are a perfect accompaniment to soup or pasta.

⅔ cup warm water
1 package dry yeast
¾ teaspoon sugar
¾ teaspoon salt
2 tablespoons butter or margarine, melted
½ cup freshly grated Parmesan cheese
2½ to 3 cups bread flour, scoop measured
6 tablespoons olive oil
2 cloves garlic, pressed

1. Measure the water into a large mixing bowl. Sprinkle on the yeast and stir to dis-

solve. Blend in the sugar, salt, and melted butter. Add the cheese and 2 cups of the flour. Beat with a wooden spoon until a smooth, stiff dough is formed. Turn out onto a floured surface and knead, working in as much additional flour as necessary to form a smooth, resilient dough. Transfer to a greased bowl and cover with plastic wrap. Secure with an elastic band and set aside to rise until double in bulk.

2. Generously grease 2 baking sheets. Punch the dough down and turn out onto a floured surface. Roll to a 9x12-inch rectangle. Trim the edges to square off the rectangle. Lift the dough to loosen it from the work surface. Using a pastry wheel, cut the dough lengthwise into eighteen ½-inch strips. Cut the strips in half crosswise. Roll each strip into an 8-inch twisted length by holding one end of the dough stationary and rolling with the palm of the other hand. (See illustration on previous page.) Transfer to the prepared sheets, placing the strips well apart. Cover with a clean kitchen towel and let stand for 20 minutes. Meanwhile, combine the oil and garlic in a small saucepan. Heat gently until the garlic begins to make a hissing sound. Remove from the heat immediately and stir. Brush the garlic oil over the lengths of dough and bake in a preheated 375°F. oven for 20 to 25 minutes, or until lightly browned. Turn the oven off and leave the door ajar, allowing the bread sticks to cool inside the oven to become crisp.   ❖

Herbed Bread Sticks

MAKES 36

Sophisticated bread sticks to serve with roast lamb or to take on a picnic.

⅔ cup warm water
1 package dry yeast
¾ teaspoon sugar
¾ teaspoon salt
2 tablespoons olive oil
1 teaspoon dried oregano

½ teaspoon dried basil
½ teaspoon dried rosemary, crushed with a mortar and pestle
2½ to 3 cups bread flour, scoop measured

1. Measure the water into a large mixing bowl. Sprinkle on the yeast and stir to dissolve. Blend in the sugar, salt, and oil. Stir in the oregano, basil, and rosemary. Add 2 cups of the flour and beat with a wooden spoon until a smooth, stiff dough is formed. Turn out onto a floured surface and knead, working in as much additional flour as necessary to form a smooth, resilient dough. Transfer to a greased bowl and cover with plastic wrap. Secure with an elastic band and set aside to rise until double in bulk.

2. Generously grease 2 baking sheets. Punch the dough down and turn out onto a floured surface. Roll to a 9x12-inch rectangle. Trim the edges to square off the rectangle. Lift the dough to loosen it from the work surface. Using a pastry wheel, cut the dough lengthwise into eighteen ½-inch strips. Cut the strips in half crosswise. Roll each strip under the palms of your hands to form an 8-inch length. (See illustration on previous page.) Transfer the strips to the prepared sheets, placing them well apart. Cover with a clean kitchen towel and let stand for 20 minutes. Brush with cold water and bake in a preheated 400°F. oven for 15 to 20 minutes. Turn the oven off and leave the door ajar, allowing the bread sticks to cool and become crisp.   ❖

Italian Bread Sticks

MAKES 36

These are the familiar bread sticks seen in the small Italian restaurants that dot New England. Often they are displayed standing in a tall glass in the center of each table.

⅔ cup warm water
1 package dry yeast
¾ teaspoon sugar
¾ teaspoon salt

2 tablespoons olive oil
2½ to 3 cups bread flour, scoop measured

1. Measure the water into a large mixing bowl. Sprinkle on the yeast and stir to dissolve. Blend in the sugar, salt, and oil. Add 2 cups of the flour and beat with a wooden spoon until a smooth, stiff dough is formed. Turn out onto a floured surface and knead, working in as much additional flour as necessary to form a smooth, resilient dough. Transfer to a greased bowl and cover with plastic wrap. Secure with an elastic band and set aside to rise until double in bulk.

2. Generously grease 2 baking sheets. Punch the dough down and turn out onto a floured surface. Roll to a 9x12-inch rectangle. Trim the edges to square off the rectangle. Lift the dough to loosen it from the work surface. Using a pastry wheel, cut the dough lengthwise into eighteen ½-inch strips. Cut the strips in half crosswise. Roll each strip under the palms of your hands to form an 8-inch length. (See illustration on page 258.) Transfer the strips to the prepared sheets, placing them well apart. Cover with a clean kitchen towel and let stand for 20 minutes. Brush with cold water and bake in a preheated 400°F. oven for 15 to 20 minutes, or until lightly browned. Turn the oven off and leave the door ajar, allowing the bread sticks to cool inside the oven to become crisp. ❖

Onion Bread Sticks

MAKES 36

Flavored with caramelized onion bits, these beautiful bread sticks may be served in place of rolls for a special occasion or a holiday dinner.

6 tablespoons butter or margarine
1 medium onion, finely chopped
1 teaspoon sugar
½ cup milk
¾ teaspoon salt
1 package dry yeast, dissolved in ¼ cup warm water
2½ to 3 cups bread flour, scoop measured

1. Melt the butter in a small saucepan. Measure out 3 tablespoons and set aside. Add the onion and sugar to the butter remaining in the saucepan. Cook over low heat until the onion is limp and golden brown. Pour in the milk. Add the salt and heat until the surface wrinkles. Transfer to a large mixing bowl to cool.

2. When the mixture is barely warm to the touch, stir in the dissolved yeast. Add 2 cups of the flour and beat with a wooden spoon until a smooth, stiff dough is formed. Turn out onto a floured surface and knead, working in as much additional flour as necessary to form a smooth, resilient dough. Transfer to a greased bowl and cover with plastic wrap. Secure with an elastic band and set aside to rise until double in bulk.

3. Generously grease 2 baking sheets. Punch the dough down and turn out onto a floured surface. Roll to a 9x12-inch rectangle. Trim the edges to square off the rectangle. Lift the dough to loosen it from the work surface. Using a pastry wheel, cut the dough lengthwise into eighteen ½-inch strips. Cut the strips in half crosswise. Roll each strip under the palms of your hands to form an 8-inch length. (See illustration on page 258.) Transfer the strips to the prepared sheets, placing them well apart. Cover with a clean kitchen towel and let stand for 20 minutes. Brush with the reserved melted butter and bake in a preheated 375°F. oven for 20 to 25 minutes, or until lightly browned. Turn the oven off and leave the door ajar, allowing the bread sticks to cool inside the oven to become crisp. ❖

Poppy Seed Bread Sticks

MAKES 36

Bread sticks studded with poppy seeds are surprisingly compatible with brunch. Try them with scrambled eggs and honey-baked ham.

⅔ cup milk
2 tablespoons butter or margarine
1 teaspoon sugar
¾ teaspoon salt
1 package dry yeast, dissolved in ¼ cup warm water
2½ to 3 cups bread flour, scoop measured
4 tablespoons poppy seeds

1. In a wide saucepan, combine the milk, butter, sugar, and salt. Place over medium heat and stir until the butter is melted. Transfer to a large mixing bowl to cool.

2. When the mixture is barely warm to the touch, stir in the dissolved yeast. Add 2 cups of the flour and beat with a wooden spoon until a smooth, stiff dough is formed. Turn out onto a floured surface and knead, working in as much additional flour as necessary to form a smooth, resilient dough. Transfer to a greased bowl and cover with plastic wrap. Secure with an elastic band and set aside to rise until double in bulk.

3. Generously grease 2 baking sheets. Punch the dough down and turn out onto a floured surface. Roll to a 9x12-inch rectangle. Trim the edges to square off the rectangle. Lift the dough to loosen it from the work surface. Using a pastry wheel, cut the dough lengthwise into eighteen ½-inch strips. Cut the strips in half crosswise. Sprinkle poppy seeds over the work surface. Then roll each strip over the poppy seeds. Create a twisted 8-inch length by holding one end of the dough stationary and rolling with the palm of the other hand. (See illustration on page 258.) Sprinkle the work surface with additional poppy seeds as needed to coat the remaining strips of dough. Transfer the strips to the prepared sheets, placing them well apart. Cover with a clean kitchen towel and let stand for 20 minutes. Bake in a preheated 400°F. oven for 15 to 20 minutes, or until lightly browned. Turn the oven off and leave the door ajar, allowing the bread sticks to cool inside the oven to become crisp. ❖

Prosciutto Bread Sticks

MAKES 36

Bread sticks are customarily served at room temperature, but these prosciutto-flecked fingers are delicious warm. Heat them wrapped in aluminum foil; they will be chewy and densely textured.

⅔ cup warm water
1 package dry yeast
¾ teaspoon sugar
½ teaspoon salt
2 tablespoons olive oil
¼ pound prosciutto, finely chopped
2½ to 3 cups bread flour, scoop measured
4 tablespoons sesame seeds

1. Measure the water into a large mixing bowl. Sprinkle on the yeast and stir to dissolve. Blend in the sugar, salt, and oil. Stir in the prosciutto. Add 2 cups of the flour and beat with a wooden spoon until a smooth, stiff dough is formed. Turn out onto a floured surface and knead, working in as much additional flour as necessary to form a smooth, resilient dough. Transfer to a greased bowl and cover with plastic wrap. Secure with an elastic band and set aside to rise until double in bulk.

2. Generously grease 2 baking sheets. Punch the dough down and turn out onto a floured surface. Roll to a 9x12-inch rectangle. Trim the edges to square off the rectangle. Lift the dough to loosen it from the work surface. Using a pastry wheel, cut the dough lengthwise into eighteen ½-inch strips. Cut the strips in half crosswise. Sprinkle sesame seeds over the work surface, then roll each strip over the seeds. Continue rolling with the palms of your

hands to form an 8-inch length. (See illustration on page 258.) Transfer the strips to the prepared sheets, placing them well apart. Cover with a clean kitchen towel and let stand for 20 minutes. Bake in a preheated 400°F. oven for 15 to 20 minutes, or until lightly browned. Turn the oven off and leave the door ajar, allowing the bread sticks to cool inside the oven to become crisp.   ❖

Caraway Rye Bread Sticks

MAKES 36

For a delicious appetizer, roll thin slices of ham around these bread sticks and serve at room temperature.

½ cup milk
2 tablespoons molasses
2 tablespoons butter or margarine
¾ teaspoon salt
1 package dry yeast, dissolved in ¼ cup warm
    water
1 tablespoon caraway seeds
1 cup rye flour, scoop measured
1½ to 2 cups bread flour, scoop measured

1. In a wide saucepan, combine the milk, molasses, butter, and salt. Place over medium heat and stir until the butter is melted. Transfer to a large mixing bowl to cool.

2. When the mixture is barely warm to the touch, stir in the dissolved yeast. Blend in the caraway seeds. Add the rye flour and 1 cup of the bread flour, and beat with a wooden spoon until a smooth, stiff dough is formed. Turn out onto a floured surface and knead, working in as much additional bread flour as needed to form a smooth, resilient dough. Transfer to a greased bowl and cover with plastic wrap. Secure with an elastic band and set aside to rise until double in bulk.

2. Generously grease 2 baking sheets. Punch the dough down and turn out onto a floured surface. Roll to a 9x12-inch rectangle. Trim the edges to square off the rectangle. Lift the dough to loosen it from the work

surface. Using a pastry wheel, cut the dough lengthwise into eighteen ½-inch strips. Cut the strips in half crosswise. Roll each strip under the palms of your hands to form an 8-inch length. (See illustration on page 258.) Transfer the strips to the prepared sheets, placing them well apart. Cover with a clean kitchen towel and let stand for 20 minutes. Brush with cold water and bake in a preheated 375°F. oven for 20 to 25 minutes. Turn the oven off and leave the door ajar, allowing the bread sticks to cool inside the oven to become crisp.   ❖

Sesame Twists

MAKES 36

Sesame seeds contribute their mild, nutty flavor to these crunchy bread sticks. Serve with fruit salad for a festive lunch.

½ cup milk
5 tablespoons butter or margarine
¾ teaspoon sugar
¾ teaspoon salt
1 package dry yeast, dissolved in ¼ cup warm
    water
1 large egg, beaten
2½ to 3 cups bread flour, scoop measured
4 tablespoons sesame seeds

1. In a wide saucepan, combine the milk, butter, sugar, and salt. Place over medium heat and stir until the butter is melted. Transfer to a large mixing bowl to cool.

2. When the mixture is barely warm to the touch, stir in the dissolved yeast. Blend in the beaten egg. Add 2 cups of the flour and beat with a wooden spoon until a smooth, stiff dough is formed. Turn out onto a floured surface and knead, working in as much additional flour as necessary to form a smooth, resilient dough. Transfer to a greased bowl and cover with plastic wrap. Secure with an elastic band and set aside to rise until double in bulk.

3. Generously grease 2 baking sheets. Punch the dough down and turn out onto a

floured surface. Roll to a 9x12-inch rectangle. Trim the edges to square off the rectangle. Lift the dough to loosen it from the work surface. Using a pastry wheel, cut the dough lengthwise into eighteen ½-inch strips. Cut the strips in half crosswise. Sprinkle sesame seeds over the work surface, then roll each strip over the seeds. Create a twisted length by holding one end of the dough stationary and rolling with the palm of the other hand. (See illustration on page 258.) Sprinkle the work surface with additional sesame seeds as needed to coat the remaining strips of dough. Transfer the strips to the prepared sheets, placing them well apart. Cover with a clean kitchen towel and let stand for 20 minutes. Bake in a preheated 375°F. oven for 20 to 25 minutes. Turn the oven off and leave the door ajar, allowing the bread sticks to cool and become crisp.　　　　　　❖

Whole Wheat Bread Sticks

MAKES 36

Hearty bread sticks, encrusted with kernels of wheat germ. These are marvelous for snacks or with a late-night supper of cold cuts and deli salads.

½ cup milk
2 tablespoons solid vegetable shortening
¾ teaspoon sugar
¾ teaspoon salt
1 package dry yeast, dissolved in ¼ cup warm water
1 cup whole wheat flour, scoop measured

1½ to 2 cups bread flour, scoop measured
4 tablespoons wheat germ

1. In a wide saucepan, combine the milk, shortening, sugar, and salt. Place over medium heat and stir until the shortening is melted. Transfer to a large mixing bowl.

2. When the mixture is barely warm to the touch, stir in the dissolved yeast. Add the whole wheat flour and 1 cup of the bread flour, and beat with a wooden spoon until a smooth, stiff dough is formed. Turn out onto a floured surface and knead, working in as much additional bread flour as needed to form a smooth, resilient dough. Transfer to a greased bowl and cover with plastic wrap. Secure with an elastic band and set aside to rise until double in bulk.

3. Generously grease 2 baking sheets. Punch the dough down and turn out onto a floured surface. Roll to a 9x12-inch rectangle. Trim the edges to square off the rectangle. Lift the dough to loosen it from the work surface. Using a pastry wheel, cut the dough lengthwise into eighteen ½-inch strips. Cut the strips in half crosswise. Sprinkle wheat germ over the work surface, then roll each strip over the wheat germ. Continue rolling with the palms of your hands to form an 8-inch length. (See illustration on page 258.) Transfer the strips to the prepared sheets, placing them well apart. Cover with a clean kitchen towel and let stand for 20 minutes. Bake in a preheated 375°F. oven for 20 to 25 minutes. Turn the oven off and leave the door ajar, allowing the bread sticks to cool inside the oven to become crisp.　　　　　　❖

❖ Steamed, Spoon, and Batter Breads ❖

PROBABLY the first bread that comes to mind when you think of New England is Boston brown bread — and with good reason. This cornmeal and molasses steamed bread dates back to the days of the Pilgrims, who were taught how to cook with cornmeal by the Indians. Boston brown bread could well be considered the most truly authentic Yankee bread.

Other kinds of steamed breads were an offshoot of steamed pudding, a classic component of England's cuisine. Colonial women favored steamed breads because they could cook them easily in a kettle of steaming water hung in the fireplace.

Spoon breads are essentially a casserole based on cornmeal and eggs. Like steamed breads, they could be baked on the hearth, so they too were among the earliest forms of New England bread. Spoon bread, however, has a spoonable, soufflélike texture, and in that respect it differs from more familiar types of bread.

Batter breads are yeast breads made from a dough with a pourable consistency. They require no kneading, so the ingredients can simply be stirred together, then set aside to rise. Batter breads are quick and easy to prepare, and for this reason they are especially popular with contemporary Yankee cooks, whose busy schedules leave little time for bread baking.

Steamed breads are exceptionally moist and therefore store better than most other types of breads. They may be wrapped in aluminum foil and packed inside an airtight metal tin. Batter breads tend to go stale faster than other breads, so it is best not to plan to keep them for long periods of time. Spoon breads must be served as soon as they are baked.

Steamed breads and batter breads freeze well when placed in a plastic bag, secured with a wire twist. Let them defrost at room temperature inside the sealed bag. Warm them if you wish by wrapping them in aluminum foil and placing them in a preheated 375°F. oven for 5 to 8 minutes. Steamed breads warm remarkably well in the microwave oven. Wrap them in absorbent paper and heat on medium power for 30 seconds, depending on the quantity. Microwaving batter breads is not recommended.

Cinnamon Apple Steamed Bread

MAKES 2 LOAVES

Dried apple slices are sold in health-food stores and the specialty-foods section of supermarkets. Here they are coarsely chopped and added to steamed bread to create a warm, flavorful loaf.

2 cups whole wheat flour, scoop measured
1½ cups all-purpose flour, scoop measured
3 teaspoons baking powder
1 teaspoon salt
1 teaspoon cinnamon
1½ cups milk
1 large egg
1 cup boiling water
½ cup honey
1 cup coarsely chopped dried apple slices

1. Generously grease two 1-pound coffee cans and set aside. Place a rack in the bottom of a large kettle. Pour in enough water to come to a depth of 1 inch. Cover the kettle and bring the water to a vigorous boil.

2. Meanwhile, in the bowl of an electric mixer, combine the whole wheat flour, all-purpose flour, baking powder, salt, and cin-namon. Run the mixer briefly on low speed to blend the dry ingredients.

3. In a separate bowl, whisk together the milk and egg. Add the water and honey, and blend well. With the mixer set at low speed, gradually pour the honey mixture into the dry ingredients. Beat until thoroughly moistened. Stir in the apple.

4. Pour the batter into the prepared cans. They will be two-thirds to three-quarters full. Cover each can with a square of aluminum foil and crimp tightly around the edge. When the water is boiling, set the cans on the rack and cover the kettle. Begin to time for doneness when the water has returned to the boil. Steam the bread for 2½ to 3 hours, or until a wooden pick inserted in the center comes out clean. Occasionally you will need to pour in additional water to maintain the depth at 1 inch. When the bread is done, transfer the cans to a cooling rack. Let stand for 20 minutes, then turn out. Serve immediately or complete cooling on the rack.   ❖

Boston Brown Bread I

MAKES 2 LOAVES

The traditional partner of Boston baked beans, this dark, rich bread is served hot with plenty of butter.

1 cup whole wheat flour, scoop measured
1 cup rye flour, scoop measured
1 cup yellow cornmeal
½ cup all-purpose flour, scoop measured
2 teaspoons baking soda
1 teaspoon salt
2¾ cups buttermilk
⅔ cup molasses
¾ cup raisins

1. Generously grease two 1-pound coffee cans and set aside. Place a rack in the bottom of a large kettle. Pour in enough water to come to a depth of 1 inch. Cover the kettle and bring the water to a vigorous boil.

2. Meanwhile, in the bowl of an electric mixer, combine the whole wheat flour, rye

flour, cornmeal, and all-purpose flour. Add the baking soda and salt, then run the mixer briefly on low speed to blend the dry ingredients thoroughly.

3. In a separate bowl, whisk together the buttermilk and molasses. With the mixer set at low speed, gradually pour the molasses mixture into the dry ingredients. Beat until well moistened. Stir in the raisins.

4. Pour the batter into the prepared cans. They will be two-thirds to three-quarters full. Cover each can with a square of aluminum foil and crimp tightly around the edge. When the water is boiling, set the cans on the rack and cover the kettle. Begin to time for doneness when the water has returned to the boil. Steam the bread for 2½ to 3 hours, or until a wooden pick inserted in the center comes out clean. Occasionally you will need to pour in additional water to maintain the depth at 1 inch. When the bread is done, transfer the cans to a cooling rack. Let stand for 20 minutes, then turn out. Serve immediately or complete cooling on the rack.   ❖

Boston Brown Bread II

MAKES 2 LOAVES

For some inexplicable reason, the customary way to slice hot brown bread is with a length of string. Position the string under the loaf. Bring the ends up, crossing them as if you were tying a shoe. Pull the ends in opposite directions and cut the loaf into ¾-inch-thick slices.

2 cups all-purpose flour, scoop measured
1½ cups yellow cornmeal
2 teaspoons baking soda
1 teaspoon salt
1⅓ cups milk
1⅓ cups buttermilk
¾ cup molasses
1 cup raisins

1. Generously grease two 1-pound coffee cans and set aside. Place a rack in the bottom of a large kettle. Pour in enough water to come to a depth of 1 inch. Cover the kettle and bring the water to a vigorous boil.

2. Meanwhile, in the bowl of an electric mixer, combine the flour, cornmeal, baking soda, and salt. Run the mixer briefly on low speed to blend the dry ingredients.

3. In a separate bowl, whisk together the milk, the buttermilk, and the molasses. With the mixer set at low speed, gradually pour the molasses mixture into the dry ingredients. Beat until thoroughly moistened. Stir in the raisins.

4. Pour the batter into the prepared cans. They will be two-thirds to three-quarters full. Cover each can with a square of aluminum foil and crimp tightly around the edge. When the water is boiling, set the cans on the rack and cover the kettle. Begin to time for doneness when the water has returned to the boil. Steam the bread for 2½ to 3 hours, or until a wooden pick inserted in the center comes out clean. Occasionally you will need to pour in additional water to maintain the depth at 1 inch. When the bread is done, transfer the cans to a cooling rack. Let stand for 20 minutes, then turn out. Serve immediately or complete cooling on the rack.   ❖

Carrot Apricot Steamed Bread

MAKES 2 LOAVES

The combination of carrots and dried apricots is particularly enjoyable in this moist, rich loaf. Serve hot, spread with softened cream cheese.

2 cups whole wheat flour, scoop measured
1½ cups all-purpose flour, scoop measured
2 teaspoons baking powder
1 teaspoon baking soda
1 teaspoon salt

2½ cups milk
1 large egg
½ cup honey
1 cup shredded raw carrot
½ cup coarsely chopped dried apricots

1. Generously grease two 1-pound coffee cans and set aside. Place a rack in the bottom of a large kettle. Pour in enough water to come to a depth of 1 inch. Cover the kettle and bring the water to a vigorous boil.

2. Meanwhile, in the bowl of an electric mixer, combine the whole wheat flour, all-purpose flour, baking powder, baking soda, and salt. Run the mixer briefly on low speed to blend the dry ingredients.

3. In a separate bowl, whisk together the milk and egg. Add the honey and blend well. With the mixer set at low speed, gradually pour the honey mixture into the dry ingredients. Beat until thoroughly moistened. Stir in the carrot and apricots.

4. Pour the batter into the prepared cans. They will be two-thirds to three-quarters full. Cover each can with a square of aluminum foil and crimp tightly around the edge. When the water is boiling, set the cans on the rack and cover the kettle. Begin to time for doneness when the water has returned to the boil. Steam the bread for 2½ to 3 hours, or until a wooden pick inserted in the center comes out clean. Occasionally you will need to pour in additional water to maintain the depth at 1 inch. When the bread is done, transfer the cans to a cooling rack. Let stand for 20 minutes, then turn out. Serve immediately or complete cooling on the rack. ❖

Fruited Brown Bread

MAKES 2 LOAVES

Bits of dried figs and dates are macerated in dark rum to lend an air of sophistication to this version of classic brown bread.

⅓ cup dark rum
½ cup coarsely chopped dates
½ cup coarsely chopped dried figs
1 cup whole wheat flour, scoop measured
1 cup all-purpose flour, scoop measured
¾ cup rye flour, scoop measured
¾ cup yellow cornmeal
2 teaspoons baking soda
1 teaspoon salt
2¼ cups buttermilk
2 large eggs
2 tablespoons butter or margarine, melted

1. Combine the rum, dates, and figs in a small bowl. Set aside for 30 minutes, stirring the fruit occasionally to encourage even maceration.

2. Generously grease two 1-pound coffee cans and set aside. Place a rack in the bottom of a large kettle. Pour in enough water to come to a depth of 1 inch. Cover the kettle and bring the water to a vigorous boil.

3. Meanwhile, in the bowl of an electric mixer, combine the whole wheat flour, all-purpose flour, rye flour, and cornmeal. Add the baking soda and salt, then run the mixer briefly on low speed to blend the dry ingredients thoroughly.

4. In a separate bowl, whisk together the buttermilk, eggs, and melted butter. With the mixer set at low speed, gradually pour the egg mixture into the dry ingredients. Beat until thoroughly moistened. Stir in the rum-soaked dates and figs.

5. Pour the batter into the prepared cans. They will be two-thirds to three-quarters full. Cover each can with a square of aluminum foil and crimp tightly around the edge. When the water is boiling, set the cans on the rack and cover the kettle. Begin to time for doneness when the water has returned to the boil. Steam the bread for 2½ to 3 hours, or until a wooden pick inserted in the center comes out clean. Occasionally you will need to pour in additional water to maintain the depth at 1 inch. When the bread is done, transfer the cans to a cooling rack. Let stand for 20 minutes, then turn out. Serve immediately or complete cooling on the rack. ❖

Maple Raisin Brown Bread

MAKES 2 LOAVES

The essence of New England is recalled in this hearty, maple-flavored bread. Try this variation with baked beans.

1½ cups whole wheat flour, scoop measured
1 cup all-purpose flour, scoop measured
1 cup yellow cornmeal
3 teaspoons baking powder
1 teaspoon salt
1⅓ cups milk
1⅓ cups cold water
1 large egg
½ cup pure maple syrup
1 cup raisins

1. Generously grease two 1-pound coffee cans and set aside. Place a rack in the bottom of a large kettle. Pour in enough water to come to a depth of 1 inch. Cover the kettle and bring the water to a vigorous boil.

2. Meanwhile, in the bowl of an electric mixer, combine the whole wheat flour, all-purpose flour, and cornmeal. Add the baking powder and salt, then run the mixer briefly on low speed to blend the dry ingredients thoroughly.

3. In a separate bowl, whisk together the milk, water, and egg. Stir in the maple syrup. With the mixer set at low speed, gradually pour the maple syrup mixture into the dry ingredients. Beat until thoroughly moistened. Stir in the raisins.

4. Pour the batter into the prepared cans. They will be two-thirds to three-quarters

full. Cover each can with a square of aluminum foil and crimp tightly around the edge. When the water is boiling, set the cans on the rack and cover the kettle. Begin to time for doneness when the water has returned to the boil. Steam the bread for 2½ to 3 hours, or until a wooden pick inserted in the center comes out clean. Occasionally you will need to pour in additional water to maintain the depth at 1 inch. When the bread is done, transfer the cans to a cooling rack. Let stand for 20 minutes, then turn out. Serve immediately or complete cooling on the rack.　　　　❖

Molasses Rye Steamed Bread

MAKES 2 LOAVES

The earthy nature of rye and molasses is evident in this full-flavored loaf. Butter while still hot and serve with stew.

2 cups rye flour, scoop measured
1 cup yellow cornmeal
½ cup all-purpose flour, scoop measured
2 teaspoons baking soda
1 teaspoon salt
2 cups buttermilk
2 large eggs
¾ cup molasses
¾ cup raisins

1. Generously grease two 1-pound coffee cans and set aside. Place a rack in the bottom of a large kettle. Pour in enough water to come to a depth of 1 inch. Cover the kettle and bring the water to a vigorous boil.

2. Meanwhile, in the bowl of an electric mixer, combine the rye flour, cornmeal, and all-purpose flour. Add the baking soda and salt, then run the mixer briefly on low speed to blend the dry ingredients.

3. In a separate bowl, whisk together the buttermilk and eggs. Stir in the molasses. With the mixer set at low speed, gradually pour the molasses mixture into the dry ingredients. Beat until thoroughly moistened. Stir in the raisins.

4. Pour the batter into the prepared cans. They will be two-thirds to three-quarters full. Cover each can with a square of aluminum foil and crimp tightly around the edge. When the water is boiling, set the cans on the rack and cover the kettle. Begin to time for doneness when the water has returned to the boil. Steam the bread for 2½ to 3 hours, or until a wooden pick inserted in the center comes out clean. Occasionally you will need to pour in additional water to maintain the depth at 1 inch. When the bread is done, transfer the cans to a cooling rack. Let stand for 20 minutes, then turn out. Serve immediately or complete cooling on the rack. ❖

Steamed Pumpkin Ginger Bread

MAKES 2 LOAVES

Sliced into hot, moist rounds, this gingery loaf makes a unique addition to the holiday bread tray.

2 cups all-purpose flour, scoop measured
½ cup light brown sugar
1½ cups whole wheat flour, scoop measured
2 teaspoons baking powder
½ teaspoon baking soda
1 teaspoon salt
1 teaspoon ground ginger
2 cups milk
2 large eggs
2 tablespoons butter or margarine, melted
1 cup pumpkin purée
1 tablespoon finely grated orange zest

1. Generously grease two 1-pound coffee cans and set aside. Place a rack in the bottom of a large kettle. Pour in enough water to come to a depth of 1 inch. Cover the kettle and bring the water to a vigorous boil.

2. Meanwhile, sift the all-purpose flour and sugar into the bowl of an electric mixer. Add the whole wheat flour, baking powder, baking soda, salt, and ginger. Run the mixer briefly on low speed to blend the dry ingredients thoroughly.

3. In a separate bowl, whisk together the milk, the eggs, and the melted butter. Stir in the pumpkin purée and orange zest. With the mixer set at low speed, gradually pour the egg mixture into the dry ingredients. Beat until thoroughly moistened.

4. Pour the batter into the prepared cans. They will be two-thirds to three-quarters full. Cover each can with a square of aluminum foil and crimp tightly around the edge. When the water is boiling, set the cans on the rack and cover the kettle. Begin to time for doneness when the water has returned to the boil. Steam the bread for 2½ to 3 hours, or until a wooden pick inserted in the center comes out clean. Occasionally you will need to pour in additional water to maintain the depth at 1 inch. When the bread is done, transfer the cans to a cooling rack. Let stand for 20 minutes, then turn out. Serve immediately or complete cooling on the rack. ❖

Spicy Steamed Bread

MAKES 2 LOAVES

Flavored with cinnamon and ginger, this steamed bread tastes remarkably like Indian pudding. Serve with clotted cream or whipped cream cheese.

2 cups whole wheat flour, scoop measured
1 cup yellow cornmeal
½ cup all-purpose flour, scoop measured
2 teaspoons baking soda
1 teaspoon salt
1 teaspoon cinnamon
½ teaspoon ground ginger
2½ cups buttermilk
¾ cup molasses

1. Generously grease two 1-pound coffee cans and set aside. Place a rack in the bottom of a large kettle. Pour in enough water to come to a depth of 1 inch. Cover the kettle and bring the water to a vigorous boil.

2. Meanwhile, in the bowl of an electric mixer, combine the whole wheat flour, corn-

meal, and all-purpose flour. Add the baking soda, salt, cinnamon, and ginger. Run the mixer briefly on low speed to blend the dry ingredients.

3. In a separate bowl, whisk together the buttermilk and molasses. With the mixer set at low speed, gradually pour the molasses mixture into the dry ingredients. Beat until thoroughly moistened.

4. Pour the batter into the prepared cans. They will be two-thirds to three-quarters full. Cover each can with a square of aluminum foil and crimp tightly around the edge. When the water is boiling, set the cans on the rack and cover the kettle. Begin to time for doneness when the water has returned to the boil. Steam the bread for 2½ to 3 hours, or until a wooden pick inserted in the center comes out clean. Occasionally you will need to pour in additional water to maintain the depth at 1 inch. When the bread is done, transfer the cans to a cooling rack. Let stand for 20 minutes, then turn out. Serve immediately or complete cooling on the rack. ❖

Cheddar Cheese Spoon Bread

SERVES 4

Just as its name implies, spoon bread is customarily served by generous spoonfuls, directly from the baking dish. You may add a pat of butter or ladle on some sauce, but spoon bread is every bit as good when unadorned.

1 cup yellow cornmeal
2½ cups milk
3 tablespoons butter or margarine, cut into small pieces
4 large eggs, separated
1½ teaspoons baking powder
1 teaspoon salt
1 cup shredded Cheddar cheese

1. Preheat the oven to 375°F. Generously butter a 2-quart soufflé dish or bowl-shaped casserole. Combine the cornmeal and ½ cup of the milk in a small bowl. Stir to moisten the cornmeal.

2. Pour the remaining 2 cups milk into a wide saucepan. Heat until the surface wrinkles, then gradually stir in the cornmeal–milk mixture. Cook over medium-low heat until the mixture is very thick. Stir frequently to prevent scorching.

3. Remove from the heat and stir in the butter until it is melted. Transfer to a large mixing bowl and set aside to cool for 3 minutes. Meanwhile, whisk the egg whites in a separate bowl until soft peaks form.

4. Add the baking powder and the salt to the cornmeal mixture, and blend well. Beat the egg yolks in one at a time, then stir in the cheese. Add the beaten egg whites and fold together. Pour into the prepared dish and bake for 35 to 45 minutes, or until the bread is puffed and richly browned. Serve immediately. ❖

Corn and Onion Spoon Bread

SERVES 4

When fresh corn is in season, try this wonderful version of spoon bread with barbecued chicken or pork spareribs.

1 cup yellow cornmeal
2½ cups milk
3 tablespoons butter or margarine
1 medium onion, finely chopped
4 large eggs, separated
1½ teaspoons baking powder
1 teaspoon salt
Freshly ground black pepper to taste
1 cup fresh corn kernels

1. Preheat the oven to 375°F. Generously butter a 2-quart soufflé dish or bowl-shaped casserole. Combine the cornmeal and ½ cup of the milk in a small bowl. Stir to moisten the cornmeal.

2. Melt the butter in a wide saucepan. Add the onion and toss to coat. Stir over medium heat until the onion is tender. Pour in the remaining 2 cups milk and heat until the surface wrinkles. Gradually stir in the cornmeal–milk mixture. Cook over medium-low heat until the mixture is very thick. Stir frequently to prevent scorching.

3. Remove from the heat and transfer to a large mixing bowl. Set aside to cool for 3 minutes. Meanwhile, whisk the egg whites in a separate bowl until soft peaks form.

4. Add the baking powder, salt, and pepper to the cornmeal mixture, and blend well. Beat the egg yolks in one at a time, then stir in the fresh corn. Add the beaten egg whites and fold together. Pour into the prepared dish and bake for 35 to 45 minutes, or until the bread is puffed and richly browned. Serve immediately.   ❖

Cranberry Orange Spoon Bread

SERVES 4

Dotted with bits of red cranberry, this slightly sweet spoon bread is delicious with roast chicken.

1 cup yellow cornmeal
2½ cups milk
½ cup orange marmalade
4 tablespoons butter or margarine, cut into
   small pieces
4 large eggs, separated
2 teaspoons baking powder
½ teaspoon salt
1 cup fresh cranberries, coarsely chopped

1. Preheat the oven to 375°F. Generously butter a 2-quart soufflé dish or bowl-shaped casserole. Combine the cornmeal and ½ cup of the milk in a small bowl. Stir to moisten the cornmeal.

2. Pour the remaining 2 cups milk into a wide saucepan. Heat until the surface wrinkles, then gradually stir in the cornmeal–milk mixture. Cook over medium-low

heat until the mixture is very thick. Stir frequently to prevent scorching.

3. Remove from the heat and stir in the marmalade and butter until the butter is melted. Transfer to a large mixing bowl and set aside to cool for 3 minutes. Meanwhile, whisk the egg whites in a separate bowl until soft peaks form.

4. Add the baking powder and the salt to the cornmeal mixture, and blend well. Beat the egg yolks in one at a time, then stir in the cranberries. Add the beaten egg whites and fold together. Pour into the prepared dish and bake for 35 to 45 minutes, or until the bread is puffed and richly browned. Serve immediately.   ❖

Herbed Spoon Bread

SERVES 4

The classic herbal trio of parsley, sage, and thyme lends a sophisticated air to this otherwise homespun dish. Offer in place of stuffing with roast game hens.

1 cup white cornmeal
1½ cups water
1 cup milk
3 tablespoons butter or margarine, cut into
   small pieces
4 large eggs, separated
1½ teaspoons baking powder
1 teaspoon salt
2 tablespoons chopped fresh parsley
1 teaspoon dried thyme
½ teaspoon dried sage

1. Preheat the oven to 375°F. Generously butter a 2-quart soufflé dish or bowl-shaped casserole. Combine the cornmeal and ½ cup of the water in a small bowl. Stir to moisten the cornmeal.

2. Pour the remaining cup of water and the milk into a wide saucepan. Heat until the mixture begins to boil. Gradually stir in the cornmeal–water mixture. Cook over medium-low heat until the cornmeal is very thick. Stir frequently to prevent scorching.

3. Remove from the heat and stir in the butter until it is melted. Transfer to a large mixing bowl and set aside to cool for 3 minutes. Meanwhile, whisk the egg whites in a separate bowl until soft peaks form.

4. Add the baking powder and the salt to the cornmeal mixture, and blend well. Beat the egg yolks in one at a time, then stir in the parsley, thyme, and sage. Add the beaten egg whites and fold together. Pour into the prepared dish and bake for 35 to 45 minutes, or until the bread is puffed and richly browned. Serve immediately.   ❖

Honey Date Spoon Bread

SERVES 4

Sweet with honey, a dollop of this spoon bread is a wonderful accompaniment to baked ham.

1 cup yellow cornmeal
2½ cups milk
½ cup honey
4 tablespoons butter or margarine, cut into small pieces
4 large eggs, separated
1½ teaspoons baking powder
½ teaspoon salt
½ cup coarsely chopped dates

1. Preheat the oven to 375°F. Generously butter a 2-quart soufflé dish or bowl-shaped casserole. Combine the cornmeal and ½ cup of the milk in a small bowl. Stir to moisten the cornmeal.

2. Pour the remaining 2 cups milk into a wide saucepan. Heat until the surface wrinkles, then gradually stir in the cornmeal–milk mixture. Cook over medium-low heat until the cornmeal is very thick. Stir frequently to prevent scorching.

3. Remove from the heat and stir in the honey and butter until the butter is melted. Transfer to a large mixing bowl and set aside to cool for 3 minutes. Meanwhile, whisk the egg whites in a separate bowl until soft peaks form.

4. Add the baking powder and the salt to the cornmeal mixture, and blend well. Beat the egg yolks in one at a time, then stir in the dates. Add the beaten egg whites and fold together. Pour into the prepared dish and bake for 35 to 45 minutes, or until the bread is puffed and richly browned. Serve immediately.   ❖

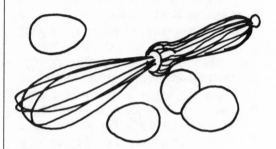

Individual Buttermilk Spoon Breads

SERVES 8

An individual spoon bread at each place setting creates a lovely effect. Pass iced curls or molded pats of butter.

1 cup yellow cornmeal
1½ cups water
1 cup buttermilk
3 tablespoons butter or margarine, cut into small pieces
4 large eggs, separated
½ teaspoon baking soda
1 teaspoon salt

1. Preheat the oven to 375°F. Generously butter 8 ramekins. Combine the cornmeal and ½ cup of the water in a small bowl. Stir to moisten the cornmeal.

2. Pour the remaining cup of water and the buttermilk into a wide saucepan. Heat until bubbles begin to appear around the edge of the pan. Gradually stir in the cornmeal–water mixture. Cook over medium-low heat until the mixture is very thick. Stir frequently to prevent scorching.

3. Remove from the heat and stir in the butter until it is melted. Transfer to a large

mixing bowl and set aside to cool for 3 minutes. Meanwhile, whisk the egg whites in a separate bowl until soft peaks form.

4. Add the baking soda and the salt to the cornmeal mixture, and blend well. Beat the egg yolks in one at a time, then fold in the beaten egg whites. Pour into the prepared ramekins and bake for 25 to 35 minutes, or until the breads are puffed and richly browned. Serve immediately.   ❖

Lemony Spoon Bread

SERVES 4

Spoon out a generous portion of this lemony bread to serve alongside grilled fish.

1 cup yellow cornmeal
2½ cups milk
3 tablespoons butter or margarine, cut into small pieces
2 tablespoons freshly squeezed lemon juice
½ cup freshly grated Parmesan cheese
4 large eggs, separated
1½ teaspoons baking powder
¾ teaspoon salt
1 teaspoon finely grated lemon zest

1. Preheat the oven to 375°F. Generously butter a 2-quart soufflé dish or bowl-shaped casserole. Combine the cornmeal and ½ cup of the milk in a small bowl. Stir to moisten the cornmeal.

2. Pour the remaining 2 cups milk into a wide saucepan. Heat until the surface wrinkles, then gradually stir in the cornmeal–milk mixture. Cook over medium-low heat until the mixture is very thick. Stir frequently to prevent scorching.

3. Remove from the heat and stir in the butter until it is melted. Blend in the lemon juice and cheese. Transfer to a large mixing bowl and set aside to cool for 3 minutes. Meanwhile, whisk the egg whites in a separate bowl until soft peaks form.

4. Add the baking powder and the salt to the cornmeal mixture, and blend well. Beat

the egg yolks in one at a time, then stir in the lemon zest. Add the beaten egg whites and fold together. Pour into the prepared dish and bake for 35 to 45 minutes, or until the bread is puffed and richly browned. Serve immediately.   ❖

Molasses Raisin Spoon Bread

SERVES 4

Here is a hearty, full-flavored spoon bread to serve for cold-weather meals. Its molasses essence pairs well with roast game or turkey.

1 cup yellow cornmeal
1½ cups water
1 cup buttermilk
½ cup molasses
4 tablespoons butter or margarine, cut into small pieces
4 large eggs, separated
½ teaspoon baking soda
1 teaspoon salt
½ cup raisins

1. Preheat the oven to 375°F. Generously butter a 2-quart soufflé dish or bowl-shaped casserole. Combine the cornmeal and ½ cup of the water in a small bowl. Stir to moisten the cornmeal.

2. Pour the remaining cup of water and the buttermilk into a wide saucepan. Heat until bubbles begin to appear around the edge of the pan. Gradually stir in the cornmeal–water mixture. Cook over medium-low heat until the mixture is very thick. Stir frequently to prevent scorching.

3. Remove from the heat and stir in the molasses and butter until the butter is melted. Transfer to a large mixing bowl and set aside to cool for 3 minutes. Meanwhile, whisk the egg whites in a separate bowl until soft peaks form.

4. Add the baking soda and the salt to the cornmeal mixture, and blend well. Beat the

egg yolks in one at a time, then stir in the raisins. Add the beaten egg whites and fold together. Pour into the prepared dish and bake for 35 to 45 minutes, or until the bread is puffed and richly browned. Serve immediately.   ❖

Spiced Pear Spoon Bread

SERVES 4

A warm, wonderful side dish for a special family meal.

1 cup yellow cornmeal
2½ cups milk
¼ cup sugar
4 tablespoons butter or margarine, cut into
    small pieces
4 large eggs, separated
1½ teaspoons baking powder
½ teaspoon salt
½ teaspoon cinnamon
¼ teaspoon allspice
2 medium pears, peeled, cored, and coarsely
    chopped

1. Preheat the oven to 375°F. Generously butter a 2-quart soufflé dish or bowl-shaped casserole. Combine the cornmeal and ½ cup of the milk in a small bowl. Stir to moisten the cornmeal.

2. Pour the remaining 2 cups milk into a wide saucepan. Heat until the surface wrinkles, then gradually stir in the corn-meal–milk mixture. Cook over medium-low heat until the mixture is very thick. Stir frequently to prevent scorching.

3. Remove from the heat and stir in the sugar and butter until the butter is melted. Transfer to a large mixing bowl and set aside to cool for 3 minutes. Meanwhile, whisk the egg whites in a separate bowl until soft peaks form.

4. Add the baking powder and salt to the cornmeal mixture, and blend well. Stir in the cinnamon and allspice. Beat the egg yolks in one at a time, then stir in the pears. Add the beaten egg whites and fold together.

Pour into the prepared dish and bake for 35 to 45 minutes, or until the bread is puffed and richly browned. Serve immediately.   ❖

Zucchini Spoon Bread

SERVES 4

Shredded zucchini and cornmeal are most compatible flavors in this pleasing spoon bread. Serve by generous spoonfuls with grilled hamburgers and cold sliced tomatoes.

1 cup yellow cornmeal
2½ cups milk
3 tablespoons butter or margarine
1 medium onion, finely chopped
4 large eggs, separated
1½ teaspoons baking powder
1 teaspoon salt
Freshly ground black pepper to taste
1 teaspoon dried basil
1 cup shredded, unpeeled zucchini

1. Preheat the oven to 375°F. Generously butter a 2-quart soufflé dish or bowl-shaped casserole. Combine the cornmeal and ½ cup of the milk in a small bowl. Stir to moisten the cornmeal.

2. Melt the butter in a wide saucepan. Add the onion and toss to coat. Stir over medium heat until the onion is tender. Pour in the remaining 2 cups milk and heat until the surface wrinkles. Gradually stir in the cornmeal–milk mixture. Cook over medium-low heat until the mixture is very thick. Stir frequently to prevent scorching.

3. Remove from the heat and transfer to a large mixing bowl. Set aside to cool for 3 minutes. Meanwhile, whisk the egg whites in a separate bowl until soft peaks form.

4. Add the baking powder, salt, pepper, and basil to the cornmeal mixture, and blend well. Beat the egg yolks in one at a time, then stir in the zucchini. Add the beaten egg whites and fold together. Pour into the prepared dish and bake for 35 to 45 minutes, or until the bread is puffed and richly browned. Serve immediately.   ❖

Cheddar Whole Wheat Batter Bread

MAKES 1 ROUND LOAF

The assertive flavor of Vermont Cheddar cheese contributes to the full-bodied character of this tasty loaf.

1 cup milk
2 tablespoons butter or margarine
1 tablespoon sugar
¾ teaspoon salt
1 package dry yeast, dissolved in ¼ cup warm water
1 large egg, beaten
1 cup shredded Cheddar cheese
1½ cups whole wheat flour, scoop measured
1½ cups all-purpose flour, scoop measured

1. In a wide saucepan, combine the milk, butter, sugar, and salt. Place over medium heat and stir until the butter is melted. Transfer to the large bowl of an electric mixer to cool.

2. When the mixture is barely warm to the touch, stir in the dissolved yeast. Blend in the beaten egg. Stir in the cheese. Add the whole wheat flour and beat on medium speed until well blended. Reduce the speed to low and gradually sprinkle in the all-purpose flour. Beat until a moist, smooth dough is formed. Scrape down the sides of the bowl and cover with plastic wrap. Secure with an elastic band and set aside to rise until double in bulk.

3. Generously grease a 2-quart soufflé dish or bowl-shaped casserole. Stir the batter down with a lightly oiled wooden spoon and pour into the prepared dish. Cover with plastic wrap and let rise. When double in bulk, bake in a preheated 375°F. oven for 40 to 45 minutes, or until the loaf sounds hollow when you tap the top. Cool on a rack for 5 minutes, then turn out. Complete cooling on the rack. ❖

Cottage Cheese and Dill Batter Bread

MAKES ONE 9x5-INCH LOAF

Bouquets of fresh dill are sold at roadside stands throughout New England during pickling season. Try some in this heady, aromatic loaf.

1 cup small-curd cottage cheese
¼ cup butter or margarine, melted
2 large eggs
2 tablespoons sugar
1 teaspoon salt
1 tablespoon dehydrated minced onion
½ cup fresh dill leaves, chopped
1 package dry yeast, dissolved in ¼ cup warm water
3½ cups all-purpose flour, scoop measured

1. In the bowl of an electric mixer, combine the cottage cheese, melted butter, and eggs, and beat until well blended. Stir in the sugar, salt, onion, and dill. Blend in the dissolved yeast. Add 2 cups of the flour and beat on medium speed until well blended. Reduce the speed to low and gradually sprinkle in the remaining 1½ cups flour. Beat until a moist, smooth dough is formed. Scrape down the sides of the bowl and cover with plastic wrap. Secure with an elastic band and set aside to rise until double in bulk.

2. Generously grease a 9x5-inch loaf pan. Stir the batter down with a lightly oiled wooden spoon and pour into the prepared pan. Cover with plastic wrap and let rise. When double in bulk, bake in a preheated 375°F. oven for 40 to 45 minutes, or until the loaf sounds hollow when you tap the top. Cool on a rack for 5 minutes, then turn out. Complete cooling on the rack. ❖

Cranberry Batter Bread

MAKES ONE 9x5-INCH LOAF

Slice this cranberry-studded loaf thinly and spread with softened cream cheese. Serve with fruit salad or scrambled eggs.

1 cup milk
¼ cup butter or margarine
¼ cup sugar
¾ teaspoon salt
1 package dry yeast, dissolved in ¼ cup warm water
1 large egg, beaten
1½ cups whole wheat flour, scoop measured
2 cups all-purpose flour, scoop measured
1 cup coarsely chopped fresh cranberries

1. In a wide saucepan, combine the milk, butter, sugar, and salt. Place over medium heat and stir until the butter is melted. Transfer to the large bowl of an electric mixer to cool.

2. When the mixture is barely warm to the touch, stir in the dissolved yeast. Blend in the beaten egg. Add the whole wheat flour and beat on medium speed until well blended. Reduce the speed to low and gradually sprinkle in the all-purpose flour. Beat until a moist, smooth dough is formed. Stir in the cranberries. Scrape down the sides of the bowl and cover with plastic wrap. Secure with an elastic band and set aside to rise until double in bulk.

3. Generously grease a 9x5-inch loaf pan. Stir the batter down with a lightly oiled wooden spoon and pour into the prepared pan. Cover with plastic wrap and let rise. When double in bulk, bake in a preheated 375°F. oven for 40 to 45 minutes, or until the loaf sounds hollow when you tap the top. Cool on a rack for 5 minutes, then turn out. Complete cooling on the rack.   ❖

English Muffin Batter Bread

MAKES 3 LOAVES

This exceptional bread has become a New England favorite. It is meant to be served thickly sliced and toasted. Buttered and spread with jam, it tastes like an English muffin.

1½ cups milk
½ cup cold water
2 tablespoons butter or margarine
2 tablespoons sugar
1 teaspoon salt
2 packages dry yeast, dissolved in ½ cup warm water
½ teaspoon baking soda, dissolved in 1 tablespoon cold water
4½ to 5 cups all-purpose flour, scoop measured

1. In a wide saucepan, combine the milk, cold water, butter, sugar, and salt. Place over medium heat and stir until the butter is melted. Transfer to the large bowl of an electric mixer to cool.

2. When the mixture is barely warm to the touch, stir in the dissolved yeast and dissolved baking soda. Add 2 cups of the flour and beat on medium speed until well blended. Reduce the speed to low and gradually sprinkle in the remaining flour, adding just enough to form a moist, smooth dough. Scrape down the sides of the bowl and cover with plastic wrap. Secure with an elastic band and set aside to rise until double in bulk.

3. Generously grease three 1-pound coffee cans and sprinkle the insides with cornmeal. Stir the batter down with a lightly oiled wooden spoon and pour into the prepared cans. Cover with plastic wrap and let rise. When double in bulk, bake in a preheated 375°F. oven for 25 to 30 minutes, or until the loaves sound hollow when you tap the tops. Cool on a rack for 5 minutes, then turn out. Complete cooling on the rack.   ❖

Fennel Bread

MAKES 1 ROUND LOAF

Redolent of fennel seeds, this high, round loaf is a savory companion for fish stew.

1 cup milk
¾ cup cold water
2 tablespoons solid vegetable shortening
¼ cup sugar
1½ teaspoons salt
1 package dry yeast, dissolved in ¼ cup warm
  water
1 tablespoon fennel seeds
1 tablespoon finely grated orange zest
2 cups whole wheat flour, scoop measured
2 cups all-purpose flour, scoop measured

1. In a wide saucepan, combine the milk, water, shortening, sugar, and salt. Place over medium heat and stir until the shortening is melted. Transfer to the large bowl of an electric mixer to cool.

2. When the mixture is barely warm to the touch, stir in the dissolved yeast. Stir in the fennel seeds and orange zest. Add the whole wheat flour and beat on medium speed until well blended. Reduce the speed to low and gradually sprinkle in the all-purpose flour. Beat until a moist, smooth dough is formed. Scrape down the sides of the bowl and cover with plastic wrap. Secure with an elastic band and set aside to rise until double in bulk.

3. Generously grease a 2-quart soufflé dish or bowl-shaped casserole. Stir the batter down with a lightly oiled wooden spoon and pour into the prepared pan. Cover with plastic wrap and let rise. When double in bulk, bake in a preheated 375°F. oven for 40 to 45 minutes, or until the loaf sounds hollow when you tap the top. Cool on a rack for 5 minutes, then turn out. Complete cooling on the rack.   ❖

Herb Batter Bread

MAKES ONE 9x5-INCH LOAF

A quick, savory loaf to serve piping hot with clam chowder.

1 cup water
2 tablespoons butter or margarine
1 tablespoon sugar
¾ teaspoon salt

1 package dry yeast, dissolved in ¼ cup warm
  water
½ teaspoon dried chervil
½ teaspoon dried tarragon
½ teaspoon dried thyme
3 cups all-purpose flour, scoop measured

1. In a wide saucepan, combine the water, butter, sugar, and salt. Place over medium heat and stir until the butter is melted. Transfer to the large bowl of an electric mixer to cool.

2. When the mixture is barely warm to the touch, stir in the dissolved yeast. Blend in the chervil, tarragon, and thyme. Add 2 cups of the flour and beat on medium speed until well blended. Reduce the speed to low and gradually sprinkle in the remaining cup of flour. Beat until a moist, smooth dough is formed. Scrape down the sides of the bowl and cover with plastic wrap. Secure with an elastic band and set aside to rise until double in bulk.

3. Generously grease a 9x5-inch loaf pan. Stir the batter down with a lightly oiled wooden spoon and pour into the prepared pan. Cover with plastic wrap and let rise. When double in bulk, bake in a preheated 375°F. oven for 40 to 45 minutes, or until the loaf sounds hollow when you tap the top. Cool on a rack for 5 minutes, then turn out. Complete cooling on the rack.   ❖

Molasses Batter Bread

MAKES ONE 9x5-INCH LOAF

Wheat germ creates an interesting grainy texture in this substantial, molasses-flavored bread.

1 cup milk
¼ cup molasses
3 tablespoons butter or margarine
1 teaspoon salt
1 package dry yeast, dissolved in ¼ cup warm
  water
1 large egg, beaten
¾ cup wheat germ

1½ cups whole wheat flour, scoop measured
1½ cups all-purpose flour, scoop measured

1. In a wide saucepan, combine the milk, molasses, butter, and salt. Place over medium heat and stir until the butter is melted. Transfer to the large bowl of an electric mixer to cool.

2. When the mixture is barely warm to the touch, stir in the dissolved yeast. Blend in the beaten egg and wheat germ. Add the whole wheat flour and beat on medium speed until well blended. Reduce the speed to low and gradually sprinkle in the all-purpose flour. Beat until a moist, smooth dough is formed. Scrape down the sides of the bowl and cover with plastic wrap. Secure with an elastic band and set aside to rise until double in bulk.

3. Generously grease a 9x5-inch loaf pan. Stir the batter down with a lightly oiled wooden spoon and pour into the prepared pan. Cover with plastic wrap and let rise. When double in bulk, bake in a preheated 375°F. oven for 40 to 45 minutes, or until the loaf sounds hollow when you tap the top. Cool on a rack for 5 minutes, then turn out. Complete cooling on the rack.   ❖

Oatmeal Raisin Batter Bread

MAKES ONE 9x5-INCH LOAF

Honey flavors this easy-to-make raisin loaf. Cut into thick slices and toast for a nourishing snack or breakfast treat.

1 cup milk
¼ cup honey
¼ cup butter or margarine
1 teaspoon salt
1 package dry yeast, dissolved in ¼ cup water
1 large egg, beaten
1 cup quick-cooking rolled oats
3 cups all-purpose flour, scoop measured
¾ cup raisins

1. In a wide saucepan, combine the milk, honey, butter, and salt. Place over medium heat and stir until the butter is melted.

Transfer to the large bowl of an electric mixer to cool.

2. When the mixture is barely warm to the touch, stir in the dissolved yeast. Blend in the beaten egg. Add the oats and 1 cup of the flour, and beat on medium speed until well blended. Reduce the speed to low and gradually sprinkle in the remaining 2 cups flour. Beat until a moist, smooth dough is formed. Stir in the raisins. Scrape down the sides of the bowl and cover with plastic wrap. Secure with an elastic band and set aside to rise until double in bulk.

3. Generously grease a 9x5-inch loaf pan. Stir the batter down with a lightly oiled wooden spoon and pour into the prepared pan. Cover with plastic wrap and let rise. When double in bulk, bake in a preheated 375°F. oven for 40 to 45 minutes, or until the loaf sounds hollow when you tap the top. Cool on a rack for 5 minutes, then turn out. Complete cooling on the rack.   ❖

Spicy Orange Batter Bread

MAKES ONE 9x5-INCH LOAF

Curiously, it is during the bleakest part of the winter that fresh oranges are at their best — or perhaps it only seems that way. In any event, one navel orange is enough to flavor this homey, comforting loaf.

¾ cup milk
¼ cup butter or margarine
¼ cup sugar
1 teaspoon salt
1 package dry yeast, dissolved in ¼ cup warm water
2 large eggs, beaten
¼ cup freshly squeezed orange juice
1 tablespoon finely grated orange zest
½ teaspoon cinnamon
¼ teaspoon nutmeg
¼ teaspoon ground cloves
3½ cups all-purpose flour, scoop measured

1. In a wide saucepan, combine the milk, butter, sugar, and salt. Place over medium heat and stir until the butter is melted.

Transfer to the large bowl of an electric mixer to cool.

2. When the mixture is barely warm to the touch, stir in the dissolved yeast. Blend in the beaten egg. Stir in the orange juice and zest. Add the cinnamon, nutmeg, cloves, and 2 cups of the flour. Beat on medium speed until well blended. Reduce the speed to low and gradually sprinkle in the remaining 1½ cups flour. Beat until a moist, smooth dough is formed. Scrape down the sides of the bowl and cover with plastic wrap. Secure with an elastic band and set aside to rise until double in bulk.

3. Generously grease a 9x5-inch loaf pan. Stir the batter down with a lightly oiled wooden spoon and pour into the prepared pan. Cover with plastic wrap and let rise. When double in bulk, bake in a preheated 375°F. oven for 40 to 45 minutes, or until the loaf sounds hollow when you tap the top. Cool on a rack for 5 minutes, then turn out. Complete cooling on the rack.   ❖

Parmesan Cheese Batter Bread

MAKES 10

Spoon this dough into 1-cup soufflé dishes to create tiny, individual breads. Turn out while hot and set one on a bread plate at each place setting.

3 tablespoons butter or margarine
1 medium onion, finely chopped
1 cup milk
1 tablespoon sugar
½ teaspoon salt
1 package dry yeast, dissolved in ¼ cup warm water
1 large egg, beaten
1 cup freshly grated Parmesan cheese, plus 2 tablespoons
3 cups all-purpose flour, scoop measured

1. Melt the butter in a wide saucepan. Add the onion and toss to coat. Stir over medium heat until the onion is tender. Pour in the milk and heat until the surface wrinkles. Add the sugar and salt, and stir to dissolve. Transfer to the large bowl of an electric mixer to cool.

2. When the mixture is barely warm to the touch, stir in the dissolved yeast. Blend in the beaten egg and 1 cup of the cheese. Add 2 cups of the flour and beat on medium speed until well blended. Reduce the speed to low and gradually sprinkle in the remaining cup of flour. Beat until a moist, smooth dough is formed. Scrape down the sides of the bowl and cover with plastic wrap. Secure with an elastic band and set aside to rise until double in bulk.

3. Generously grease 10 individual soufflé dishes. Stir the batter down with a lightly oiled wooden spoon and pour into the prepared dishes. Cover loosely with plastic wrap and let rise. When double in bulk, sprinkle the tops with the remaining 2 tablespoons cheese. Bake in a preheated 375°F. oven for 30 to 35 minutes, or until the tops are nicely browned. Cool on a rack for 5 minutes, then turn out. Serve immediately or complete cooling on the rack.   ❖

Streusel Batter Bread

MAKES ONE 9x5-INCH LOAF

Nubbly with cinnamon streusel, this rich, sweet bread makes marvelous toast.

3¾ cups all-purpose flour, scoop measured
2 tablespoons light brown sugar
1 teaspoon cinnamon
2 tablespoons butter or margarine, cut into small pieces, plus ¼ cup
1 cup milk
½ cup granulated sugar
¾ teaspoon salt
1 package dry yeast, dissolved in ¼ cup warm water
2 large eggs, beaten
¼ teaspoon nutmeg
½ cup golden raisins

1. In a small bowl, combine ¼ cup of the flour, the brown sugar, ½ teaspoon of the

cinnamon, and 2 tablespoons of the butter. Cut in the butter until the mixture is crumbly. Set aside.

2. In a wide saucepan, combine the milk, the remaining ¼ cup butter, the granulated sugar, and the salt. Place over medium heat and stir until the butter is melted. Transfer to the large bowl of an electric mixer to cool.

3. When the mixture is barely warm to the touch, stir in the dissolved yeast. Blend in the beaten egg. Add the remaining ½ teaspoon cinnamon, the nutmeg, and 2 cups of the flour. Beat on medium speed until well blended. Reduce the speed to low and gradually sprinkle in the rest of the flour. Beat until a moist, smooth dough is formed. Stir in the raisins. Scrape down the sides of the bowl and cover with plastic wrap. Secure with an elastic band and set aside to rise until double in bulk.

4. Generously grease a 9x5-inch loaf pan. Sprinkle the reserved streusel mixture over the batter and stir with a lightly oiled wooden spoon. Pour into the prepared pan. Cover with plastic wrap and let rise. When double in bulk, bake in a preheated 375°F. oven for 40 to 45 minutes, or until the loaf sounds hollow when you tap the top. Cool on a rack for 5 minutes, then turn out. Complete cooling on the rack.   ❖

Triticale Batter Bread

MAKES ONE 9x5-INCH LOAF

Triticale is a high-protein hybrid grain flour available at most health-food stores. It contributes robust flavor and a pleasing texture to this honey-sweetened loaf.

1 cup milk
¼ cup honey
3 tablespoons butter or margarine
1 teaspoon salt
1 package dry yeast, dissolved in ¼ cup warm water
1 large egg, beaten
1 cup triticale flour, scoop measured

½ cup whole wheat flour, scoop measured
2 cups all-purpose flour, scoop measured

1. In a wide saucepan, combine the milk, honey, butter, and salt. Place over medium heat and stir until the butter is melted. Transfer to the large bowl of an electric mixer to cool.

2. When the mixture is barely warm to the touch, stir in the dissolved yeast. Blend in the beaten egg. Add the triticale flour and whole wheat flour and beat on medium speed until well blended. Reduce the speed to low and gradually sprinkle in the all-purpose flour. Beat until a moist, smooth dough is formed. Scrape down the sides of the bowl and cover with plastic wrap. Secure with an elastic band and set aside to rise until double in bulk.

3. Generously grease a 9x5-inch loaf pan. Stir the batter down with a lightly oiled wooden spoon and pour into the prepared pan. Cover with plastic wrap and let rise. When double in bulk, bake in a preheated 375°F. oven for 40 to 45 minutes, or until the loaf sounds hollow when you tap the top. Cool on a rack for 5 minutes, then turn out. Complete cooling on the rack.   ❖

Whole Wheat Batter Bread

MAKES ONE 9x5-INCH LOAF

Since batter breads skip the kneading step and are simply poured into the pan rather than shaped into a loaf, this is a superquick way to keep homemade whole wheat bread on hand.

1 cup milk
¼ cup honey
¼ cup solid vegetable shortening
1 teaspoon salt
1 package dry yeast, dissolved in ¼ cup warm water
1 large egg, beaten
2 cups whole wheat flour, scoop measured
1¾ cups all-purpose flour, scoop measured

1. In a wide saucepan, combine the milk, honey, shortening, and salt. Place over medium heat and stir until the shortening is melted. Transfer to the large bowl of an electric mixer to cool.

2. When the mixture is barely warm to the touch, stir in the dissolved yeast. Blend in the beaten egg. Add the whole wheat flour and beat on medium speed until well blended. Reduce the speed to low and gradually sprinkle in the all-purpose flour. Beat until a moist, smooth dough is formed. Scrape down the sides of the bowl and cover with plastic wrap. Secure with an elastic band and set aside to rise until double in bulk.

3. Generously grease a 9x5-inch loaf pan. Stir the batter down with a lightly oiled wooden spoon and pour into the prepared pan. Cover with plastic wrap and let rise. When double in bulk, bake in a preheated 375°F. oven for 40 to 45 minutes, or until the loaf sounds hollow when you tap the top. Cool on a rack for 5 minutes, then turn out. Complete cooling on the rack. ❖

Zucchini Batter Bread

MAKES ONE 9x5-INCH LOAF

At harvest time, New England gardens fairly burst with zucchini squash. Batter bread is a speedy way to incorporate it into a yeast loaf.

1 cup milk
3 tablespoons butter or margarine
1 tablespoon sugar
1 teaspoon salt
1 package dry yeast, dissolved in ¼ cup warm water
1 large egg, beaten
½ cup yellow cornmeal
¼ cup freshly grated Parmesan cheese
3 cups all-purpose flour, scoop measured
1 cup grated, unpeeled zucchini

1. In a wide saucepan, combine the milk, butter, sugar, and salt. Place over medium heat and stir until the butter is melted. Transfer to the large bowl of an electric mixer to cool.

2. When the mixture is barely warm to the touch, stir in the dissolved yeast. Blend in the beaten egg. Stir in the cornmeal and cheese. Add 1 cup of the flour and beat on medium speed until well blended. Reduce the speed to low and gradually sprinkle in the remaining 2 cups flour. Beat until a moist, smooth dough is formed. Stir in the zucchini. Scrape down the sides of the bowl and cover with plastic wrap. Secure with an elastic band and set aside to rise until double in bulk.

3. Generously grease a 9x5-inch loaf pan. Stir the batter down with a lightly oiled wooden spoon and pour into the prepared pan. Cover with plastic wrap and let rise. When double in bulk, bake in a preheated 375°F. oven for 40 to 45 minutes, or until the loaf sounds hollow when you tap the top. Cool on a rack for 5 minutes, then turn out. Complete cooling on the rack. ❖

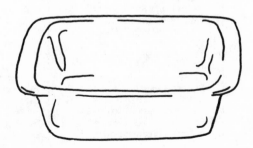

❖ Index ❖